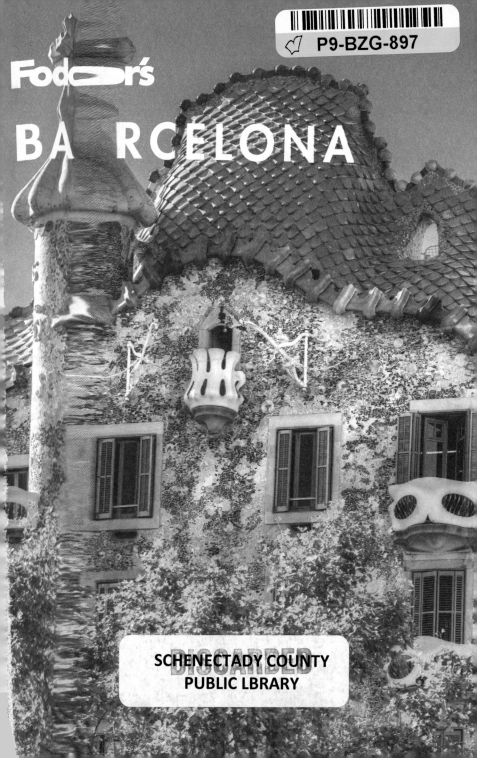

Fodor's

BARCELONA

Welcome to Barcelona

The capital of Catalonia is a banquet for the senses, with its beguiling mix of ancient and modern architecture, tempting cafés and markets, and sun-drenched Mediterranean beaches. A stroll along La Rambla and through waterfront Barceloneta, as well as a tour of Gaudí's majestic Sagrada Família and his other unique creations, are part of a visit to Spain's second-largest city. Modern art museums and chic shops call for attention, too. Barcelona's vibe stays lively well into the night, when you can linger over regional wine and cuisine at buzzing tapas bars.

TOP REASONS TO GO

★ **Gaudí:** The iconic Sagrada Família, undulating Casa Batlló, and playful Park Güell.

★ **Food:** From the Boqueria market's bounty to tapas bars to avant-garde restaurants.

★ **Museums:** Museu Picasso and the Museu Nacional d'Art de Catalunya lead the list.

★ **Architecture:** Roman and medieval in the Barri Gòtic, Moderniste in the Eixample.

★ **Shopping:** Stylish fashion boutiques and innovative design emporia tempt buyers.

★ **Beautiful Beaches:** Sandy havens and surfing hubs delight urban sun worshippers.

Contents

MAPS

Fodor's Features

Chapter 1

EXPERIENCE BARCELONA

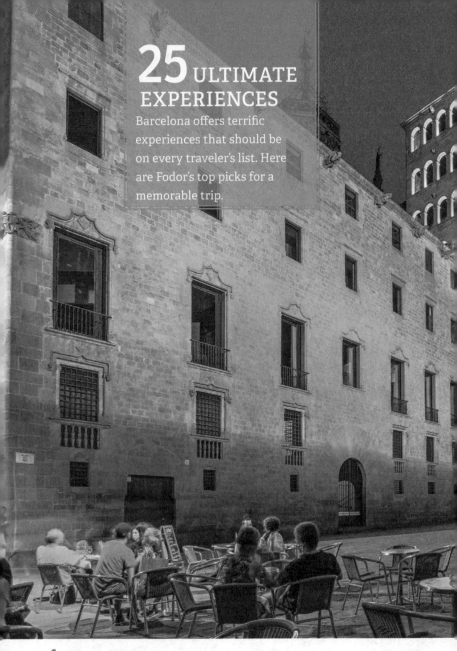

25 ULTIMATE EXPERIENCES

Barcelona offers terrific experiences that should be on every traveler's list. Here are Fodor's top picks for a memorable trip.

1 People Watch at Plaça del Rei

Located in the heart of Barri Gòtic, Plaça del Rei was once the center of all noble activity in Barcelona. In fact, when Christopher Columbus returned from the New World, it was here that the Catalan-Aragonese monarchs received him. *(Ch. 4)*

2 Find Hidden Tapas Bars

What better way to get to know a city than by sampling its most delectable dishes in miniature? Find smaller bars away from the center to fill up on meat-filled bombas.

3 Hit the Beach at La Barceloneta

What Barcelona's famed seaside district lacks in natural beauty, it makes up for in liveliness. Think: Kites, vendors, music, people-watching, and seaside dining. *(Ch. 7)*

4 Wander La Rambla

No visit to Barcelona would be complete without a stroll through La Rambla, the wide, shady boulevard that runs through the heart of the city from Plaça de Catalunya down to Port Vell. *(Ch. 3)*

5 Explore MACBA

With a collection spanning from the mid-20th century to today, the Museu d'Art Contemporani de Barcelona showcases Catalonia's most celebrated contemporary artists and emerging talent. *(Ch.5)*

6 Hang out in Park Güell

With the Collserola foothills as his canvas, Gaudí's architectural park features columns that shoot up like tree trunks and fountains guarded by giant lizards with scales fashioned out of mosaic tiles. *(Ch. 9)*

7 Feast in Gràcia

Forgo English-menu-touting restaurants and chain stores for the mom-and-pop joints, trendy restaurants, and hip little bars and cafés tucked away in the jumble of Gràcia's streets. *(Ch. 9)*

8 Visit Fundació Joan Miró

A gift from the artist Joan Miró to his native city, this airy museum perched on Montjuïc, offers more than 10,000 of Miro's playful and colorful masterpieces. *(Ch. 11)*

9 Marvel at La Sagrada Família

If/when it's completed in 2026, after 150 years of construction, Gaudí's basilica will be the tallest religious building in Europe. Skip the crowds and visit for Sunday mass. *(Ch. 8)*

10 Shop in Barri Gòtic

The Barri Gòtic was built on cottage industries and there are still plenty of artisans at work along its stone streets. Look for handmade espadrilles, leather goods, and the Mercat Gòtic. *(Ch. 4)*

11 Say Salud to Cava

Prosecco and other budget sparklers rely on industrial carbonization to make their wines bubble. But Catalan cava, like fine Champagne, gets its effervescence and complexity from bottle fermentation.

12 Worship at Camp Nou

Join the millions of soccer fans who make the pilgrimage to Barcelona each year to cheer on Barcelona's home team, Futbol Club Barcelona ("Barça" for short) at Camp Nou. *(Ch. 10)*

13 Stroll Carrer de les Aigues

A slice of serenity completely off the tourist track, Carretera de les Aigües is an ancient road that winds around the mountains overlooking the city and the Mediterranean. *(Ch. 10)*

14 Enjoy El Palau de la Música Catalana

One of the world's grandest music halls and a UNESCO World Heritage site, you'll want to take a tour of this incredible auditorium if you can't catch a performance. *(Ch. 6)*

15 Chill in Parc de la Ciutadella

After a promenade under the trees in this lush 19th-century park, take a moment to admire the handiwork of the central fountain, a neoclassical work designed by Josep Fontserè. *(Ch. 7)*

16 Taste Everything at La Boqueria

A major tourist attraction, La Boqueria welcomes more than 45,000 visitors a day with its abundant and artful displays of the region's finest cheeses, charcuterie, seafood, and produce *(Ch. 3)*

17 The Santa María del Mar

To gain perspective on this soaring Gothic temple, consider that each boulder used in the church's construction was hauled one at a time from surrounding mountainsides by ordinary civilians. *(Ch. 6)*

18 Take a Day Trip

Popular daytrip destinations include Girona for its Gothic architecture, Figueres for its theater-museum designed by Salvador Dalí, and Sitges, a beach paradise with bumping nightlife. *(Ch. 12)*

19 Explore Casa Milà

Better known as La Pedrera, Casa Milà features wavy interior patios, curved walls, slanting columns, and a rooftop with plunging stairways and sculptural chimneys. *(Ch. 8)*

20 Wander the Museu Nacional D'Art de Catalunya

MNAC's Romanesque collection is one of the most exhaustive in the world and chronicles the pre-Gothic beginnings of religious art in Catalonia. *(Ch. 11)*

21 Visit the Museu Picasso

Picasso's early works in sculpture, paint, and engraving are not the only draw at Museu Picasso; the five adjoining 13th- and 14th-century residences that comprise the museum are incredible, too. *(Ch. 6)*

22 Climb Tibidabo

Towering above Barcelona's northern rim, the 1,700-foot peak of Tibidabo is the best vantage point to take in panoramic views of the cityscape against the cobalt-blue backdrop of the Mediterranean. *(Ch. 10)*

23 Barhop at Passeig del Born

Like a less-touristy version of La Rambla, this tree-lined promenade is lined with bars of all types where you can sample zippy Menorca-style pomadas, ice-cold gin and lemonade cocktails, and tapas. *(Ch. 6)*

24 Catedral de la Seu

Gargoyles, flying buttresses, and barrel vaults accent this Gothic structure, which predates La Sagrada Família by six centuries. Enjoy them—and the city skyline—on a rooftop tour. *(Ch. 4)*

25 Vote on Manzana de la Discòrdia

Name your style on one city block on Passeig de Gràcia known for its four different interpretations of Modernisme architecture, including Gaudí's Casa Batlló. *(Ch. 8)*

WHAT'S WHERE

1 La Rambla. The city's most emblematic promenade was once a seasonal watercourse that flowed along the outside of the 13th-century city walls. A stroll on La Rambla—where tourists mix with pickpockets, buskers, street performers, and locals—passes the Boqueria market, the Liceu opera house, and, at the port end, Drassanes, the medieval shipyards. Just off La Rambla is Plaça Reial, a stately neoclassical square; off the other side is Gaudí's masterly Palau Güell.

2 Barri Gòtic. The medieval Gothic Quarter surrounds the Catedral de la Seu on the high ground that the Romans settled in the 1st century BC. The medieval Jewish quarter, the antiquers' row, Plaça Sant Jaume, and the Sant Just neighborhood are quintessential Barcelona.

3 El Raval. Once a slum, this area west of La Rambla has brightened considerably, thanks partly to the Barcelona Museum of Contemporary Art, designed by Richard Meier. Behind the Boqueria market is the stunning Antic

Hospital de la Santa Creu, with its high-vaulted Gothic Biblioteca de Catalunya reading room; just steps away is Sant Pau del Camp, Barcelona's earliest church.

4 Sant Pere and La Ribera. Northeast of La Rambla, Sant Pere is the city's old textile neighborhood. The narrow cobblestone streets of La Ribera are filled with interesting shops and restaurants; this area is known for the grand urban palaces of Barcelona's medieval nobles and merchant princes—five of which linked together now house the Picasso Museum.

5 La Ciutedella and Barceloneta. This waterfront neighborhood, just east of Born-Ribera, was open water until the mid-18th century, when it was filled in to provide housing for those displaced by the construction of Ciutadella—at the time the largest fortress in Europe and a symbol of the hated Bourbon regime. Some of the city's best seafood restaurants make Barceloneta a favorite for Sunday-afternoon paella gatherings.

6 The Eixample. The Eixample (Expansion) is the post-1860 grid square of city blocks uphill from Ciutat Vella containing

WHAT'S WHERE

most of Barcelona's Moderniste (Art Nouveau) architecture, including Gaudí's unfinished work, the Sagrada Família church. Passeig de Gràcia is the city's premier shopping street. It also offers more Gaudí at Casa Batlló, Casa Milà (La Pedrera), and Casa Calvet.

7 Gràcia. This former outlying village begins at Gaudí's playful Park Güell and continues past his first commissioned house, Casa Vicens, through two markets and various pretty squares such as Plaça de la Vila de Gràcia (formerly Plaça de Rius i Taulet) and Plaça del Sol. Carrer Gran de Gràcia, though narrow and noisy, is lined with buildings designed by Gaudí's assistant Francesc Berenguer i Mestres.

8 Upper Barcelona. Sarrià was an independent village until it was incorporated into the burgeoning metropolis in 1927. It still feels very much like a village, though present-day gentrification has endowed it with a gratifying number of gourmet shops and fine restaurants. Nearby is the Monestir de Pedralbes, a 14th-century

architectural gem with a rare triple-tiered cloister; not far away are Gaudí's Col·legi de les Teresianes and his Torre Bellesguard. Tibidabo, Barcelona's perch, has little more to offer at the summit than its retro kitschy amusement park—but do take the *Tramvia Blau* (Blue Tram) at least to the lower end of the funicular that goes up to the park: the square in front of the terminus has restaurants and bars with views over the city.

9 Montjuïc and Poble Sec. Located on the western edge of the city, Montjuïc is Barcelona's playground: a sprawling complex of parks and gardens, sports facilities, open-air theater spaces, and museums. Among the latter are the Museu Nacional d'Art de Catalunya (MNAC) in the Palau Nacional, repository of a thousand years of Catalonia's artistic treasures; the Joan Miró Foundation collection of contemporary art and sculpture; the Mies van der Rohe Barcelona Pavilion; and the CaixaForum. Between Montjuïc and the port, Poble Sec is one of the oldest neighborhoods in Barcelona and is slowly making a name for itself with an up-and-coming food scene.

Map labels:

DABO, VALLUIDRERA, OLLSEROLE HILLS

Park Güell

Plaça de Lesseps

Trav. de Dalt
C. de Sant Salvador
C. de les Camèlies
C. de la Providència

Carrer Gran de Gràcia

Ronda del Guinardó

GRÀCIA

Plaça del Sol 7

C. de Balmes

Plaça de la Vila de Gràcia

Passeig de S. Joan

Plaça de Joan Carles I

Avda. de Gaudí

C. de Cartagena

SECTIONS 1-6

Av. Diagonal

C. d'Aragó
C. d'Aragó

Plaça de les Glòries

Gran Via de les Corts Catalanes

Plaça Tetuán

P. de Carles I

BARRI GÒTIC

Avda. de la Meridiana

BORN-RIBERA

Parc de la Ciutadella

C. de Wellington

Vila Olímpica

Moll d'Espanya

BARCELONETA

Parc de Mar

Mediterranean Sea

What to Eat and Drink in Barcelona

restaurants cook the slender onions over open flame until blackened on the outside and tender and sweet within.

ESCALIVADA
Escalivada is the ultimate poster child of the Mediterranean diet: it's a simple medley of roasted late-summer vegetables (eggplant, tomatoes, and bell peppers) rounded out with nothing more than garlic and olive oil. It's particularly delectable spooned on crusty bread at the no-frills bar En Diagonal; goat-cheese lovers shouldn't miss the nontraditional gratinéed version served at Cervecería Catalana.

BOMBAS
Mashed-potato fritters stuffed with succulent ground beef and drenched in *allioli* and spicy *salsa brava* are the bomb. Try a nongreasy, juicy rendition at La Cova Fumada, the bar that created the dish in 1955, or a duck-confit version at Arola.

ALLIOLI
Barcelona takes its allioli seriously—after all, the creamy, garlicky spread is said to have been invented in Catalonia. Try it over *patatas bravas* at Elsa y Fred, alongside black rice with squid ink at Paella Bar in La Boqueria market, or spread on toast at any number of neighborhood restaurants as a requisite first course.

CAVA
Catalan cava gets its effervescence and complexity from bottle fermentation. Taste some of the region's best bubblies at La Vinya del Senyor, a cozy, understated restaurant with several by-the-glass boutique cavas to choose from. If you're lucky enough to snag a table on the plaça, you'll be rewarded with views of Santa María del Mar's 14th-century facade.

VERMUT
On sunny weekend afternoons, neighborhood bars fill up with locals out to *fer el vermut*, the Catalan ritual of catching up with friends over a few dainty glasses of the herbaceous, garnet-red aperitif, customarily garnished with an orange slice and an olive. Barcelona's best vermouth bars, like Morro Fi, blend their own vermouths by infusing fortified wine with any range of botanicals, and pour them on draft. Or look for a quality Catalan brand such as Vermut Yzaguirre.

CALÇOTS
Short of scoring an invite to a *calçocada*, a Catalan-style barbecue centering on grilled spring onions (calçots), you can get your allium fix at a number of Barcelona *braserías* such as Casa Pamplinas and Taverna El Glop. From November to April, calçot season, these grill-centric

TORRÓ
Come Christmastime, Barcelona's bakeries and pastry shops brim with one of southern Europe's most addictive sweets, *torró* ("turrón" in Spanish and "torrone" in Italian), a crunchy confection of toasted nuts bound with egg whites and honey. Turrones Sirvent, founded in 1920, is a one-stop shop for all your torró needs.

Ibérico ham

IBÉRICO HAM
Though most *jamón ibérico*—the world-famous dry-cured ham made from indigenous black-footed pigs—hails from western and southern Spain, the delicacy is relished in restaurants across Barcelona. Sample the best of the best at Cinco Jotas Rambla, a ham lover's paradise operated by the eponymous brand known for using only purebred ibérico hogs fattened on acorns.

TORTILLA ESPAÑOLA
If there's one thing almost all Spaniards can get behind, it's the country's most popular dish, *tortilla española*. A hubcap-size omelet filled with melty olive oil–poached potatoes and caramelized onions, it can be eaten hot or cold and at breakfast, lunch, or dinner. Tuck into a made-to-order slice at Belmonte in the Gothic Quarter; or choose from 140 different tortilla types at Les Truites in Sarrià.

PA AMB TOMÀQUET
Anyone can make *pa amb tomàquet* (literally "bread with tomato"), but it's elevated to an art form at La Bodegueta, whose thick-crusted *payés* bread gives the dish an extra crunch.

CROQUETAS
The best *croquetas* have a shatteringly crisp exterior and a molten béchamel center flavored with whatever's handy: chopped ham ends, flaked *bacalao*, leftover roast chicken—you name it. Find classic croqueta nirvana at Bodega Sepúlveda, whose meticulous cooks change the breading type depending on the croqueta add-in, or have your mind blown at Catacroquet, with fillings like monkfish and sherry-braised pork jowl.

PAELLA
You can't leave Spain's Mediterranean coast without trying one of the region's most famous dishes: paella. Catalans love arguing about what consti-tutes an *"autèntica"* paella, but you can't go wrong at rice-focused restaurants like Cafetí, a hidden gem in the Raval neighborhood famous for its seafood preparations, or Can Solé, a white-tablecloth Barcelo-neta institution that's been packed since 1903.

FIDEUÁ
Imagine paella made with pasta instead of rice and you have *fideuá*, a Catalan specialty that's typical Sunday lunch fare. It's worth shelling out the euros for the impeccable, seafood-packed version at La Mar Salada, which gets its *abuela*-level comfort-food deliciousness from homemade fish stock.

What to Buy in Barcelona

ESPARDENYES
You'll see *espardenyes*, the rope-soled sandals also called espadrilles or *alpargatas*, all over the world, but to take home a pair of the originals, you have to visit Catalonia, where locals have been donning them since at least the 14th century. Find a perfect pair at La Manual in the Barri Gotic.

VERMOUTH
L'hora del vermut is sacred in Barcelona—that hour-long window just before lunch when locals flood the bodegas (wine bars) to catch up over icy glasses of vermouth and heaping plates of olives. Emulate that signature Mediterranean *alegria* at home by throwing your own tapas and vermut party; when in Barcelona, scoop up a bottle or two of the local stuff, like Morro Fi (rich with chocolate and coffee notes) or Casa Mariol (heady with rosemary and thyme plucked from the surrounding mountains), available for purchase at their namesake bars.

DESIGNER DECORATIONS
Support local artisans and impress your friends by investing in one-of-a-kind design pieces made in Barcelona. If home entertaining is your thing, pop into Luesma & Vega, the haute plate showroom where the likes of Andoni Aduriz (of three-star Mugaritz) shop for the latest nature-inspired dinnerware. Art enthusiasts, on the other hand, should seek out handmade works by Catalan studio Apparatu, whose modern ceramic sculptures and furniture are turning heads in fine-art circles across the Continent. Find a solid selection of Apparatu wares at Domésticoshop in the Eixample neighborhood—and while you're up there, stop by Matèria to purchase butter-soft blankets and shawls by Teixidors, a family-run company that trains developmentally disabled people to weave on traditional wooden looms.

CAVA
Prosecco and other budget sparklers rely on industrial carbonization to make their wines fizz, but cava, bottled in the Penedès region just south of Barcelona, gets its effervescence from a long and leisurely fermentation—the same process used in fine Champagne. You can probably find cava on the shelves of your local wine shop, but chances are, it pales in comparison to the complex *Gran Reserva* gems on offer at Barcelona wine purveyors like Cellarer and Vila Viniteca, whose staff will lovingly pack your purchases so they don't explode in transit.

CAGANER FIGURINE
A defecating workman is perhaps the world's most unholy—and improbable—symbol of Christmas. Come holiday season, families across Catalonia adorn their household nativity scenes with *caganer* (literally "crapper" or "pooper") figurines. The origins and meaning of the tongue-in-cheek tradition are unknown, but that doesn't stop barcelonins from keeping it alive. Elicit a few laughs next December by setting out your own caganer purchased at

Pessebres Puig, an artisan shop that's been painting these lilliputian poopers by hand since 1933.

PAINTED CERAMICS

The Moors brought exquisite ceramic craftsmanship to the Iberian Peninsula in the 8th century with their florid mosaics and *azulejos*, and the tradition further blossomed in Renaissance Spain with Barcelona as Catalonia's leading hub of production. Though you won't find specimens from the city's glory days of pottery outside museums, the modern reproductions that line the walls at Itaca L'Art del Poble are a close approximation and make excellent souvenirs. Choose from playfully decorated pitchers, ancient-looking wine jugs, ornately patterned bowls, and more.

FC BARCELONA T-SHIRT

Millions of soccer fans make the pilgrimage to Barcelona each year to cheer on Barcelona's home team, Futbol Club Barcelona. But even if you don't make it to the bleachers at Camp Nou stadium, you can flaunt your Barça pride by sporting a jersey with your favorite *futbolista's* name on the back. Avoid counterfeit swag by shopping in an official store, of which there are several in the city center. A Messi shirt, in homage to Barcelona's most famous resident and perhaps soccer's biggest star, is an obvious but classic choice for any soccer fan.

L'ESCALA ANCHOVIES

These plump, umami-packed fillets from the Catalan coast will make you question everything you ever thought you knew about anchovies. With just the right amount of salt and funk, they're as satisfying eaten straight from the can over the kitchen sink—we won't snitch—as they are draped over toasted, garlic-rubbed slices of baguette (as you'll find them in Barcelona tapas bars). Find them at any of the gourmet *conserves* stalls in neighborhood markets like Mercat de Santa Caterina or Mercat de Sants.

OLD-SCHOOL MORTAR AND PESTLE

A fixture in home kitchens the city over, the mortar and pestle is an essential tool for making Catalonia's favorite mother sauces such as allioli (the garlicky mayonnaise invented by the Catalans) and *romescu* (roasted peppers pounded with garlic and almonds). Spanish-style *morteros*, which you can find in any neighborhood hardware store in Barcelona, are canary-yellow with bright green splotches—making them as aesthetically pleasing as they are practical.

A PIECE OF GAUDÍ

If Gaudí's physics-defying constructions bursting with colors, patterns, and textures leave you inspired—and how could they not!—consider taking home a memento that will get your creative juices flowing. At the well-appointed gift shops inside La Pedrera and

Mortar and pestle

Casa Batlló, take your pick from Moderniste-style jewelry, kitchenware, posters, and decorations made by local artisans. The coffee mugs with gilded handles modeled after the doorknobs at La Pedrera are particularly eye-catching. Also, look for Gaudí tiles: the decorative hexagonal tiles now lining Passeig de Gràcia were originally designed by Gaudí to pave the floors of Casa Milà and they represent the two constants in his work—geometry and symbolism. You can purchase Gaudí tiles at most Gaudí property gift shops as well as tile-inspired handbags and purses. If you need even more Gaudí gifts, there's an excellent gift shop in La Sagrada Família with a wide selection of Gaudí-related items.

The Best Museums in Barcelona

MUSEU MARÍTIM DE BARCELONA

Spain's reputation as a seafaring nation is legendary and—for better or worse—Spanish explorers crossed the globe and established a powerful empire. Inside this museum's enormous vaulted chambers, you'll find navigational tools, nautical maps, paintings, and even entire ships.

POBLE ESPANYOL

Poble Espanyol was designed to highlight artistry from all over Spain, and the village was so successful the government decided not to dismantle it. Today, visitors can stroll along its stone streets and buy traditional crafted goods like textiles, painted glass, and jewelry from artisans with small shops.

FUNDACIÓN MAPFRE

Nonprofit Fundación MAPFRE's Barcelona Exhibition Hall, Casa Garriga Nogués, shows early pictoral modern painting and photography, focusing on the works of Catalan artists.

MUSEU PICASSO

While Pablo Picasso the man is a controversial figure, his art remains iconic both in terms of skill and originality of vision. The Museu Picasso, housed in five adjoining medieval stone mansions, has over 4,000 works in its permanent collection, making it one of the best places to explore the artist's legacy.

MUSEU NACIONAL D'ART DE CATALUNYA

The palatial MNAC was built as part of the 1929 Barcelona International Exposition. Today the classical-style building—whose dome was modeled after St. Peter's Basilica—houses a massive and diverse collection of Catalan and Spanish art from multiple styles and centuries, including medieval, Renaissance, and Modernist. At more than 50,000 square feet, there's a lot of ground to cover.

FUNDACIÓ ANTONI TÀPIES

Atop the Catalan Modernist building which houses Antoni Tàpies's museum and foundation sits Cloud and Chair, an enormous nest of steel and aluminum designed to represent a chair emerging from a large cloud. This piece of art, as with the collections inside of the museum—both permanent and rotating—reflects the abstract and avant-garde sensibilities of the artist, which are said to have been birthed during two teenage years spent recuperating from a tuberculosis-related heart attack. This is an important center of art in Barcelona and a must-stop

Museu Nacional d'Art de Catalunya

for those interested in Catalan Modernism.

MUSEU D'ART CONTEMPORANI DE BARCELONA (MACBA)

A temple of modern Spanish and Catalan art, the MACBA houses a rotating collection of approximately 5,000 pieces of art representing three eras beginning in the mid-20th century. While the collection itself is noteworthy, the same can be said for the large, "fridgelike" building whose enormous glass front is both an architectural feature and a way of allowing in natural light. The MACBA is a distinctive museum perfect for those looking for a broad exposure to Spanish Modernism.

MUSEU D'HISTÒRIA DE CATALUNYA

Dedicated to the history of Catalonia, this museum's exhibits examine the cultural, social, and political evolution of the region, from the Paleolithic era all the way to contemporary society. Housed inside a former warehouse, the photographs, artifacts, and historical re-creations make it an interesting departure from other museums in Barcelona.

FUNDACIÓ JOAN MIRÓ

Located on Montjuïc hill (with a lovely city view from its terrace), and designed by architect Josep Lluís Sert with Miró, this minimalist building houses hundreds of paintings, sculptures, ceramics, and tapestries from the icon.

PALAU DE LA MÚSICA CATALANA

This Catalan Art Nouveau concert hall, designed and built by the Modernist architect Lluís Domènech i Montaner in the first years of the 1900s, is so spectacular that it's been designated a UNESCO World Heritage site. While open for tours, it also remains an active music venue.

Best Day Trips from Barcelona

Zaragoza

THE BEACHES OF SITGES
A pleasant coastal town situated directly on the Mediterranean, Sitges is about an hour south of Barcelona and easily accessible by car, bus, and train. There are numerous reasons to visit Sitges but its 17 clean, beautiful beaches are a significant draw.

SEASIDE AT CAMBRILS
Located about an hour and a half by either car or train from Barcelona, Cambrils is a peaceful and demure setting known for its Michelin-starred restaurants and clean beaches with calm, cerulean-colored waters. All nine of the town's beaches are Blue Flag certified, meaning that they're clean, ecologically maintained, and well labeled.

GIRONA
An hour and a half north of Barcelona by car or train, Girona is a vision from the Middle Ages with its brooding castle, soaring cathedral, its labyrinth of climbing cobblestone streets and connecting staircases, and dreamy riverside setting. No wonder it was one of the filming locations for the sixth season of *Game of Thrones*.

Girona

ZARAGOSA

The capital of the Spanish region of Aragon, Zaragoza is about 90 minutes from Barcelona by car or train and has everything you could want from a day-trip destination: fabulous fountains, wonderful tapas restaurants with extensive outdoor seating, gorgeous avenues and wandering narrow side streets, and multiple museums.

MONTSERRAT

Montserrat is an easy, unique, and popular daytrip from Barcelona, and home to the world-famous La Moreneta (the Black Virgin of Montserrat), which resides in a Benedictine monastery nestled into the mountain and surrounded by jagged peaks. Take a funicular to view the monastery from above and to experience breathtaking views that stretch to the Pyrenees.

COLÒNIA GÜELL

Colònia Güell is a remnant from a time when the villages (called colonies) were built around rural industrial centers and factories. This particular colony remains intact in part because it features the spectacular Güell Crypt, one of Gaudí's least known works. The crypt—a UNESCO World Heritage site—is both architecturally unique and incredibly beautiful, making it a great option for an afternoon trip. It's easily accessible via public transportation and lies just outside Barcelona.

SALVADOR DALÍ MUSEUMS TOUR

Salvador Dalí was a native son of Catalonia who spent a good portion of his life north of Barcelona. Appropriately, several museums related to his work exist close to his hometown of Figueres: the

Gala Dalí Castle Púbol, a medieval estate dedicated to his wife Gala; the Dalí Theatre-Museum (where his body is entombed beneath the theater's stage); and the Salvador Dalí House in Portlligat. You may want to rent a car to visit all of them.

PARC NATURAL DE LA ZONA VOLCÀNICA DE LA GARROTXA

Garrotxa Volcanic Zone Natural Park is a massive natural park covering over 12,000 hectares. While the landscape is varied, its most remarkable features are the 40 dormant volcanic cones which dot the landscape. Incredibly vast, this park offers a plethora of outdoor activities which include trekking its scenic trails either on foot or via horse, cycling and mountain biking, and carriage rides.

Free Things to Do in Barcelona

FREE HOURS AT MUSEUMS

Many museums in Barcelona offer free admission on the first Sunday of the month including, MNAC (also free Saturday after 3), Palau Güell, Museu Frederic Marès, and Museu Picasso (also free Thursday evening).

CATEDRAL DE BARCELONA

This Gothic cathedral is a serene (and free) alternative to La Sagrada Família. Its broad front courtyard offers an unobstructed view of the cathedral's facade. You can call ahead of time if you'd like to arrange for a tour.

MONTJUÏC MAGIC FOUNTAIN

Built in the 1920s, the Montjuïc Magic Fountain offers a music-and-light show choreographed with undulating jets of water. It's a lively spot and a beautiful setting, even if it is a little kitschy, particularly if the evening's featured music is an '80s hits parade.

PARK GÜELL

Park Güell is another of Catalan architect Antoni Gaudí's beautiful creations. The hillside park features gorgeous mosaics as well as prime examples of Gaudí's architectural vision, and it's also home to multiple museums which require a ticket to enter. Don't be fooled into thinking that you have to pay to enter the park though—while the "monumental core" (i.e., the section of the park with the museums) requires a ticket there are sections you can enter free of charge.

WALKING TOUR

Barcelona is a beautiful city perfect for walking and there are multiple companies offering free walking tours. Sandemans New Europe and Runner Bean are both solid operations with knowledgeable tour guides and nice itineraries. (While these tours are free there is an expectation you'll tip your guide at the end.)

PARC DE LA CIUTADELLA

While this leafy park is home to several institutions which require tickets (such as the Museu d'Art Modern, the zoo, Museum of Natural Sciences, and the Museu de Geologia) one could argue that the main attraction is the park itself. It's also a popular place for runners and walkers alike, who are drawn in by its fountains, beautiful staircases, and towering palm trees.

Park Güell

FOOD MARKETS

Barcelona is justifiably known for its markets filled with vendors selling high-quality food, drink, and merchandise, and even if you don't buy anything they're a great way to experience the city's culture. The most famous by far is La Boquería, but lesser known (and trafficked) options include Mercat de la Llibertat, Mercat de Santa Caterina, and Mercat de Sant Antoni.

PARC DEL LABERINT

Free on Wednesday and Sunday, this park is the oldest remaining architectural park in Barcelona and is known for being off the beaten tourist path. Wander its terraces and you'll find not just the sculpted topiaries which make up the maze but other hidden gems as well, such as temples dedicated to the Greek gods Artemis and Danae and a statue of Dionysus, the god of wine. The park complex is also located inside of a Mediterranean forest, enhancing its peaceful nature.

CONCERT IN A PARK

Barcelona's Music in the Parks Festival is a yearly summer series of free concerts hosted in green spaces across the city. The performances, which provide a platform for young up-and-coming musicians, feature a variety of musical styles and act as a way of drawing people into the parks on summer evenings. It's a lovely way to listen to some free music, and to experience Barcelona's many parks.

THE BEACH

One of Barcelona's many charms is its free municipal beaches, such as Barceloneta and Sant Miguel. The weather is good year round; the beaches are centrally located and mostly populated with locals; and there are lots of amenities.

What's New in Barcelona

Capital of the autonomous Community of Catalonia, bilingual Barcelona (Catalan and Spanish) is the unrivaled visitor destination in Spain, and with good reason: dazzling art and architecture, creative cuisine, great weather, and warm hospitality are just part of what the city offers. Barcelona is proud of its cultural past and confident about its future.

A TALE OF TWO CITIES

Restive for centuries in the shadow of Madrid, where Spain ruled from the center—more often than not, with an iron hand—Barcelona has a drive to innovate and excel that stems largely from a determination to eclipse its long-time rival. A powerful sense of national identity (Catalans consider themselves a "nation" and decidedly not a province of Spain) motivates designers, architects, merchants, and industrialists to ever-higher levels of originality and achievement. Especially since the success of the 1992 Olympic Games, national pride and confidence have grown stronger and stronger, and today nearly half the Catalan population believes the nation would be better served—whatever implications that might have for membership in the European Union—by complete independence.

CUISINE: HAUTE AND HOT

Since Ferran Adrià's northern Catalonian phenomenon elBulli closed, *chef d'auteur* successes in Barcelona have proliferated. Some two dozen superb restaurants (and more on the way) have won international recognition, so keeping abreast of the city's culinary rock stars can be a dizzying pursuit. Here's a quick primer: Adrià disciple Sergi Arola, at his eponymous Arola Restaurant in the Hotel Arts, and Disfrutar—the project of three former elBulli chefs, Oriol Castro, Eduard Xatruch, and Mateu Casañas—remain at the frontier of Adrià-inspired

molecular gastronomy. Rising stars such as Jordi Artal of Cinc Sentits, Jordi Vilà of Alkimia, and Jordi Herrera of Manairó, join established masters Carles Gaig and Mey Hofmann in a dazzling galaxy of gastronomical creativity. Meanwhile, Raül Balam from Sant Pol de Mar and Martin Berasategui from San Sebastián have opened award-winning hotel restaurants in, respectively, the Mandarin Oriental (Moments), and the Monument Hotel (Lasarte). Add to this list up-and-comers like Jordi Cruz of the restaurant ÀBaC, the Torres twins of Cocina Hermanos Torres, and Romain Fornell of Caelis, and you begin to appreciate what a gastronomic haven Barcelona has become.

DESIGN AND ARCHITECTURE

Barcelona's cutting-edge achievements in interior design and couture continue to threaten the traditional dominance of Paris and Milan, while "starchitect" landmarks like Jean Nouvel's Torre Agbar, Norman Foster's communications tower on the Collserola skyline, and Ricardo Bofill's W Barcelona hotel (nicknamed Vela: the Sail) on the waterfront transform the city into a showcase of postmodern visual surprises.

Visitors can now marvel at some recently reopened Catalan Modernisme masterworks: Puig i Cadafalch's landmark Casa de les Punxes and Gaudí's Casa Vicens are open to the public and the restoration of Domènech i Montaner's Hospital de Sant Pau (now Europe's largest Art Nouveau architectural complex, rechristened the Sant Pau Recinte Modernista) is complete and a must-visit.

BREAKING NEW GROUND

With a new airport terminal, a behemoth new convention center complex, and a new AVE high-speed train connection to Madrid, Barcelona is again on the move. City planners predict that the recent redesign of Plaça de les Glòries will someday shift the city center eastward, and that the new Barcelona hub will surround the Torre Agbar and the Fòrum at the Mediterranean end of the Diagonal.

POLITICAL PROGRESS

The approval of Catalonia's controversial Autonomy Statute in 2008 ushered in a wave of change in Catalonia. Bitterly opposed by the right-wing Partido Popular, the autonomy agreement gives Catalonia a larger slice of local taxes and more control of its own infrastructure.. Perhaps more importantly, the new statute reinforces the use of the Catalan language and formally establishes Catalonia as one of the most progressive societies in Europe, with special provisions safeguarding human rights on same-sex marriage, euthanasia, and abortion that would win scant support in other more traditional regions of Spain. The Partido Popular, coming into power in 2011, rolled back many of the progressive laws passed in the previous eight years of Socialist government, and its austerity measures have hit a lot of people where it hurts; support grew steadily through 2017 for a referendum which eventually took place in October of the same year. Of those who voted, 90% supported independence; however, only 43% of all voters turned out, as many who opposed the split refused to vote in a referendum that is illegal under the present Spanish Constitution. A subsequent declaration of independence from Spain resulted in the Catalan leader, Carles Puigdemont, being exiled and several other members of the Catalan Parliament arrested and imprisoned. While protests are commonplace, the ongoing political crisis will not impact your visit.

What We're Talking About

In 2015, newly elected mayor Ada Colau imposed a moratorium on new hotels, part of an effort to limit growth of the city's tourist industry. Residents were generally happy with the idea, while hoteliers were not. More recently, another contentious subject for locals are the rising rents due to a boom in tourist rentals—people buying properties only to rent out to tourists at inflated prices, forcing locals out of the center, and leading to fears that the gentrification of the city's old town has turned it into an open-air museum.

The Sagrada Família, Gaudí's masterpiece that's been in the works since 1882, is finally nearing completion, expected to be finished by the centenary of Gaudí's death, in 2026. The basilica was consecrated by Pope Benedict XVI in 2010, and today the nave and transept of the interior are open to visitors. Drawing some 3 million visitors a year, it is Barcelona's most iconic structure.

Can FC Barcelona continue to dominate world *fútbol*? When beloved coach Pep Guardiola left the team for German Bundesliga club Bayern Munich in 2012, Barça faltered for a while; three coaches later, Guardiola protégé Luis Enrique (who retired at the end of the 2016–17 season) brought the team back as the Liga powerhouse. The latest coach, Ernesto Valverde, continues the legacy.

What to Watch and Read Before Your Trip

HOMAGE TO CATALONIA BY GEORGE ORWELL

George Orwell's life was strongly influenced by his time in Spain fighting against the Nationalist army led by future Fascist dictator Francisco Franco. Orwell's journals directly document his time at war in Catalonia and his first-person narrative provides a view of war-torn Barcelona.

THE SHADOW OF THE WIND BY CARLOS RUIZ ZAFÓN

Daniel Sempere is 10 years old when his father, a bookseller in post–civil war Barcelona, takes him to a mysterious labyrinth filled with treasured but forgotten tomes and tells him to pick one that he will then dedicate his life to preserving. What follows is a tale of a young man who discovers a mysterious person—or perhaps creature—is destroying all remaining works of Julián Carax, the author whose book he now protects. *The Shadow of the Wind*'s story of life, death, and history may be fictional, but its setting in a war-torn Spain is forceful, and the fact that it's sold more than 15 million copies hints at its compelling universe.

THE BEST THING THAT CAN HAPPEN TO A CROISSANT BY PABLO TUSSET

Pablo "Baloo" Miralles is the lazy, debaucherous scion of a well-to-do Spanish family. When his elder (and more accomplished) brother inexplicably disappears, Baloo suddenly finds himself pulled into the dealings of the family's powerful financial firm, a turn of events which inspires him to try to locate his missing sibling. Within this satirical quasi-detective story is a modern-day tale about the city of Barcelona.

THE CITY OF MARVELS BY EDUARDO MENDOZA

The tale of a boy who rises from abject poverty to great wealth and power and a city—Barcelona—that expands from a small provincial capital to a metropolitan city. The action spans the years between Barcelona's two economically disastrous World's Fairs of 1888 and 1929.

HOMAGE TO BARCELONA BY COLM TÓIBÍN

Irish author Colm Tóibín moved to Barcelona in 1975 when he was twenty. In this book, written with deep affection and knowledge, Tóibín celebrates one of Europe's greatest cities and explores its history, moving from its foundations through to nationalism, civil war, and the transition from dictatorship to democracy. He looks at the lives of Barcelona's great artists—Gaudí, Miró, Picasso, Casals, and Dali. Tóibín is the perfect guide to Barcelona and this is a sensuous and beguiling portrait of a unique Mediterranean port and an adopted home.

MARKS OF IDENTITY BY JUAN GOYTISOLO

A searing masterpiece from Spain's greatest living novelist describes the return of an exile to Barcelona. Goytisolo comes to the conclusion that every man carries his own exile about with him, wherever he lives. The narrator (Goytisolo) rejects Spain itself and searches instead for poetry. This is a shocking and influential work, and an affirmation of the ability of the individual to survive the political tyrannies of the last century and the current one. *Marks of Identity* was banned in Spain until after Franco's death.

THE TIME OF THE DOVES BY MERCÈ RODOREDA

Written by exiled Catalan writer Mercè Rodoreda, *The Time of the Doves* is a novel about a shopkeeper named Natalia who endures a controlling husband and an increasingly challenging life during the Spanish Civil War. This is widely considered a classic of Catalan literature and is required reading in Catalan secondary schools. It's a story about hope and endurance in the face of great adversity. After the Spanish Civil War, when the Catalan language was banned in public and the culture harshly suppressed,

Rodoreda went into exile. In 1962 she published La plaça del Diamant (translated as The Time of the Doves by David Rosenthal in 1981), widely regarded as her masterpiece and a masterpiece of Catalan literature. It is not your usual account of the civil war in that there is no fighting and no scenes from the front. We learn about the war from the perspective of a woman whose husband is fighting with the Republicans while she works hard to feed herself and her two children. Gabriel García Márquez learned Catalan just to read this book and declared it "the most beautiful novel that's been published in Spain after the Civil War." The author, who died in 1983, is also known for her first novel, *Aloma*.

NADA BY CARMEN LAFORET

In the aftermath of the Spanish Civil War a young woman named Andrea moves to Barcelona so that she can attend university on a government scholarship. Once there she finds herself living in the home of her grandmother, a decrepit building haunted by the emotionally and physically violent confrontations and betrayals of the array of family members who reside there. Nada is considered to be a Catalan Existentialist classic, a rare volume from a time when Franco's censors suppressed novels from Catalan writers and tamped down on anything which showed how desperate life could be.

TODO SOBRE MI MADRE (ALL ABOUT MY MOTHER) DIRECTED BY PEDRO ALMODÓVAR

After Manuela's 17-year-old son Esteban is killed before her eyes she decides to move to Barcelona in order to find his father, a transvestite named Lola who doesn't know that Esteban exists. It's a brilliantly directed tale which sensitively examines a variety of complex topics such as bereavement, addiction, gender identity, and the impacts of HIV. It also earned director Pedro Almodóvar the Best Director award at the 1999 Cannes Film Festival and the Academy Award for Best Foreign Language Film in 2000.

BIUTIFUL DIRECTED BY ALEJANDRO GONZÁLEZ IÑÁRRITU

Iñárritu's first feature since *Babel*, and his fourth moving film is the story of a single father of two (Javier Bardem) in Barcelona who finds out he has terminal cancer and tries to find someone to care for his children before his death. While melancholy, this is also a story of redemption as a father seeks a better life for his children.

A GUN IN EACH HAND DIRECTED BY CESC GAY

Catalan director Cesc Gay recruited some top-notch Spanish actors and actresses for this comedy. Told through a series of vignettes, *A Gun in Each Hand* explores how changing gender roles in Spain affect modern relationships—typically by having the central male

characters either embarrass themselves directly, or suffer some form of emasculation at the hands of their much more clever female counterparts. It speaks to how Spanish ideas about masculinity and relationships are changing, and how the an evolution can benefit women in Spain.

SUMMER 1993 DIRECTED BY CARLA SIMÓN

Director Carla Simón was only six years old when she went to live with her aunt and uncle after her parents died of AIDS. In her debut film, *Summer 1993*, the character of Frida shares the same fate and goes to live in the Catalan countryside outside of Barcelona. In the mid-'90s, Spain had the highest number of AIDS cases in Europe, and this film is a courageous and personal exploration of the tragedy of Spain's AIDS crisis.

JULIA IST DIRECTED BY ELENA MARTIN

When Julia, a university student in Barcelona, decides to move to Berlin, she anticipates a life of escape, where she'll blossom away from her family and longtime boyfriend. It's only after settling in Berlin that she realizes it's not the vibrant place she anticipated, or that she might not be the person she thought she was. Inspired by the lives of the four screenwriters who produced this film, and shot on a limited budget, *Julia Ist* is a story of growth, identity, and independence, topics that Spain—and Catalonia in particular—still struggle with.

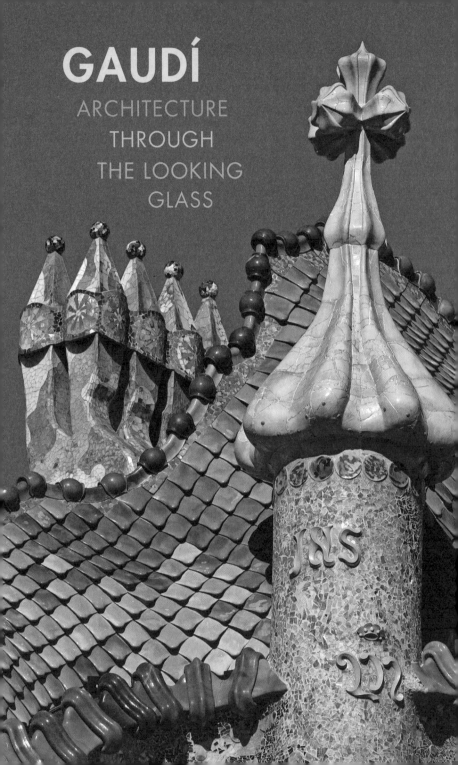

GAUDÍ

ARCHITECTURE THROUGH THE LOOKING GLASS

(left) The undulating rooftop of Casa Batlló. (top) Right angles are notably absent in the Casa Milà façade.

Before his 75th birthday in 1926, Antoni Gaudí was hit by a trolley car while on his way to Mass. The great architect—initially unidentified—was taken to the medieval Hospital de la Santa Creu in Barcelona's Raval and left in a pauper's ward, where he died two days later without regaining consciousness. It was a dramatic and tragic end for a man whose entire life seemed to court the extraordinary and the exceptional.

Gaudí's singularity made him hard to define. Indeed, eulogists at the time, and decades later, wondered how history would treat him. Was he a religious mystic, a rebel, a bohemian artist, a Moderniste genius? Was he, perhaps, all of these? He certainly had a rebellious streak, as his architecture stridently broke with tradition. Yet the same sensibility that created the avant-garde benchmarks Park Güell and La Pedrera also created one of Spain's greatest shrines to Catholicism, the *Temple Expiatori de la Sagrada Família* (Expiatory Temple of the Holy Family), which archi-

tects agree is one of the world's most enigmatic structures; work on the cathedral continues to this day. And while Gaudí's works suggest a futurist aesthetic, he also reveled in the use of ornamentation, which 20th century architecture largely eschewed.

What is no longer in doubt is Gaudí's place among the great architects in history. Eyed with suspicion by traditionalists in the 1920s and 30s, vilified during the Franco regime, and ultimately redeemed as a Barcelona icon after Spain's democratic transition in the late 70s, Gaudí has finally gained universal admiration.

THE MAKING OF A GENIUS

Gaudí was born in 1852 the son of a boilermaker and coppersmith in Reus, an hour south of Barcelona. As a child, he helped his father forge boilers and cauldrons in the family foundry, which is where Gaudí's fascination with three-dimensional and organic forms began. Afflicted from an early age with reoccuring rheumatic fever, the young architect devoted his energies to studying and drawing flora and fauna in the natural world. In school Gaudí was erratic: brilliant in the subjects that interested him, absent and disinterested in the others. As a seventeen-year-old architecture student in Barcelona, his academic results were mediocre. Still, his mentors agreed that he was brilliant.

Unfortunately being brilliant didn't mean instant success. By the late 1870s, when Gaudí was well into his twenties, he'd only completed a handful of projects, including the Plaça Reial lampposts, a flower stall, and the factory and part of a planned workers' community in Mataró. Gaudí's career got the boost it needed when, in 1878, he met Eusebi Güell, heir to a textiles fortune and a man who, like Gaudí, had a refined sensibility. (The two bonded over a mutual admiration for the visionary Catalan poet Jacint Verdaguer.) In 1883 Gaudí became Güell's architect and for the next three decades, until Güell's death in 1918, the two collaborated on Gaudí's most important architectural achievements, from high-profile endeavors like Palau Güell, Park Güell, and Pabellones Güell to smaller projects for the Güell family.

(top) Interior of Casa Batlló. (bottom) Chimneys on rooftop of Casa Milà recall helmeted warriors or veiled women.

GAUDÍ TIMELINE

1883–1884

Gaudí builds a summer palace, *El Capricho* in Comillas, Santander for the brother-in-law of his benefactor, Eusebi Güell. Another gig comes his way during this same period when Barcelona ceramics tile mogul Manuel Vicens hires him to build his town house, Casa Vicens, in the Gràcia neighborhood.

El Capricho

1884–1900

Gaudí whips up the Pabellones Güell, Palau Güell, the Palacio Episcopal of Astorga, Barcelona's Teresianas school, the Casa de los Botines in León, Casa Calvet, and Bellesguard. These have his classic look of this time, featuring interpretation of Mudéjar (Moorish motifs), Gothic, and Baroque styles.

Palacio Episcopal

BREAKING OUT OF THE T-SQUARE PRISON

If Eusebi Güell had not believed in Gaudí's unusual approach to Modernisme, his creations might not have seen the light of day. Güell recognized that Gaudí was imbued with a vision that separated him from the crowd. That vision was his fascination with the organic. Gaudí had observed early in his career that buildings were being composed of shapes that could only be drawn by the compass and the T-square: circles, triangles, squares, and rectangles—shapes that in three dimensions became prisms, pyramids, cylinders and spheres. He saw that in nature these shapes are unknown. Admiring the structural efficiency of trees, mammals, and the human form, Gaudí noted ". . . neither are trees prismatic, nor bones cylindrical, nor leaves triangular." The study of natural forms revealed that bones, branches, muscles, and tendons are all supported by internal fibers. Thus, though a surface curves, it is supported from within by a fibrous network that Gaudí translated into what he called "ruled geometry," a system of inner reinforcement he used to make hyperboloids, conoids, helicoids, or parabolic hyperboloids.

These tongue-tying words are simple forms and familiar shapes: the femur is hyperboloid; the way shoots grow

Hyperboloid

Hyperbolic Paraboloid

The top of the gatehouse in Park Güell at the main entrance; note the mushroom-like form.

off a branch is helicoidal; the web between your fingers is a hyperbolic paraboloid. To varying degrees, these ideas find expression in all of Gaudí's work, but nowhere are they more clearly stated than in the two masterpieces La Pedrera and Park Güell.

1900–1917

Gaudí's Golden Years—his most creative, personal, and innovative period. Topping each success with another, he tackles Park Güell, the reform of Casa Batlló, the Güell Colony church, Casa Milà (La Pedrera), and the Sagrada Família school.

Casa Batlló's complex chimneys

1918–1926

A crushing blow: Gaudí suffers the death of his assistant, Francesc Berenguer. Grieving and rudderless, he devotes himself fully to his great unfinished opus, la Sagrada Família—to the point of obsession. On June 10th, 1926, he's hit by a trolley car. He dies two days later.

La Sagrada Família

KEY

◄ **0.8mi**	Mile Marker
◇	Metro Stations
┼	Railway Lines
i	Tourist Information

0 ————— 1/4 mile

0 ————— 1/2 km

Collegi de les Teresianes

● Bellesguard Tower

Park Güell

Park Güell

Ronda del General Mitre

C. de Madrell

C. de Muntaner

C. de Saragossa

C. de Vallirana

C. de Menéndez Pelayo

C. de Verdi

C. de Alzina

SARRIÀ

LESSEPS

Plaça de Lesseps

Trav. de Dalt

C. de Sant Salvador

C. de Santa Agata

C. d'Asturies

Casa Vicens

FONTANA

C. Gran de Gràcia

GRÀCIA

Via Augusta

Avda. Diagonal

Travessera de Gràcia

GRÀCIA

Plaça de Joan Carles I

C. de Còrsega

i

DIAGONAL

C. del Rosselló

● Casa Milà (La Pedrera)

C. de Provença

C. de Mallorca

C. de València

Avda. Diagonal

C. d'Aragó

C. de Consell de Cent

SAGRADA FAMÍLIA

● Sagrada Família

C. de Sardenya

C. de Marina

C. de Balmes

Rambla de Catalunya

Passeig de Gràcia

C. de Pau Claris

EIXAMPLE

Casa Batlló ●

PASSEIG DE GRÀCIA

Plaça Universitat

C. de la Diputació

Plaça de Catalunya

Gran Vía de les Corts Catalanes

Ronda S. Pere

C. de Casp

● Casa Calvet

Pl. Urquinaona

Pelai

CATALUNYA

C. Sta. Anna

URQUINAONA

C. del Carme

La Rambla

ARC DE TRIOMF

C. dels Almogàvers

Passeig de Lluís Companys

Avda. de la Meridiana

P. de Carles

MARIN

C. de Hospital

LICEU

C. Ferran

BARRI GÒTIC

C. Princesa

Passeig Pujades

i

Parc de la Ciutadella

C. Nou de la Rambla

Plaça Reial

Passeig del Born

Pg. Picasso

Palau Güell

C. Ample

DRASSANES

Rambla de Santa Mónica

Pg. de Colom

Pl. d'Antoni López

BARCELONETA

C. de Wellington

Plaça Portal de la Pau

Rambla de Mar

Moll d'Espanya

BARCELONETA

Avda. d'Icària

CIUTADELLA-VILA OLÍMPICA

Passeig Marítim

Mile markers: **1 mi**, **0.22mi**, **0.15mi**, **0.22mi**, **0.82mi**, **0.3 mi**, **0.9 mi**, **0.2 mi**, **0.25 mi**, **0.25 mi**, **0.6 mi**, **0.23 mi**, **0.32 mi**, **0.25 mi**, **0.8 mi**

Park Güell.
A mosaic dragon greets visitors on Park Güell's central staircase.

La Sagrada Família.
Tubular bell towers over the Nativity façade were designed by Gaudí for an innovative carillon musical system.

Palau Güell. The rooftop chimneys display organic form. Using colorful broken tiles, each is a unique structure almost like a topiary garden.

Casa Calvet. Gaudí forewent his trademark Moorish and medieval touches for a simpler (but still Moderniste) structure.

Casa Milà (La Pedrera). The undulating stone façade seems to reflect the Mediterranean's rolling surface.

HOW TO SEE GAUDÍ IN BARCELONA

Few architects have left their stamp on a major city as thoroughly as Gaudí did in Barcelona. Paris may have the Eiffel Tower, but Barcelona has Gaudí's still unfinished masterpiece, the **Temple Expiatori de la Sagrada Família,** the city's most emblematic structure. Dozens of other buildings, parks, gateways and even paving stones around town bear Gaudí's personal Art Nouveau signature, but the continuing progress on his last and most ambitious project makes his creative energy an ongoing part of everyday Barcelona life in a unique and almost spectral fashion.

In Barcelona, nearly all of Gaudí's work can be visited on foot or, at most, with a couple of metro or taxi rides. A walk from **Palau Güell** near the Mediterranean end of the Rambla, up past **Casa Calvet** just above Plaça Catalunya, and on to **Casa Batlló** and **Casa Milà** is an hour's stroll, which, of course, could take a full day with thorough visits to the sites. **Casa Vicens** is a half hour's walk up into Gràcia from

(top) The serpentine ceramic bench at Park Güell, designed by Gaudí collaborator Josep Maria Jujol, curves sinuously around the edge of the open square. (bottom) Sculptures by Josep María Subirachs grace the temple of the Sagrada Família.

Casa Milà. Park Güell is another thirty- to forty-minute walk up from that. **La Sagrada Família,** on the other hand, is a good hour's hike from the next nearest Gaudí point and is best reached by taxi or metro. The **Teresianas** school, the **Bellesguard Tower,** and **Pabellones Güell** are within an hour's walk of each other, but to get out to Sarrià you will need to take the comfortable Generalitat (FGC) train.

Chapter 2

TRAVEL SMART

Updated by
Steve Tallantyre
and Jacob Dean

★ **CAPITAL**
Madrid

⚥ POPULATION
48,958,159

LANGUAGE
Spanish

$ CURRENCY
Euro

☎ **COUNTRY CODE**
34

⚠ **EMERGENCIES**
112

🚗 **DRIVING**
On the right side

✦ **ELECTRICITY**
220 volts/50 cycles; electrical
plugs have two round prongs

🕐 **TIME**
Six hours ahead of New York

⊕ **WEB RESOURCES**
www.spain.info
www.parador.es

What You Need to Know Before You Go

Should you tip? When can you eat? Should you skip the touristy bits? We've got answers and a few tips to help you make the most of your visit to this beautiful city.

CATALAN CULTURE IS STRONG

Before the rise of modern-day Spain there was Aragon, a kingdom on the Iberian Peninsula whose territories included the regions we know as Catalonia and Aragon, as well as Roussillon, a part of southern France. The Catalan people and their culture are tenacious and Barcelona—the capital of Catalonia—remains strongly Catalan. This means that you'll see signage printed in both Spanish and Catalan and will also hear Catalan being spoken. While you won't be expected to learn the language, it's a sign of respect to learn at least a few Catalan words. As a visitor you should also keep in mind that the Catalan bid for independence remains an unresolved and politically sensitive issue for a number of people, and the polite thing to do is avoid talking about Spanish politics in public.

YOU DON'T NEED TO TIP (BUT ROUNDING UP IS NICE)

Service industry jobs in Europe tend to pay better than they do in the United States, and in Spain tipping is neither expected nor required. Rounding up a euro or two in a restaurant where you had good service is a nice and appreciated gesture though, and the same goes for throwing in an extra euro for a cab ride, or even just letting your driver keep the change.

MEALS ARE LATE AND LONG

The Spanish internal clock is set about three hours behind that of America, which means late lunches and even later dinners. Brunch starts at noon, lunch starts at 2 or 3, and dinner starts at 10 or 11. Keep in mind that meals, and particularly dinners, can be multihour affairs as well, with the potential for more than one round of food and certainly multiple drink orders. If you're not up for adopting the Spanish meal schedule you can of course eat whenever you want, but you won't always have the same restaurant options available off-hours, especially for lunch.

WATCH OUT FOR THIEVES

For all of its charms Barcelona is also a place where petty theft is common. Pickpocketing, mugging, and bag snatching remain a chronic, daily problem in Barcelona, and this is particularly true in any place where you'll find crowds of distracted people, such as train platforms and on La Rambla. Leave original documents—especially plane tickets, your ID, and your passport—in your place of lodging and instead carry photocopies if you think you'll need to show ID. As with any major city, keep bags and purses closed at all times and wear them on your front. If you are the victim of theft, dial "112" (which offers services in English) or visit the Help Centre for Tourists at 43 La Rambla: it's open 24 hours a day.

GO AHEAD AND ORDER THE BOTTLE

You already know that Spanish wine is world famous, but you might be surprised—and delighted—to hear that in Spain it's also wildly inexpensive. Spain offers some of the best wine values in all of Europe, and ordering a bottle of wine in a tapas bar could easily mean spending less than 10 euros, with that same bottle costing half of that in a shop. Even better, northern Spain has fabulous wines and many quality appellations (areas producing distinct wines). A particularly good one is DO (Denominación de Origen) Cariñena, a wine-producing area near the city of Zaragoza.

FC BARCELONA IS EVERYTHING

Not only is FC Barcelona one of the single best football (soccer) teams on the planet, it also has an incredibly successful youth soccer program designed to groom the next generation of sports idols. FC Barcelona fandom is basically a religion here and if you want to worship alongside fans, you should buy tickets in advance online or at kiosks throughout the city as well as at ATMs at Caixa de Catalunya banks. Inside tip: if you don't have tickets but want the local FC Barcelona experience, find a bar during a match and enjoy the experience of watching—and *feeling*—a game with locals.

THE BEACHES ARE FREE, BUT BUSY

Barcelona is a seaside city and that means easy access to the beach … which means everyone goes. For that reason, the most central beaches—Barceloneta and Sant Miguel—are also the most crowded and chaotic. If you're looking for a stretch of sand that isn't completely crammed with people, leave the city entirely: there are beautiful, clean beaches just outside of the city that are perfect for a day trip.

THE RESTAURANTS ARE GREAT, BUT YOU'LL WANT TO EAT AT THE MARKET

While it might be hard to turn yourself away from one of Barcelona's countless restaurants, at least one of your meals should be a picnic made up of ingredients like jamón

ibérico, olives, cheese, olive oil, bread, and tomatoes—or whatever strikes your fancy at one of the city's many incredible markets. Barcelona's most famous open-air food market is La Boqueria, but other top options include Mercat Santa Caterina in La Ribera, Tutusaus in Upper Barcelona, and Plaça del Pi in Barri Gòtic.

LA RAMBLA IS SUPER CROWDED

Once upon a time the wide avenue called La Rambla was considered one of Barcelona's essential tourism destinations, and then everyone went there, all at once! La Rambla now maintains a reputation as a loud tourist trap known for its illegal betting and drinking, pickpockets, and thieves. It's not exactly an unsafe area, but it's also not exactly fun in peak tourist season. Regardless, you will find yourself absolutely compelled to visit La Rambla because it has to be done. In summer especially, do yourself a favor and visit early in the day.

SUNDAY IS A DAY OF REST

Spain is a Catholic majority country and while Barcelona doesn't completely shut down on Sundays it is a day when a significant number of businesses close. This doesn't mean that you can't still have fun or find a place to eat, but your options will definitely be limited and stores (including supermarkets) will likely not be open.

EAT PAELLA ON SUNDAY

Paella is Valencian, not Catalan, but Sunday paella in La Barceloneta, usually with seafront views, is a local family tradition. Excellent La Barceloneta options include Pez Vela Chiringuito, Xiringuito Escriba, La Barraca, and Restaurante la Barca del Salamanca. Make reservations in advance to avoid disappointment. When ordering, know that paella marinera is a seafood rice boiled in fish stock and seasoned with clams, mussels, prawns, and jumbo shrimp, while traditional paella valenciana omits seafood and includes chicken, rice, and snails. Paella feeds a minimum of two diners, and is usually enough for three people to share.

PLAN AHEAD

There are a few major attractions in Barcelona that rank highly on most traveler bucket lists and if you are hoping to check some of the world's top attractions off your list, too, you'll need to plan ahead. For big-ticket sights like the the Sagrada Família, Parc Güell, and the Picasso Museum, you will need to book tickets before you arrive. Also plan ahead if you wish to attend a performance at the Palau de la Música Catalana.

Getting Here and Around

With some planning, finding your way around in Barcelona can be simple. All of Barcelona's Ciutat Vella (Old City), including the Barri Gòtic (Gothic Quarter), can be explored on foot. Your transport needs will be mainly to get to Sarrià, Gràcia, Park Güell, Gaudí's Sagrada Família, Montjuïc, and the Auditori near Plaça de les Glòries. The metro system will normally get you wherever you need to go. The commuter trains on the Catalan regional government's FGC system are also handy. The municipal metro lines are useful, air-conditioned, and safe. Buses are practical for certain runs, and taxis are rarely much more than €15 for a complete crosstown ride.

Modern Barcelona, above Plaça de Catalunya, is built on a grid system. The Old City, however, from Plaça de Catalunya to the port, is a labyrinth of narrow streets, so you'll need a good street map (or GPS) and a good pair of shoes to explore it. Whenever possible, it's best to avoid driving in the city. *(For information about driving, see Car Travel.)* Maps of the bus and metro routes are available free from the main tourist information office on Plaça de Catalunya.

✈ Air Travel

Transatlantic flying time to Barcelona's El Prat Airport averages about 7 hours and 30 minutes from New York's JFK Airport. Other U.S. cities with direct flights to Barcelona are Atlanta, Chicago, Miami, Newark, and Philadelphia. Low-cost carrier Norwegian Airlines also has direct routes from Fort Lauderdale, Oakland, Newark, and Los Angeles. Flying from other cities in North America usually requires a connection.

Nonstop flights from London to Barcelona average 2 hours and 30 minutes. Flights from the United Kingdom to a number of destinations in Spain are frequent and offered at competitive fares, particularly on low-cost carriers such as Ryanair or easyJet.

For air travel within the regions covered in this book there are numerous regular flights, but rates tend to be high, so consider alternative ways of getting around. Bilbao, Pamplona, and San Sebastián all have small airports, and flights do run from Barcelona to each of them. For travel between those cities, given the short distances involved, most people elect to go by train or car.

Iberia operates a shuttle, the *puente aereo,* between Barcelona and Madrid from 6:50 am to 9:45 pm; planes depart from Terminal 1 hourly, and more frequently in the morning and afternoon commuter hours. Flying time is about an hour and a half; given the time you need for airport transfers, many commuters now prefer the high-speed rail connection between Estació de Sants in Barcelona and Atocha Station in Madrid. You don't need to reserve ahead for the shuttle flight; you can buy your tickets at the counter when you get to the airport.

Charter flights of varying prices routinely fly in and out of El Prat Airport. Top charter companies include NetJets, Global Jet Concept, and Luxaviation.

AIRPORTS

Most connecting flights arriving in Spain from the United States and Canada pass through Madrid's Barajas Airport (MAD), but the major gateway to Catalonia and other regions in this book is Spain's second-largest airport, Barcelona's spectacular glass, steel, and marble El Prat del Llobregat (BCN). The second of two terminals, the T1 terminal, which opened in 2009, is a sleek ultramodern facility that uses solar panels for sustainable energy and offers a spa, a fitness center, restaurants and cafés, and VIP lounges. This airport is about 12 km (7½ miles) southwest from the center of Barcelona and is served by numerous international carriers, but Catalonia also has two other airports that handle passenger traffic, including charter flights. One is Girona-Costa Brava Airport (GRO) 12½ km (8 miles) southwest of Girona, 90 km (56 miles) north of Barcelona and convenient to the resort towns of the Costa Brava. Bus and train connections from Girona to Barcelona are convenient and affordable, provided you have the time. The other Catalonia airport is the tiny Reus Airport (REU), 110 km (68 miles) south of Barcelona and a gateway to neighboring Tarragona, Port Adventura theme park, and the beaches of the Costa Daurada. Both airports are considerably smaller than El Prat and offer the bare essentials: a limited number of duty-free shops, restaurants, and car hire services. Flights to and from the major cities in Europe and Spain also fly into and out of Bilbao's Loiu (BIL) airport. For information about airports in Spain, consult ⊕ www.aena.es.

GROUND TRANSPORTATION

Check first to see if your hotel in Barcelona provides airport-shuttle service. If not, visitors typically get into town by train, bus, taxi, or rental car.

Cab fare from the airport into town is €30–€35, depending on traffic, the part of town you're heading to, and the amount of baggage you have (there's a €3.10 surcharge for airport pickups/drop-offs, and a €1 surcharge for each suitcase that goes in the trunk). If you're driving your own car, follow signs to the Centre Ciutat, from which you can enter the city along Gran Vía. For the port area, follow signs for the Ronda Litoral. The journey to the center of town can take 25–45 minutes, depending on traffic.

The Aerobus leaves Terminal 1 at the airport for Plaça de Catalunya every 10 minutes 5:35–7:20 am and 10:25 pm–1:05 am, and every 5 minutes 7:30 am–10:20 pm. From Plaça de Catalunya the bus leaves for the airport every 5 or 10 minutes between 5 am and 12:10 am. The fare is €5.90 one way and €10.20 round-trip. Aerobuses for Terminals 1 and 2 pick up and drop off passengers at the same stops en route, so if you're outward bound make sure that you board the right one. The A1 Aerobus for Terminal 1 is two-tone light and dark blue; the A2 Aerobus for Terminal 2 is dark blue and yellow.

The train's only drawback is that it's a 10- to 15-minute walk from your gate through Terminal 2 over the bridge. From Terminal 1 a shuttle bus drops you at the train. Trains leave the airport every 30 minutes between 5:42 am and 11:38 pm, stopping at Estació de Sants, for transfer to the Arc de Triomf, then at Passeig de Gràcia and finally at El Clot–Aragó. Trains going to the airport begin at 5:21 am from El Clot, stopping at Passeig de Gràcia at 5:27 am, and Sants at 5:32 am. The trip takes about half an hour, and the fare is €4.10. But the best bargain is the T10 subway card; it gives you free connections within Barcelona plus nine more rides, all for €10.20. Add an extra hour if you take the train to or from the airport.

TRANSFERS BETWEEN AIRPORTS

To get to Girona Airport from Barcelona Airport by train you have to first catch the RENFE train that leaves from the airport and then change at Barcelona Sants station. From Barcelona Sants

Getting Here and Around

you need to catch the train for Figueres and get off at Girona, two stops before. Travel times vary between 38 minutes and 2 hours 10 minutes depending on the train line. From there you will have to take a 30-minute bus ride, or a 17-minute taxi ride to the airport for around €25–€30. Allow yourself 30 minutes from the RENFE Girona station to the airport.

Sagales runs the Barcelona Bus shuttle buses between Girona airport and El Prat. The trip takes about 1 hour and 15 minutes. The schedules, set up to coincide with RyanAir arrivals and departures at Girona, are a bit tortuous; consult the Sagales website or call ☎ 902/130014 for bus information.

FLIGHTS

If you are traveling from North America, consider flying a British or other European carrier, especially if you are traveling directly to Barcelona or Bilbao. Though you may have to change planes in London, Paris, Amsterdam, Zurich, or even Rome, savings can be significant.

The least expensive airfares to Barcelona are priced for round-trip travel and must usually be purchased in advance. Airlines generally allow you to change your return date for a fee; most low-fare tickets, however, are nonrefundable.

On certain days of the week, Iberia offers minifares (*minitarifas*), which can save you 40% on domestic flights. Tickets must be purchased at least two days in advance, and you must stay over at your destination on a Saturday night.

American, United/Continental, Delta, and Iberia fly to Madrid and Barcelona; Norwegian Air Shuttle flies to Barcelona from San Francisco, Los Angeles, New York, Miami, and Orlando; US Airways and Air Europa fly to Madrid. Within Spain, Iberia is the main domestic airline;

two independent airlines, Air Europa and Vueling, fly a number of domestic routes at somewhat lower prices.

🚢 Boat Travel

There are regular ferry services between the United Kingdom and northwestern Spain. Brittany Ferries sails from Portsmouth to Bilbao and Santander. The trip is more than 24 hours, so not practical unless you love the ocean and have some extra time on your hands. Spain's major ferry line, Trasmediterránea, links mainland Spain (including Barcelona) with the Balearics and the Canary Islands. This ferry's fast catamaran service takes half the time of the standard ferry, but catamarans are often canceled because they can navigate only in very calm waters. Trasmediterránea and Balearia operate overnight ferries from Barcelona, Valencia, and Dénia to the islands of Mallorca, Menorca, and Ibiza. Formentera can be reached from Ibiza via Balearia and Transmapi, a local ferry company. At 7 hours, 30 minutes from Barcelona via ferry crossing, Mallorca is the closest island. Long-stretch ferries are equipped with a choice of seating options including sleepers, a restaurant, several bars, and small shopping area.

You can pick up schedules and buy tickets at the ferry ticket office in the port.

CRUISE TRAVEL

Barcelona is Europe's busiest cruise port, and the fourth largest in the world. Vessels dock at the Port Vell facility, which has seven terminals catering to cruise-ship traffic. All terminals are equipped with duty-free shops, telephones, bar/restaurants, information desks, and currency-exchange booths. The ships docking closest to the terminal entrance are a 10-minute walk from the southern end of La Rambla (the Rambla), but those docked at the farthest end require passengers to catch a shuttle bus (the Autobús Azul, a distinctive blue bus) to the port entrance. The shuttle, which runs every 20 minutes, links all terminals with the public square at the bottom of the Rambla. If you walk up La Rambla, after about 10 minutes you'll reach Drassanes metro station for onward public transport around the city. The shuttle runs about every 30 minutes.

🚌 Bus Travel

Barcelona's main bus station for intra-Spain routes is Estació del Nord, a few blocks east of the Arc de Triomf. Buses also depart from the Estació de Sants for long-distance and international routes, as well as from the depots of Barcelona's various private bus companies. Spain's major national long-haul company is ALSA. Grup Sarbus serves Catalonia and, with its subsidiary Sarfa, the Costa Brava. Bus timetables are complicated and confusing; trying to get information by phone will probably get you put on interminable hold. Better to plan your bus trip online or through a local travel agent, who can quickly book you the best way to your destination.

Within Spain, private companies provide comfortable and efficient bus services between major cities. Fares are lower than the corresponding train fares, and service is more extensive: if you want to get somewhere not served by rail, you can be sure a bus will go there. *See the planner section in Chapter 12 for companies serving Catalonia.*

Most larger bus companies have buses with comfortable seats and adequate legroom; on longer journeys (two to three hours or more) a movie is shown on board, and earphones are provided. Except for smaller, regional buses that travel short hops, buses have bathrooms on board. Smoking is prohibited. Most long-haul buses stop at least once every two to three hours for a snack and bathroom break. Although buses are subject to road and traffic conditions, highways in Catalonia and the Basque Country, particularly along major routes, are well maintained. That may not be the case in more rural areas, where you could be in for a bumpy ride.

You can get to Spain by bus from London, Paris, Rome, Frankfurt, Prague, and other major European cities. It is a long journey, but the buses are modern and inexpensive. Eurolines, the main carrier, connects many European cities with Barcelona.

ALSA, Spain's largest national bus company, has two luxury classes in addition to its regular coach services. The top of the line is Supra Clase, with roomy leather seats, free Wi-Fi Internet connection, and onboard meals; in this class you also have the option of *asientos individuales,* single-file seats along one side of the bus. The next class is the Eurobus, with comfy seats and plenty of legroom, but no asientos individuales or onboard meals. The Supra Clase and Eurobus cost up to one-third and one-quarter more, respectively, than the regular coaches.

Some smaller, regional bus lines (Sarfa, for example, which connects Barcelona to destinations on the Costa Brava) offer multitrip bus passes, which are worthwhile if you plan on making multiple trips between two destinations. Generally, these tickets offer a savings of 20% per journey; you can buy them only in the bus station (not on the bus).

Getting Here and Around

In Barcelona you can pick up schedule and fare information at the tourist information offices in Plaça de Catalunya, Plaça Sant Jaume, or at the Sants train station. A better and faster solution is to check online at ⊕ *www.barcelonanord.com.*

At bus-station ticket counters, major credit cards (except for American Express) are universally accepted. You must pay in cash for tickets purchased on the bus. Traveler's checks are almost never accepted.

During peak travel times (Easter, August, and Christmas), it's always a good idea to make a reservation at least three to four days in advance.

City buses run daily 5:30 am–11:30 pm. Route maps are displayed at bus stops. Note that those with a red band always stop at a central square—Catalunya, Universitat, or Urquinaona—and blue, with an N prefix on the bus number, indicates a night bus. Barcelona's 17 night buses generally run until about 5 am.

🚡 Cable Car and Funicular Travel

The Montjuïc Funicular is a cog railway that runs from the junction of Avinguda Paral.lel and Nou de la Rambla (Ⓜ *Paral. lel)* to Montjuïc Castle, with stops en route at Parc de Monjuïc and Miramar. It operates weekdays 7:30 am–8 pm and weekends 9 am–9 pm; the fare is €2.15, or one ride on a T10 card.

A Transbordador Aeri del Port (Harbor Cable Car) runs between Miramar and Montjuïc across the harbor to Torre de Jaume I, on Barcelona's *moll* (quay), and on to Torre de Sant Sebastià, at the end of Passeig Joan de Borbó in Barceloneta. You can board at either stage. One-way fare is €11; round-trip fare is

€16.50. The car runs every eight minutes, November–February 11 am–5:30 pm, March–May and September and October 11 am–7 pm, and June–August 11 am–8 pm.

To reach the summit of Tibidabo, take the metro to Avinguda de Tibidabo, then the Tramvía Blau (€5.50 one way) to Peu del Funicular, and finally the Tibidabo Funicular (€7.70 round-trip; €4.10 with purchase of admission to the Tibidabo Amusement Park) from there to the top. The Tramvia runs daily March–December, and weekends only in February. Generally it runs every 15–30 minutes, beginning at 10 am and finishing at dusk (around 6 pm in winter and 8 pm in summer).

🚗 Car Travel

Major routes throughout Spain bear heavy traffic, especially in peak holiday periods, so be extremely cautious; Spain has one of the highest traffic accident rates in Europe, and the roads are shared by a mixture of local drivers, immigrants en route elsewhere from Eastern Europe and North Africa, and non-Spanish travelers on vacation, some of whom are more accustomed to driving on the left-hand side of the road. Watch out for heavy truck traffic on national routes. Expect the near-impossibility of on-street parking in the major cities. Parking garages are common and affordable, and provide added safety to your vehicle and possessions.

The country's main cities are well connected by a network of four-lane *autovías* (freeways). The letter N stands for a national route (*carretera nacional)*, either four- or two-lane. An *autopista* (AP) is a toll road. At the tollbooth plazas (the term in Castilian is *peaje;*

in Catalan, *peatge*), there are three systems to choose from—*automàtic,* with machines for credit cards or coins; *manual,* with an attendant; or *telepago,* an automatic chip-driven system mostly used by Spanish drivers.

GETTING AROUND AND OUT OF BARCELONA

Arriving in Barcelona by car from the north along the AP7 autopista or from the west along the AP2, follow signs for the Ronda Litoral (the coastal ring road—but beware: it's most prominently marked "Aeroport," which can be misleading) to lower and central Barcelona along the waterfront, or the Ronda de Dalt (the upper-ring road) along the edge of upper Barcelona to Horta, the Bonanova, Sarrià, and Pedralbes. For the center of town, take the Ronda Litoral and look for Exit 21 ("Paral.lel–Les Ramblas") or 22 ("Barceloneta–Via Laietana–Hospital de Mar"). If you are arriving from the Pyrenees on the C1411/E9 through the Tunel del Cadí, the Tunels de Vallvidrera will put you on the upper end of Via Augusta with off-ramps to Sarrià, Pedralbes, and La Bonanova. The Eixample and Ciutat Vella are 10–15 minutes farther if traffic is fluid. Watch out for the new variable speed limits on the approaches to Barcelona. While 80 kph (48 mph) is the maximum speed on the *rondas,* flashing signs over the motorway sometimes cut the speed limit down to 40 kph (24 mph) during peak hours.

Barcelona's main crosstown traffic arteries are Diagonal (running diagonally through the city) and the midtown avenues, Carrer d'Aragó, and Gran Via de les Corts Catalanes, both cutting northeast–southwest through the heart of the city. Passeig de Gràcia, which becomes Gran de Gràcia above Diagonal, runs all the way from Plaça de Catalunya up to Plaça Lesseps, but the main up-and-down

streets, for motorists, are Balmes, Muntaner, Aribau, and Comtes d'Urgell. The general urban speed limit is 50 kph (30 mph).

Getting around Barcelona by car is generally more trouble than it's worth. It's better to walk or travel via subway, taxi, or bus.

Leaving Barcelona is not difficult. Follow signs for the rondas, do some advance mapping, and you're off. Follow signs for Girona and França for the Costa Brava, Girona, Figueres, and France. Follow Via Augusta and signs for Tunels de Vallvidrera or E9 and Manresa for the Tunel del Cadí and the Pyrenean Cerdanya valley. Follow Diagonal west and then the freeway AP7 signs for Lleida, Zaragoza, Tarragona, and Valencia to leave the city headed west. Look for airport, Castelldefells, and Sitges signs to head southwest down the coast for these beach points on the Costa Daurada. This C32 freeway to Sitges joins the AP7 to Tarragona and Valencia.

For travel outside Barcelona, the freeways to Girona, Figueres, Sitges, Tarragona, and Lleida are surprisingly fast. The distance to Girona, 97 km (58 miles), is a 45-minute shot. The French border is an hour away. Perpignan, at 188 km (113 miles) away, is an hour and 20 minutes.

ⓜ Metro Travel

In Barcelona the underground metro, or subway, is the fastest, cheapest, and easiest way to get around. Metro lines run Monday–Thursday and Sunday 5 am–midnight, Friday to 2 am, Saturday and holiday evenings all night. The FGC trains run 5 am to just after midnight on weekdays and to 1:52 am on weekends and the eves of holidays. Sunday trains run on weekday schedules.

Getting Here and Around

Ticket/Pass	Price
Single Fare	€2.20
10-Ride Pass	€10.20

Transfers from a metro line to the FGC (or vice versa) are free within an hour and 15 minutes. Note that in many stations, you need to validate your ticket at both ends of your journey. Maps showing bus and metro routes are available free from the tourist information office in Plaça de Catalunya.

SUBWAY INFO Transports Metropolitans de Barcelona (*TMB*). ☎ *93/214–8000, 93/298–7000* ⊕ *www.tmb.cat/en/home.*

Taxi Travel

In Barcelona taxis are black and yellow and show a green rooftop sign on the front right corner when available for hire. The meter currently starts at €2.10 and rises in increments of €1.07 every kilometer. These rates apply 6 am–10 pm weekdays. At hours outside of these, the rates rise 20%. There are official supplements of €1 per bag for luggage.

Trips to or from a train station entail a supplemental charge of €2.10; a cab to or from the airport, or the Barcelona Cruise Terminal, adds a supplemental charge of €4.20, as do trips to or from a football match. The minimum price for taxi service to or from the Barcelona airport is €20 for terminals T1, T2, and T3, and €39 from T4. There are cabstands (*parades*, in Catalan) all over town, and you can also hail cabs on the street, though if you are too close to an official stand they may not stop. You can call for a cab by phone 24 hours a day. Drivers do not expect a tip, but rounding up the fare is standard.

 Train Travel

International overnight trains to Barcelona arrive from many European cities, including Paris, Grenoble, Geneva, Zurich, and Milan; the four-a-day high-speed trains to and from Paris take about 5½ hours, and advance-purchase tickets online are competitive with flight prices. Almost all long-distance trains arrive at and depart from Estació de Sants, though many make a stop at Passeig de Gràcia that comes in handy for hotels in the Eixample or in the Ciutat Vella. Estació de França, near the port, handles only a few regional trains within Catalonia. Train service connects Barcelona with most other major cities in Spain; in addition a high-speed Euromed route connects Barcelona to Tarragona and Valencia.

Spain's intercity services (along with some of Barcelona's local train routes) are the province of the government-run railroad system—RENFE (Red Nacional de Ferrocarriles Españoles). The high-speed AVE train now connects Barcelona and Madrid (via Lleida and Zaragoza) in less than three hours. (Spain has more high-speed tracks in service than any other country in Europe.) The fast TALGO and ALTARIA trains are efficient, though local trains remain slow and tedious. The Catalan government's FGC (Ferrocarril de la Generalitat de Catalunya) also provide train service, notably to Barcelona's commuter suburbs of Sant Cugat, Terrassa, and Sabadell.

Information on the local/commuter lines (*rodalies* in Catalan, *cercanias* in Castilian) can be found at ⊕ *www.renfe. es/cercanias.* Rodalies go, for example, to Sitges from Barcelona, whereas you would take a regular RENFE train to, say, Tarragona. It's important to know whether you are traveling on RENFE or on rodalies (the latter distinguished by a stylized C), so you don't end up in the wrong line.

Both Catalonia and the Basque Country offer scenic railroad excursions. The day train from Barcelona to Madrid runs through bougainvillea-choked towns before leaping out across Spain's central *meseta* (plateau) via Zaragoza, most trains arriving at Atocha Station in Madrid in about 2½ hours. The train from Barcelona's Plaça de Catalunya north to Sant Pol de Mar and Blanes runs along the edge of the beach.

First-class train service in Spain, with the exception of the *coche-cama* (Pullman) overnight service, barely differs from second class or *turista*. The TALGO or the AVE trains, however, are much faster than second-class carriers like the slowpoke Estrella overnight from Barcelona to Madrid, both with limited legroom and general comforts. The AVE is the exception: these sleek, comfortable bullet trains travel between Barcelona and Madrid or between Madrid and Seville. Some 30 AVE trains a day connect Barcelona and Madrid, with departures from 5:50 am to 9:15 pm. Trips take from 2 hours 30 minutes to 3 hours 10 minutes.

During peak travel times (Easter, August, and Christmas), it's important to make a reservation weeks or even months in advance; on routes between major cities (Barcelona to Bilbao or Madrid, for example), it's a good idea to reserve well in advance, especially for overnight trips.

Where to Stay?

	NEIGHBORHOOD VIBE	PROS	CONS
Barri Gòtic and Born-Ribera	With lamps glowing in the Roman and Gothic corners, this is a romantic part of town. The Picasso Museum and Santa Maria del Mar are nearby.	Plaça Sant Jaume, the cathedral, Plaça del Rei, and the Born-Ribera district are among the main reasons to visit the city.	It's easy to lose yourself in this labyrinth of narrow cobblestone streets. It can also be noisy, with echoes reverberating around this ancient sound chamber.
El Raval	A rough-and-tumble part of town, but the nightlife is exciting and the diversity of the neighborhood is exemplary. It's just steps from the Boqueria market.	El Raval has a buzz all its own. A contemporary art museum, the medieval hospital, and the Mercat de Sant Antoni offer plenty to explore.	El Raval can seem dangerous, and demands street-sense, especially at night.
La Rambla	Constantly bustling, La Rambla is a virtual anthology of Barcelona street life.	Boqueria market, flower stalls, the Liceu opera house, and Plaça Reial are all quintessential Barcelona sites.	The crowds can be overwhelming, especially if FC Barcelona wins a championship match.
Barceloneta and Port Olímpic	At one time the fishermen's quarter, Barceloneta retains its informal and working-class ambience.	Near the beach, this part of town has a laid-back feel. It's where to go for casual seafood restaurants.	Barceloneta offers few accommodations beyond the W Hotel; Port Olímpic is a bit isolated.
Eixample	Casa Milà and Casa Battló are here, on the Passeig de Gràcia alogn with great restaurants and shopping.	Art Nouveau architecture is everywhere. La Sagrada Família is within walking distance.	Too few buildings here have street numbers; the neighborhood can be difficult to navigate.
Upper Barcelona	Leafy and residential, Pedralbes is Barcelona's wealthiest residential quarter; Sarrià is the rustic little village next door.	A 15-minute train ride connects Sarrià with the middle of the Eixample and La Rambla.	Staying in upper Barcelona involves a 15-minute trip, at least, to the most important attractions. After midnight on weeknights will require a taxi.

Before You Go

🌐 Passports

Visitors from the United States, Australia, Canada, New Zealand, and the United Kingdom need a valid passport to enter Spain. No visa is required for U.S. passport holders for a stay of up to three months; for stays exceeding three months, contact the Consulate of Spain nearest you. Australians require a visa for stays longer than one month; you should obtain it from the Spanish Embassy before you leave.

📅 When to Go

For optimal weather and fewer tourists, visit Barcelona, Catalonia, and Bilbao from April through June and mid-September through mid-December. Expect traffic at the start and end of August when locals leave for vacation. Major cities are relaxed and empty except for tourists in August, though Gràcia's Festa Major in Barcelona and Semana Grande in Bilbao keep these two cities alive during summer. Some shops and restaurants shut down for part of the month, but museums remain open, and music and theater festivals ensure that there's never a cultural lull.

Barcelona summers can be very hot, but temperatures rarely surpass 100°F (38°C), and air-conditioning is becoming more widespread. Dining alfresco on a warm summer night is one of northern Spain's finest pleasures. Spring and fall offer the best temperatures at both ends of the Pyrenees. Barcelona winters—chilly, but never freezing—are ideal for fireside dining and hearty cuisine.

➕ Safety

Petty crime is a perennial problem in Barcelona. Pickpocketing and thefts from parked cars are the most common offenses. The lower Raval and parts of Poble Nou are particularly prone to these problems. Be especially cautious in train and bus stations, getting on and off the metro, and on La Rambla, where masses of people sometimes offer camouflage for petty thieves.

💼 What to Pack

If you can imagine getting by with what you wear on your back plus the contents of a rolling carry-on bag, you will save yourself waiting, lost baggage, and the frustration of stumbling over multiple suitcases. Although baggage carts are free and plentiful in most Spanish airports, they're rare in train and bus stations. Summer will be hot nearly everywhere; winter, fall, and spring call for warm clothing and, in winter, sturdy walking shoes or boots. On the whole, Spanish people dress up more than Americans or the British. It makes sense to wear casual, comfortable clothing and shoes for sightseeing, but you'll want to dress up a bit in Barcelona and Bilbao, especially in the evening.

Good walking shoes make all the difference for exploring Barcelona. In summer, sturdy sandals that you might even wear hiking are best for city trekking. On the beach, anything goes; it's common to see females of all ages wearing only bikini bottoms, and many of the more remote beaches allow nude sunbathing. Regardless of your style, bring a cover-up for when you leave the beach. Shorts are acceptable, though light skirts and summery dresses are the norm.

Essentials

🧭 Addresses

Abbreviations used in the book for street names are Av. for *avinguda* in Catalan; *avenida* in Spanish, and Ctra. for *carreter* (or *carretera* in Spanish). The letters *s/n* following an address mean *sin número* (without a street number). *Carrer* (*calle* in Spanish) is often dropped entirely or not abbreviated at all. *Camí* (*camino* in Spanish) is abbreviated to *C. Passeig* (*paseo* in Spanish) is sometimes abbreviated as P., but is usually written out in full. Plaça/plaza is usually not abbreviated (in this book it is abbreviated as Pl.).

Addresses in Barcelona may include the street name, building number, floor level, and apartment number. For example, Carrer Balmes 155, 3°, 1ª indicates that the apartment is on the *tercero* (third) floor, *primera* (first) door. In older buildings, the first floor is often called the *entresuelo*; one floor above it is *principal* (sometimes called the *planta baja*), and above this, the first floor (*primera*). The top floor of a building is the *ático*; occasionally there is a floor above that, called the *sobreàtico*. In more modern buildings there is often no *entresuelo* or *principal*.

💲 Tipping

While tipping isn't expected in Spain, it is always welcome, and if you feel so inclined you can be sure that your contribution will be appreciated. On the other hand, if you experience bad or surly service, don't feel obligated to leave a tip.

Restaurant checks always include service. The bill may not tell you that the service is included, but it is. An extra tip of 5% to 10% of the bill is icing on the cake. Leave tips in cash, even if paying by credit card. If you eat tapas or sandwiches at a bar, just round up the bill

to the nearest euro. Tip cocktail servers €0.50 a drink, depending on the bar. In a fancy establishment, leave no more than a 10% tip even though service is included—likewise if you had a great time.

Taxi drivers expect no tip and are happy if you round up in their favor. A tip of 5% of the total fare is considered generous. Long rides or extra help with luggage may merit a tip, but if you're short of change, you'll never hear a complaint. On the contrary, your driver may sometimes round down in *your* favor instead of ransacking his pockets for exact change.

Tip hotel porters €1 a bag, and the bearer of room service €1. A doorman who calls a taxi for you gets €1. If you stay in a hotel for more than two nights, tip the maid about €1 per night. A concierge should receive a tip for service, from €1 for basic help to €5 or more for special assistance such as getting reservations at a popular restaurant.

Tour guides should be tipped about €2, barbers €1, and women's hairdressers at least €2 for a wash and style. Restroom attendants (though you won't see many of them today) are tipped €1 or whatever loose change is at hand.

🧭 Tours

SPECIAL-INTEREST TOURS
ART TOURS

The Ruta del Modernisme (Moderniste Route), a self-guided tour, provides an excellent guidebook (available in English) that interprets 116 Moderniste sites from the Sagrada Família and the Palau de la Música Catalana to Art Nouveau building facades, lampposts, and paving stones. The €12 Guide, sold at the Pavellons Güell and the Institut Municipal del Paisatge Urbà (*Av. Drassanes 6*), comes with a book of vouchers good for discounts up to 50% on admission to most of the Moderniste buildings and sites in the Guide in Barcelona and 13 other towns and cities in Catalonia, as well as free guided tours in English at Pavellons Güell (daily 10:15 and 12:15) and the Hospital de Sant Pau (daily at 10, 11, noon, and 1).

The Palau de la Música Catalana offers guided tours in English every hour on the hour from 10 to 3:30. Sagrada Família guided tours cost extra. Casa Milà offers one guided tour daily (6 pm weekdays, 11 am weekends). Architect Dominique Blinder of Urbancultours specializes in explorations of the Barcelona Jewish Quarter but can also provide tours of the Sagrada Família or virtually any architectural aspect of Barcelona.

CONTACTS Centre del Modernisme, Pavellons Güell. ✉ *Av. de Pedralbes 7, Pedralbes* ☎ *93/317–7652* ⊕ *www.rutadelmodernisme. com* Ⓜ *L3 Palau Real, Maria Cristina.* **Recinte Modernista de Sant Pau.** ✉ *Carrer Sant Antoni Maria Claret 167, Eixample* ☎ *93/553–7801* ⊕ *www.santpaubarcelona.org/en* Ⓜ *L5 Sant Pau/Dos de Maig.* **Urbancultours.** ⊕ *www. urbancultours.com.*

CULINARY
Aula Gastronómica (Cooking Classroom) has different culinary tours, including tours of the Boqueria and Santa Catarina markets with breakfast, cooking classes, and tastings, for €12 per person and up. The locals you'll meet on the tours may struggle a bit in English, but between the guides and the help of fellow travelers, everyone manages. Jane Gregg, founder of Epicurean Ways, offers gourmet and wine tours of Barcelona and Catalonia. Teresa Parker of Spanish Journeys organizes cooking classes, seasonal specials, custom cultural or culinary tours, corporate cooking retreats, or off-the-beaten-path travel.

CONTACTS Aula Gastronómica. ✉ *Carrer Sagristans 5, Entresuelo, Barri Gòtic* ☎ *93/301–1944* ⊕ *www.aulagastronomica. com/cooking-classes* Ⓜ *L4 Jaume I.* **Epicurean Ways.** ☎ *434/738–2293 in U.S., 93/802–2688 in Spain* ⊕ *www.epicureanways.com.* **Spanish Journeys.** ☎ *508/349–9769* ⊕ *www. spanishjourneys.com.*

DAY TOURS AND GUIDES
BOAT TOURS
Golondrina harbor boats make short trips from the Portal de la Pau, near the Columbus monument. The fare is €7.70 for a 40-minute "Barcelona Port" tour of the harbor and €15.20 for the "Barcelona Sea," 90-minute ride out past the beaches and up the coast to the Fòrum at the eastern end of Diagonal. Departures are spring and summer (Easter week–September), daily 11:15 am–5:15 pm for the Port tour, 12:30 pm and 3:30 pm for the Sea tour; fall and winter, weekends and holidays only, 11 am–5 pm. It's closed mid-December–early January.

FEES AND SCHEDULES Las Golondrinas. ✉ *Pl. Portal de la Pau s/n, Moll de les Drassanes, La Rambla* ☎ *93/442–3106* ⊕ *lasgolondrinas.com/en* Ⓜ *L3 Drassanes.*

BUS TOURS
The Bus Turístic (9 or 9:30 am to 7 or 8 pm every 5–25 minutes, depending on the season), sponsored by the tourist office, runs on three circuits with stops at all the important sights. The blue route covers upper Barcelona; the red route tours lower Barcelona; and the green route runs from the Port Olímpic along Barcelona's beaches to the Fòrum at the eastern end of Diagonal (April through September only). A one-day ticket can be bought online (with a 10% discount) for €27 (a two-day ticket is €36). An additional €11.25 ticket (for sale on the same website) covers the fare for the Tramvía Blau, funicular, and Montjuïc cable car across the port. You receive a booklet

Essentials

with discount vouchers for various attractions. The blue and red bus routes start at Plaça de Catalunya near Café Zurich. The green route starts at Port Olímpic next to the Hotel Arts. Passengers can jump off and catch a later bus at any stop along the way; some stops are "hubs" where you can switch to a bus on one of the other routes. Audio coverage is provided in 10 languages. A competing bus tour, Barcelona Hop On Hop Off Tours, also leaves from Plaça de Catalunya near the corner of Ronda de la Universitat.

The product and prices are all but identical, though the Bus Turístic is the official tourist office tour, offering discount vouchers and superior service. In the event of long lines or delays on the Bus Turístic, Hop On Hop Off Tours is a good alternative.

CONTACTS Bus Turístic. ✉ *Pl. de Catalunya 3, Eixample* ☎ *93/285–3832* ⊕ *www.barcelon-abusturistic.cat* Ⓜ *Catalunya.* **Barcelona Hop On Hop Off Tours.** ✉ *Eixample* ☎ *871/180–005* ⊕ *www.hop-on-hop-off-bus.com/barcelo-na-bus-tours.* **Julià Travel.** ✉ *Carrer Balmes 5, Eixample* ☎ *93/402–6900* ⊕ *www.juliatravel.com/destinations/barcelona* Ⓜ *Catalunya, L1/L2 Universitat.*

PRIVATE GUIDES

Guides from the organizations listed below are generally competent, though the quality of language skills and general showmanship may vary. For customized tours, including access to some of Barcelona's leading chefs, architects, art historians, and artists, Heritage Tours will set it all up from New York.

CONTACTS Barcelona Guide Bureau. ✉ *Via Laietana 54, 2–2, Born-Ribera* ☎ *93/268–2422, 667/419140 on weekends* ⊕ *www.barcelona-guidebureau.com* Ⓜ *Urquinaona.* **Heritage Tours.** ✉ *121 W. 27th St., Suite 1201, New York* ☎ *800/378–4555 toll-free in U.S., 212/206–8400 in U.S.* ⊕ *www.heritagetours.com.*

SEGWAY TOURS

Barcelona Segway Tours, with an office near the cathedral, puts you up on one of its futuristic two-wheelers for a two-hour tour (€55) of the Barri Gòtic, La Rambla, and the seafront; its longer three-hour excursion (€75) includes the Ciutadella Park as well. Tours depart daily at 9:30 and 10 am, and 12:30, 3, 4:30, and 6 pm; the Early Bird tour, at 8 am, includes breakfast. Helmets are provided; children must be more than 10 years of age; learn more at ⊕ *www.barcelonasegwaytour.com.*

WALKING TOURS

Turisme de Barcelona offers weekend walking tours of the Barri Gòtic, the Waterfront, Picasso's Barcelona, Modernisme, a shopping circuit, and Gourmet Barcelona in English (at 10:30 am). Prices range from €15 to €21, with 10% discounts for purchases online. For private tours, Julià Travel and Pullmantur *(Bus Tours)* both lead walks around Barcelona. Tours leave from their offices, but you may be able to arrange a pickup at your hotel. Prices per person are €35 for half a day and €90 for a full day, including lunch.

For the best English-language walking tour of the medieval Jewish Quarter, Dominique Tomasov Blinder, of Urbancultours *(Art Tours)* is an architect with 13 years experience in Jewish heritage. Her tour of Jewish Barcelona is a unique combination of history, current affairs, and personal experience; learn more at ⊕ *www.urbancultours.com.*

Great Itineraries

Ciutat Vella, Quintessential Barcelona

Stroll La Rambla and see the colorful Boqueria market before cutting over to the Catedral de la Seu in Barri Gòtic, unrivaled for its medieval buildings and monuments. Detour through stately Plaça Sant Jaume where the Palau de la Generalitat, Catalonia's seat of government, faces the Ayuntamiento (City Hall). The Gothic Plaça del Rei and the neoclassical Plaça Reial are short walks from Plaça Sant Jaume. The Museu Picasso is five minutes from the loveliest example of Catalan Gothic architecture, the basilica of Santa Maria del Mar. An evening concert at the Palau de la Música Catalana after a few tapas is an unbeatable way to end the day.

Budget a whole day for the Raval, behind the Boqueria, for the Museu d'Art Contemporani de Barcelona, the medieval Antic Hospital de la Santa Creu, the Sant Pau del Camp church, and the medieval shipyards at Drassanes Reiales. Palau Güell, just off the lower Rambla, is an important Gaudí work. Nearby, the waterfront Barceloneta neighborhood is a prime venue for a paella.

The Post-1860 Checkerboard Eixample

A day touring the Eixample starts early and begins at Gaudí's magnum opus, the Temple Expiatori de la Sagrada Família (while there, include a side trip up Avinguda Gaudí to the Hospital de Sant Pau); if you buy your tickets ahead of time, you can avoid the lengthy queue. After, head to the central Passeig de Gràcia; en route swing past Moderniste architect Puig i Cadafalch's Casa Terrades and his Palau

Baró de Quadras. Spend the afternoon in the Eixample with the undulating facades of Casa Milà and Casa Batlló. Other masterpieces include Gaudí's Casa Calvet, not far from Plaça de Catalunya, the Fundació Tàpies, and more far-flung gems such as the Casa Golferichs, and the Casa de la Papallona (the "Butterfly House") out toward Plaça de Espanya. Parallel to the Passeig de Gràcia is the Rambla Catalunya, a tree-shaded promenade lined with shops and cafés.

Upper Barcelona: Gràcia and Sarrià

For a more restful excursion, try the formerly outlying towns of Gràcia and Sarrià. Gràcia is home to Gaudí's first private residential commission, Casa Vicens, and his playful Park Güell above Plaça Lesseps; the tree-lined lower reaches of this bustling neighborhood are filled with houses by Gaudí's right-hand man, Francesc Berenguer. Sarrià is a village long since absorbed by the city, an intimate warren of narrow streets, small shops, and restaurants. A bit removed from the village itself are the Monestir de Pedralbes, with its superb Gothic cloister, Gaudí's Torre Bellesguard, and his Col·legi de les Teresianes (a convent school, not open to the public).

Art in Montjuïc

Montjuïc is home to the Museu Nacional d'Art de Catalunya; the nearby Fundació Miró features Catalan artist Joan Miró's colorful paintings and textiles and a stellar Calder mobile. Down the stairs toward Plaça d'Espanya are the Mies van der Rohe Barcelona Pavilion and the restored Casaramona textile mill, now the Caixa-Forum cultural center and gallery.

On the Calendar

Where to Get Information

To find out what's on (in Spanish or Catalan), check "*Ocio y cultura*" listings in Barcelona's leading daily newspapers' online versions: *La Vanguardia* (⊕ *www.lavanguardia.com*) and *El Periódico* (⊕ *www.elperiodico.com*) or the English-language edition of *TimeOut* (⊕ *www.timeout.com/barcelona*). *Le Cool* (⊕ *barcelona.lecool.com*) offers a curated list of events and activities online (available in English). *Barcelona Metropolitan* magazine updates its online "what's on" section regularly, and features a monthly print version, available for free in English-language bookstores and hotel lobbies (⊕ *www.barcelona-metropolitan.com*). Barcelona city hall's culture website (⊕ *barcelonacultura.bcn.cat*) also publishes an English edition of events listings and highlights.

Annual Festivals

Barcelona Acció Musical (BAM). Held over a week toward late September, this musical celebration forms part of the lively La Mercé festival, an annual event honoring Our Lady of Mercy, Barcelona's patron saint. BAM showcases emerging talent (both national and international) in dance, rock, pop, and electronic genres; acts perform in parks, squares, and venues around the city. ☎ *010 Barcelona information: daily 24 hrs (local call)* ⊕ *www.barcelona.cat/bam.*

Ciutat Flamenco. Held annually in May, this lively festival, co-organized by the Taller de Músics (Musicians' Workshop) and the Mercat de les Flors, offers visitors a chance to experience authentic flamenco instrumental, song, and dance performances by both local and international artists. ✉ *Mercat de les Flors,* *Carrer de Lleida 59, Poble Sec* ☎ *93/443-4346 Taller de Músics, 93/256–2600 Mercat de les Flors* ⊕ *ciutatflamenco. com* Ⓜ *Poble Sec, Plaça Espanya.*

Festival del Grec. Barcelona's monthlong summer arts festival in July features acts from the world of dance, performance art, music, and theater. Performances take place in such historic venues as Mercat de les Flors and the Teatre Grec on Montjuïc—an open-air theater built for the 1929 Barcelona International Exposition, which gives the festival its name and serves as the main venue. ✉ *Barcelona* ☎ *93/316–1000* ⊕ *lameva.barcelona.cat/grec.*

Guitar Bcn. Held between mid-February and late July, this annual festival features concerts in the Palau de la Música Catalana and other venues by master guitarists of all musical genres and styles. Folk, jazz, classical, and flamenco are all well represented. ☎ *93/481–7040* ⊕ *www.guitarbcn.com.*

International Jazz Festival. One of Europe's oldest jazz festivals, this festive gathering takes place from late September to early December, with concerts all around the city in illustrious venues like the Palau de la Musica, L'Auditori, and smoky side-street bars such as the Harlem Jazz Club. Highlights include vocal and instrumental jazz renditions from around the globe. ☎ *93/481–7040* ⊕ *www.barcelona-jazzfestival.com.*

Primavera Sound. From its modest beginnings at the architectural miniature museum Poble Espanyol, this event has evolved into one of the biggest and most exciting music festivals in Spain, attracting more than 200,000 visitors each year. Concerts are organized in small venues around the city during the weeks leading up to the event, but the main stint takes place over four days in late May or early June at the Parc del Fòrum. Everybody who's anybody, from Nine Inch Nails to The National, has played here, and you can rest assured that whoever is doing the big summer festival circuit will pass through Primavera. Festival tickets can be bought online. ⊠ *Parc del Fòrum, Poblenou* ⊕ *www.primaverasound.com* Ⓜ *El Maresme Fòrum.*

Sónar. For more than a decade, Sónar has grown from a niche festival for electronic and dance music fans to one of Barcelona's largest and most celebrated happenings. Over three days in summer (sometimes mid-June, sometimes mid-July), thousands descend upon the city, turning Plaça Espanya—the site of the festival's principal venues—into a huge rave. The celebration is divided into "Day" and "Night" activities. Sónar by Day sees sets by international DJs, record fairs, and digital art exhibits at the Fira Montjuïc. Sónar by Night takes place in the Fira Gran Via Hospitalet for acts on the forefront of the dance-music scene like Skrillex, Die Antwoord, and The Chemical Brothers. It's best to purchase tickets early via the festival website. ⊕ *www.sonar.es.*

Off Sónar. Whilst Sónar itself is a definite must, OffSónar is like the cooler, younger sibling that scores more bragging rights. Bringing together labels and artists at the cutting edge of dance music for Europe's biggest party week, OFF Sónar presents nine parties over four days in the idyllic venues of Poble Espanyol. Unlike Sónar which is hosted at two fixed locations, Off Sónar's "Off Parties" take place in a variety of locations throughout the city, including rooftops, bars, nightclubs, and the beautiful open-air spaces of Poble Espanyol museum. ⊕ *offsonar.co*

Pride Barcelona. One of Spain's most popular gay festivals. Pride Barcelona brings together the local LGBTQIA community, friends, and allies to the Gay Village for a weekend of culture, activities, and parties. The highlight is the parade on Saturday afternoon, followed by a massive party. ⊕ *www. pridebarcelona.org*

Brunch in the Park. Brunch in the Park is exactly what you hope it will be and more: a festival that is outdoors and includes waffles. Every Sunday from June to September local and international DJ's play at this local-friendly event which takes place in Jardins de Joan Brossa on Montjuïc, with its beautiful view over the city. There are food trucks, small stores, bars, and family-friendly activities. ⊕ *barcelona. brunch-in.com/park*

Contacts

✈ Air Travel

Aeroport de Girona–Costa Brava (*GRO*). ✉ *17185 Vilobi de Onyar, Girona* ☎ *902/404704 general info on Spanish airports* ⊕ *www.girona-airport. cat.* **Aeropuerto de Madrid (Adolfo Suárez Madrid-Barajas)** (*MAD*). ✉ *Av. de la Hispanidad s/n, Madrid* ☎ *902/404704 general info on Spanish airports* ⊕ *www.aeropuerto-madrid-barajas.com/eng.* **Aeropuerto de Reus** (*REU*). ✉ *Autovía Tarragona–Reus, Reus* ☎ *902/404704 general info on Spanish airports* ⊕ *www.aena.es/ en/reus-airport/reus.html.* **Aeropuerto Internacional de Bilbao** (*BIL*). ✉ *Loiu 48180, Bilbao* ☎ *902/404704 general info on Spanish airports* ⊕ *www. aeropuertodebilbao.net/ en.* **Barcelona El Prat de Llobregat** (*BCN*). ✉ *C–32B s/n* ☎ *902/404704 general info on Spanish airports* ⊕ *www.aena.es/en/barcelona-airport/index.html.*

🚍 Bus Travel

ALSA. ☎ *902/422242* ⊕ *www.alsa.es.* **Grup Sarbus.** ✉ *Estació d'Autobusos Barcelona–Nord, Carrer d' Alí Bei 80, Eixample* ☎ *902/302025* ⊕ *www.sarfa.com* Ⓜ *L1 Arc de Triomf.* **Julià Travel.** ✉ *Carrer Balmes 5,* *Eixample* ☎ *93/317–6454* ⊕ *www.juliatravel.com.*

BUS TERMINALS
Estació de Sants. ✉ *Pl. dels Països Catalans s/n, Eixample* ☎ *902/432343, 902/240505 bookings and sales* Ⓜ *L3/L5 SantsEstació.* **Estació del Nord.** ✉ *Carrer d'Ali Bei 80, Eixample* ☎ *902/260606* ⊕ *www. barcelonanord.com.*

🚕 Taxi Travel

Barna Taxi. ☎ *93/322222* ⊕ *barnataxi.com.* **Radio Taxi 033.** ☎ *93/303–3033 to call a cab* ⊕ *radiotaxi033. com.* **Taxi Class Rent.** ☎ *93/307–0707* ⊕ *www. taxiclassrent.com/en.*

🚆 Train Travel

Estació de França. ✉ *Av. Marquès de l'Argentera 1, Born-Ribera* ☎ *912/320320 RENFE station info* ⊕ *www.renfe.com* Ⓜ *L4 Barceloneta.* **Estació de Passeig de Gràcia.** ✉ *Passeig de Gràcia/ Carrer Aragó, Eixample* ☎ *912/432343 station info, 912/320320 RENFE general info* ⊕ *www. renfe.com* Ⓜ *L2/L3/L4 Passeig de Gràcia.* **Estació de Sants.** ✉ *Pl. dels Països Catalans s/n, Les Corts* ☎ *912/432343 station info, 902/320320 RENFE general info* ⊕ *www. renfe.com* Ⓜ *L3/L5 Sants* *Estació.* **Ferrocarrils de la Generalitat de Catalunya (FGC).** ✉ *Carrer Vergos 44, Sarrià* ☎ *93/366–3000* ⊕ *www.fgc.cat/eng/index. asp* Ⓜ *Sarrià (FGC).* **RENFE.** ☎ *912/320320* ⊕ *www. renfe.com.*

TRAIN PASSES
Eurail. ⊕ *www.eurail.com.* **Rail Europe.** ☎ *800/622–8600* ⊕ *www.raileurope. com* ☎ *800/622–8600* ⊕ *www.raileurope.ca.*

📍 Tourist Offices

Plaça Sant Jaume. ✉ *Carrer de la Ciutat 2, Ajuntament de Barcelona, Barri Gòtic* ☎ *93/285–3834* ⊕ *www. barcelonaturisme.com* Ⓜ *L3 Liceu, L4 Jaume I.* **Sants Estació.** ✉ *Pl. dels Països Catalans s/n, Eixample* ☎ *93/285–3834* ⊕ *www.barcelonaturisme.com* Ⓜ *L3/L5 Sants Estació.* **Servei d'Informació Cultural–Palau de la Virreina** (*Tiquet Rambles*). ✉ *Rambla 99, La Rambla* ☎ *93/316–1000, 93/316–1111* ⊕ *lameva.barcelona. cat/tiquetrambles* Ⓜ *Catalunya, L3 Liceu.*

Chapter 3

LA RAMBLA

Updated by
Elizabeth Prosser and
Steve Tallantyre

👁 Sights	🍴 Restaurants	🛏 Hotels	🛍 Shopping	🍸 Nightlife
★★★★★	★★★☆☆	★★★★☆	★★★☆☆	★★★★☆

NEIGHBORHOOD SNAPSHOT

TOP EXPERIENCES

■ **La Boqueria:** Wander and graze the stalls of this glass-and-steel market hall, packed with culinary riches.

■ **Gran Teatre del Liceu:** Plan to take in an opera at one of Europe's leading opera houses or at least take a tour of its spectacular rooms and halls.

■ **Palau Güell:** This extraordinary Gothic mansion, built for Gaudí's wealthy patron, is a magnificent example of the architect's imagination.

■ **Strolling La Rambla:** A stroll here, with thousands of visitors from around the world, is sensory overload, and should be experienced both in the early morning and late at night.

■ **Carrer Petitxol:** Enjoy a hot chocolate and pastry on one of Barcelona's most charming streets.

GETTING HERE

The Plaça de Catalunya metro stop will put you at the head of La Rambla in front of the Café Zurich, Barcelona's most famous rendezvous point. From here it's just a few steps down to the fountain on the right side of La Rambla de Canaletes.

PLANNING YOUR TIME

Allow three to four hours, including stops, for exploring La Rambla. The best times to find things open are 9 am–2 pm and 4 pm–8 pm, although this popular promenade has a life of its own 24 hours a day. Not all museums remain open through the lunch hour—go online or ask at your nearest tourist information office to check. Most church hours are 9 am–1:30 pm and 4:30 pm–8 pm.

QUICK BITES

■ **Café de l'Opera.** Across La Rambla from the Liceu opera house, Café de l'Opera is a favorite Barcelona hangout. The waiters are seasoned pros, the tapas come in ample portions, and the Thonet chairs and etched mirrors give the café historic charm. ✉ *La Rambla 74, La Rambla* ⊕ *www.cafeoperabcn.com* Ⓜ *Liceu*

■ **Café Viena.** There are nine Viena cafés in Barcelona, but this particular branch is always packed with international travelers trying what Mark Bittman of the *New York Times* once consecrated as "the best sandwich in the world." ✉ *La Rambla 115, La Rambla* ⊕ *www.viena.es* Ⓜ *Catalunya*

■ **Amorino.** Yes, you're in Spain, but it doesn't mean you can't enjoy delicious, refreshing, and all-natural Italian gelato. You can also get hot drinks and crepes here. ✉ *La Rambla 125, La Rambla* Ⓜ *Liceu*

The promenade in the heart of pre-modern Barcelona was originally a watercourse, dry for most of the year, that separated the walled Ciutat Vella from the outlying Raval. In the 14th century, the city walls were extended and the arroyo was filled in, so it gradually became a thoroughfare where peddlers, farmers, and tradesmen hawked their wares. (The watercourse is still there, under the pavement. From time to time a torrential rain will fill it, and the water rises up through the drains.) The poet-playwright Federico García Lorca called this the only street in the world he wished would never end—and in a sense, it doesn't.

Down the watercourse now flows a river of humanity, gathered here and there around the mimes, acrobats, jugglers, musicians, puppeteers, portrait artists, break dancers, rappers, and rockers competing for the crowd's attention. Couples sit at café tables no bigger than tea trays while nimble-footed waiters dodge traffic, bringing food and drink from kitchens. With the din of taxis and motorbikes in the traffic lanes on either side of the promenade, the revelers and rubberneckers, and the Babel of languages, the scene is as animated at 3 am as it is at 3 pm.

Barcelona's most famous boulevard boasts a generous pedestrian strip down the middle and it is a tourist magnet. Much as you may want to avoid the crowds and the tacky, touristy shops and eateries that now cater to the crush of visitors, a stroll here is essential to your Barcelona experience. From the rendezvous point at the head of La Rambla at Café Zurich to La Boqueria produce market, the Liceu opera house, or La Rambla's lower reaches, there are crowds but also gems along this spinal column of Barcelona street life.

◉ Sights

Carrer dels Escudellers

NEIGHBORHOOD | Named for the *terris-saires* (earthenware potters) who worked here making *escudellas* (bowls or stew pots), this colorful loop is an interesting subtrip off La Rambla. Go left at Plaça del Teatre and you'll pass the landmark **Grill Room** at No. 8, an Art Nouveau saloon with graceful wooden decor and an ornate oak bar; next is **La Fonda Escudellers,** another lovely, glass- and stone-encased dining emporium. (Alas, the food is not especially good at either.) At Nos. 23–25 is Barcelona's most comprehensive ceramics display, **Art Escudellers.** Farther down, on the right, is **Los Caracoles,** once among the most traditional of Barcelona's restaurants and now mainly the choice of tourists with deep pockets. Still, the bar and the walk-through kitchen on the way in are picturesque, as are the dining rooms and the warren of little stairways between them. Another 100 yards down Carrer Escudellers is **Plaça George Orwell,** named for the author of *Homage to Catalonia,* a space created to bring light and air into this formerly iffy neighborhood. The little flea market that hums along on Saturday is a great place to browse.

Take a right on on the narrow Carrer de la Carabassa—a street best known in days past for its houses of ill fame, and one of the few remaining streets in the city still entirely paved with cobblestones. It is arched over with two graceful bridges that once connected the houses with their adjacent gardens. At the end of the street, looming atop her own basilica, is **Nostra Senyora de la Mercè** (Our Lady of Mercy). This giant representation of Barcelona's patron saint is a 20th-century (1940) addition to the 18th-century Església de la Mercè; the view of La Mercè gleaming in the sunlight, babe in arms, is one of the Barcelona waterfront's most impressive sights. As you arrive at Carrer Ample, note the **15th-century door** with a winged Sant Miquel Archangel delivering a backhand blow to a scaly Lucifer; it's from the Sant Miquel church, formerly part of City Hall, torn down in the early 19th century. From the Mercè, a walk out Carrer Ample (to the right) leads back to the bottom of La Rambla. The *colmado* (grocery store) on the corner as you make the turn, **La Lionesa** (Carrer Ample 21), is one of Barcelona's best-preserved 19th-century shops: a prime location for Spanish wines and liquors, artisanal cheeses, and charcuterie. At No. 7 is the **Calçats Artesans Solé** shoe store, known for nearly a century for its handmade footwear. You might recognize Plaça Medinaceli, next on the left, from Pedro Almodóvar's film *Todo Sobre Mi Madre* (*All About My Mother*). ⊠ *Carrer dels Escudellers, Barcelona* Ⓜ *L3 Drassanes.*

Carrer Petritxol

NEIGHBORHOOD | Just steps from La Rambla and one of Barcelona's most popular streets, lined with art galleries, *xocolaterías* (chocolate shops), and stationers, this narrow passageway dates back to the 15th century, when it was used as a shortcut through the backyard of a local property owner. Working up Petritxol from Plaça del Pi, stop to admire the late-17th-century sgraffito design (mural ornamentation made by scratching away a plaster surface), some of the city's best, on the facade over the **Ganiveteria Roca** knife store, *the* place for cutlery in Barcelona. Next on the right at Petritxol 2 is the 200-year-old **Dulcinea**, with a portrait of the great Catalan playwright Àngel Guimerà (1847–1924) over the fireplace; drop in for the house specialty, the *suizo* ("Swiss" hot chocolate and whipped cream). Also at Petritxol 2 is the **Llibreria Quera,** one of the city's best hiking and mountaineering bookstores.

Note the plaque to Àngel Guimerà over No. 4 and the **Art Box** gallery at Nos. 1–3 across the street. At No. 5 is **Sala Parès,** founded in 1840, the dean of Barcelona's art galleries, where major figures like

Isidre Nonell, Santiago Russinyol, and Picasso have shown their work, and its affiliated **Galeria Trama**, which shows more contemporary work. **Xocoa** at No. 9 is another popular chocolate shop. Look carefully at the "curtains" carved into the wooden door at No. 11 and the floral ornamentation around the edges of the ceiling inside; the store is **Granja la Pallaresa,** yet another enclave of chocolate and *ensaimada* (a light-looking but deadly sweet Mallorcan pastry, with confectioner's sugar dusted on top). Finally on the left at No. 17 is the **Rigol** fine arts supply store. ✉ *Carrer Petrixol, Barcelona* Ⓜ *L3 Liceu, Pl. Catalunya.*

Casa Bruno Cuadros

BUILDING | Like something out of an amusement park, this former umbrella shop was whimsically designed (assembled is more like it) by Josep Vilaseca in 1885. A Chinese dragon with a parasol, Egyptian balconies and galleries, and a Peking lantern all reflect the Eastern style that was very much in vogue at the time of the Universal Exposition of 1888. Now housing a branch office of the Banco Bilbao Vizcaya Artentaria, this prankster of a building is much in keeping with Art Nouveau's eclectic playfulness, though it has never been taken very seriously as an expression of Modernisme and is generally omitted from most studies of Art Nouveau architecture. ✉ *La Rambla 82, La Rambla* Ⓜ *L3 Liceu.*

Església de Betlem

RELIGIOUS SITE | The Church of Bethlehem is one of Barcelona's few baroque buildings, and hulks stodgily on La Rambla just above Rambla de les Flors. Burned out completely at the start of the Civil War in 1936, the church is unremarkable inside; the outside, spruced up, is made of what looks like quilted stone. If you find this less than a must-see, worry not: you have all of Barcelona for company, with the possible exception of Betlem's parishioners. This was where Viceroy Amat claimed the hand of the young virreina-to-be when in 1780 she was left in the lurch by the viceroy's nephew. In a sense, Betlem has compensated the city with the half century of good works the young widow was able to accomplish with her husband's fortune. The Nativity scenes on display down the stairs at the side entrance on La Rambla at Christmastime are an old tradition here, allegedly begun by St. Francis of Assisi, who assembled the world's first such crèche in Barcelona in the early 13th century. ✉ *Carrer del Carme 2, La Rambla* ☎ *93/318–3823* Ⓜ *Pl. Catalunya.*

★ Gran Teatre del Liceu

ARTS VENUE | Barcelona's opera house has long been considered one of the most beautiful in Europe, a rival to La Scala in Milan. First built in 1848, this cherished cultural landmark was torched in 1861, later bombed by anarchists in 1893, and once again gutted by an accidental fire in early 1994. During that most recent fire, Barcelona's soprano Montserrat Caballé stood on La Rambla in tears as her beloved venue was consumed. Five years later, a restored Liceu, equipped for modern productions, opened anew. Even if you don't see an opera, you can take a tour of the building; some of the Liceu's most spectacular halls and rooms, including the glittering foyer known as the Saló dels Miralls (Room of Mirrors), were untouched by the fire of 1994, as were those of Spain's oldest social club, El Círculo del Liceu—established in 1847 and restored to its pristine original condition after the fire. The Espai Liceu downstairs in the annex has a restaurant and cafeteria and a gift shop with a wide selection of opera-related books and recordings. ✉ *La Rambla 51–59, La Rambla* ☎ *93/485–9914 express and guided tour information and reservations, 93/485–9931 premium visit reservations* ⊕ *www.liceubarcelona.cat* ✉ *Variety of tours from €16* Ⓜ *L4 Liceu.*

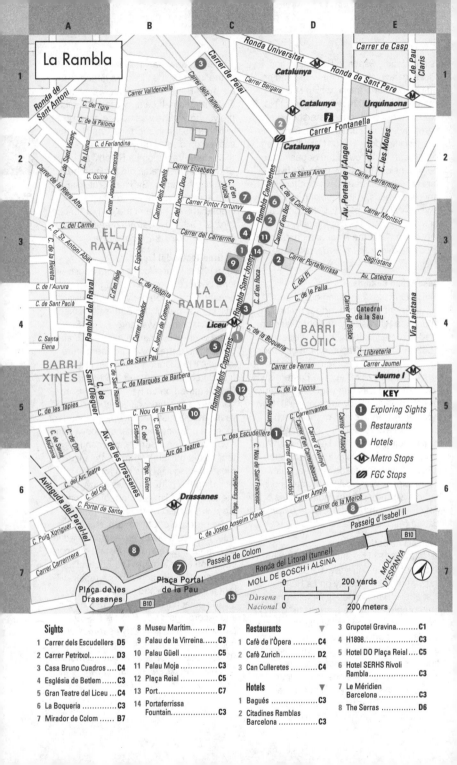

La Rambla

Sights ▼

1 Carrer dels Escudellers **D5**
2 Carrer Petritxol **D3**
3 Casa Bruno Cuadros **C4**
4 Església de Betlem **C3**
5 Gran Teatre del Liceu **C4**
6 La Boqueria **C3**
7 Mirador de Colom **B7**
8 Museu Marítim **B7**
9 Palau de la Virreina **C3**
10 Palau Güell **C5**
11 Palau Moja **C3**
12 Plaça Reial **C5**
13 Port **C7**
14 Portaferrissa Fountain **C3**

Restaurants ▼

1 Cafè de l'Òpera **C4**
2 Cafè Zurich **D2**
3 Can Culleretes **C4**

Hotels ▼

1 Bagués **C3**
2 Citadines Ramblas Barcelona **C3**
3 Grupotel Gravina **C1**
4 H1898 **C3**
5 Hotel DO Plaça Reial **C5**
6 Hotel SERHS Rivoli Rambla **C3**
7 Le Méridien Barcelona **C3**
8 The Serras **D6**

Visit La Boqueria market early (it opens at 8 am) to avoid the crowds as you discover all this colorful institution has to offer.

★ La Boqueria

MARKET | Barcelona's most spectacular food market, also known as the Mercat de Sant Josep, is an explosion of life and color, with tapas bar-restaurants (counter seating only). Stall after stall of fruit, herbs, veggies, nuts, candied preserves, cheese, ham, fish, poultry, and provender of all kinds greet you as you turn in from La Rambla and wade through the throng of shoppers and casual visitors. (The market has become such a popular venue that tourist groups of 15 people or more are banned from 8 am to 3 pm, Friday and Saturday. To avoid crowds, go before 8 am or after 5 pm.) Under a Moderniste hangar of wrought-iron girders and stained glass, the market occupies a neoclassical square built in 1840, after the original Sant Josep convent was torn down, by architect Francesc Daniel Molina. The Ionic columns around the edges of the market were part of the mid-19th-century square, uncovered in 2001 after more than a century of neglect. Highlights include the sunny greengrocers' market outside (to the right if you enter from La Rambla), along with **Pinotxo** (Pinocchio), just inside to the right, where owner Juanito Bayén and his family serve some of the best food in Barcelona. The secret? "Fresh, fast, hot, salty, and garlicky." If it's too crowded to find a seat, the **Kiosko Universal,** over toward the port side of the market, and **Quim de la Boqueria,** both offer delicious alternatives. Don't miss the *fruits del bosc* (fruits of the forest) specialty stand at the back of the market, with its display of wild mushrooms, herbs, nuts, and berries. ⊠ *La Rambla 91, La Rambla* ☎ *93/318–2017 information desk, Tues.–Thurs. 8–3, Fri. and Sat. 8–5, 93/318–2584* ⊕ *www.boqueria.info* ⊘ *Closed Sun.* Ⓜ *Liceu.*

Mirador de Colom (*Columbus Monument*)

MEMORIAL | This Barcelona landmark to Christopher Columbus sits grandly at the foot of La Rambla along the wide harbor-front promenade of Passeig de Colom, not far from the very shipyards (Drassanes Reials) that constructed two of the ships of his tiny but immortal fleet. Standing atop the 150-foot-high iron column—the base of which is aswirl with gesticulating angels—Columbus seems to be looking out at "that far-distant shore" he discovered; in fact he's pointing, with his 18-inch-long finger, in the general direction of Sicily. The monument was erected for the 1888 Universal Exposition to commemorate the commissioning of Columbus's voyage in Barcelona by the monarchs Ferdinand and Isabella, in 1491. Since the royal court was at that time itinerant (and remained so until 1561), Barcelona's role in the discovery of the New World is at best circumstantial. In fact, Barcelona was consequently excluded from trade with the Americas by Isabella, so Catalonia and Columbus have never really seen eye to eye. For a bird's-eye view of La Rambla and the port, take the elevator to the small viewing platform (*mirador*) at the top of the column. The entrance is on the harbor side. ⊠ *Pl. Portal de la Pau s/n, Port Olímpic* ☎ *93/285–3832* 🎫 *€6* Ⓜ *L3 Drassanes.*

★ Museu Marítim

BUILDING | FAMILY | The superb Maritime Museum is housed in the 13th-century **Drassanes Reials** (Royal Shipyards), at the foot of La Rambla adjacent to the harbor front. This vast covered complex launched the ships of Catalonia's powerful Mediterranean fleet directly from its yards into the port (the water once reached the level of the eastern facade of the building). Today these are the world's largest and best-preserved medieval shipyards; centuries ago, at a time when the region around Athens was a province of the House of Aragón (1311–90), they were of crucial importance to the sea power of Catalonia (then the heavyweight in an alliance with Aragón). On the Avinguda del Paral·lel side of Drassanes is a completely intact section of the 14th- to 15th-century walls—Barcelona's third and final ramparts—that encircled El Raval along the Paral·lel and the Rondas de Sant Pau, Sant Antoni, and Universitat. (*Ronda,* the term used for the "rounds," or patrols

Geometrical Barcelona

Barcelona's three geometrically named avenues, the Diagonal, the Meridiana, and the Paral·lel, were devised by Ildefons Cerdà (the urban planner who designed the post-1860 Eixample) as high-speed urban thoroughfares that would funnel traffic through and beyond the checkerboard of his urban grid. The Paral·lel is so named because it parallels the equator. The Meridiana is perpendicular to the Paral·lel and parallels the Greenwich Meridian. The Diagonal runs at an oblique angle across the Eixample.

soldiers made atop the defensive walls, became the name for the avenues that replaced them.)

The Museu Marítim is filled with vessels, including a spectacular collection of ship models. The life-size reconstruction of the galley of Juan de Austria, commander of the Spanish fleet in the Battle of Lepanto, is perhaps the most impressive display in the museum. Figureheads, nautical gear, early navigational charts, and medieval nautical lore enhance the experience, and headphones and infrared pointers provide a first-rate self-guided tour. Concerts are occasionally held in this acoustic gem. The cafeteria-restaurant Norai, open daily 9 am to 8 pm, is Barcelona's hands-down winner for dining in a setting of medieval elegance, and has a charming terrace. Admission to the museum includes a visit to the schooner *Santa Eulàlia,* a meticulously restored clipper built in 1918, which is moored nearby at the Port Vell. ⊠ *Av. de les Drassanes s/n, La Rambla* ☎ *93/342–9920* ⊕ *www.mmb.cat* 🎫 *€10 (includes admission to Santa Eulàlia clipper); free Sun. after 3* ☸ *Closed Mon.* Ⓜ *L3 Drassanes.*

A shipshape collection of nautical wonders is on display at the Museu Marítim.

Palau de la Virreina (*La Virreina Centre de la Imatge*)

CASTLE/PALACE | The baroque Virreina Palace, built by a viceroy to Peru in the late 18th century, is now a major center for themed exhibitions of contemporary art, film, and photography. The **Tiquet Rambles** office on the ground floor, run by the city government's Institut del Cultura (ICUB), open daily 10–8:30, is the place to go for information and last-minute tickets to concerts, theater and dance performances, gallery shows, and museums. The portal to the palace, and the pediments carved with elaborate floral designs, are a must-see. ✉ *Rambla de les Flors 99, La Rambla* ☎ *93/316–1000* ⊕ *lavirreina.bcn. cat* 🎟 *Free; €3 charge for some exhibits* 🕐 *Closed Mon.* Ⓜ *Liceu.*

★ **Palau Güell**

BUILDING | Gaudí built this mansion in 1886–89 for textile baron Count Eusebi de Güell Bacigalupi, his most important patron. (The prominent four bars of the *senyera,* the banner of Catalunya, on the facade between the parabolic arches

of the entrance attest to the nationalist fervor the two men shared.) Gaudí's principal obsession in this project was to find a way to illuminate this seven-story house, hemmed in as it is by other buildings in the cramped quarters of El Raval. The dark facade is a dramatic foil for the brilliance of the inside, where spear-shape Art Nouveau columns frame the windows, rising to support a series of detailed and elaborately carved wood ceilings.

The basement stables are famous for the "fungiform" (mushroomlike) columns carrying the weight of the whole building. Note Gaudí's signature parabolic arches between the columns and the way the arches meet overhead, forming a canopy of palm fronds. (The beauty of the construction was probably little consolation to the political prisoners held here during the 1936–39 Civil War.) The patio where the horses were groomed receives light through a skylight, one of many devices Gaudí used to brighten the space. Don't miss the figures of the faithful hounds, with the rings in their mouths for hitching horses, or the wooden bricks laid down in lieu of cobblestones in the entryway upstairs and on the ramp down to the basement grooming area, to deaden the sound of horses' hooves.

Upstairs are three successive receiving rooms; the wooden ceilings are progressively more spectacular in the complexity of their richly molded floral motifs. The room farthest in has a jalousie in the balcony: a double grate through which Güell was able to observe—and eavesdrop on—his arriving guests. The main hall, with the three-story-tall tower reaching up above the roof, was for parties, dances, and receptions. Musicians played from the balcony; the overhead balcony window was for the principal singer. Double doors enclose a chapel of hammered copper with retractable priedieux; around the corner is a small organ, the flutes in rectangular tubes climbing the central shaft of the building.

The dining room is dominated by a beautiful mahogany banquet table seating 10, an Art Nouveau fireplace in the shape of a deeply curving horseshoe arch, and walls with floral and animal motifs. From the outside rear terrace, the polished Garraf marble of the main part of the house is exposed; the brick servants' quarters are on the left. The passageway built toward La Rambla was all that came of a plan to buy an intervening property and connect three houses into one grand structure, a scheme that never materialized.

Gaudí is most himself on the roof, where his playful, polychrome ceramic chimneys seem like preludes to later works like the Park Güell and La Pedrera. Look for the flying-bat weather vane over the main chimney, a reference to the Catalan king Jaume I, who brought the house of Aragón to its 13th-century imperial apogee in the Mediterranean. Jaume I's affinity for bats is said to have stemmed from his Mallorca campaign, when, according to one version, he was awakened by a fluttering *rat penat* (literally, "condemned mouse") in time to stave off a Moorish night attack. ⊠ *Nou de la Rambla 3–5, La Rambla* ☎ *93/472–5771, 93/472–5775* ⊕ *www.palauguell.cat/en* ⊠ *€12; free 1st Sun. of month, 5–8 pm* ☉ *Closed Mon.* ☞ *Guided tours (1 hr) in English Fri. at 10:30 am and Sat. at 2:30 pm at no additional cost* Ⓜ *L3 Drassanes, Liceu.*

Palau Moja

CASTLE/PALACE | The first palace to occupy this corner on La Rambla was built in 1702 and inhabited by the Marquès de Moja. The present austere palace was completed in 1784 and, with the Betlem church across the street, forms a small baroque-era pocket along La Rambla. Now housing offices of the Cultural Heritage Department of the Catalan Ministry of Culture (with a tourist information center on the ground floor), the Palau is normally open to the public only on rare occasions, such as special exhibitions, when visitors also have the chance to see the handsome mural and painted ceiling by Francesc Pla, the 18th-century painter known as El Vigatà (meaning "from Vic," a town 66 km [40 miles] north of Barcelona, where he was born). In the late 19th century the Palau Moja was bought by Antonio López y López, Marquès de Comillas, and it was here that Jacint Verdaguer, Catalonia's national poet and chaplain of the marquess's shipping company, the Compañia Transatlántica, wrote his famous patriotic epic poem "L'Atlàntida." ⊠ *Carrer de la Portaferrissa 1, La Rambla* ☎ *93/316–2740* Ⓜ *Pl. Catalunya.*

Plaça Reial

PLAZA | Nobel Prize–winning novelist Gabriel García Márquez, architect and urban planner Oriol Bohigas, and Pasqual Maragall, former president of the Catalonian Generalitat, are among the many famous people said to have acquired apartments overlooking this elegant square, a chiaroscuro masterpiece in which neoclassical symmetry clashes with big-city street funk. Plaça Reial is bordered by stately ocher facades with

Barcelona's Lovers' Day

One of the best days to spend in Barcelona is April 23: St. George's Day, La Diada de Sant Jordi, Barcelona's "Valentine's Day." A day so sweet and playful, so goofy and romantic, that 6 million Catalans go giddy from dawn to dusk.

Legend has it that the patron saint of Catalonia, the knight-errant St. George (Sant Jordi in Catalan) slew a dragon that was about to devour a beautiful princess in the little village of Montblanc, south of Barcelona. From the dragon's blood sprouted a rosebush, from which the hero plucked the prettiest blossom for the princess. Hence the traditional Rose Festival celebrated in Barcelona since the Middle Ages, to honor chivalry and romantic love, and a day for men to present their true loves with roses. In 1923 the festival merged with International Book Day to mark the anniversary of the all-but-simulta-neous deaths of Miguel de Cervantes and William Shakespeare, on April 23, 1616; it then became the custom for the ladies to present their flower-bearing swains with a book in return.

More than 4 million roses and half a million books are sold in Catalonia on Sant Jordi's Day. In Barcelona, bookstalls run the length of nearly every major thoroughfare, and although it's an official workday, nearly everybody manages to duck out for at least a while and go brows-ing. There is a 24-hour reading of *Don Quixote*. Authors come to bookstalls to sign their works. Given Barcelona's importance as a publishing capital, the literary side of the holiday gets special attention.

A Roman soldier martyred for his Christian beliefs in the 4th century, St. George is venerated as the patron saint of 15 European countries—England, Greece, and Romania among them. Images of St. George are everywhere in Barcelona—most notably, perhaps, on the facade of the Catalonian seat of government, the Generalitat. Art Nouveau sculptor Eusebi Arnau depicted Sant Jordi skewering the unlucky dragon on the facade of the Casa Amatller, and on the corner of Els Quatre Gats café. Gaudí referenced the story with an entire building, the Casa Batlló, with the saint's cross implanted on the scaly roof and the skulls and bones of the dragon's victims framing the windows.

Sant Jordi's Day roses are tied with a spike of wheat (for his association with springtime and fertility) and a little red and yellow *senyera*, the Catalonian flag.

In Sarrià there are displays of 45 varieties of rose, representing 45 different kinds of love, from impos-sible to unrequited, from platonic to filial and maternal. In the Plaça Sant Jaume the Generalitat, its patio filled with roses, opens its doors to the public. Choral groups sing love songs in the Barri Gòtic; jazz combos play in Plaça del Pi. La Rambla is packed solid from the Diagonal to the Mediter-ranean, with barcelonins basking in the warmth of spring and romance. Rare is the woman anywhere in town without a rose in hand, bound with a red-and-yellow ribbon that says "*t'estimo*": I love you.

balconies overlooking the wrought-iron **Fountain of the Three Graces,** and an array of lampposts designed by Gaudí in 1879. Cafés and restaurants—several of them excellent—line the square. Plaça Reial is most colorful on Sunday morning, when collectors gather to trade stamps and coins; after dark it's a center of downtown nightlife for the jazz-minded, the young, and the adventurous (it's best to be streetwise touring this area in the late hours). Bar Glaciar, on the uphill corner toward La Rambla, is a booming beer station for young international travelers. Tarantos has top flamenco performances, and Jamboree offers world-class jazz. ⊠ *La Rambla* Ⓜ *L3 Liceu.*

Port

MARINA | Beyond the Columbus monument—behind the ornate Duana (now the Barcelona Port Authority headquarters)—is **La Rambla de Mar,** a boardwalk with a drawbridge designed to allow boats into and out of the inner harbor. La Rambla de Mar extends out to the **Moll d'Espanya,** with its Maremagnum shopping center (open on Sunday, unusual for Barcelona) and the excellent **Aquarium.** Next to the Duana you can board a Golondrina boat for a tour of the port and the waterfront or, from the Moll de Barcelona on the right, take a cable car to Montjuïc or Barceloneta. Trasmediterránea and Baleària passenger ferries leave for Italy and the Balearic Islands from the Moll de Barcelona; at the end of the quay is Barcelona's World Trade Center and the Eurostars Grand Marina Hotel. ⊠ *Port Olímpic* Ⓜ *Drassanes.*

Portaferrissa Fountain

FOUNTAIN | Both the fountain and the ceramic representation of Barcelona's second set of walls and the early Rambla are worth studying carefully. If you can imagine pulling out the left side of the ceramic scene and looking broadside at the amber yellow 13th-century walls that ran down this side of the Rambla, you will see a clear picture of what this spot

looked like in medieval times. The sandy Rambla ran along outside the walls, while the portal looked down through the ramparts into the city. As the inscription on the fountain explains, the Porta Ferrica, or Iron Door, was named for the iron measuring stick attached to the wood and used in the 13th and 14th centuries to establish a unified standard for measuring goods. The fountain itself dates to 1680; the ceramic tiles are 20th century. ⊠ *Rambla and Carrer Portaferrissa, La Rambla* Ⓜ *L3 Pl. Catalunya, Liceu.*

🍴 Restaurants

Cafè de l'Òpera

$ | **CAFÉ** | Directly across from the Liceu opera house, this high-ceiling Art Nouveau café has welcomed operagoers and performers for more than 100 years. It's a central point on the Rambla tourist traffic pattern, so locals are increasingly hard to find, but the café has hung onto its atmosphere of faded glory nonetheless. **Known for:** Art Nouveau decor; good for a drink; late-night hours. Ⓢ *Average main: €12* ⊠ *La Rambla 74, La Rambla* ☎ *93/317–7585* ⊕ *www.cafeoperabcn. com* Ⓜ *Liceu.*

Cafè Zurich

$ | **CAFÉ** | This traditional café at the top of La Rambla and directly astride the main metro and transport hub remains the city's prime meeting point. Forget the food and enjoy a beer or coffee at a table on the terrace, perhaps the best spot in the city to observe street life. **Known for:** people-watching far better than the food; sunny terrace; watch for pickpockets. Ⓢ *Average main: €10* ⊠ *Pl. de Catalunya 1, La Rambla* ☎ *93/317–9153* Ⓜ *Catalunya.*

Can Culleretes

$ | **CATALAN** | Just off La Rambla in the Barri Gòtic, this family-run restaurant founded in 1786 displays tradition in both decor and culinary offerings. Generations of the Manubens and Agut families have kept this unpretentious spot—Barcelona's oldest restaurant, listed in the *Guinness World Records*—popular for more than two centuries. **Known for:** Barcelona's oldest restaurant; traditional Catalan cuisine; large portions. [$] *Average main: €10* ✉ *Quintana 5, La Rambla* ☎ *93/317–3022* 🌐 *www.culleretes.com* 🕓 *Closed Mon., and 4 wks in July and 2 wks in Aug. No dinner Sun.* [M] *Liceu.*

Hotels

Bagués

$$$$ | HOTEL | The luxury of the Eixample has worked is way down to La Rambla, as this boutique gem (formerly the shop and atelier of the well-known Art Nouveau jeweler of the same name) bears ample witness. **Pros:** steps from the opera house; view of the cathedral and port from the rooftop terrace; free entrance to the Egyptian Museum of Barcelona. **Cons:** rooms a bit small for the price. [$] *Rooms from: €291* ✉ *La Rambla 105, La Rambla* ☎ *93/343–5000* 🌐 *www.hotelbagues.com* 🛏 *28 rooms, 3 suites* 🍴 *No meals* [M] *Pl. Catalunya, L3 Liceu.*

Citadines Ramblas Barcelona

$$$$ | HOTEL | FAMILY | Located in two buildings at the upper end of La Rambla, Citadines is an excellent choice for families, groups of friends, or long-term visitors; the accommodations consist of apartments with sitting rooms and one-room studios with kitchenettes and small dining areas. **Pros:** central location; spacious rooms; pet-friendly. **Cons:** basic amenities; no pool; rooms only cleaned during six-night stays (and only once). [$] *Rooms from: €280* ✉ *La Rambla 122, La Rambla* ☎ *93/270–1111* 🌐 *www.citadines.com* 🛏 *115 studios, 16 apartments* 🍴 *No meals* [M] *Catalunya.*

Grupotel Gravina

$ | HOTEL | On a side street near the Plaça de Catalunya and just five minutes from the MACBA and the Raval, this modern hotel offers comfort and prime location at a very affordable price. **Pros:** great location; room with private terrace for extra €30; friendly, competent staff. **Cons:** rooms are a bit small; generic furniture. [$] *Rooms from: €120* ✉ *Gravina 12, La Rambla* ☎ *93/301–6868* 🌐 *www.grupotelgravina.com* 🛏 *84 rooms* 🍴 *No meals* [M] *Catalunya, L1/L2 Universitat.*

★ H1898

$$$$ | HOTEL | Overlooking La Rambla, this imposing mansion (once the headquarters of the Compañiá General de Tabacos de Filipinas) couldn't be better located—especially for opera fans, with the Liceu just around the corner. **Pros:** impeccable service; ideal location for exploring the Barri Gòtic; historic spaces plus modern amenities like a spa and roof deck. **Cons:** subway rumble discernible in lower rooms on the Rambla side; no pets; some street noise from the Rambla in lower rooms. [$] *Rooms from: €238* ✉ *La Rambla 109, La Rambla* ☎ *93/552–9552* 🌐 *www.hotel1898.com* 🛏 *169 rooms* 🍴 *No meals* [M] *Catalunya, Liceu.*

Hotel DO Plaça Reial

$$$$ | HOTEL | Just at the entrance to the neoclassical Plaça Reial, this charming addition to Barcelona's growing collection of boutique hotels—with its three restaurants, La Terraza (under the arcades on the square), El Terrat, and La Cuina (downstairs under graceful brick vaulting)—is a find for foodies and lovers of tasteful design. **Pros:** walking distance from old city center; helpful multilingual staff; 24-hour room service. **Cons:** neighborhood can be rowdy at night; no pets; street noise discernible in lower rooms. [$] *Rooms from: €340* ✉ *Pl. Reial 1, La Rambla* ☎ *93/481–3666* 🌐 *www.hoteldoreial.com* 🛏 *18 rooms* 🍴 *Free Breakfast* [M] *L3 Liceu.*

Hotel SERHS Rivoli Rambla

$$$ | HOTEL | Behind this traditional upper-Rambla facade lies a surprisingly whimsical intérior with marble floors and artwork by well-known Barcelona artist Perico Pastor in the lobby. **Pros:**

ideal location; Room 601 is the best in the house; good views from the rooftop terrace. **Cons:** service inconsistent; no pool or spa; two-night minimum stay for online bookings. $ *Rooms from: €205* ⊠ *La Rambla 128, La Rambla* ☎ *93/481–7676* ⊕ *www.hotelserhsrivolirambla.com* ➽ *126 rooms* |○| *No meals* Ⓜ *Catalunya, L3 Liceu.*

★ Le Méridien Barcelona

$$$$ | **HOTEL** | There's no dearth of hotels along La Rambla in the heart of the city, but few rival the upscale Le Méridien, popular with businesspeople and visiting celebrities alike for its suites overlooking the promenade and cozy amenities. **Pros:** central location; soaker tubs in deluxe rooms; Mediterranean suites have large private terraces. **Cons:** no pool; rooms small for the price; €60-per-day surcharge for pets. $ *Rooms from: €249* ⊠ *La Rambla 111, La Rambla* ☎ *93/318–6200* ⊕ *www.lemeridien.com/barcelona* ➽ *231 rooms* |○| *No meals* Ⓜ *Catalunya L3 Liceu.*

The Serras

$$$$ | **HOTEL** | Picasso had his first studio here (on the sixth floor) when the building was all walk-up flats; today, designer Eva Martinez has found ingenious, tasteful ways to make the best of the space and its limits: a small lobby with a comfortable sofa suite leads back to the long, narrow El Informal, the hotel's excellent restaurant presided over by award-winning young chef Marc Gascons; a mezzanine hosts the 24-hour lounge bar and a small gym. **Pros:** romantic "El Sueño" rooftop terrace with DJ on weekends; fun in-room amenities like yoga mats; excellent restaurant El Formal. **Cons:** no sauna or spa; hard on the budget. $ *Rooms from: €350* ⊠ *Passeig Colom 9, La Rambla* ☎ *93/169–1868* ⊕ *www.hoteltheserrasbarcelona.com* ➽ *28 rooms* |○| *Free Breakfast* Ⓜ *L4 Barceloneta.*

🍸 Nightlife

The liveliest pedestrian promenade in the city bustles with a dizzying array of tourist-baiting shops, eateries, and arched paths to Plaça Reial's euphoric nightlife scene. Casual and unpretentious, the scene erupts nightly with a parade of rambunctious crowds of expats, curious interlopers, and assorted celebrations.

BARS
Boadas

BARS/PUBS | Barcelona's oldest cocktail bar opened its doors in 1933 and quickly gained a reputation as the only place to enjoy a genuine mojito. The faithful—who still include a few of the city's luminaries—have been flocking ever since, despite the bar's decidedly lackluster decor. The space has the look and feel of an old-fashioned private club and is still the spot to watch old-school barmen in dapper duds mixing drinks the way tradition dictates. ⊠ *Tallers 1, La Rambla* ☎ *93/318–9592* ⊕ *boadascocktails.com* Ⓜ *Catalunya.*

Jamboree-Jazz and Dance-Club

MUSIC CLUBS | This legendary nightspot has hosted some of the world's most influential jazz musicians since its opening in 1960. Decades later, the club continues to offer two nightly shows and remains a notable haven for new generations of jazz and blues aficionados. After the last performance, the spot transforms into a late-night dance club playing soul, hip-hop, and R&B. ⊠ *Pl. Reial 17, La Rambla* ☎ *93/319–1789* ⊕ *www.masimas.com/en/jamboree* Ⓜ *Liceu.*

🎭 Performing Arts

ART GALLERIES
Palau de la Virreina

ART GALLERIES—ARTS | This beautiful edifice right on the bustling Rambla is an important Barcelona art hub, resource, and outpost of the Institut de Cultura, with photography on display at the Espai Xavier Miserachs, temporary exhibits on the patio, and cultural events held regularly in the space. ⊠ *La Rambla 99, La Rambla* ☏ *93/316–1000* ⊕ *ajuntament.barcelona. cat/lavirreina/en* Ⓜ *Catalunya, Liceu.*

THEATER
Teatre Poliorama

THEATER | Originally built as a cinema in the late 1890s, Teatre Poliorama has also been immortalized in George Orwell's *Homage to Catalonia*, where the celebrated author describes it as the site of a shoot-out between opposing sides during the Spanish Civil War. In sharp contrast to its sinister past most of the productions offered focus on lighthearted comedy and musical plays in Spanish or Catalan, as well as flamenco and opera. ⊠ *Rambla del Estudis 115, La Rambla* ☏ *93/317–7599* ⊕ *www.teatrepoliorama. com* Ⓜ *Catalunya.*

Shopping

Although not exactly a shopping mecca—unless you're after a Sagrada Família snow globe from one of the dozens of tacky souvenir shops—La Rambla has a few establishments that make up with convenience what they may lack in style. The diamond in the rough is La Boqueria, one of the world's great food markets.

DEPARTMENT STORES AND MALLS
El Triangle

DEPARTMENT STORES | The Triangle d'Or or Golden Triangle at the top end of the Rambla on Plaça Catalunya is a stylish and popular complex and home for, among other stores, FNAC, where afternoon book presentations and CD launches bring together crowds of literati and music lovers. ⊠ *Pl. Catalunya 1–4 and Pelai 13-39, La Rambla* ☏ *93/318–0108* ⊕ *www.eltriangle.es* Ⓜ *Catalunya.*

Maremàgnum

SHOPPING CENTERS/MALLS | This modern shopping complex sits on an artificial "island" in the harbor and is accessed by Rambla del Mar, a wooden swing bridge.

The shops inside are fairly run-of-the-mill, but this mall is one of the few places in Barcelona where you can be sure to shop on Sunday. On the first floor, there's a good food court with fine water views. ⊠ *Moll d'Espanya 5, Port Vell, La Rambla* ☏ *93/225–8100* ⊕ *www.maremagnum. klepierre.es* Ⓜ *Drassanes.*

FOOD
Pastelería Escribà

FOOD/CANDY | Barcelona's wave of creative cake makers owe a lot to Antoni Escribà, a pastry chef who elevated the craft to an art form, especially in the field of chocolate sculptures. His three sons—Cristian, Joan, and Jordi—keep his spirit alive in the Casa Figueras, a jewel box of a shop awash in mosaic murals, curly copper work, and other fanciful Art Nouveau detailing. Tortes, chocolate kisses, and candy rings are just some of the edible treasures here that delight and surprise. A second Escribà shop, which has a café area, is at Gran Vía 546 in the Eixample. ⊠ *Rambla de les Flores 83, La Rambla* ☏ *93/301–6027* ⊕ *www.escriba. es* Ⓜ *Liceu.*

Activities

SAILING

On any day of the week in Barcelona you can see midday regattas taking place off the Barceloneta beaches or beyond the *rompeolas* (breakwater) on the far side of the port. Believe it or not, Olympic-level sailors are being trained for competition just a stone's throw (or two) from La Rambla.

Reial Club Marítim de Barcelona

SAILING | Barcelona's most exclusive and prestigious yacht club can advise visitors on maritime matters, from where to charter yachts and sailboats to how to sign up for sailing programs. ⊠ *Moll d'Espanya s/n, Port Vell* ☏ *932/217394* ⊕ *www.maritimbarcelona.org* Ⓜ *L3 Drassanes.*

Chapter 4

THE BARRI GÒTIC

4

Updated by
Elizabeth Prosser and
Steve Tallantyre

 Sights
★★★★★

 Restaurants
★★★★☆

 Hotels
★★★☆☆

 Shopping
★★★★☆

 Nightlife
★★☆☆☆

NEIGHBORHOOD SNAPSHOT

TOP EXPERIENCES

■ **Casa de l'Ardiaca:** Take in the 4th-century Roman wall, serene courtyard, and views of La Catedral from this 15th-century building.

■ **The Jewish Quarter:** Discover one of Europe's oldest synagogues, secret Jewish baths, and the dark history of Barcelona's Jewish community in the fascinating quarter of El Call.

■ **Catedral de la Seu:** Don't miss La Seu's leafy 14th-century cloister with its tropical garden and pool populated by 13 white swans.

■ **Els Quatre Gats–Casa Martí:** Linger over a coffee at this historic café, once the meeting place for Barcelona's bohemians, such as Picasso and Gaudí.

■ **Plaça Reial** Wander the narrow streets off the Gothic Quarter, particularly the less-crowded area between Plaça Reial's square and the seafront.

■ **Sardana Dancing:** Catch a traditional Catalan *sardana* dance performance at Plaça Sant Jaume on Sunday afternoons.

GETTING HERE

The best way to get to the Barri Gòtic and the cathedral is to start down La Rambla from the Plaça de Catalunya metro stop. Take your first left on Carrer Canuda and walk past Barcelona's Ateneu Barcelonès at No. 6, through Plaça Villa de Madrid and its Roman tombstones, then through Passatge and Carrer Duc de la Victoria and out Carrer Boters (where the boot makers were located in medieval times) to Plaça Nova.

PLANNING YOUR TIME

Exploring the Barri Gòtic should take about three hours, depending on how often you stop and how long you linger. Allow another hour or two for the Museum of the History of the City. Plan to visit before 1:30 or after 4:30, or you'll miss a lot of street life; some churches are closed mid-afternoon as well.

QUICK BITES

■ **Mesón del Café.** For a coffee or tapas, look for this amiable (if pricey) gingerbread-house-like hole-in-the-wall steps from the Plaça Sant Jaume. ✉ *Carrer de la Llibreteria 16, Barri Gòtic* Ⓜ *Jaume*

■ **Café de l'Acadèmia.** With its brick arches and exposed-beam ceilings, the Café de l'Acadèmia is an intimate, relaxing place for lunch or dinner, popular with government workers from nearby Plaça Sant Jaume and visitors alike ✉ *Carrer Lledo 1, Barri Gòtic* Ⓜ *Jaume*

■ **Cafe Caelum.** Enjoy a variety of delicacies made in Spanish convents and monasteries and be sure to check out the remains of the medieval baths in the basement. ✉ *Carrer de la Palla 8, Barri Gòtic* Ⓜ *Jaume*

No city in Europe has an ancient quarter to rival Barcelona's Barri Gòtic in its historic atmosphere and the sheer density of its monumental buildings. It's a stroller's delight, where you can expect to hear the strains of a flute or a classical guitar from around the next corner. Thronged with sightseers by day, the quarter can be eerily quiet at night, a stone oasis of silence at the eye of the storm.

A labyrinth of medieval buildings, squares, and narrow cobblestone streets, the Barri Gòtic comprises the area around the Catedral de la Seu, built over Roman ruins you can still visit and filled with the Gothic structures that marked the zenith of Barcelona's power in the 15th century. On certain corners you feel as if you're making a genuine excursion back in time.

The Barri Gòtic rests squarely atop the first Roman settlement. Sometimes referred to as the *rovell d'ou* (the yolk of the egg), this high ground the Romans called Mons Taber coincides almost exactly with the early 1st- to 4th-century fortified town of Barcino. Sights to see here include the Plaça del Rei, the remains of Roman Barcino underground beneath the Museum of the History of the City, the Plaça Sant Jaume and the area around the onetime Roman Forum, the medieval Jewish Quarter, and the ancient Plaça Sant Just.

 Sights

Ajuntament de Barcelona

BUILDING | The 15th-century city hall on Plaça Sant Jaume faces the Palau de la Generalitat, with its mid-18th-century neoclassical facade, across the square once occupied by the Roman Forum. The Ajuntament is a rich repository of sculpture and painting by the great Catalan masters, from Marès to Gargallo to Clarà, from Subirachs to Miró and Llimona. Inside is the famous Saló de Cent, from which the Consell de Cent, Europe's oldest democratic parliament, governed Barcelona between 1373 and 1714. The Saló de les Croniques (Hall of Chronicles) is decorated with Josep Maria Sert's immense black-and-burnished-gold murals (1928) depicting the early-14th-century Catalan campaign in Byzantium and Greece under the command of Roger de Flor. Sert's perspective technique makes the paintings seem to follow you around the room. The city hall is open to visitors on Sunday mornings 10–1:30, with guided visits in

The Barri Gòtic

Map labels:

G · H · I · J

Carrer de Roger
C. d'Ausiàs Marc
Carrer del Bruc
Carrer de Girona
Carrer de Ballén
Ronda de Sant Pere
Carrer de Trafalgar
C. de les Jonqueres
Carrer d'Alí Bei
Carrer d'Ortigosa
Carrer de Trafalgar
Carrer de Trafalgar
Carrer de Girona
ptge. Sant Benet
Carrer Sant Pere més Alt
Carrer fonglilar
Carrer del Rec Carrermtal
Carrer de Sant Pere Mes Biax
SANT PERE
Carrer de Montcada
Av. F. Cambó
Carrer del Portal Nou
Passeig de Lluís companys
Plaça de Joan Capri
Carrer Carrerrders
Carrer del Comerç
Carrer Carrerrders
Carrer de la Princèsa
Carrer Banyes Valls
Carrer de Montcada
Museu Picasso
C. Cirera
C. del Rec
Passeig de Picasso
LA RIBERA
Carrer Argentaria
Carrer Mosques
Plaça de Santa Maria
C. Santa Maria
C. dels Agullers
Carrer Consolat de Mar
Av. Marquès de l'Argenterá
Estació de França

0 — 200 yards
0 — 200 meters

Sights ▼

1 Ajuntament de Barcelona E6
2 Baixada de Santa Eulàlia D5
3 Casa de l'Ardiaca E5
4 Catedral de la Seu E5
5 Columnes del Temple d'August ... E6
6 Col·legi d'Arquitectes E4
7 Els Quatre Gats–Casa Martí E3
8 Gaudí Exhibition Center E5
9 Generalitat de Catalunya E6
10 Museu d'Història de Barcelona... F6
11 Palau del Lloctinent F5
12 Plaça del Rei F5
13 Plaça Sant Felip Neri D5
14 Plaça Sant Jaume E6
15 Plaça Sant Just F6
16 Santa Maria del Pi C5

Restaurants ▼

1 Agut E8
2 Caelis F3
3 Cafè de L'Acadèmia F7
4 Cuines Santa Caterina G5
5 Irati Taverna Basca C5
6 Koy Shunka F4
7 La Cerería D6
8 La Palma E7
9 La Plassohla F3
10 MariscCO C6
11 Pla E7

Hotels ▼

1 Arai 4* Aparthotel Barcelona D7
2 Catalunya Portal d'Angel E3
3 Colón F4
4 Duquesa de Cardona E9
5 el Jardí C5
6 Grand Hotel Central F5
7 Hotel Neri D5
8 Hotel Ohla F3
9 Mercer Hotel Barcelona F7
10 Mercer House Boria Bcn G6

4

The Barri Gòtic

KEY

1 Exploring Sights
1 Restaurants
1 Hotels
Ⓜ Metro Stops
Ⓕ FGC Stops

English at 10; on local holidays; and for occasional concerts or events in the Saló de Cent. ✉ *Pl. Sant Jaume 1, Barri Gòtic* ☎ *93/402–7000* ⊕ *ajuntament.barcelona. cat/en* 🎫 *Free* Ⓜ *L4 Jaume I, L3 Liceu.*

Baixada de Santa Eulàlia

RELIGIOUS SITE | Down Carrer Sant Sever from the side door of the cathedral cloister, past Carrer Sant Domènec del Call and the Església de Sant Sever, is a tiny shrine, in an alcove overhead, dedicated to the 4th-century martyr Santa Eulàlia, patron saint of the city. Down this hill, or *baixada* (descent), Eulàlia was rolled in a barrel filled with—as the Jacint Verdaguer verse in ceramic tile on the wall reads— *glavis i ganivets de dos talls* (swords and double-edged knives), the final of the 13 tortures to which she was subjected before her crucifixion at Plaça del Pedró. ✉ *Carrer Sant Sever s/n, Barri Gòtic* Ⓜ *Liceu, Jaume I.*

Casa de l'Ardiaca *(Archdeacon's House)*

BUILDING | The interior of this 15th-century building, home of the Municipal Archives (upstairs), has superb views of the remains of the 4th-century Roman watchtowers and walls. Look at the Montjuïc sandstone carefully, and you will see blocks taken from other buildings carved and beveled into decorative shapes, proof of the haste of the Romans to fortify the site as the Visigoths approached from the north, when the Pax Romana collapsed. The marble letter box by the front entrance was designed in 1895 by Lluís Domènech i Montaner for the Lawyer's Professional Association; as the story goes, it was meant to symbolize, in the images of the doves, the lofty flight to the heights of justice and, in the images of the turtles, the plodding pace of administrative procedures. In the center of the lovely courtyard here, across from the Santa Llúcia chapel, is a fountain; on the day of Corpus Christi in June the fountain impressively supports *l'ou com balla,* or "the dancing egg," a Barcelona tradition in which eggs are set to bobbing atop jets of water in various places around the city. ✉ *Carrer de Santa Llúcia 1, Barri Gòtic* ☎ *93/256–2255* Ⓜ *L3 Liceu, L4 Jaume I.*

★ Catedral de la Seu

BUILDING | Barcelona's cathedral is a repository of centuries of the city's history and legend—although as a work of architecture visitors might find it a bit of a disappointment, compared to the Mediterranean Gothic Santa Maria del Mar and Gaudí's Moderniste Sagrada Família. It was built between 1298 and 1450; work on the spire and neo-Gothic facade began in 1892 and was not completed until 1913. Historians are not sure about the identity of the architect: one name often proposed is Jaume Fabre, a native of Mallorca. The building is perhaps most impressive at night, floodlit with the stained-glass windows illuminated from inside; book a room with a balcony at the Hotel Colon, facing the cathedral square, and make the most of it.

This is reputedly the darkest of all the world's great cathedrals—even at high noon the nave is enveloped in shadows, which give the appearance that it's larger than it actually is—so it takes a while for your eyes to adjust to the rich, velvety pitch of the interior. Don't miss the beautifully carved choir stalls of the Knights of the Golden Fleece; the intricately and elaborately sculpted organ loft over the door out to Plaça Sant Iu (with its celebrated Saracen's Head sculpture); the series of 60-odd wood sculptures of evangelical figures along the exterior lateral walls of the choir; the cloister with its fountain and geese in the pond; and, in the crypt, the tomb of Santa Eulàlia.

St. Eulàlia, originally interred at Santa Maria del Mar—then known as Santa Maria de les Arenes (St. Mary of the Sands)—was moved to the cathedral in 1339, and venerated here as its patron and protector. Eulalistas (St. Eulàlia devotees, rivals of a sort to the followers of La Mercé, or Our Lady of Mercy) celebrate

El Call: The Jewish Quarter

Barcelona's Jewish Quarter, El Call (a name derived from the Hebrew word *qahal, or* "meeting place"), is just to the Rambla side of the Palau de la Generalitat. Carrer del Call, Carrer de Sant Domènec del Call, Carrer Marlet, and Arc de Sant Ramón del Call mark the heart of the medieval ghetto. Confined by law to this area at the end of the 7th century (one reason the streets in Calls or Aljamas were so narrow was that their inhabitants could only build into the streets for more space), Barcelona's Jews were the private bankers to Catalonia's sovereign counts (only Jews could legally lend money). The Jewish community also produced many leading physicians, translators, and scholars in medieval Barcelona, largely because the Jewish faith rested on extensive Talmudic and textual study, thus promoting a high degree of literacy. The reproduction of a plaque bearing Hebrew text on the corner of Carrer Marlet and Arc de Sant Ramón del Call was the only physical reminder of the Jewish presence here until the medieval synagogue reopened as a historical site in 2003.

The **Sinagoga Major de Barcelona** (✉ *Carrer Marlet 2, Barri Gòtic* ⊕ *www.calldebarcelona.org* 🎟 *€2.50* ⊙ *Weekdays 11–5:30, weekends 11–3*), the restored original synagogue at the corner of Marlet and Sant Domènec del Call, is virtually all that survives of the Jewish presence in medieval Barcelona. Tours are given in English, Hebrew, and Spanish, and a booklet in English (€3) explains the history of the community.

The story of Barcelona's Jewish community came to a bloody end in August 1391, when during a time of famine and pestilence a nationwide outbreak of anti-Semitic violence reached Barcelona, with catastrophic results: nearly the entire Jewish population was murdered or forced to convert to Christianity.

the fiesta of La Laia (the nickname for Eulàlia) for a few days around her feast day on February 12, and would like to see the cathedral named after her, but for the moment it is known simply as La Catedral, or in Catalan La Seu (the See, or seat of the bishopric).

Enter from the front portal (there are also entrances through the cloister and from Carrer Comtes down the left side of the apse), and the first thing you see are the high-relief sculptures of the **story of St. Eulàlia,** on the near side of the choir stalls. The first scene, on the left, shows St. Eulàlia in front of Roman Consul Decius with her left hand on her heart and her outstretched right hand pointing at a cross in the distance. In the next, she is tied to a column and being whipped by the consul's thugs. To the right of the door into the choir the unconscious Eulàlia is being hauled away, and in the final scene on the right she is being lashed to the X-shape cross upon which she was crucified in mid-February in the year 303. To the right of this high relief is a sculpture of the martyred heroine, resurrected as a living saint.

Among the two dozen ornate and gilded chapels in the basilica, pay due attention to the **Capella de Lepant,** dedicated to Sant Crist de Lepanto, in the far right corner as you enter through the front door. According to legend, the 15th-century polychrome wood sculpture of a battle-scarred, dark-skinned Christ, visible on the altar of this 100-seat chapel behind a black-clad Mare de Deu dels Dolors

The ornate Gothic interior of the Catedral de la Seu is always enclosed in shadows, even at high noon.

(Our Lady of the Sorrows), was the bowsprit of the flagship Spanish galley at the battle fought between Christian and Ottoman fleets on October 7, 1571.

Outside the main nave of the cathedral to the right, you'll find the leafy, palm tree–shaded **cloister** surrounding a tropical garden, and a pool populated by 13 snow-white geese, one for each of the tortures inflicted upon St. Eulàlia in an effort to break her faith. Legend has it that they are descendants of the flock of geese from Rome's Capitoline Hill, whose honking alarms roused the city to repel invaders during the days of the Roman Republic. Don't miss the fountain with the bronze sculpture of an equestrian St. George, hacking away at his perennial foe, the dragon, on the eastern corner of the cloister. On the day of Corpus Christi, this fountain is one of the more spectacular displays of the traditional l'ou com balla (dancing egg).

In front of the cathedral is the grand square of **Plaça de la Seu,** where on Saturday from 6 pm to 8 pm, Sunday morning, and occasional evenings, barcelonins gather to dance the sardana, the circular folk dance performed for centuries as a symbol-in-motion of Catalan identity and the solidarity of the Catalan people. Nimble-footed oldsters share the space with young esbarts (dance troupes), coats and bags piled in the center of the ring, all dancing together to the reedy music of the cobla (band) in smooth, deceptively simple, heel-and-toe sequences of steps. This is no tourist attraction: Catalans dance the sardana just for themselves. Also check local listings for the annual series of evening organ concerts held in the cathedral. ⊠ Pl. de la Seu s/n, Barri Gòtic ☎ 93/342–8262 ⊕ www.catedral-bcn.org ☜ Free weekdays 8–12:45 and 5:45–7:30, Sat. 8–12:45 and 5:15–8, Sun. 8–1:30 and 5:15–8; €7 donation weekdays 1–5:30, Sat. 1–5, Sun. 2–5; choir €3; rooftop €3 Ⓜ L4 Jaume I.

Col·legi d'Arquitectes

COLLEGE | Barcelona's College of Architects, designed by Xavier Busquets and opened in 1962, houses three important gems: a superb library located across the street, where for a small fee the college's bibliographical resources are at your disposal for research; a bookstore specializing in architecture, design, and drafting supplies; and a decent restaurant (one of the city's best-kept secret lunch options for the weary explorer). The Picasso friezes on the facade of the building were designed by the artist in 1960; inside are two more, one a vision of Barcelona and the other dedicated to the sardana, Catalonia's traditional folk dance. The glass-and-concrete modernity of the building itself raises hackles: how could *architects,* of all people, be so blithely unconcerned—even contemptuous—about the aesthetics of accommodation to the Gothic setting around it? ⊠ *Pl. Nova 5, Barri Gòtic* ☎ *93/301–5000, 93/306–7803* ⊕ *www.coac.net* ☾ *Closed Sun.* Ⓜ *L3 Jaume I.*

Columnes del Temple d'August (*Columns of the Temple of Augustus*)

ARCHAEOLOGICAL SITE | The highest point in Roman Barcelona is marked with a circular millstone at the entrance to the Centre Excursionista de Catalunya, a club dedicated to exploring the mountains and highlands of Catalonia on foot and on skis. Inside the entryway on the right are some of the best-preserved 1st- and 2nd-century Corinthian Roman columns in Europe. Massive, fluted, and crowned with the typical Corinthian acanthus leaves in two distinct rows under eight fluted sheaths, these columns remain only because Barcelona's early Christians elected, atypically, not to build their cathedral over the site of the previous temple. The Temple of Augustus, dedicated to the Roman emperor, occupied the northwest corner of the Roman Forum, which coincided approximately with today's Plaça Sant Jaume. ⊠ *Centre Excursionista de Catalunya, Carrer Paradís 10, Barri Gòtic* ☎ *93/315–2311 Centre Excursionista* Ⓜ *L4 Jaume I.*

Els Quatre Gats–Casa Martí

ARTS VENUE | Built by Josep Puig i Cadafalch for the Martí family, this Art Nouveau house, a three-minute walk from the cathedral, was the fountainhead of bohemianism in Barcelona. It was here in 1897 that four friends, notable dandies all—Ramon Casas, Pere Romeu, Santiago Russinyol, and Miguel Utrillo—started a café called the Quatre Gats (Four Cats), meaning to make it *the* place for artists and art lovers to gather. (One of their wisest decisions was to mount a show, in February 1900, for an up-and-coming young painter named Pablo Picasso.) The exterior was decorated with figures by sculptor Eusebi Arnau (1864–1934). Inside, Els Quatre Gats hasn't changed one iota: pride of place goes to the Casas self-portait, smoking his pipe, comically teamed up on a tandem bicycle with Romeu. Drop in for a café au lait and you just might end up seated in Picasso's chair. Venture to the dining room in back, with its unusual gallery seating upstairs; this room where Miró used to produce puppet theater is charming, but the food is nothing to rave about. *Quatre gats* in Catalan is a euphemism for "hardly anybody," but the four founders were each definitely somebody. ⊠ *Carrer Montsió 3 bis, Barri Gòtic* ☎ *93/302–4140* ⊕ *www.4gats.com* Ⓜ *Pl. Catalunya, L4 Jaume I, L4 Urquinaona.*

Gaudí Exhibition Center (*Casa de la Pia Almoina–Museu Diocesà de Barcelona*)

BUILDING | Set virtually into the city's ancient Roman wall, this 11th-century Gothic building, now a museum, once served soup to the city's poor; hence its popular name, the "House of Pious Alms." The museum (originally housing a collection of religious sculpture, paintings, and liturgical implements) is now dedicated to the works of the master architect Antoni Gaudí. For a tour of the Roman walls, consult the excellent relief map/scale model of Roman Barcelona in the vestibule; copies of the map and model are for sale in the nearby **Museu**

d'Història de la Ciutat (Museum of the History of the City). Inside, Roman stones are clearly visible in this much-restored structure, the only octagonal tower of the 82 that ringed 4th-century Barcino. The museum is behind the massive floral iron grate in the octagonal Roman watchtower to the left of the stairs of the Catedral de la Seu. ⊠ *Av. de la Catedral 4, Barri Gòtic* ☏ *93/315–2213* ⊕ *www.gaudiexhibitioncenter.com* ✉ *€15 (€17 with virtual reality/hologram headset and commentary)* Ⓜ *L4 Jaume I.*

Generalitat de Catalunya

GOVERNMENT BUILDING | Opposite city hall, the Palau de la Generalitat is the seat of the autonomous Catalan government. Seen through the front windows of this ornate 15th-century palace, the gilded ceiling of the Saló de Sant Jordi (St. George's Hall), named for Catalonia's dragon-slaying patron saint, gives an idea of the lavish decor within. Carrer del Bisbe, running along the right side of the building from the square to the cathedral, offers a favorite photo op: the ornate gargoyle-bedecked Gothic bridge overhead, connecting the Generalitat to the building across the street. The Generalitat opens to the public on the second and fourth weekends of the month, with free one-hour guided tours in English (request in advance), through the Generalitat website. The building is also open to visitors on Día de Sant Jordi (St. George's Day: April 23), during the Fiesta de la Mercé in late September, and on the National Day of Catalonia (September 11). There are carillon concerts here on Sunday at noon, another opportunity to see inside. ⊠ *Pl. de Sant Jaume 4, Barri Gòtic* ☏ *93/402–4600* ⊕ *www.gencat.cat* Ⓜ *L4 Jaume I, L3 Liceu.*

★ Museu d'Història de Barcelona

(*Museum of the History of Barcelona [MUHBA]*)
ARCHAEOLOGICAL SITE | This fascinating museum just off Plaça del Rei traces Barcelona's evolution from its first Iberian settlement through its Roman and Visigothic ages and beyond. The Romans took the city during the Punic Wars, and you can tour underground remains of their Colonia Favencia Iulia Augusta Paterna Barcino (Favored Colony of the Father Julius Augustus Barcino) via metal walkways. Some 43,000 square feet of archaeological artifacts, from the walls of houses, to mosaics and fluted columns, workshops (for pressing olive oil and salted fish paste), and street systems, can be found in large part beneath the plaça. See how the Visgoths and their descendants built the early medieval walls on top of these ruins, recycling chunks of Roman stone and concrete, bits of columns, and even headstones. In the ground-floor gallery is a striking collection of marble busts and funerary urns discovered in the course of the excavations. The price of admission to the museum includes entry to the other treasures of the **Plaça del Rei,** including the **Palau Reial Major,** the splendid **Saló del Tinell,** and the chapel of **Santa Àgata.** Also included are visits to other sites maintained by the museum: the most important and central of these are the Temple of Augustus, the Door of the Sea (the largest of the Roman-era city gates) and Dockside Thermal Baths, the Roman Funeral Way in the Plaça de la Vila de Madrid, and the Call (medieval Barcelona's Jewish quarter). The admission ticket also gives visitors a 21% discount on entrance to Park Güell. ⊠ *Palau Padellàs, Pl. del Rei s/n, Barri Gòtic* ☏ *93/256–2100* ⊕ *ajuntament.barcelona.cat/museuhistoria/en/* ✉ *From €7 (free with Barcelona Card, 1st Sun. of month, and all other Sun. after 3)* ☉ *Closed Mon.* Ⓜ *L4 Jaume I, L3 Liceu.*

Palau del Lloctinent (*Lieutenant's Palace*)

CASTLE/PALACE | The three facades of the Palau face Carrer dels Comtes de Barcelona on the cathedral side, the Baixada de Santa Clara, and Plaça del Rei. Typical of late Gothic–early Renaissance Catalan design, it was constructed by Antoni Carbonell between 1549 and 1557, and remains one of the Gothic Quarter's most graceful buildings. The heavy stone arches over the entry, the central patio, and the intricately coffered wooden roof over the stairs are all good examples of noble 16th-century architecture. The door on the stairway is a 1975 Josep Maria Subirachs work portraying scenes from the life of Sant Jordi and the history of Catalonia. The Palau del Lloctinent was inhabited by the king's official emissary or viceroy to Barcelona during the 16th and 17th centuries; it now houses the historical materials of the Archivo de la Corona de Aragón (Archive of the Crown of Aragon), and offers an excellent exhibit on the life and times of Jaume I, one of early Catalonia's most important figures. The patio also occasionally hosts early-music concerts, and during the Corpus Christi celebration is one of the main venues for the ou com balla, when an egg "dances" on the fountain amid an elaborate floral display. ⊠ *Carrer dels Comtes de Barcelona 2, Barri Gòtic* ☎ *93/485–4285 archives office* ⊕ *www. mecd.gob.es* Ⓜ *L4 Jaume I.*

★ **Plaça del Rei**

ARCHAEOLOGICAL SITE | This little square is as compact a nexus of history as anything the Barri Gòtic has to offer. Long held to be the scene of Columbus's triumphal return from his first voyage to the New World—the precise spot where Ferdinand and Isabella received him is purportedly on the stairs fanning out from the corner of the square (though evidence indicates that the Catholic Monarchs were at a summer residence in the Empordá)—the **Palau Reial Major** (admission included in the €7 entrance fee for the Museu d'Història de Barcelona; closed Mon.) was the official royal residence in Barcelona. The main room is the **Saló del Tinell,** a magnificent banquet hall built in 1362. To the left is the **Palau del Lloctinent** (Lieutenant's Palace); towering overhead in the corner is the dark 15th-century **Torre Mirador del Rei Martí** (King Martin's Watchtower).

The 14th-century **Capella Real de Santa Àgueda** (Royal Chapel of St. Agatha) is on the right side of the stairway, and behind and to the right as you face the stairs is the **Palau Clariana-Padellàs,** moved to this spot stone by stone from Carrer Mercaders in the early 20th century and now the entrance to the **Museu d'Història de Barcelona.** ⊠ *Pl. del Rei s/n, Barri Gòtic* Ⓜ *L3 Liceu, L4 Jaume I.*

Plaça Sant Felip Neri

PLAZA | A tiny square just behind **Plaça de Garriga Bachs** off the side of the cloister of the Catedral de la Seu, this was once a burial ground for Barcelona's executed heroes and villains, before all church graveyards were moved to the south side of Montjuïc, the present site of the municipal cemetery. The church of San Felip Neri here is a frequent venue for classical concerts. Fragments of a bomb that exploded in the square during the Civil War made the pockmarks on the walls of the church. ⊠ *Pl. Sant Felip Neri, Barri Gòtic* Ⓜ *L3 Liceu, L4 Jaume I.*

Plaça Sant Jaume

GOVERNMENT BUILDING | Facing each other across this oldest epicenter of Barcelona (and often on politically opposite sides as well) are the seat of Catalonia's regional government, the Generalitat de Catalunya, in the **Palau de La Generalitat,** and the City Hall, the Ajuntament de Barcelona, in the **Casa de la Ciutat.** This square was the site of the Roman forum 2,000 years ago, though subsequent construction filled the space with buildings. The square was cleared in the 1840s, but the two imposing government buildings are actually much older: the Ajuntament dates back to the 14th century, and the Generalitat was built between the 15th and mid-17th century. ⊠ *Barri Gòtic* ⊙ *Closed weekdays* ☞ *Tours of Ajuntament (in Catalan, Spanish, and English) weekends 10–2; tours of Generalitat on 2nd and 4th weekends of month 10:30–1, by reservation only (bring your passport)* Ⓜ *Jaume I.*

Plaça Sant Just

PLAZA | Off to the left side of city hall down Carrer Hèrcules (named for the mythical founder of Barcelona) are this square and the site of the Església de Sant Just i Pastor, one of the city's oldest Christian churches. Unfortunately, nothing remains of the original church, founded in 801 by King Louis the Pious; the present structure dates to 1342. Christian catacombs are reported to have been found beneath the plaça. The Gothic fountain was built in 1367 by the patrician Joan Fiveller, then Chief Minister of the city administration. (Fiveller's major claim to fame was to have discovered a spring in the Collserola hills and had the water piped straight to Barcelona.) The fountain in the square bears an image of St. Just, and the city and sovereign count-kings' coats of arms, along with a pair of falcons. The excellent entryway and courtyard to the left of Carrer Bisbe Caçador is the Palau Moixó, the town house of an important early Barcelona family; down Carrer Bisbe Caçador is the Acadèmia de Bones Lletres, the Catalan Academy of Arts and Letters. The church is dedicated to the boy martyrs Just and Pastor; the Latin inscription over the door translates into English as "Our pious patron is the black and beautiful Virgin, together with the sainted children Just and Pastore." ⊠ Pl. Sant Just, Barri Gòtic Ⓜ Jaume I.

Santa Maria del Pi (*St. Mary of the Pine*)

BUILDING | Sister church to Santa Maria del Mar and to Santa Maria de Pedralbes, this early Catalan Gothic structure is perhaps the most fortresslike of all three: hulking, dark, and massive, and perforated only by the main entryway and the mammoth rose window, said to be the world's largest. Try to see the window from inside in the late afternoon to get the best view of the colors. The church was named for the lone *pi* (pine tree) that stood in what was a marshy lowland outside the 4th-century Roman walls. An early

Bats in the Belfry

Spain, like the United States, chose the eagle as its national bird, but Catalonia's aerial mascot, oddly enough, is the bat—allegedly because King Jaume I was a fan ever since bats alerted his troops to repel a dawn attack during his Balearic campaign. Barcelona bats hang from the chandeliers in the City Hall's Saló de Cent, are sculpted into the Triumphal Arch on Passeig Lluís Companys, and preside over the main Carrer Hospital entrance to the medieval hospital.

church dating back to the 10th century preceded the present Santa Maria del Pi, which was begun in 1322 and finally consecrated in 1453. The interior compares poorly with the clean and lofty lightness of Santa Maria del Mar, but there are two interesting things to see: the original wooden choir loft, and the Ramón Amadeu painting *La Mare de Deu dels Desamparats* (*Our Lady of the Helpless*), in which the artist reportedly used his wife and children as models for the Virgin and children. The church is a regular venue for classical guitar concerts by well-known soloists. Tours of the basilica and bell tower are available in English, by reservation. The adjoining squares, **Plaça del Pi** and **Plaça de Sant Josep Oriol,** are two of the liveliest and most appealing spaces in the Ciutat Vella, filled with much-frequented outdoor cafés and used as a venue for markets selling natural products or paintings, or as an impromptu concert hall for musicians. The handsome entryway and courtyard at No. 4 Plaça de Sant Josep Oriol across from the lateral facade of Santa Maria del Pi is the **Palau Fivaller,** now seat of the Agricultural Institute, an interesting patio to have a look through. Placeta del Pi, tucked in behind the church, has outdoor tables

Did You Know?

The Barri Gòtic actually sits on top of the first Roman settlement. Roman walls are visible around the edges of the neighborhood.

and is convenient for a coffee or tapas. ✉ *Pl. del Pi 7, Barri Gòtic* ☎ *93/318–4743* 🌐 *basilicadelpi.com* 🍽 *From €4* Ⓜ *L3 Liceu.*

 ## Restaurants

Agut

$$ | CATALAN | Wainscoting and 1950s canvases are the background for the mostly Catalan crowd in this homey restaurant in the lower reaches of the Barri Gòtic. Agut was founded in 1924, and its popularity has never waned—after all, hearty Catalan fare at a fantastic value is always in demand. **Known for:** must-try civet of wild boar; local wines; local favorite. 💲 *Average main: €17* ✉ *Gignàs 16, Barri Gòtic* ☎ *93/315–1709* 🕐 *Closed Mon., and 3 wks in Aug. No dinner Sun.* Ⓜ *Jaume I.*

Caelis

$$$$ | CATALAN | Situated in the Hotel Ohla Barcelona, near the Palau de la Música Catalana, Caelis keeps its starred, fine-dining style and adds the pizzazz of open-kitchen show cooking. The two tasting menus (€92 and €135) change regularly and you can pick a course from them as an à la carte alternative. **Known for:** refined fine dining; open kitchen; Michelin-starred. 💲 *Average main: €42* ✉ *Via Laietana 49, Barri Gòtic* ☎ *93/510–1205* 🌐 *www.caelis.com* 🕐 *Closed Sun. and Mon. No lunch Tues.* Ⓜ *Urquinaona.*

Cafè de l'Acadèmia

$$ | CATALAN | With wicker chairs, stone walls, and classical music, this place is sophisticated-rustic in style. Contemporary Mediterranean cuisine specialties such as *timbal d'escalibada amb formatge de cabra* (roast vegetable salad with goat cheese) make it more than just a café. **Known for:** lively terrace; great set lunch; private wine cellar for larger groups. 💲 *Average main: €16* ✉ *Lledó 1, Barri Gòtic* ☎ *93/319–8253* 🕐 *Closed weekends, and 3 wks in Aug.* Ⓜ *Jaume I.*

Cuines Santa Caterina

$ | ECLECTIC | A lovingly restored market designed by the late Enric Miralles and completed by his widow Benedetta Tagliabue provides a spectacular setting for one of the city's most original dining operations. Under the undulating wooden superstructure of the market, the breakfast and tapas bar offers a variety of international culinary specialties. **Known for:** open all day; vegetarian options; Mediterranean fare. 💲 *Average main: €14* ✉ *Av. Francesc Cambó 16, Born-Ribera* ☎ *93/268–9918* 🌐 *www.grupotragaluz.com* Ⓜ *Urquinaona, Jaume I.*

Irati Taverna Basca

$$ | BASQUE | There's only one drawback to this lively Basque bar between Plaça del Pi and La Rambla: it's narrow at the street end, and harder to squeeze into than the Barcelona metro at rush hour. Skip the tapas on the bar and opt for the plates brought out piping-hot from the kitchen. **Known for:** quick bites; Basque specialties; txakoli sparkling wine. 💲 *Average main: €21* ✉ *Cardenal Casañas 17, Barri Gòtic* ☎ *93/302–3084* 🌐 *www.iratitavernabasca.com* Ⓜ *Liceu.*

Koy Shunka

$$$$ | JAPANESE | Two blocks away from their mothership Shunka, partners Hideki Matsuhisa and Xu Changchao have done it again. This time, with more space to work with, the Japanese-Chinese team of master chefs has organized a tribute to Asian fusion cooking based on products from the Catalan larder. **Known for:** inventive fusion cuisine; contemporary atmosphere; scrumptious cerdo ibérico. 💲 *Average main: €30* ✉ *Copons 7, Barri Gòtic* ☎ *93/412–7939* 🌐 *www.koyshunka.com* 🕐 *Closed Mon., Sun., 3 wks in Aug., and 2 wks at Christmas* Ⓜ *Urquinaona.*

La Cereria

$ | VEGETARIAN | At the corner of Baixada de Sant Miquel and Passatge de Crèdit, this humble terrace and musical instrument store/café has charm to spare. The tables in the Passatge itself are shady

A Primer on Barcelona's Cuisine

Menus in Catalan are as musical as they are aromatic, with rare ingredients such as *salicornia* (seawort, or sea asparagus) with *bacalao* (cod), or fragrant wild mushrooms such as *rossinyols* (chanterelles) and *moixernons* (St. George's mushroom) accompanying dishes like *mandonguilles amb sepia* (meatballs with cuttlefish).

Four sauces grace the Catalan table: *sofregit* (fried onion, tomato, and garlic—a base for nearly everything); *samfaina* (a ratatouille-like sofregit with eggplant and sweet red peppers); *picada* (garlic, almonds, bread crumbs, olive oil, pine nuts, parsley, saffron, or chocolate); and *allioli* (pounded garlic and virgin olive oil).

The three *e*'s deserve a place in any Catalan culinary anthology: *escalibada* (roasted red peppers, eggplants, and tomatoes served in garlic and olive oil); *esqueixada* (shredded salt-cod salad served raw with onions, peppers, olives, beans, olive oil, and vinegar); and *escudella* (a winter stew of meats and vegetables with noodles and beans).

Universal specialties are *pa amb tomaquet* (toasted bread with squeezed tomato and olive oil), *espinaques a la catalana* (spinach cooked with raisins, garlic, and pine nuts), and *botifarra amb mongetes* (pork sausage with white beans).

The *mar i muntanya* (Catalan "surf 'n' turf") has been a standard since Roman times. Rice dishes are simply called *arròs*, and range from standard seafood paella to the *arròs a banda* (paella with shelled prawns, shrimp, and mussels), to *arròs negre* (paella cooked in cuttlefish ink) or *arròs caldós* (a brothy risotto-like dish often made with lobster). *Fideuà* is a paella made of vermicelli noodles, not rice.

Fresh fish such as *llobarro* (sea bass, *lubina* in Spanish) or *dorada* (gilthead bream) cooked *a la sal* (in a shell of salt) are standards, as are grilled *llenguado* (sole) and *rodaballo* (turbot). Duck, goose, chicken, and rabbit frequent Catalan menus, as do *cabrit* (kid or baby goat), *xai* (lamb), *porc* (pork), *vedella* (young beef), and *bou* (mature beef). Finally come the two Catalan classic desserts, *mel i mató* (honey and fresh cream cheese) and *crema catalana* (a crème brûlée–like custard with a caramelized glaze).

A typical session *à table* in Barcelona might begin with *pica-pica* (hors d'oeuvres), a variety of delicacies such as *jamón ibérico de bellota* (acorn-fed ham), *xipirones* (baby squid), *pimientos de Padrón* (green peppers, some spicy), or *bunyols de bacallà* (cod fritters or croquettes), and pa amb tomaquet. From here you can order a starter such as *canelones* (cannelloni) or you can go straight to your main course.

and breezy in summer, and the vegetarian and vegan cuisine is organic and creative. **Known for:** creative vegetarian and vegan cuisine; tasty escalivada; next to birthplace of Catalan painter Joan Miró. [$] *Average main: €10* ✉ *Baixada de Sant Miquel 3–5, Barri Gòtic* ☎ *93/301–8510* ⏲ *Closed Mon.* [M] *Liceu.*

La Palma

$ | **CAFÉ** | Behind the Plaça Sant Jaume's ajuntament (city hall), toward the post office, sits this cozy and ancient café. An old favorite of 20th-century artists ranging from Salvador Dalí to Pablo Picasso, it has marble tables, wine barrels, sausages hanging from the ceiling, and newspapers to pore over. **Known for:** local wines; historic setting; authentic tapas. [$] *Average main: €12* ✉ *Palma Sant Just 7, Barri Gòtic* ☎ *93/315–0656* 🌐 *www.bodegalapalma.com* 💳 *No credit cards* 🕒 *Closed Sun.* [M] *Jaume I.*

La Plassohla

$ | **TAPAS** | A trendy international crowd packs this place, sampling tapas such as free-range eggs cooked at low temperature with mushrooms, and charcoal-grilled fresh mussels with tomato sauce. The stylish, high-ceilinged space keeps noise levels under control, and huge windows allow both natural light and views of passing street life. **Known for:** sophisticated atmosphere; open late; cheap fixed lunch. [$] *Average main: €15* ✉ *Via Laietana 49, Barri Gòtic* ☎ *93/504–5100* 🌐 *www.ohlabarcelona.com* [M] *Urquinaona.*

MariscCO

$$ | **SEAFOOD** | The only tolerable dining choice in the elegant Plaça Reial—a square filled with sunny cafés serving mediocre fare—this restaurant specializes in fresh fish and rice dishes. Quality can be variable but prices are competitive, and there are set menus ranging from €35 to €50 to make ordering less daunting. **Known for:** fresh seafood; sunny terrace. [$] *Average main: €14* ✉ *Pl. Reial 8, La Rambla* ☎ *93/412–4536* 🌐 *www.mariscco.com* 🕒 *Closed 2 wks Jan.* [M] *Liceu.*

Pla

$$ | **CATALAN** | Filled with couples night after night, this combination music, drinking, and dining place is candlelit and sleekly designed in glass over ancient stone, brick, and wood. The cuisine is light and contemporary, featuring inventive salads and fresh seafood, as well as options for vegetarians and vegans. **Known for:** romantic ambience; extensive wine list; vegetarian options. [$] *Average main: €18* ✉ *Bellafila 5, Barri Gòtic* ☎ *93/412–6552* 🌐 *www.restaurantpla.cat* 🕒 *No lunch weekdays* [M] *Jaume I.*

Hotels

★ **Arai 4* Aparthotel Barcelona** (*Arai-Palau Dels Quatre Rius Monument*)

$$$$ | **HOTEL** | **FAMILY** | You couldn't ask for a better location from which to explore Barcelona's Barri Gòtic—or for a bivouac more elegant—than one of the aparthotel suites in this stunning restoration. **Pros:** warm and attentive service; historic character retained in former palace; welcome set with a bottle of wine. **Cons:** somewhat seedy area; on busy street; rooms on the top floor lack historic charm. [$] *Rooms from: €370* ✉ *Avinyó 30, Barri Gòtic* ☎ *93/320–3950* 🌐 *www.hotelarai.com* 🛏 *31 rooms* 🍴 *No meals* [M] *L3 Liceu.*

Catalunya Portal d'Angel

$$$ | **HOTEL** | Converted in 1998 from a historic stately home dating back to 1825, the Catalunya Portal d'Angel beckons with its neoclassic facade and original grand marble staircase. **Pros:** pet-friendly; includes walking tours of the Old City and the Eixample; pleasant breakfast pavilion in the garden. **Cons:** small rooms; faces busy pedestrian mall; lighting needs improvement. [$] *Rooms from: €200* ✉ *Av. Portal d'Angel 17, Barri Gòtic* ☎ *93/318–4141* 🌐 *www.hoteles-catalonia.com* 💳 *No credit cards* 🛏 *82 rooms, 1 suite* 🍴 *No meals* [M] *Pl. Catalunya.*

Colón

$$$$ | **HOTEL** | Around since 1951, the quiet and conservative Colón feels like it's been around forever, and is reasonably priced for the location: near the Catedral de la Seu, which is spectacular when illuminated at night. **Pros:** central location; some rooms have balconies overlooking square; rooftop terrace with heated Jacuzzi. **Cons:** can feel a bit stodgy; narrow bathrooms. [$] *Rooms from: €240* ✉ *Av. Catedral 7, Barri Gòtic* ☎ *93/301–1404* 🌐 *www.hotelcolon.es* 🛏 *141 rooms* 🍴 *No meals* [M] *L4 Jaume I.*

Barcelona's Sweet Tooth

For a long time, desserts were the Achilles heel of the Barcelona culinary scene. Diners groaning in anticipation after devouring their lovingly prepared starters and entrées often experienced disappointment when the final course arrived at the table—straight from the local supermarket's deep freeze. Occasionally, the waiter delivered a good, homemade *crema catalana* (crème brûlée), but the odds of a truly memorable ending to one's meal weren't favorable. To find Barcelona's sweet spot, you needed to skip the *postres* and head to the local *pastiseria*.

These neighborhood bakeries have always supplied Catalans with a cornucopia of seasonal treats. Some of the most beloved delectables include *xuixos* (pastries stuffed with, yes, crema catalana) and *pastissets de cabell d'àngel* (half-moon pastries). *Coques* are flatbreads, usually enjoyed around Easter, Christmas, or on saints' days. They're often topped with pine nuts and candied fruit, or even some delicious sweet-and-savory combinations, such as pork crackling and sugar. *Panellets* are another local favorite, worth seeking out in autumn: balls of baked marzipan and pine nuts served with a sweet wine.

More acclaimed establishments have raised the bar for Barcelona desserts, and local chefs are applying the lessons learned in prestigious local cooking schools. One of them, the dazzlingly innovative school-restaurant Espai Sucre (Sugar Space), specializes in all things sweet.

For the best treats in town, try the chocolate. Oriol Balaguer sells pure black gold at his two shops, which look more like exquisite jewelry stores than food retailers. Often rated among the world's top chocolatiers, he competes with Enric Rovira for the crown of Catalonia's best. Another contender for top haute confectioner is Cacao Sampaka, founded by Quim Capdevilla. Travelers with children should consider a trip to the Museu de la Xocolata (Chocolate Museum) in El Born, where they can enjoy some finger-licking fun in the workshops, and shop for delicious sweets in the museum shop.

4

The Barri Gòtic

★ Duquesa de Cardona

$$ | HOTEL | A refurbished 17th-century town house, built when the Passeig de Colom in front was lined with the summer homes of the nobility, this hotel on the waterfront is a five-minute walk from everything in the Barri Gòtic and Barceloneta, and no more than a 30-minute walk to the Eixample. **Pros:** 24-hour room service; menu of fragrances to order for your room; glass of cava on check-in. **Cons:** rooms on the small side; no spa; no parking. $ *Rooms from:* €147 ✉ *Passeig de Colom 12, Barri Gòtic*

☎ *93/268–9090* ⊕ *www.hduquesade-cardona.com* 🛏 *51 rooms* ⦿ *No meals* Ⓜ *L4 Barceloneta, L3 Drassanes.*

★ el Jardí

$ | HOTEL | FAMILY | Facing charming Plaça del Pi and Plaça Sant Josep Oriol, in a pair of conjoined buildings that date to 1860, this family-friendly little budget hotel couldn't be better situated for exploring La Rambla and the Barri Gòtic. **Pros:** central location; friendly English-speaking staff; some rooms have balconies overlooking the square. **Cons:** no room service; no pool, gym, or spa; no place for suitcases in small rooms. $ *Rooms from: €100* ✉ *Pl. Sant Josep Oriol 1, Barri Gòtic* ☎ *93/301–5900* ⊕ *www.eljardi-barcelona.com* ⤴ *40 rooms* ‖ *No meals* Ⓜ *L3 Liceu, L4 Jaume I, Catalunya.*

Grand Hotel Central

$$$$ | HOTEL | FAMILY | At the edge of the Gothic Quarter, very near the Barcelona cathedral, this fashionable midtown hotel is popular with business and pleasure travelers alike, with contemporary decor and upscale amenities. **Pros:** excellent location between the Gothic Quarter and the Born; infinity pool with city views; Mediterranean City Bar and Restaurant on-site. **Cons:** no pets; busy thoroughfare outside; pricey breakfast. $ *Rooms from: €300* ✉ *Via Laietana 30, Barri Gòtic* ☎ *93/295–7900* ⊕ *www.grandhotelcentral.com* ⤴ *147 rooms* ‖ *No meals* Ⓜ *L4 Jaume I.*

★ Hotel Neri

$$$$ | HOTEL | Just steps from the cathedral, in the heart of the city's old Jewish Quarter, this elegant, upscale, boutique hotel, part of the prestigious Relais & Chateaux hotel group, marries ancient and avant-garde designs. **Pros:** central location (close to Barri Gòtic); barbecue and occasional live music on the rooftop terrace; 24-hour room service. **Cons:** noisy on summer nights and school days; pets allowed only in deluxe rooms with terraces (pricey surcharge); lighting over beds could improve. $ *Rooms from: €350* ✉ *Carrer Sant Sever 5, Barri Gòtic* ☎ *93/304–0655* ⊕ *www.hotelneri.com/en* ⤴ *22 rooms* ‖ *No meals* Ⓜ *L3 Liceu, L4 Jaume I.*

Hotel Ohla

$$$$ | HOTEL | One of Barcelona's top design hotels (also with incredible food), the Ohla has a neoclassical exterior (not counting the playful eyeballs stuck to the facade) that belies its avant-garde interior, full of witty, design-conscious touches. **Pros:** rooftop terrace and pool; remarkable restaurant Caelis on-site; high-end

wines at Vistro 49. **Cons:** adjacent to noisy Via Laietana; uncomfortable furniture in lobby. $ *Rooms from: €280* ✉ *Via Laietana 49, Barri Gòtic* ☎ *93/341–5050* ⊕ *www.ohlabarcelona.com* ⤴ *74 rooms* ‖ *Free Breakfast* Ⓜ *L4 Urquinaona.*

Mercer Hotel Barcelona

$$$$ | HOTEL | On a narrow side street near Plaça Sant Jaume, this romantic boutique hotel, a medieval town house, is among the latest examples of Barcelona's signature genius for the redesign and rebirth of historical properties. **Pros:** minutes from the Old City; comfortable rooftop terrace with a plunge pool and (in season) a bar-café; breakfast in glassed-in patio. **Cons:** very pricey; no gym or spa; expensive breakfast. $ *Rooms from: €480* ✉ *Carrer dels Lledó 5, Barri Gòtic* ☎ *93/310–7480* ⊕ *www.mercerhoteles.com* ⤴ *28 rooms* ‖ *No meals* Ⓜ *L4 Jaume I.*

Mercer House Bòria Bcn

$$$ | HOTEL | FAMILY | Blink and you miss it: on a small side street between the Santa Caterina market and the Picasso Museum, this boutique hotel (just six rooms and five suites) announces itself with no more than a name etched in the glass on its discreet front door. **Pros:** walking distance to great attractions; pleasant rooftop terrace and solarium; en suite kitchens in suites and lofts. **Cons:** no restaurant or bar; no room service; no pool. $ *Rooms from: €179* ✉ *Carrer de la Bòria 24–26, Barri Gòtic* ☎ *93/295–5893* ⊕ *www.boriabcn.com* ⤴ *6 double rooms, 5 suites* ‖ *No meals* Ⓜ *L4 Jaume I.*

☉ Nightlife

Medieval Barri Gòtic is a wanderer's paradise filled with ancient winding streets, majestic squares, and myriad period-perfect wine bars and dimly lighted pubs found in the hidden corners of labyrinthine alleyways. The adjoining La Rambla, the liveliest pedestrian promenade in the city, bustles with a dizzying array of tourist-baiting shops, eateries, and arched paths to Plaça Reial's euphoric nightlife scene. Casual and unpretentious, the scene erupts nightly with a parade of rambunctious crowds of expats, curious interlopers, and assorted celebrations.

BARS

El Paraigua

BARS/PUBS | This eatery's stunning Moderniste facade—intricately carved wood, an exquisite vintage register, and other delicate reminders of its former incarnation as a turn-of-the-20th-century umbrella shop—is usually enough to lure newcomers inside for a closer look. But for fiesta-loving night owls, the real attraction is downstairs in the arched, exposed-brick cocktail club, a former convent basement offering first-rate cocktails and weekend jazz concerts in a note-perfect setting. ✉ *Carrer del Pas de l'Ensenyança 2, Barri Gòtic* ☎ *93/317–1479* ⊕ *www.elparaigua.com* Ⓜ *Jaume I.*

Harlem Jazz Club

MUSIC CLUBS | Located on a rare tree-lined street in the Barri Gòtic, this club attracts patrons of all ages and musical tastes. Listen to live Cuban salsa, swing, and reggae while enjoying killer cocktails in a relaxed and friendly atmosphere. Most concerts start at 10 pm and finish around 1 am, and many people linger until closing time. ✉ *Comtessa de Sobradiel 8, Barri Gòtic* ☎ *93/310–0755* ⊕ *www. harlemjazzclub.es* Ⓜ *Jaume I, Liceu.*

La Vinateria del Call

WINE BARS—NIGHTLIFE | Located in the heart of Barcelona's former Jewish Quarter, this rustic charmer serves a wide variety of hearty national wines paired with regional cheeses, meats, and tapas. Popular with wine-loving romantics for its antique carved-wood furnishings and candlelit setting, the venue also attracts visitors and regulars looking for a respite from the area's chaotic pace. ✉ *Sant Domènec del Call 9, Barri Gòtic* ☎ *93/302–6092* ⊕ *www.lavinateriadelcall. com* Ⓜ *Liceu, Jaume I.*

Marula Café

DANCE CLUBS | After a decade in the business, Marula Café has remained steadfast in its ambitious quest to keep Barcelona grooving with funk and all its sister sounds. No electronic music will enter this slick, red-curtained venue with back-lighted glass walls: once past the bouncer, it's just funk, disco, and Latin spiced up with Afro-funk licks. The crowd is a mix of funk-loving locals who come to dance and foreigners who've stumbled in from the tourist circuit off Plaça Reial. There is also a regular lineup of DJ sessions and concerts. Check out the regularly updated website. ✉ *Escudellers 49, Barri Gòtic* ☎ *93/318–7690* ⊕ *www. marulacafe.com/bcn* Ⓜ *Liceu, Drassanes.*

Milk

BARS/PUBS | Resembling a prim parlor lounge with touches of kitsch, this cozy bar bistro with plush sofas, gilded mirrors, handmade knickknacks, and tastefully worn tapestry wallpaper has been a favorite hangout for young expats for more than a decade. Offering a perfect setup for cocktails and conversation until 2 am, Milk serves the usual classics (as well as beer and wine) with a dab of personality—the Michelada, for one, is a dramatic alternative Bloody Mary reserved for the strongest constitutions: Corona beer mixed with hot sauce, Worcestershire, and tomato juice. ✉ *Gignas 21, Barri Gòtic* ☎ *93/268–0922* ⊕ *www.milkbarcelona.com* Ⓜ *Jaume I.*

★ Ocaña

BARS/PUBS | Located in a trio of ancient mansions on buzzy Plaça Reial's southern flank, this venue is dedicated to Jose Peréz Ocaña, a cross-dressing artist and proud bohemian, and a dominating figure of Barcelona's decadent post-Franco explosion of alternative culture. With an adjoining Mexican restaurant, as well as a sizable café bar, club, and cocktail lounge, Ocaña also has the fiercest drag queen hostesses on the square. The showstopping interior was conceived as an homage to the establishment's namesake, via a *mise en scene* of decaying period elegance scattered with head-turning pop art. It's a wonderful place for people-watching on the terrace, followed by dinner in one of two distinctive spaces and cocktails at the Moorish-chic Apotheke bar downstairs. ⊠ *Pl. Reial 13–15, Barri Gòtic* ☎ *93/676–4814* ⊕ *www.ocana.cat* Ⓜ *Drassanes.*

Sidecar Factory Club
BARS/PUBS | A mainstay of the decadent nightlife centered on Plaça Reial, this long-running music club has never fallen out of fashion—in fact, it attracts new fans just as the old ones bow out. With a firm focus showcasing up-and-coming indie talent, the venue offers à way to discover new favorites in moody neon red surroundings. ⊠ *Pl. Reial 7, Barri Gòtic* ☎ *93/317–7666* ⊕ *www.sidecarfactoryclub.com* Ⓜ *Drassanes.*

Sor Rita
BARS/PUBS | Beyond kitschy, this wacky joint is inspired by the "anything goes" antiestablishment spirit of director Pedro Almodóvar's most memorable characters. The decor is a mishmash of pop culture quirk: stilettos stuck on the ceiling, a wall of framed retro icons, a Barbie-head lamp, and other off-the-wall treasures. For the open-minded, several nights a week are dedicated to the pursuit of mindless mischief; Mondays are for spicy cocktails and tarot readings; Tuesdays mean all-you-can-eat salads and beer; Thursdays are host to karaoke stylings of iconic cheeseball (mostly Spanish) songs. Meanwhile, any night of the week, patrons—mostly locals—get in the mood by wearing one of several wigs available at the bar. Though anyone is welcome, it's recommended to leave the day's stress at the door. ⊠ *Mercé 27, Barri Gòtic* ☎ *93/176–6266* ⊕ *www.sorritabar.es* Ⓜ *Jaume I.*

🎭 Performing Arts

ART GALLERIES
Col·legi Oficial d'Arquitectes de Catalunya
ART GALLERIES—ARTS | The architectural temporary exhibitions (see the website for details of the program) on the ground floor of the School of Architecture focus on urbanism and notable architects. The design and architecture bookshop in the basement is reason alone to visit. The stick figure frieze on the exterior of the building was designed by Picasso during his exile, and executed by the Norwegian artist Carl Nesjar in 1955. ⊠ *Pl. Nova 5, Barri Gòtic* ☎ *93/301–5000* ⊕ *www.arquitectes.cat* Ⓜ *Liceu, Catalunya.*

FLAMENCO
Barcelona's flamenco scene is surprisingly vibrant for a culture so far removed from Andalusia. Los Tarantos, in Plaça Reial, is a must for its authentic flamenco performances.

Los Tarantos
DANCE | This small basement boîte spotlights some of Andalusia's best flamenco in 30-minute shows of dance, percussion, and song. These shows are a good intro to the art and feel much less touristy than most standard flamenco fare. Shows are daily at 7:30, 8:30, and 9:30 pm, with an additional 10:30 pm show June–September. ⊠ *Pl. Reial 17, Barri Gòtic* ☎ *93/304-1210* ⊕ *www.masimas.com/en/tarantos* Ⓜ *Liceu.*

🛍 Shopping

The Barri Gòtic was built on trade and cottage industries, and there are plenty of nimble fingers producing artisan goods in the old-world shops along its stone streets. Start at the cathedral and work your way outward.

ART GALLERIES
Base Elements Urban Art Gallery
ART GALLERIES | Robert Burt, a talented painter and restorer of found objects originally from California, founded this gallery

in 2003 to provide a space where young street artists and graffiti-meisters could display their talents without risking jail time. The gallery serves a workshop and hangout for young artists, and paintings can be shipped all over the world. ⊠ *Palau 6, Barri Gòtic* ☎ *93/268–8312* ⊕ *www. baseelements.net* Ⓜ *Jaume I.*

Sala Parès

ART GALLERIES | The dean of Barcelona's art galleries, this place is the oldest art gallery in Barcelona. It opened in 1840 as an art-supplies shop; as a gallery, it dates to 1877 and has shown every Barcelona artist of note since then. Picasso and Miró exhibited their work here, as did Casas and Rossinyol before them. Nowadays, Catalan artists like Perico Pastor and Carlos Morago get pride of place. ⊠ *Petritxol 5, Barri Gòtic* ☎ *93/318–7020* ⊕ *salapares.com* Ⓜ *Liceu, Catalunya.*

BOOKS AND STATIONERY

Llibreria Quera

BOOKS/STATIONERY | This is the bookstore to seek out if you're interested in the Pyrenees or in exploring any part of the Catalonian hinterlands. Maps, charts, and books detailing everything from Pyrenean ponds and lakes to Romanesque chapels are available in this diminutive giant of a resource. ⊠ *Petritxol 2, Barri Gòtic* ☎ *93/318–0743* Ⓜ *Liceu.*

Papirvm

BOOKS/STATIONERY | Exquisite hand-printed papers, marbleized blank books, and writing implements await you at this tiny, medieval-tone shop. ⊠ *Baixada de la Llibreteria 2, Barri Gòtic* ☎ *93/310–5242* ⊕ *papirumbcn.com* Ⓜ *Jaume I.*

CERAMICS AND GLASSWARE

★ Art Escudellers

CERAMICS/GLASSWARE | Ceramic pieces from all over Spain are on display at this large store across the street from the restaurant Los Caracoles; more than 140 different artisans are represented, with maps showing what part of Spain the work is from. Wine, cheese, and

Catalan Flamenco

Barcelona has a burgeoning and erudite flamenco scene, even if the dance is imported from Andalusia. For the best flamenco in Barcelona, consult listings and concierges and don't be put off if the venue seems touristy—these venues often book the best artists. Barcelona-born *cantaors* include Mayte Martín and Miguel Poveda. Keep an eye on the billboards for such names as Estrella Morente (daughter of the late, great Enrique Morente) and Chano Domínguez (who often appears at the Barcelona Jazz Festival).

ham tastings are held downstairs, and you can even throw a pot yourself in the workshop. There are four other branches of Art Escudellers in the old city, including one on the Carrer Avinyó. ⊠ *Escudellers 23–25, Barri Gòtic* ☎ *93/412–6801* ⊕ *www.artescudellers.com* Ⓜ *Liceu, Drassanes.*

Caixa de Fang

CERAMICS/GLASSWARE | Glazed tiles, glass objects, and colorful sets of cups and saucers are on sale at this little shop just off Plaça Sant Jaume. Translatable as "Box of Mud" in Catalan, Caixa de Fang shows handmade earthenware cooking vessels from all over Spain, as well as boxwood and olive-wood kitchen utensils. ⊠ *Freneria 1, Barri Gòtic* ☎ *93/315–1704* Ⓜ *Jaume I.*

CLOTHING

Decathlon

SPORTING GOODS | **FAMILY** | Whether you're planning a trek through the Pyrenees or a beach yoga session, this mega–sports emporium should be your first port of call. From waterproof clothing to footballs to bike repairs, it caters to every conceivable sport and active hobby. Affordable and always busy, Decathlon is the best place to pick up practical travel clothing, such as that forgotten fleece jacket for a sudden cold snap. ⊠ *Canuda 20, Barri Gòtic* ☎ *93/342–6161* ⊕ *www.decathlon. es* Ⓜ *Catalunya.*

L'Arca
ANTIQUES/COLLECTIBLES | This store sells vintage clothing, fabrics, and accessories, with a focus on wedding dresses, veils, and lace. Despite the found-object attitude and ambience of the place, they're not giving away these vintage baubles, so don't be surprised at the hefty price tags. You'll also find a collection of their own bridal gowns, newly made but in romantic, old-fashioned styles. ⊠ *Banys Nous 20, Barri Gòtic* ☎ *93/302–1598* ⊕ *www.larca.es* Ⓜ *Liceu.*

Sombrereria Obach
CLOTHING | This *sombrerería* (hat shop) is as much part of the Barri Gòtic's landscape as any of its medieval churches. Occupying a busy corner in El Call—the old Jewish district—curved glass windows display the sort of hats, caps, and berets that have been dressing heads in Barcelona since 1924. Styles are classic and timeless, from traditional Basque berets to Stetsons and panamas. ⊠ *Call 2, Barri Gòtic* ☎ *93/318–4094* ⊕ *www. sombrereriaobach.com* Ⓜ *Jaume I, Liceu.*

FOOD

Caelum
FOOD/CANDY | At the corner of Carrer de la Palla and Banys Nous, this café and shop sells wines and foodstuffs such as honey, biscuits, chocolates, and preserves made in convents and monasteries all over Spain. You can pop in to pick up an exquisitely packaged pot of jam, or linger longer in the tearoom, part of which is housed in an old medieval bathhouse in the candlelit basement. ⊠ *De la Palla 8, Barri Gòtic* ☎ *93/302–6993* ⊕ *www. caelumbarcelona.com* Ⓜ *Liceu, Jaume I.*

Formatgeria La Seu
FOOD/CANDY | Scotswoman Katherine McLaughlin has put together the Gothic Quarter's most delightful cheese-tasting sanctuary on the site of an ancient buttery. (A 19th-century butter churn is visible in the back room.) A dozen artisanal cow, goat, and sheep cheeses from all over Spain, and olive oils, can be tasted and taken home. La Seu is named for a combination of La Seu Cathedral, as the "seat" of cheeses, and for cheese-rich La Seu d'Urgell in the Pyrenees. Katherine's wrapping paper, imaginatively chosen sheets of newspaper, give a final flourish to purchases. ⊠ *Dagueria 16, Barri Gòtic* ☎ *93/412–6548* ⊕ *www. formatgerialaseu.com* Ⓜ *Jaume I.*

La Casa del Bacalao
FOOD/CANDY | This cult store decorated with cod-fishing memorabilia specializes in salt cod and books of codfish recipes. Slabs of salt and dried cod, used in a wide range of Catalan recipes (such as esqueixada, in which shredded strips of raw salt cod are served in a marinade of oil and vinegar) can be vacuum-packed for portability. ⊠ *Comtal 8 , just off Porta de l'Àngel, Barri Gòtic* ☎ *93/301–6539* Ⓜ *Catalunya.*

GIFTS AND SOUVENIRS

Artesania Catalunya – CCAM
GIFTS/SOUVENIRS | In 2010 the Catalan government created the registered trademark Empremtes de Catalunya to represent Catalan artisans and to make sure that visitors get the real deal when buying what they believe to be genuine products. The official shop now sells jewelry re-created from eras dating back to pre-Roman times, Gaudí-inspired sculptures, traditional Cava mugs, and some bravely avant-garde objects from young artisans—all officially sanctioned as fit to represent the city. ⊠ *Banys Nous 11, Barri Gòtic* ☎ *93/653–7214* ⊕ *www. bcncrafts.com/en/* Ⓜ *Jaume I, Liceu.*

Cereria Subirà

GIFTS/SOUVENIRS | Known as the city's oldest shop, having remained open since 1761 (though it was not always a candle store), this "waxery" (*cereria*) offers candles in all sizes and shapes, ranging from wild mushrooms to the Montserrat massif, home of the Benedictine abbey dear to the heart of every barcelonin. ✉ *Baixada Llibreteria 7, Barri Gòtic* ☎ *93/315–2606* ⊕ *www.cereriasubira.cat/en/* Ⓜ *Jaume I.*

Coses de Casa

GIFTS/SOUVENIRS | The 19th-century windows of this lovely corner shop overlooking Plaça del Pi burst with all sorts of home textiles—from humble, superb-quality tea towels to country-chic patchwork quilts. If they don't stock the cushion cover you're after, it probably doesn't exist, although the most unique take-home item is a gingham bread bag—a sausage-shaped carrier for your morning baguette. ✉ *Pl. Sant Josep Oriol 5, Barri Gòtic* ☎ *93/302–7328* ⊕ *www.cosesdecasa.com* Ⓜ *Liceu.*

★ Ganiveteria Roca

GIFTS/SOUVENIRS | Directly opposite the giant rose window of the Santa Maria del Pi church, the knife store (*ganivet* is Catalan for knife) beneath this lovely sgraffito-decorated facade takes cutlery culture to a new level. Knives, razors, scissors, hatchets, axes, swords, nail clippers, tweezers, and penknives are all displayed in this comprehensive, cutting-edge emporium. ✉ *Pl. del Pi 3, Barri Gòtic* ☎ *93/302–1241* ⊕ *www.ganiveteriaroca.cat* Ⓜ *Liceu.*

Guantería y Complementos Alonso

GIFTS/SOUVENIRS | The storefront and interiors of this ancient little glove and accessory shop is well worth the visit. Lovely antique cabinets painstakingly stripped of centuries of paint display gloves, fans, shawls, mantillas, and a miscellany of textile crafts and small gifts. ✉ *Calle Santa Ana 27, Barri Gòtic* ☎ *93/317–6085* ⊕ *www.tiendacenter.com* Ⓜ *Catalunya.*

MARKETS

Mercat Gòtic

OUTDOOR/FLEA/GREEN MARKETS | A browser's bonanza, this interesting if somewhat pricey Thursday market for antique clothing, jewelry, and art objects occupies the plaza in front of the cathedral. ✉ *Av. Plaça de la Catedral, Barri Gòtic* ⊕ *www.mercatgoticbcn.com* Ⓜ *Jaume I, Urquinaona.*

Plaça del Pi

OUTDOOR/FLEA/GREEN MARKETS | This little square fills with the interesting tastes and aromas of a natural-produce market (honeys, cheeses) throughout the month, while neighboring Plaça Sant Josep Oriol holds a painter's market every Sunday. ✉ *Pl. del Pi, Barri Gòtic* Ⓜ *Catalunya, Liceu.*

SHOES, LUGGAGE, LEATHER GOODS, AND ACCESSORIES

★ La Manual Alpargatera

SHOES/LUGGAGE/LEATHER GOODS | If you appreciate old-school craftsmanship in footwear and reasonable prices, visit this boutique just off Carrer Ferran. Handmade rope-sole sandals and espadrilles are the specialty, and this shop has sold them to everyone—including the pope. The flat, beribboned espadrilles model used for dancing the sardana is available, as are fashionable wedge heels with peep toes and comfy slippers. The cost of a pair of espadrilles here might put you back about $50, which is far less than the same quality shoes in the United States. ✉ *Avinyó 7, Barri Gòtic* ☎ *93/301–0172* ⊕ *www.lamanualalpargatera.es* Ⓜ *Liceu, Jaume I.*

TOBACCO

Estanc Gimeno

TOBACCO | Smoking items of every kind along with pipes and cigarettes of all sorts are sold in this tobacco sanctuary, but cigars from Havana are the top draw. ✉ *Rambla 100, Barri Gòtic* ☎ *93/302–0983* ⊕ *www.gimenocigars.com* Ⓜ *Catalunya, Liceu.*

Activities

BICYCLES

Bike Tours Barcelona

BICYCLING | This company offers a three-hour bike tour (in English) for €25, with a drink included. Just look for the guide with a bike and a blue flag at the northeast corner of the Casa de la Ciutat in Plaça Sant Jaume, outside the Tourist Information Office. Tours depart at 11 am daily; there is an additional tour at 4:30 pm Friday–Monday, April 1–September 15. The company will also organize private guided tours through the Barri Gòtic, parks, the Port Olímpic and Barceloneta, the Ruta Moderniste, and other itineraries on request. Touring on your own? The company also rents bikes by the hour or the day, at its shop in Carrer Esparteria. ⊠ *Carrer Esparteria 3, Barri Gòtic* ☎ *932/682105* ⊕ *biketoursbarcelona.com* Ⓜ *Jaume I.*

Fat Tire Bike Tours

BICYCLING | Four-hour guided city tours with this company start in Plaça Sant Jaume daily at 11 am and 4 pm (from mid-October to mid-April, morning tours only), covering—with a lunch break—the usual suspects: the Barri Gòtic, Sagrada Família, Ciutadella Park, the port, and Barceloneta. Reservations can be made on the website. ⊠ *Calle Marlet 4, Barri Gòtic* ☎ *933/429275* ⊕ *www.fattirebike-tours.com* 🎫 *€28* Ⓜ *Jaume I.*

Steel Donkey Bike Tours

BICYCLING | Groups up to eight people can take four-hour "alternative" bike tours with this outfit on Tuesday, Friday, and Saturday mornings, meeting at the shop on Calle Ample at 10 am. The tours (€35 per person, including bike and helmet rentals) are quirky, offering sights and experiences a bit off the beaten path from the standard itineraries. Call for reservations. ⊠ *Carrer de Cervantes 5, Barri Gòtic* ☎ *657/286854* ⊕ *www.steeldonkeybiketours.com* Ⓜ *Jaume I.*

HIKING

The Collserola hills behind the city offer well-marked trails, fresh air, and lovely views. Take the San Cugat, Sabadell, or Terrassa FGC train from Plaça de Catalunya and get off at Baixador de Vallvidrera; the information center, 10 minutes uphill next to Vil·la Joana (now the Jacint Verdaguer Museum), has maps of this mountain woodland just 20 minutes from downtown. The walk back into town can take two to five hours depending on your speed and the trails you choose. For longer treks, try the 15-km (9-mile) Sant Cugat–to–Barcelona hike, or take the train south to Sitges and make the three-day pilgrimage walk to the Monastery of Montserrat.

Centre Excursionista de Catalunya

HIKING/WALKING | The center has information on hiking throughout Catalunya and the Pyrenees, gives mountaineering and technical climbing courses, organizes excursions, and provides guides for groups. ⊠ *Carrer del Paradis 10, Barri Gòtic* ☎ *933/152311* ⊕ *www.cec.cat* Ⓜ *Jaume I.*

EL RAVAL

Updated by
Elizabeth Prosser and
Steve Tallantyre

● Sights	🍴 Restaurants	🛏 Hotels	🛍 Shopping	🍸 Nightlife
★★★★☆	★★★☆☆	★★☆☆☆	★★★☆☆	★★★☆☆

NEIGHBORHOOD SNAPSHOT

TOP EXPERIENCES

■ **Antic Hospital de la Santa Creu:** The 15th-century chapel of the hospital showcases the works of up-and-coming artists.

■ **Sant Pau del Camp:** Catch a musical performance in Barcelona's oldest church and linger by the fountain at the tiny cloister.

■ **Botero's bronze cat:** Stroke the famous bearlike and bronze El Gato del Raval, a favorite meeting spot on the Rambla del Raval.

■ **Museo d'Art Contemporani de Barcelona:** Take a guided tour of MACBA's incredible collection of contemporary art and then take in the skateboarders performing outside on the plaza.

■ **Bar crawl:** From Casa Almirall on lively Joaquin Costa to La Confitería's vintage bar in a former pastry shop to little-changed Marsella, a onetime haunt for artistic notables such as Gaudí, Picasso, and Hemingway, you'll want to pace yourself for a leisurely crawl of El Raval's bars.

GETTING HERE

Begin at Plaça de Catalunya, with its convenient metro stop. Walk down La Rambla and take your first right into Carrer Tallers, working your way through to the MACBA.

PLANNING YOUR TIME

The Raval covers a lot of ground. Plan on a four-hour walk or break your exploration into multiple two-hour hikes. The cloister of Sant Pau del Camp, not to be missed, is closed Monday morning, Saturday afternoon, and all day Sunday, except for during Mass.

QUICK BITES

■ **Bar Castells.** Enjoy tapas, coffee, and other light items at Bar Castells, which has a lovely marble counter and a gorgeous wood-framed mirror behind the bar. ✉ *Pl. Bonsuccés 1, El Raval* ⊕ *www. barcastells.com* Ⓜ *Catalunya, Liceu*

■ **Nomad Coffee Every Day.** A tiny spot good with only a few seats but perfect for a quality takeaway flat white coffee and pastry. ✉ *Carrer de Joaquim Costa 26, El Raval* ⊕ *nomadcoffee. es* Ⓜ *Catalunya, Liceu*

El Raval (from arrabal, meaning "suburb" or "slum") is the area to the west of La Rambla, on the right as you walk toward the port. Originally a rough quarter outside the second set of city walls that ran down the left side of La Rambla, El Raval was once notorious for its Barri Xinès (or Barrio Chino) red-light district, the lurid attractions of which are known to have fascinated a young Pablo Picasso.

Gypsies, acrobats, prostitutes, and *saltimbanques* (clowns and circus performers) who made this area their home soon found immortality in the many canvases Picasso painted of them during his Blue Period. It was the ladies of the night on Carrer Avinyó, not far from the Barri Xinès, who may have inspired one of the 20th-century's most famous paintings, Picasso's *Les Demoiselles d'Avignon,* an important milestone on the road to Cubism. Not bad for a city slum.

El Raval, though still rough-and-tumble, has been gentrified and much improved since 1980, largely as a result of the construction of the Museu d'Art Contemporani de Barcelona (MACBA) and other cultural institutions nearby, such as the Centre de Cultura Contemporània (CCCB), Filmoteca, and the Convent dels Àngels. La Rambla del Raval has been opened up between Carrer de l'Hospital and Drassanes, bringing light and air into the streets of the Raval for the first time in a thousand years. The medieval Hospital de la Santa Creu, Plaça del Pedró, the Mercat de Sant Antoni, and Sant Pau del Camp are highlights of this funky,

rough-edged part of Barcelona. The only area to consider avoiding is the lower part between Carrer de Sant Pau and the back of the Drassanes Reials shipyards on Carrer del Portal Santa Madrona.

◉ Sights

★ **Antic Hospital de la Santa Creu i Sant Pau**
BUILDING | Founded in the 10th century, this is one of Europe's earliest medical complexes, and contains some of Barcelona's most impressive Gothic architecture. The buildings that survive today date back mainly to the 15th and 16th centuries; the first stone for the hospital was laid by King Martí el Humà (Martin the Humane) in 1401. From the entrance on Carrer del Carme, the first building on the left is the 18th-century **Reial Acadèmia de Medicina** de Catalunya (Royal Academy of Medicine); the surgical amphitheater is kept just as it was in the days when students learned by observing dissections. (One assumes that the paupers' hospital next door was always ready to oblige with cadavers.) The Academy is open to the public for guided tours on Wednesday

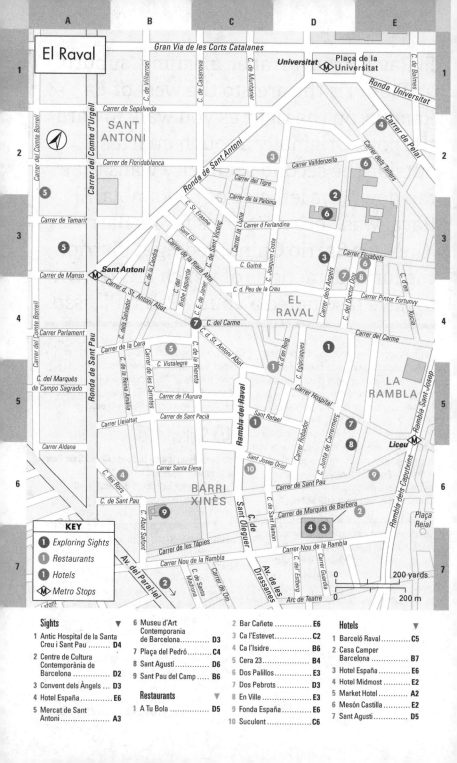

El Raval

KEY
- ① Exploring Sights
- ① Restaurants
- ① Hotels
- Ⓜ Metro Stops

Sights ▼

1 Antic Hospital de la Santa Creu i Sant Pau **D4**
2 Centre de Cultura Contemporània de Barcelona **D2**
3 Convent dels Àngels ... **D3**
4 Hotel España **E6**
5 Mercat de Sant Antoni **A3**
6 Museu d'Art Contemporania de Barcelona............ **D3**
7 Plaça del Pedró **C4**
8 Sant Agustí **D6**
9 Sant Pau del Camp **B6**

Restaurants ▼

1 A Tu Bola **D5**
2 Bar Cañete **E6**
3 Ca l'Estevet............. **C2**
4 Ca l'Isidre.............. **B6**
5 Cera 23................. **B4**
6 Dos Palillos **E3**
7 Dos Pebrots **D3**
8 En Ville **E3**
9 Fonda España............ **E6**
10 Suculent **C6**

Hotels ▼

1 Barceló Raval **C5**
2 Casa Camper Barcelona **B7**
3 Hotel España **E6**
4 Hotel Midmost **E2**
5 Market Hotel **A2**
6 Mesón Castilla **E2**
7 Sant Agustí **D5**

One of the earliest medical complexes in Europe is the Antic Hospital de la Santa Creu i Sant Pau.

and Saturday. Across the way on the right is the gateway into the patio of the **Casa de la Convalescència,** where patients who survived their treatment in the hospital were moved for recuperation; it now houses the Institute for Catalan Studies. The walls of the forecourt are covered with brightly decorated scenes of the life of St. Paul in blue and yellow ceramic tiles; the story begins with the image to the left of the door to the inner courtyard, recounting the moment of the saint's conversion: *Savle, Savle, quid me persegueris?* ("Saul, Saul, why do you persecute me?"). The ceramicist, Llorenç Passolas, also designed the late-17th-century tiles around the inner patio. The image of St. Paul in the center of the pillared courtyard, over what was once a well, pays homage to the building's first benefactor, Pau Ferran. Look for the horseshoes, two of them around the keyholes, on the double wooden doors in the entryway: tokens of good luck for the afflicted who came here to recover—again, in reference to benefactor Ferran, from *ferro* (iron), as in *ferradura* (horseshoe).

Through a gate to the left of the Casa de Convalescència is the garden-courtyard of the hospital complex, the **Jardins de Rubió i Lluc,** centered on a baroque cross and lined with orange trees. On the right is the **Biblioteca de Catalunya** (✉ *Carrer de l'Hospital 56* ☎ *93/2702300* ⊕ *www. bnc.cat* ⊙ *Weekdays 9–8, Sat. 9–2*), Catalonia's national library and—with some 2 million volumes in its collection—second only to Madrid's Biblioteca Nacional. The stairway under the arch, leading up to the library, was built in the 16th century; the Gothic well to the left of the arch is from the 15th century, as is the little Romeo-and-Juliet balcony in the corner to the left of the doors to the Escola Massana academy of design. The library itself is spectacular: two parallel halls—once the core of the hospital—230 feet long, with towering Gothic arches and vaulted ceilings, designed in the 15th century by the architect of the church of Santa Maria del Pi, Guillem Abiell. This was the hospital where Antoni Gaudí was taken, unrecognized and assumed to be a pauper, after he was struck by a trolley on June 7, 1926. Among the library's collections are archives recording Gaudí's admittance and photographs of the infirmary and the private room where he died. The staggering antiquarian resources here go back to the earliest history of printing, and range from silver medieval book covers to illuminated manuscripts from the *Llibre Vermell* (*Red Book*) of medieval Catalonian liturgical music, to rare editions of Cervantes. (Reserve guided group tours by appointment on the Biblioteca website.)

Leave the complex through the heavy wooden doors to Carrer Hospital, and turn left toward La Rambla. The next set of doors leads to the **Capella** (Chapel) of the Hospital, an interesting art space well worth a visit. Built in the early 15th century, on the site of what had been the old Hospital de Colom (founded in 1219), it is now a showcase for promising young artists, chosen by a jury of prominent museum directors and given this impressive space, with its Romanesque tunnel vault and medieval arches, to exhibit their work.

✉ *Carrer Hospital 56 (or Carrer del Carme 45), El Raval* ☎ *93/317–1686 Reial Acadèmia de Medecina, 93/270–2300 Biblioteca de Catalunya* ⊕ *www.bnc. cat* ✉ *From €8* ☉ *Royal Academy of Medicine: closed Sun.–Tues., Thurs., and Fri; Biblioteca de Catalunya and Capella: closed Sun.* Ⓜ *L3 Liceu.*

Centre de Cultura Contemporània de Barcelona (*CCCB*)

ARTS VENUE | Just next door to the MACBA, this multidisciplinary gallery, lecture hall, and concert and exhibition space offers a year-round program of cultural events and projects. The center also has a remarkable film archive of historic shorts and documentaries, free to the public. Housed in the restored and renovated Casa de la Caritat, a former medieval convent and hospital, the CCCB, like the Palau de la Música Catalana, is one of the city's shining

examples of contemporary flare added to traditional architecture and design. A smoked-glass wall on the right side of the patio, designed by architects Albert Villaplana and Helio Piñon, reflects out over the rooftops of El Raval to Montjuïc and the Mediterranean beyond. ✉ *Carrer Montalegre 5, El Raval* ☎ *93/306–4100* ⊕ *www.cccb.org* ✉ *Exhibitions €6; Sun. 3–8, free. Admission to the CCCB Film Archive is free* ☉ *Closed Mon.* Ⓜ *L1/L2 Universitat, Catalunya.*

Convent dels Àngels (*La Capella*)

ARTS VENUE | This former Augustinian convent directly across from the main entrance to the MACBA, built by Bartolomeu Roig in the middle of the 16th century, has been converted into additional exhibition space for the MACBA, with a performing arts venue and an exhibition hall (El Fòrum dels Àngels) rented out on occasion for special events. The Fòrum dels Àngels is an impressive space, with magnificent Gothic arches and vaulted ceilings. ✉ *Pl. dels Àngels 5, El Raval* ☎ *93/412–0810, 93/481–7922* ⊕ *www. macba.cat* Ⓜ *Pl. Catalunya, L3 Liceu.*

Hotel España

BUILDING | Just off La Rambla behind the Liceu opera house on Carrer Sant Pau is the Hotel España, remodeled in 1904 by Lluís Domènech i Montaner, architect of the Moderniste flagship Palau de la Música Catalana. Completely refurbished in 2010, the interior is notable for its Art Nouveau decor. The sculpted marble Eusebi Arnau fireplace in the bar, the Ramon Casas undersea murals in the salon (mermaids singing each to each), and the lushly ornate dining room are the hotel's best artistic features. The España is so proud of its place in the cultural history of the city—and justly so—it opens to the public for 40-minute guided tours, usually twice a week. Check their website for times. (Note that tours are usually in Spanish or Catalan, but English can be requested.) ✉ *Carrer Sant Pau 9–11, El Raval* ☎ *93/550–0000* ⊕ *www. hotelespanya.com* ☕ *Tour €5* Ⓜ *L3 Liceu.*

Mercat de Sant Antoni

MARKET | A mammoth hangar at the junction of Ronda de Sant Antoni and Comte d'Urgell, designed in 1882 by Antoni Rovira i Trias, the Mercat de Sant Antoni is considered the city's finest example of wrought-iron architecture. The Greek-cross-shaped market covers an entire block on the edge of the Eixample, and some of the best Moderniste stall facades in Barcelona distinguish this exceptional space. Fully functioning as of 2017 after years of painstaking restoration to incorporate medieval archaeological remains underneath, the market is a foodie paradise of fruit, vegetables, fish, cheeses, and more. On Sunday morning, visit Sant Antoni, and wander the outdoor stalls of the weekly flea market full of stamps and coins, comic books and trading cards, VHS, CDs, vinyl, and vintage clothing. ✉ *Carrer Comte d'Urgell s/n, El Raval* ☎ *93/426–3521* ⊕ *www. mercatdesantantoni.com* ⊙ *Closed Sun.* Ⓜ *L2 Sant Antoni.*

★ Museu d'Art Contemporani de Barcelona

(*Barcelona Museum of Contemporary Art, MACBA*)

MUSEUM | FAMILY | Designed by American architect Richard Meier in 1992, this gleaming explosion of light and geometry in El Raval houses a permanent collection of contemporary art, and regularly mounts special thematic exhibitions of works on loan. Meier gives a nod to Gaudí (with the Pedrera-like wave on one end of the main facade), but his minimalist building otherwise looks unfinished. That said, the MACBA is unarguably an important addition to the cultural capital of this once-shabby neighborhood. Skateboarders weave in and out around Basque sculptor Jorge Oteiza's massive sculpture, *La Ola* (*The Wave*), in the courtyard; the late Eduardo Chillida's *Barcelona* (donated by the Sara Lee Corporation) covers half the wall in the little square off Calle Ferlandina, on the left of the museum, in the sculptor's signature primitive black geometrical patterns. The MACBA's 20th-century art collection (Calder, Rauschenberg, Oteiza, Chillida, Tàpies) is excellent, as is the guided tour in English (at 4 pm on Mondays): a useful introduction to the philosophical foundations of contemporary art as well as the pieces themselves. The museum also offers wonderful workshops and activities for kids. ✉ *Pl. dels Àngels 1, El Raval* ☎ *93/412–0810* ⊕ *www.macba.cat* ☕ *€10 (valid for 1 month)* ⊙ *Closed Tues.* Ⓜ *L1/L2 Universitat, L1/L3 Catalunya.*

Plaça del Pedró

PLAZA | This landmark in medieval Barcelona was the dividing point where ecclesiastical and secular paths parted. The high road, Carrer del Carme, leads to the cathedral and the seat of the bishopric; the low road, Carrer de l'Hospital, heads down to the medieval hospital and the Boqueria market, a clear choice between body and soul. Named for a stone pillar, or *pedró* (large stone), marking the fork in the road, the square became a cherished landmark for Barcelona Christians after

Santa Eulàlia, co-patron of Barcelona, was crucified there in the 4th century after suffering the legendary 13 ordeals designed to persuade her to renounce her faith—which, of course, she heroically refused to do. As the story goes, an overnight snowfall chastely covered her nakedness with virgin snow. The present version of Eulàlia and her cross was sculpted by Barcelona artist Frederic Marès and erected in 1951. The bell tower and vacant alcove at the base of the triangular square belong to the **Capella de Sant Llàtzer** church, originally built in the open fields in the mid-12th century and used as a leper hospital and place of worship after the 15th century when Sant Llàtzer (St. Lazarus) was officially named patron saint of lepers. Flanked by two ordinary apartment buildings, the Sant Llàtzer chapel has a tiny antique patio and apse visible from the short Carrer de Sant Llàtzer, which cuts behind the church between Carrer del Carme and Carrer Hospital. ⊠ *Pl. del Pedró, El Raval* Ⓜ *L2 Sant Antoni.*

Sant Agustí

RELIGIOUS SITE | This unfinished church is one of Barcelona's most unusual structures, with jagged stone sections projecting down the left side, and the upper part of the front entrance on Plaça Sant Agustí waiting to be covered with a facade. The church has had an unhappy history: originally part of an Augustinian monastery, it was first built between 1349 and 1700. It was later abandoned and rebuilt only to be destroyed in 1714 during the War of the Spanish Succession, rebuilt again, then burned in the antireligious riots of 1825 when the cloisters were demolished. The church was looted and torched once more in the closing days of the Civil War. Sant Agustí comes alive on May 22, feast day of Santa Rita, patron saint of *"los imposibles,"* meaning lost causes. Unhappily married women, unrequited lovers, and all-but-hopeless sufferers of every sort form long lines through the square and down Carrer Hospital. Each carries a rose that will be blessed at the chapel of Santa Rita on the right side of the altar. ⊠ *Pl. Sant Agustí s/n, El Raval* ☎ *93/318–3863* Ⓜ *L3 Liceu.*

★ **Sant Pau del Camp**

BUILDING | Barcelona's oldest monastic church was originally outside the city walls (*del camp* means "in the fields") and was a Roman cemetery as far back as the 2nd century, according to archaeological evidence. A Visigothic belt buckle found in the 20th century confirmed that Visigoths used the site as a cemetery between the 2nd and 7th centuries. What you see now was built in 1127 and is the earliest Romanesque structure in Barcelona. Elements of the church—the classical marble capitals atop the columns in the main entry—are thought to be from the 6th and 7th centuries. Sant Pau is bulky and solid, featureless (except for what may be the smallest stained-glass window in Europe, high on the facade facing Carrer Sant Pau), with stone walls 3 feet thick or more; medieval Catalan churches and monasteries were built to be refuges for the body as well as the soul, bulwarks of last resort against Moorish invasions—or marauders of any persuasion. Check local events listings for musical performances here; the church is an acoustical gem. The tiny cloister is Sant Pau del Camp's best feature, and one of Barcelona's hidden treasures. Look carefully at the capitals that support the Moorish-influenced Mudejar arches, carved with biblical scenes and exhortations to prayer. This penumbral sanctuary, barely a block from the heavily trafficked Avinguda del Paral·lel, is a gift from time. ⊠ *Carrer de Sant Pau 101, El Raval* ☎ *93/441–0001* 🎟 *Free when Masses are celebrated; guided tour Sun. at 12:45, €3* ⊙ *Cloister closed Sun. during Mass; no tours Sun. in mid-Aug.* Ⓜ *L3 Paral.lel.*

🍴 Restaurants

A Tu Bola

$ | ISRAELI | Fresh, falafel-like balls of meat, fish, and vegetables in unique, mouthwatering combinations are prepared with laser-sharp focus by Israeli

Skateboarders enjoy practicing in front of the Museu d'Art Contemporani de Barcelona.

chef Shira. Everything from the *harissa* (spicy chili paste) to the hummus is made by hand, elevating the standard far beyond that of typical street food in the surrounding Raval. **Known for:** quality street food; quick snacks; amazing chocolate ball dessert. [$] *Average main: €12* ✉ *Hospital 78, El Raval* ☎ *93/315–3244* 🌐 *www.atubolarest.com* 🕓 *Closed Tues.* [M] *Liceu.*

Bar Cañete

$$$ | **TAPAS** | A superb tapas and *platillos* (small plates) emporium, this spot is just around the corner from the Liceu opera house. The long bar overlooking the burners and part of the kitchen leads down to the 20-seat communal tasting table at the end of the room. **Known for:** Spanish ham specialists; superb tapas; secreto ibérico. [$] *Average main: €24* ✉ *Unió 17, El Raval* ☎ *93/270–3458* 🌐 *www.barcanete.com/en* 🕓 *Closed Sun.* [M] *Liceu.*

Ca l'Estevet

$$ | **CATALAN** | This restaurant has been serving up old-school Catalan cuisine to local and loyal customers since 1940 (and under a different name for 50 years before that), and the practice has been made perfect. Tuck into the likes of grilled botifarra sausages or roasted kid. **Known for:** Catalan specialties; large portions of escudella i carn d'olla (meat stew); historic location. [$] *Average main: €16* ✉ *Valldonzella 46, El Raval* ☎ *93/301–2939* 🌐 *www.restaurantestevet.com* 🕓 *No dinner Sun.* [M] *Universitat.*

★ **Ca l'Isidre**

$$$$ | **CATALAN** | A throwback to an age before foams and food science took over the gastronomic world, this restaurant has elevated simplicity to the level of the spectacular since the early 1970s. Isidre and Montserrat share their encyclopedic knowledge of local cuisine with guests, while their daughter Núria cooks traditional Catalan dishes. **Known for:** once frequented by Miró and Dalí; locally sourced produce; art collection. [$] *Average main: €36* ✉ *Flors 12, El Raval* ☎ *93/441–1139* 🌐 *www.calisidre.com* 🕓 *Closed Sun., and 1st 2 wks of Aug.* [M] *Paral.lel.*

Cera 23

$$ | **SPANISH** | Top pick among a crop of modern restaurants putting the razzle back into the run-down Raval, Cera 23 offers a winning combination of great service and robust cooking in a fun, friendly setting; stand at the bar and enjoy a blackberry mojito while you wait for your table. The open kitchen is in the dining area, so guests can watch the cooks create contemporary presentations of traditional Spanish dishes. **Known for:** volcano black rice; open kitchen viewable to diners; exceptional service. [$] *Average main: €16* ✉ *Cera 23, El Raval* ☎ *93/442–0808* 🌐 *www.cera23.com* 🕒 *No lunch weekdays* [M] *Sant Antoni.*

Dos Palillos

$$$$ | **ECLECTIC** | After 10 years as the chief cook and favored disciple of pioneering chef Ferran Adrià, Albert Raurich opened this outstanding Asian-fusion restaurant with an eclectic assortment of tastes and textures. Past the typical Spanish bar in the front room, the Japanese dining room inside is a canvas of rich black surfaces bordered with red chairs. **Known for:** creative pan-Asian cooking with interesting wine pairings; gin- and chocolate-filled doughnuts; Michelin star. [$] *Average main: €30* ✉ *Elisabets 9, El Raval* ☎ *93/304–0513* 🌐 *www.dospalillos.com* 🕒 *Closed Sun. and Mon., 3 wks Aug., and 2 wks at Christmas. No lunch Tues. and Wed.* [M] *Catalunya, Universitat.*

★ **Dos Pebrots**

$$ | **MEDITERRANEAN** | Albert Raurich of Dos Palillos has transformed his favorite neighborhood haunt into a retro cutting-edge tapas bar that explores the history of Mediterranean cuisine. Everything from the Roman condiment *garum* to 10th-century Xarab fruit salad gets reinvented in a contemporary context. **Known for:** historical-themed tapas; unique dishes like pigs' nipples; restored original exterior. [$] *Average main: €20* ✉ *Doctor Dou 19, El Raval* ☎ *93/853–9598* 🌐 *www.dospebrots.com* 🕒 *Closed Mon. and Tues. No lunch Wed. and Thurs. Closed 2 wks at Christmas.* [M] *Catalunya.*

En Ville

$$ | **BISTRO** | With pan-Mediterranean cuisine and reasonable prices, this attractive bistro 100 yards west of the Rambla in the MACBA section of El Raval is a keeper. The inexpensive lunch menu attracts in-the-know locals, and à la carte choices like scallops with pea foam are tempting and economical. **Known for:** value lunch menu; romantic setting; gluten-free cuisine. [$] *Average main: €17* ✉ *Doctor Dou 14, El Raval* ☎ *93/302–8467* 🌐 *www.envillebarcelona.es/en* 🕒 *Closed Sun., and 1 wk in Jan.* [M] *Catalunya, Liceu, Universitat.*

Fonda España

$$ | **CATALAN** | The sumptuous glory of this restored late-19th-century Art Nouveau dining room now has food to match, courtesy of superstar chef Martín Berasategui. Go for broke with the "gastronomic voyage" tasting menu or feast à la carte on updated period dishes such as "the mermaids"—a smooth cod pil pil (a Basque sauce)—and pigeon with a liver paté heart. **Known for:** Art Nouveau decor; satisfying traditional dishes; excellent set lunches. [$] *Average main: €22* ✉ *Sant Pau 9, El Raval* ☎ *93/550–0000* 🌐 *www.hotelespanya.com* 🕒 *No dinner Sun. No lunch in Aug.* [M] *Liceu.*

★ **Suculent**

$$ | **CATALAN** | This is a strong contender for the crown of Barcelona's best bistro, as chef Antonio Romero continues to turn out Catalan tapas and dishes that have roots in rustic classics but reach high modern standards of execution. The name is a twist on the Catalan *sucar lent* (to dip slowly), and excellent bread is duly provided to soak up the sauces. **Known for:** obligatory set menus, except at the bar; must-try steak tartare on marrow bone; big, bold flavors. [$] *Average main: €18* ✉ *Rambla del Raval 45, El Raval* ☎ *93/443–6579* 🌐 *www.suculent.com* 🕒 *Closed Mon. and Tues.* [M] *Liceu.*

Hotels

Barceló Raval

$$$ | **HOTEL** | With an edgy contemporary design, reasonable rates, and location in one of Barcelona's most colorful neighborhoods, Barceló Raval is a welcome addition to the city's hotel scene. **Pros:** 10 minutes from La Rambla; 360-degree vistas from rooftop terrace; DJ during Sunday brunch. **Cons:** Rambla del Raval a bit dicey at night; mood lighting not to everyone's taste; pool on terrace is very small. [$] *Rooms from: €200* ✉ *Rambla del Raval 17–21, El Raval* ☎ *93/320–1490* 🌐 *www.barcelo.com/en-us/hotels/spain/barcelona/barcelo-raval* 🛏 *186 rooms* 🍴 *No meals* [M] *L3 Liceu.*

★ **Casa Camper Barcelona**

$$$ | **HOTEL** | **FAMILY** | A marriage between the Camper footwear empire and the (now defunct) Vinçon design store produced this 21st-century hotel halfway between La Rambla and the MACBA (Museum of Contemporary Art), with a focus on sustainability (think solar panels and water recycling) and a unique "one big family" feel. **Pros:** great buffet breakfast with dishes cooked to order; just steps from MACBA and the Boqueria; complimentary 24-hour snack bar. **Cons:** expensive for what you get; extra per person charge for children over three years old; no in-room minibar. [$] *Rooms from: €220* ✉ *Carrer Elisabets 11, El Raval* ☎ *93/342–6280* 🌐 *www.casacamper.com* 🛏 *40 rooms* 🍴 *Free Breakfast* [M] *Catalunya, L3 Liceu.*

★ **Hotel España**

$$$$ | **HOTEL** | This beautifully renovated Art Nouveau gem is the second oldest (after the nearby Sant Agustí) and among the best of Barcelona's smaller hotels. **Pros:** near Liceu opera house and La Rambla; alabaster fireplace in the bar lounge; lavish breakfast buffet. **Cons:** lower rooms facing Carrer Sant Pau get some street noise; bed lighting could be improved; no views. [$] *Rooms from: €250* ✉ *Carrer Sant Pau 9–11, El Raval* ☎ *93/550–0000* 🌐 *www.hotelespanya.com* 🛏 *83 rooms* 🍴 *No meals* [M] *L4 Liceu.*

Hotel Midmost

$$ | **HOTEL** | New management took over this handsome Moderniste property (formerly the Inglaterra) in 2016 and gave it an extensive makeover; rooms feature parquet floors, white walls, and touches of Mediterranean blue; amenities include robes and slippers. **Pros:** near El Raval, the Rambla, and the MACBA; superior doubles have private terrace; small "Wellness" room for massages and treatments. **Cons:** noisy avenue in front of hotel; tiny lobby; small rooms, but good value for price. [$] *Rooms from: €139* ✉ *Carrer Pelai 14, El Raval* ☎ *93/505–1100* 🌐 *www.hotelmidmost.com* 🛏 *56 rooms* 🍴 *No meals* [M] *L1/L3 Catalunya, L1/L2 Universitat, FGC Catalunya.*

Market Hotel

$ | **HOTEL** | Wallet-friendly and design conscious, this boutique hotel named for the Mercat de Sant Antoni (a block away) is one of Barcelona's best bargains and walking distance from all of El Raval and the Gothic Quarter sites and attractions. **Pros:** excellent-value Catalan cuisine at on-site restaurant; friendly staff; great showers. **Cons:** standard rooms on lower floors are a little cramped; soundproofing needs upgrade; some rooms have no views. [$] *Rooms from: €100* ✉ *Carrer del Comte Borrell 68, El Raval* ☎ *93/325–1205* 🌐 *www.hotelmarketbarcelona.com* 🛏 *68 rooms* 🍴 *No meals* [M] *L2 Sant Antoni, L1 Urgell.*

★ **Mesón Castilla**

$$ | **HOTEL** | **FAMILY** | A few steps down Carrer Tallers from the top of La Rambla, on a short side street, there's almost nothing Barcelona about the Mesón Castilla, which feels like a well-appointed country hotel or a parador in Castile or La Mancha: classically Spanish, with mosaic tile floors and sconces, painted coffered ceilings and coats of arms, rooms with antique carved headboards and painted wooden armoires. **Pros:** close to medieval

Barcelona and the Eixample; spotlessly kept; lush patio for dining in warm weather. **Cons:** no terrace, pool, or spa; no laundry or room service; bathrooms a bit cramped. $ *Rooms from: €130* ⊠ *Carrer Valldonzella 5, El Raval* ☎ *93/318–2182* ⊕ *www.atiramhotels.com* ⇥ *57 rooms* ❍❘ *No meals* Ⓜ *Catalunya, L1/L2 Universitat.*

Sant Agustí

$$ | HOTEL | FAMILY | In a leafy square just off La Rambla, the Sant Agustí bills itself as the oldest billet in Barcelona—it was built in the 1720s for the library of the adjacent convent and reborn as a hotel in 1840. **Pros:** steps from the Boqueria market, La Rambla, and the Liceu opera house; intimate breakfast room; very good value for price. **Cons:** Plaça Sant Agusti can be a homeless hangout; not enough closet space; safe boxes too small for laptops. $ *Rooms from: €150* ⊠ *Pl. Sant Agustí 3, El Raval* ☎ *93/318–1658* ⊕ *www.hotelsa.com* ⇥ *80 rooms* ❍❘ *Free Breakfast* Ⓜ *L3 Liceu.*

▼ Nightlife

El Raval has slowly evolved from a forgotten, seedy no-man's-land into one of the choicest districts to enjoy provocative modern art and a pulsating, boho-glam party scene. Though not to everyone's taste, hippie students, tattooed misfits, artists, and more recently trend-seeking nomads routinely bar crawl up and down a stretch of nightlife-friendly streets (Joaquin Costa is one) featuring a wide assortment of divey dens, music bars, pubs, and funky *coctelerias.*

BARS

Ambar

BARS/PUBS | Right off the tree-lined Rambla del Raval, the clientele at this popular watering hole is as colorful as the snazzy, red-quilted bar and moody green-blue lighting: expat students and pierced young artists rub shoulders with visiting rabble-rousers warming up for

a wild night out. With its basic menu of classic cocktails and long drinks, the main attraction is arguably the space itself. The dim interior is spacious, strewn with a calculated mix of modern and retro; shabby sofas and antique lamps are in perfect harmony with the contempo floor-to-ceiling windows, artless frames, and slick metallic stools. ⊠ *Sant Pau 77, El Raval* ☎ *93/441-3725.*

Casa Almirall

BARS/PUBS | The twisted wooden fronds framing the bar's mirror, an 1888 vintage bar-top iron statue of a muse, and Art Nouveau touches such as curvy door handles make this one of the most authentic bars in Barcelona. It's also the second oldest, dating to 1860. (The oldest is the Marsella, another Raval favorite.) It's a good spot for evening drinks after hitting the nearby MACBA (Museu d'Art Contemporani de Barcelona) or for a prelunch *vermut* (vermouth) on weekends. ⊠ *Joaquín Costa 33, El Raval* ☎ *93/318–9917* ⊕ *www.casaalmirall.com/en* Ⓜ *Universitat.*

La Confitería

BARS/PUBS | Located in a former pastry shop, this vintage bar has retained so much of the 19th-century Moderniste facade and interior touches (onetime cake display cases are now filled with period memorabilia) that visitors undoubtedly experience the sensation of time standing still. Divided into two equally inviting spaces and open unconventionally late for a bar (3 am), the front is usually packed with regulars, while the granite-and-metal tables in the back are popular with couples and small groups of friends enjoying a few beers or a bottle of cava. Sunday afternoons features live music during the traditional vermouth hour (1–2 pm). ⊠ *Sant Pau 128, El Raval* ☎ *93/140–5435* ⊕ *www.confiteria.cat* Ⓜ *Paral.lel.*

Manchester

BARS/PUBS | There's no doubt about what the name of this laid-back Raval hangout pays tribute to: that of the early '80s

Manchester scene, with the Joy Division and Happy Mondays and the Stone Roses. The sheer number of people (both locals and foreigners) crowding around the wood tables and dancing in the spaces in between suggest that a tribute is welcome. ⊠ *Valldonzella 40, El Raval* ☎ *627/733-081* Ⓜ *Catalunya.*

Marsella

BARS/PUBS | Inaugurated in 1820, this historic venue, a favored haunt for artistic notables such as Gaudí, Picasso, and Hemingway, has remained remarkably unchanged since its celebrated heyday. The chipped paint on the walls and ceiling, cracked marble tables, and elaborate spiderwebs on chandeliers and bottles all add to the charm, but the main reason patrons linger is one special shot: Marsella is one of few establishments serving homemade absinthe (*absenta* in Spanish), a potent aniseed-flavored spirit meant to be savored and rumored to enhance productivity. ⊠ *Sant Pau 65, El Raval* ☎ *93/442–7263* Ⓜ *Liceu.*

Negroni

BARS/PUBS | This cocktail bar is for no-nonsense sophisticates of all ages: pared down to mostly black decor and a shiny varnished bar. What sets Negroni apart and keeps it popular even a decade after its inception is the talented barmen's dedication to the art of cocktail creation; no menus, just reveal your favorite spirit and have a little trust. ⊠ *Joaquin Costa 46, El Raval* ☎ *615/498465* ⊕ *www. negronicocktailbar.com* Ⓜ *Universitat.*

33/45

BARS/PUBS | From the street, this indie-cool hipster haven seems too brightly lighted for gritty-glam Raval. But upon closer inspection, a copious, cushy area with oversize pillows; ratty, mismatched sofas; and a cocktail menu available day and night make it tempting enough to linger. Featuring weekly live music sessions and occasional pop-up expositions, it's the establishment's chill vibe and eclectic selection of flavored gins, tequila blends,

and imported beer that attract a steady flow of lounge lizards. ⊠ *Joaquin Costa 4, El Raval* ☎ *93/187–4138* Ⓜ *Sant Antoni.*

Ultramarinos

BARS/PUBS | Gintonic (in Spanish it's all one word), the cocktail of choice for many a hip barcelonin, is the undisputed star of this retro-fabulous neighborhood bar. Old-school aficionados favor the saucy collection of signature Hendricks blends, but for those with more curious palates, more than 175 international gins are flavored, perfumed, and/or mixed into no less than 25 killer concoctions. Beyond the gin, a varied selection of spirits and cocktails are on offer and a rotating lineup of local DJs keep the joint jumping by playing everything from classic jazz to the more obscure (Latin tropical disco anyone?). ⊠ *Sant Pau 126, El Raval* ☎ *653/582424* Ⓜ *Parallel.*

MUSIC CLUBS: JAZZ AND BLUES

Jazz Sí Club

MUSIC CLUBS | Run by the Barcelona contemporary music school next door, this workshop and (during the day) café is a forum for musicians, teachers, and fans to listen to and debate their art. There is jazz on Monday; pop, blues, and rock jam sessions on Tuesday; jazz Wednesday; Cuban salsa on Thursday; flamenco on Friday; and rock and pop on weekends. The small cover charge (€6–€10, depending on which night you visit) includes a drink; Wednesday has no cover charge. Gigs start between 6:30 and 8:45 pm. ⊠ *Requesens 2, El Raval* ☎ *93/329–0020* ⊕ *tallerdemusics.com/en/jazzsi-club* Ⓜ *Sant Antoni.*

🎭 Performing Arts

THEATER

Teatre Apolo

DANCE | This historic player in Barcelona's theater life stages musicals, comedies, and dramas. ⊠ *Av. del Paral·lel 59, El Raval* ☎ *93/441–9944* ⊕ *www.teatreapolo.com* Ⓜ *Paral.lel.*

Shopping

Shopping in the Raval reflects the district's multicultural and bohemian vibe. Around MACBA (Barcelona Museum of Contemporary Art) you'll find dozens of designer-run start-ups selling fashion, crafts, and housewares, while the edgier southernmost section has an abundance of curious establishments chock-full of ethnic foods (along Calles Hospital and Carme) and vintage clothing (on Calle Riera Baixa).

ANTIQUES AND COLLECTIBLES

Holala! Plaza

CLOTHING | Holala! is more a lifestyle than a vintage store. Its owners travel the world in search of garments for the next trend, or wave of nostalgia. This huge space is chockablock with clothing, furniture, objects, knickknacks, and other flotsam of the distant and not-so-distant past. Hawaiian surfboards, high-waisted Levis, nubby 1980s knits—it's all put into a postmodern context at Holala!—and the kids lap it up. Holala! has a smaller shop selling clothes only at Tallers 73, also in the Raval. ⊠ *Pl. de la Castella 2 (with Calle de Valldonzella), El Raval* ☎ *93/302–0593* ⊕ *www.holala-ibiza.com* Ⓜ *Catalunya.*

BOOKS

La Central del Raval

BOOKS/STATIONERY | This luscious bookstore in the former chapel of the Casa de la Misericòrdia sells books amid stunning architecture and holds regular cultural events. ⊠ *C/Elisabets 6, El Raval* ☎ *933/189979* ⊕ *www.lacentral.com* Ⓜ *Catalunya.*

CLOTHING

Home on Earth

CLOTHING | Housewares and children's clothing with a homespun sensibility are on offer in this charming store run by a Scandinavian couple. Bags made of Thai tapestries, wooden instruments, felt baskets, and handmade lamp shades are among the accessories worth checking out here. There is a second shop in the Barri Gòtic at Boqueria 14. ⊠ *Hospital 76, C. Boqueria 14, El Raval* ⊕ *Closest metro: Liceu* ☎ *93/315–8558* ⊕ *www.homeonearth.com.*

Med Winds

CLOTHING | Made locally, this casual-chic clothing for men and women is constructed with natural cotton and wool in loose silhouettes to create an effortlessly cool look loved by El Raval's armies of hipsters. Lovely leather bags and backpacks are available, too. ⊠ *Elisabets 7, El Raval* ☎ *93/619–0179* ⊕ *www.medwinds. com* Ⓜ *Catalunya, Liceu.*

MARKETS

Flea Market BCN

OUTDOOR/FLEA/GREEN MARKETS | Barcelona's current rage for retro and vintage reaches its pinnacle once a month on a little square behind the medieval shipyards. Flea Market BCN sees hipsters and hippies, dads and dealers empty out their wardrobes and garages. When the sun is shining, it makes for a fun morning out as you rummage through racks of last season's Zara for diamonds in the rough. Stick with it, and you may walk away with an art-deco wall clock or 1970s hand mixer. Flea Market BCN is held on the second Sunday of every month, while the smaller Fleedonia takes places on the Plaça Salvador Seguí on the first Sunday of every month. ⊠ *Pl. Blanquerna* ⊕ *www.fleamarketbcn.com* Ⓜ *Drassanes.*

Mercat de Sant Antoni

FOOD/CANDY | Just outside the Raval at the end of Ronda Sant Antoni, this steel hangar colossus is an old-fashioned food and secondhand clothing and books (many in English) market. Sunday morning is the most popular time to browse through the used-book and video game market. ⊠ *Comte d'Urgell 1, El Raval* ⊕ *www.mercatdesantantoni.com* Ⓜ *Sant Antoni.*

SANT PERE AND LA RIBERA

Updated by
Elizabeth Prosser and
Steve Tallantyre

👁 **Sights**
★★★★★

🍴 **Restaurants**
★★★★★

🛏 **Hotels**
★★★★☆

🛍 **Shopping**
★★★★★

🍸 **Nightlife**
★★★★★

NEIGHBORHOOD SNAPSHOT

TOP EXPERIENCES

■ **Museu Picasso:** Reserve tickets in advance to visit the stunning five medieval palaces that house the works of young Picasso.

■ **Palau de la Música Catalana:** If you can't fit a performance into your itinerary, you owe it to yourself to at least take a tour of this amazing building—the only concert hall in the world to be declared a UNESCO World Heritage site.

■ **Santa Maria del Mar:** Attend a concert or requiem Mass at this surprisingly light and serene church.

■ **Cal Pep:** Squeeze through the door and enjoy a bottle of Albariño while you wait for some of the city's best tapas.

■ **Casa Gispert:** Browse the olive oils, spices, chocolates, and fruits, and be sure to buy roasted nuts that have been prepared in the same wood-fired roaster for over 160 years.

GETTING HERE

From the central Plaça de Catalunya metro hub, it's a 10-minute walk over and down to the Palau de la Música Catalana for the beginning of this tour. The yellow L4 metro stop at Jaume I is closer to Santa Maria del Mar, but it's a hassle if you have to change trains; Plaça de Catalunya is close enough, and makes for a pleasant stroll.

PLANNING YOUR TIME

Depending on the number of museum visits and stops, exploring these neighborhoods can take a full day. Count on at least four hours of actual walking time. Catching Santa Maria del Mar open is key (it's closed daily 1:30–4:30). If you make it to Cal Pep for tapas before 1:30, you might get a place at the bar; if you don't, it's well worth the wait. The Picasso Museum is at least a two-hour visit.

QUICK BITES

■ **La Vinya del Senyor.** Relax on the patio of La Vinya del Senyor and sample top wines from around the world. Must-tries include Spanish reds from Montsant, Priorat, and Rioja, best enjoyed by the glass, along with light tapas like the Ibérico ham. ⊠ *Pl. de Santa Maria 5, Born-Ribera* Ⓜ *Jaume I*

■ **Museu de la Xocolata.** This beautiful shop and café in an 18th-century former monastery offers rich hot and cold chocolate drinks, boxes and bars of artisanal chocolate, and house-made cakes and pastries. ⊠ *Carrer del Comerç 36, Born-ribera* ⊕ *www.museuxocolata.cat* Ⓜ *Jaume I*

The textile and waterfront neighborhoods are home to some of the city's most iconic buildings, from the Gothic 14th-century basilica of Santa Maria del Mar to the over-the-top Moderniste Palau de la Música Catalana. At the Museu Picasso, works of the 20th-century master are displayed in five adjoining Renaissance palaces.

Sant Pere, Barcelona's old textile neighborhood, is centered on the church of Sant Pere. A half mile closer to the port, the Barri de la Ribera and the former market of El Born, now known as the Born-Ribera district, were at the center of Catalonia's great maritime and economic expansion of the 13th and 14th centuries. Surrounding the basilica of Santa Maria del Mar, the Born-Ribera area includes Carrer Montcada, lined with 14th- to 18th-century Renaissance palaces; Passeig del Born, where medieval jousts were held; Carrer Flassaders and the area around the early mint; the antiques shop- and restaurant-rich Carrer Banys Vells; Plaça de les Olles; and Pla del Palau, where La Llotja, Barcelona's early maritime exchange, housed the fine-arts school where Picasso, Gaudí, and Domènech i Montaner all studied, as did many more of Barcelona's most important artists and architects.

Long a depressed neighborhood, La Ribera began to experience a revival in the 1980s; now replete with intimate bars, cafés, and trendy boutiques, it continues to enjoy the blessings of gentrification. An open excavation in the center of El Born, the onetime market restored as a multipurpose cultural center, offers a fascinating view of pre-1714 Barcelona, dismantled by the victorious troops of Felipe V at the end of the War of the Spanish Succession. The Passeig del Born, La Rambla of medieval Barcelona, is once again a pleasant leafy promenade.

⊙ Sights

Biblioteca Francesca Bonnemaison (*Women's Public Library*)
LIBRARY | Barcelona's (and probably the world's) first library established exclusively for women, the Biblioteca Popular de la Dona was founded in 1909, evidence of the city's early-20th-century progressive attitudes and tendencies. Over the opulently coffered main reading room, the stained-glass skylight reads "Tota dona val mes quan letra apren" (Any woman's worth more when she learns how to read), the first line of a ballad by the 13th-century Catalan troubadour Severí de Girona. Once Franco's Spain composed of church, army, and oligarchy had restored law and order after the Spanish Civil War, the center was taken

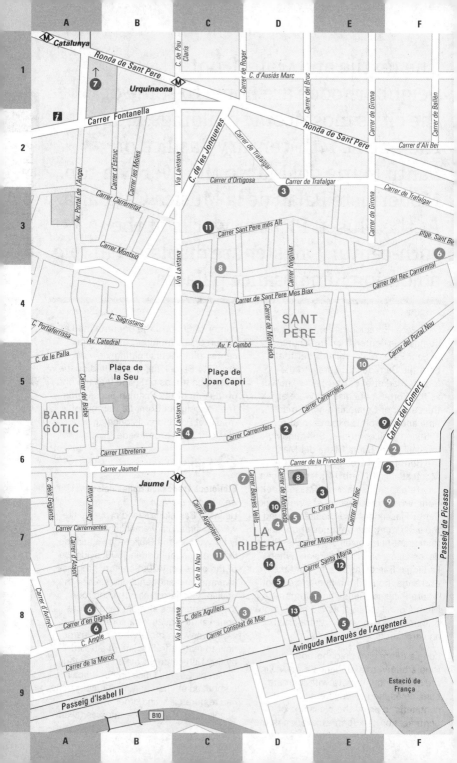

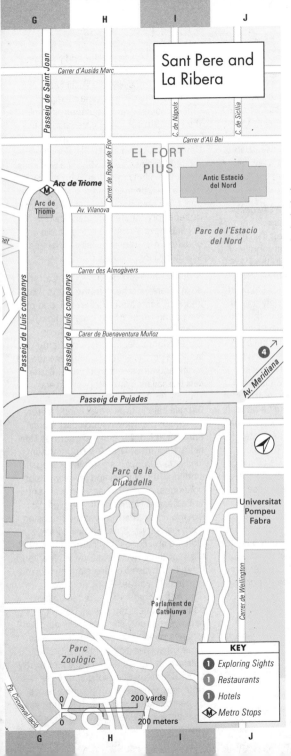

6

Sant Pere and La Ribera

over by Spain's one legal political party, the Falange, and women's activities were reoriented toward more domestic pursuits such as sewing and cooking. Today the library complex includes a small theater and offers a lively program of theatrical and cultural events. ⊠ *Centro de Cultura, Carrer Sant Pere Més Baix 7, Sant Pere* ☎ *93/268–7360* ⊕ *www.barcelona.cat/bibfbonnemaison.cat* ⊘ *Closed Sun.* Ⓜ *L1/L4 Urquinaona.*

Capella d'en Marcús (*Marcús Chapel*)
RELIGIOUS SITE | This Romanesque hermitage looks as if it had been left behind by some remote order of hermit-monks who meant to take it on a picnic in the Pyrenees. The tiny chapel, possibly—along with Sant Llàtzer—Barcelona's smallest religious structure, and certainly one of its oldest, was originally built in the 12th century on the main Roman road into Barcelona, the one that would become Cardo Maximo just a few hundred yards away as it passed through the walls at Portal de l'Àngel. Bernat Marcús, a wealthy merchant concerned with public welfare and social issues, built a hospital here for poor travelers; the hospital chapel that bears his name was dedicated to the Mare de Déu de la Guia (Our Lady of the Guide). As a result of its affiliation, combined with its location on the edge of town, the chapel eventually became the headquarters of the Confraria del Correus a Cavall (Brotherhood of the Pony Express), also known as the *troters* (trotters), that made Barcelona the key link in overland mail between the Iberian Peninsula and France. ⊠ *Carrer Carders 2 (Placeta d'en Marcús), Born-Ribera* ☎ *93/310–2390* Ⓜ *Jaume I.*

Carrer Flassaders
COMMERCIAL CENTER | Named for the weavers and blanket makers whom this street belonged to in medieval times, Carrer Flassaders begins on Carrer Montcada opposite La Xampanyet, one of La Ribera's most popular bars for tapas and cava. Duck into the short, dark Carrer

Arc de Sant Vicenç; at the end you'll find yourself face to face with **La Seca,** the Royal Mint (officially, the Reial Fàbrica de la Moneda de la Corona d'Aragó), where money was manufactured until the mid-19th century. Coins bearing the inscription, in Castilian, "Principado de Cataluña" (Principality of Catalonia) were minted here as late as 1836. La Seca has been exquisitely restored, with the original wooden beams, pillars, and brickwork intact; it's now home to a small avant-garde repertory theater company called Espai Brossa. Adjacent is the studio and showroom of internationally acclaimed sculptor Manel Alvarez.

Turn left on Carrer de la Seca to Carrer de la Cirera; overhead to the left is the image of **Santa Maria de Cervelló**, one of the patron saints of the Catalan fleet, on the back of the Palau Cervelló on Carrer Montcada. Turn right on Carrer de la Cirera past the Otman shop and tearoom, and arrive at the corner of **Carrer dels Flassaders.** Walk left past several shops—**Re-Born** at Flassaders 23; cozy **La Báscula** café in the former candy factory at No. 30; the upbeat food court **Mercat Princesa** at No. 21; and the gourmet **Montiel** restaurant at No. 19. Wander down Flassaders through a gauntlet of elegant clothing, furnishings, and jewelry design boutiques, and you'll pass the main entry to La Seca at No. 40, with the gigantic Bourbon coat of arms over the imposing archway. At No. 42 is **Loisaida** (vintage clothing and curios: the name is Spanglish for the Lower East Side in New York City). The stylish Cortana clothing store is across the street. Look up to your right at the corner of the gated Carrer de les Mosques, famous as Barcelona's narrowest street. The mustachioed countenance peering down at you was once a medieval advertisement for a brothel. **Hofmann,** at No. 44, is the excellent pastry shop of famous Barcelona chef Mey Hofmann, whose cooking school is over on nearby Carrer Argenteria. (Don't pass up the mascarpone croissants.) A right on Passeig del Born will take you back to Santa Maria del Mar. ⊠ *Carrer Flassaders, Born-Ribera* Ⓜ *Jaume I.*

★ Disseny Hub

MUSEUM | This center of activity represents the efforts of Barcelona's urban planners to put all the city's designer eggs in one basket and to plant an eye-catching architectural anchor in the long-delayed renewal project on Plaça de les Glòries. The new building is home to no less than four museum collections: the **Museu de Arts Tèxtil i Indumentària** (Textiles and Clothing Museum) of fashion, embroidery, jewelry, and accessories from ancient times to modern haute couture; the **Museu de Ceràmica** (Ceramics Museum), tracing the evolution of ceramic arts from 13th-century Moorish influences to the present, with a number of pieces by Miró and Picasso; the **Museu de les Arts Decoratives** (Museum of Decorative Arts), devoted mainly to the historical high arts of furniture and furnishings; and the **Gabinet de les Arts Gràfiques** (Graphic Arts Collection) of posters, packaging, typographic styles, and printed papers. The DHUB store has a fine selection of books on design as well as reproductions that make great gifts to take home. The building itself, by MBM Arquitectes (Oriol Bohigas, doyen of the firm, was the prime mover in much of Barcelona's makeover for the 1992 Olympics), juts out like a multistoried wedge into the Plaça de les Glòries, anchoring a traffic hub where the Diagonal meets the Avenida Meridiana. Originally built to be the new city center, the Glòries (designed by Eixample architect Ildefons Cerdà) had been run-down and unnavigable for decades. Next door to the Hub is the **Mercat dels Encants** open-air flea market (open Monday, Wednesday, Friday, and Saturday 9–8), Barcelona's biggest, reborn in the same project that produced the museum, with a whimsical, undulating mirrored roof. The Mercat is prime grazing land for old furniture, vintage clothing, and bric-a-brac of all sorts. ⊠ *Edific DHUB, Pl. de les Glòries Catalans 37–8, Sant Martí* ☎ *93/256–6800* ⊕ *www.museudeldisseny.cat* 🎫 *€6, valid for 2 days; free Sun. 3–8 and all day 1st Sun. every month; 30% discount with Bus Turístic tickets* ☉ *Closed Mon.* Ⓜ *L1 Glòries.*

Fossar de les Moreres (*Cemetery of the Mulberry Trees*)

MEMORIAL | This low marble monument runs across the eastern side of the church of Santa Maria del Mar. It honors defenders of Barcelona who gave their lives in the final siege that ended the War of the Spanish Succession on September 11, 1714. The inscription (in English: "in the cemetery of the mulberry trees no traitor lies") refers to the graveyard keeper's story. He refused to bury those on the invading side, even when one turned out to be his son. This is the traditional gathering place for the most radical elements of Catalonia's nationalist (separatist) movement, on the Catalonian national day, which celebrates the heroic defeat.

From the monument, look back at Santa Maria del Mar. The lighter-color stone on the lateral facade was left by the 17th-century Pont del Palau (Palace Bridge), erected to connect the Royal Palace in the nearby Pla del Palau with the Tribuna Real (Royal Box) over the right side of the Santa Maria del Mar altar, so that nobles and occupying military officials could get to Mass without the risk of walking in the streets. The bridge, regarded as a symbol of imperialist oppression, was finally dismantled in 1987. The steel arch with its eternal flame was erected in 2002. ⊠ *Pl. de Santa Maria, Born-Ribera* Ⓜ *L4 Jaume I.*

Hash Marihuana Cáñamo & Hemp Museum

HOUSE | Legendary Dutch cannabis pioneer Ben Dronkers acquired the historic Palau Mornau, in the Gothic Quarter, and opened it in 2012 after a major renovation as the world's largest museum devoted to this controversial crop. The building alone makes this a must-visit: a 16th-century noble palace later reconfigured in exuberant Moderniste style by architect Manuel Raspell, a contemporary of Gaudí and student of both Domènech i Montaner and Puig i Cadafalch, with jewel-box-like details of stained glass, carved wood door lintels, coffered ceilings, and ceramic tile. The museum collection of art and artifacts celebrates the history, cultivation, processing, and consumption of hemp in all its industrial, medicinal, and recreational aspects. Alas: no take-away samples. ✉ *Carrer Ample 35, Born-Ribera* ☎ *93/319–7539* ⊕ *hashmuseum.com* 🖘 *€9* Ⓜ *L4 Jaume 1.*

La Llotja (*Maritime Exchange*)
BUILDING | Barcelona's maritime trade center, the Casa Llotja de Mar, was designed to be the city's finest example of civil architecture, built in the Catalan Gothic style between 1380 and 1392. At the end of the 18th century the facades were (tragically) covered in the neoclassical uniformity of the time, but the interior, the great Saló Gòtic (Gothic Hall), remained unaltered, and was a grand venue for balls and celebrations throughout the 19th century. The Gothic Hall was used as the Barcelona stock exchange until 1975, and until late 2001 as the grain exchange. The hall, with its graceful arches and columns and floors of light Carrara and dark Genovese marble, has now been brilliantly restored. The building, which is not typically open to the general public, now houses the Barcelona Chamber of Commerce.

The Escola de Belles Arts (School of Fine Arts) occupied the southwestern corner of the Llotja from 1849 until 1960. Many illustrious Barcelona artists studied here, including Gaudí, Miró, and Picasso. The **Reial Acadèmia Catalana de Belles Arts de Sant Jordi** (Royal Catalan Academy of Fine Arts of St. George) still has its seat in the Llotja, and its museum is one of Barcelona's semisecret collections of art, from medieval paintings by unknown artists to

modern works by members of the Academy itself; a 17th-century *Saint Jerome* by Joan Ribalta is especially fine. To slip into the Saló Gòti, walk down the stairs from the museum to the second floor, then take the marble staircase down and turn right. Guided visits to the museum collection (free) are offered for groups of 10–25 persons. ✉ *Casa Llotja, Passeig d'Isabel II 1, Born-Ribera* ☎ *93/319–2432 Reial Acadèmia, 670/466260 guided visits to museum* ⊕ *www.racba.org* 🖘 *Free* 🕐 *Museum closed weekends* Ⓜ *L4 Barceloneta.*

Museu de la Xocolata

MUSEUM | **FAMILY** | The elaborate, painstakingly detailed chocolate sculptures, which have included everything from La Sagrada Família to Don Quixote's windmills, delight both youthful and adult visitors to this museum, set in an imposing 18th-century former monastery and developed by the Barcelona Provincial Confectionery Guild. Other exhibits here touch on Barcelona's centuries-old love affair with chocolate, the introduction of chocolate to Europe by Spanish explorers from the Mayan and Aztec cultures in the New World, and both vintage and current machinery and tools used to create this sweet delicacy. The beautiful shop and café offers rich hot and cold chocolate drinks, boxes and bars of artisanal chocolate, and house-made cakes and pastries. Classes on making and tasting chocolate are offered, too. ✉ *Carrer del Comerç 36, Born-Ribera* ☎ *93/268–7878* ⊕ *www.museuxocolata.cat* 🖘 *€6* Ⓜ *L4 Jaume 1, L1 Arc de Triomf.*

★ **Museu Picasso** (*Picasso Museum*)
MUSEUM | The Picasso Museum is housed in five adjoining 13th- to 15th-century palaces on Carrer Montcada, a street known for Barcelona's most elegant medieval mansions. Picasso spent his formative years in Barcelona (1895–1904), and this collection, while it does not include a significant number of his best paintings, is particularly

strong on his early work. The museum was begun in 1962 on the suggestion of Picasso's crony Jaume Sabartés, and the initial donation was from the Sabartés collection. Later Picasso donated his early works, and in 1981 his widow, Jacqueline Roque, added 141 pieces.

HIGHLIGHTS

Displays include childhood sketches, works from the artist's Rose and Blue periods, and the famous 1950s cubist variations on Velázquez's *Las Meninas* (in Rooms 22–26). The lower-floor sketches, oils, and schoolboy caricatures from Picasso's early years in A Coruña are perhaps the most fascinating part of the whole museum, showing the facility he seemed to possess from birth. His *La Primera Communión* (*First Communion*), painted at the age of 16, gives an idea of his early accomplishments. On the second floor you see the beginnings of the mature Picasso and his Blue Period in Paris.

TIPS

Expect long lines on days that offer free admission.

All other days, buy tickets for specific times online in advance.

Stop at the terrace café and restaurant for a light Mediterranean meal to break up the day. ⊠ *Carrer Montcada 15–19, Born-Ribera* ☎ *93/256–3000, 93/256–3022 guided tour and group reservations* ⊕ *www.museupicasso.bcn.cat* 🖃 *€12; free Thurs. 6–9:30 pm, and 1st Sun. of month* 🕙 *Closed Mon.* ☞ *Guided tours of permanent collection (in English) Wed. at 3 and Sun. at 11 (except Aug.); free with admission* Ⓜ *L4 Jaume I, L1 Arc de Triomf.*

Palau Dalmases

ARTS VENUE | If you can get through the massive wooden gates that open onto Carrer Montcada (at the moment, the only opportunity is when the first-floor café-theater Espai Barroc is open) you'll find yourself in Barcelona's best 17th-century Renaissance courtyard, built into a former 15th-century Gothic palace. Note the door knockers up at horseback level; then take a careful look at the frieze of "The Rape of Europa" running up the stone railing of the elegant stairway at the end of the patio. It's a festive abduction: Neptune's chariot, cherubs, naiads, dancers, tritons, and musicians accompany Zeus, in the form of a bull, as he carries poor Europa up the stairs and off to Crete. The stone carvings in the courtyard, the 15th-century Gothic chapel, with its reliefs of angelic musicians, and the vaulting in the reception hall and salon, are all that remain of the original 15th-century palace. Espai Barroc, on the ground floor, is a café-theater (flamenco, jazz, opera *concertante*) with baroque-era flourishes, period furniture, and musical performances. ⊠ *Carrer Montcada 20, Born-Ribera* ☎ *93/310–0673 Espai Barroc* ⊕ *palaudalmases.com* 🖃 *Shows €25 (includes 1 drink)* Ⓜ *L4 Jaume I.*

★ Palau de la Música Catalana

ARTS VENUE | On Carrer Amadeus Vives, just off Via Laietana, a 10-minute walk from Plaça de Catalunya, is one of the world's most extraordinary music halls. The Palau is a flamboyant tour de force, a riot of color and form designed in 1908 by Lluís Domènech i Montaner. Its sponsors, the Orfeó Català musical society, wanted it to celebrate the importance of music in Catalan culture and the life of its ordinary people (as opposed to the Liceu opera house, with its Castilian-speaking, monarchist, upper-class patrons, and its music from elsewhere), but the Palau turned out to be anything but commonplace; it and the Liceu were for many decades opposing crosstown forces in Barcelona's musical as well as philosophical discourse. If you can't fit a performance into your itinerary, you owe it to yourself to at least take a tour of this amazing building.

The exterior is remarkable. The Miquel Blay sculptural group over the corner of

Amadeu Vives and Sant Pere Més Alt is a hymn in stone to Catalonia's popular traditions, with hardly a note left unsung: St. George the dragon-slayer (at the top), women and children at play and work, fishermen with oars over their shoulders—a panoply of everyday life. Inside, the decor of the Palau assaults your senses before the first note of music is ever heard. Wagner's Valkyries burst from the right side of the stage over a heavy-browed bust of Beethoven; Catalonia's popular music is represented by the graceful maidens of Lluís Millet's song *Flors de Maig* ("Flowers of May") on the left. Overhead, an inverted stained-glass cupola seems to channel the divine gift of music straight from heaven; painted rosettes and giant peacock feathers adorn the walls and columns; across the entire back wall of the stage is a relief of muselike Art Nouveau musicians in costume. The visuals alone make music sound different here, be it a chamber orchestra, a renowned piano soloist, a gospel choir, or an Afro-Cuban combo. ⊠ *Carrer Palau de la Música 4–6, Born-Ribera* ☎ *93/295–7200, 902/442882 box office* ⊕ *www.palaumusica.cat/en* 🎫 *Tour €20* Ⓜ *L1/L4 Urquinaona.*

★ Passeig del Born

ARCHAEOLOGICAL SITE | Once the site of medieval jousts and autos-da-fé of the Inquisition, the passeig, at the end of Carrer Montcada behind the church of Santa Maria del Mar, was early Barcelona's most important square. Late-night cocktail bars and miniature restaurants with tiny spiral stairways now line the narrow, elongated plaza. The numbered cannonballs under the public benches are the work of the "poet of space"—a 20th-century specialist in combinations of letters, words, and sculpture—the late Joan Brossa. The cannonballs evoke the 1714 siege of Barcelona that concluded the 14-year War of the Spanish Succession, when Felipe V's conquering Castilian and French troops attacked the city ramparts at their lowest, flattest flank.

After their victory, the Bourbon forces obliged residents of the Barri de la Ribera (Waterfront District) to tear down nearly a thousand of their own houses, some 20% of Barcelona at that time, to create fields of fire so that the occupying army of Felipe V could better train its batteries of cannon on the conquered populace and discourage any nationalist uprisings. Thus began Barcelona's "internal exile" as an official enemy of the Spanish state.

Walk down to the Born itself—a great iron hangar, once a produce market designed by Josep Fontseré, in the Plaça Comercial, across the street from the end of the promenade. The initial stages of the construction of a public library in the Born uncovered the remains of the lost city of 1714, complete with blackened fireplaces, taverns, wells, and the canal that brought water into the city. The Museu d'Història de la Ciutat opened a museum here in 2013, the El Born Centre de Cultura i Memòria, kicking off a year of events concluding with the September 11, 2014, commemoration of Barcelona's defeat. The streets of the 14th- to 18th-century Born-Ribera lie open in the sunken central square of the old market; around it, on the ground level, are a number of new multifunctional exhibition and performance spaces; these give the city one of its newest and liveliest cultural subcenters. ⊠ *Passeig del Born, Born-Ribera* ☎ *93/256–6851 El Born Centre de Cultura i Memòria* ⊕ *elborn-culturaimemoria.barcelona.cat* 🎫 *Free to upper galleries, €6 to the archaeological site* ⊗ *Closed Mon.* Ⓜ *L4 Jaume I/ Barceloneta.*

Plaça de les Olles

PLAZA | This pretty little square named for the makers of *olles,* or pots, has been known to host everything from topless sunbathers to elegant Viennese waltzers to the overflow from the popular nearby tapas bar Cal Pep. Notice the balconies at No. 6 over Café de la Ribera, oddly with colorful blue and yellow tile on the second and top floors. The house with the turret over the street on the right at the corner leading out to Pla del Palau (at No. 2 Plaça de les Olles) is another of Enric Sagnier i Villavecchia's retro-Moderniste works. ⊠ *Pl. de les Olles, Born-Ribera* Ⓜ *L4 Jaume I/Barceloneta.*

★ Santa Maria del Mar

BUILDING | An example of early Catalan Gothic architecture, Santa Maria del Mar is extraordinary for its unbroken lines and elegance. At what was then the water's edge, the church was built by stonemasons who chose, fitted, and carved each stone hauled down from the same Montjuïc quarry that provided the sandstone for the 4th-century Roman walls. The medieval numerological symbol for the Virgin Mary, the number eight (or multiples thereof), runs through every element of the basilica: the 16 octagonal pillars are 2 meters in diameter and spread out into rib vaulting arches at a height of 16 meters; the painted keystones at the apex of the arches are 32 meters from the floor; and the central nave is twice as wide as the lateral naves (8 meters each).

The church survived the fury of anarchists who in 1936 burned nearly all of Barcelona's churches as a reprisal against the alliance of army, church, and oligarchy during the military rebellion. The basilica, then filled with ornate side chapels and choir stalls, burned for 11 days, nearly crumbling. Restored after the Civil War by a series of Bauhaus-trained architects, the church is now an architectural gem. Climb the towers for magnificent rooftop views (guided tours only), or join a guided tour for entrance to other areas that are usually closed to visitors, such as the crypt.

Highlights

The paintings in the keystones overhead represent the Coronation of the Virgin, the Nativity, the Annunciation, the equestrian figure of the father of Pedro IV, King Alfons, and the Barcelona coat of arms.

The 34 lateral chapels are dedicated to different saints and images. The first chapel to the left of the altar (No. 20) is the Capella del Santo Cristo (Chapel of the Holy Christ), its stained-glass window an allegory of Barcelona's 1992 Olympic Games.

An engraved stone riser beside the door onto Carrer Sombrerers commemorates where San Ignacio de Loyola, founder of the Jesuit Order, begged for alms in 1524 and 1525.

Tips

Set aside at least a half hour to see Santa Maria del Mar. *La Catedral del Mar* (*The Cathedral of the Sea*) by Ildefonso Falcons chronicles the construction of the basilica and 14th-century life in Barcelona. Check the leisure announcements in weekly magazines for concerts in the basilica; the setting and the acoustics here make performances an unforgettable experience. ⊠ *Pl. de Santa Maria 1, Born-Ribera* ☎ *93/310–2390* ⊕ *www.santamariadelmarbarcelona.org* ▨ *Tour from €10* Ⓜ *L4 Jaume I.*

🍴 Restaurants

Cal Pep

$$ | TAPAS | A two-minute walk east of Santa Maria del Mar, Cal Pep has been in a permanent feeding frenzy for more than 30 years, intensified even further by the hordes of tourists who now flock here. Pep serves a selection of tapas, cooked and served hot over the counter. **Known for:** excellent fish fry; delicious potato omelet; lively counter scene. ⓢ *Average main: €22* ⊠ *Pl. de les Olles 8, Born-Ribera* ☎ *93/310–7961* ⊕ *www.calpep.com* ⊘ *Closed Sun., and 3 wks in Aug. No lunch Mon.* Ⓜ *Jaume I, Barceloneta.*

El Foro

$$ | ECLECTIC | Painting and photographic exhibits line the walls of this large and lively Born restaurant, and the menu is

A wooden door leads to Barcelona's best 17th-century patio in the Palau Dalmases.

dominated by meat cooked over coals, pizzas, and salads. Flamenco and jazz performances downstairs are a good post-dinner diversion. **Known for:** Argentine meat; live jazz. [$] *Average main: €18* ✉ *Princesa 53, Born-Ribera* ☎ *93/310–1020* 🌐 *www.restauranteelforo.com* 🕓 *Closed Mon.* [M] *Jaume I.*

El Passadís d'en Pep

$$$ | **SEAFOOD** | Hidden away at the end of a narrow unmarked passageway off the Pla del Palau, near the Santa Maria del Mar church, this restaurant is a favorite with well-heeled and well-fed gourmands who tuck in their napkins before devouring some of the city's best traditional seafood dishes. Sit down and waiters will begin serving delicious starters of whatever's freshest that day in the market in rapid-fire succession. **Known for:** fresh seafood; starters served in rapid-fire succession; no menu, but you can prebook a set menu online. [$] *Average main: €28* ✉ *Pl. del Palau 2, Born-Ribera* ☎ *93/310–1021* 🌐 *www.passadis.com* 🕓 *Closed Sun., and 3 wks in Aug.* [M] *Jaume I.*

El Xampanyet

$ | **TAPAS** | Just down the street from the Museu Picasso, dangling *botas* (leather wineskins) announce one of Barcelona's liveliest and most visually appealing taverns, with marble-top tables and walls decorated with colorful ceramic tiles. It's usually packed to the rafters with a rollicking mob of local and out-of-town celebrants. **Known for:** perfect Iberian ham; mouthwatering pa amb tomàquet; real cava. [$] *Average main: €12* ✉ *Montcada 22, Born-Ribera* ☎ *93/319–7003* 💳 *No credit cards* 🕓 *Closed Mon., and 2 wks in Aug. No dinner Sun.* [M] *Jaume I.*

Euskal Etxea

$$$ | **BASQUE** | An elbow-shaped, pine-paneled space, this bar-restaurant (one of the Sagardi group of Basque restaurants) is one of the better grazing destinations in the Born, with a colorful array of tapas and canapés on the bar, ranging from the olive-pepper-anchovy on a toothpick to chunks of tortilla. Other good bets include the *pimientos de piquillo* (red piquillo peppers) stuffed with codfish paste. **Known**

Picasso's Barcelona

The city's claim to Pablo Picasso (1881–1973) has been contested by Málaga (the painter's birthplace), as well as by Madrid, where *La Guernica* hangs, and by the town of Gernika, victim of the 1937 Luftwaffe saturation bombing that inspired the famous canvas. Fervently anti-Franco, Picasso refused to return to Spain after the Civil War; in turn, the regime allowed no public display of his work until 1961, when the artist's *Sardana* frieze on Barcelona's Architects' Guild building was unveiled. Picasso never set foot on Spanish soil for his last 39 years.

Picasso spent a sporadic but formative period of his youth in Barcelona between 1895 and 1904, after which he moved to Paris. His father was an art professor at the Reial Acadèmia de Belles Arts in La Llotja—where his son, a precocious draftsman, began advanced classes at the age of 15. The 19-year-old Picasso first exhibited at Els Quatre Gats, a tavern on Carrer Montsió that looks today much as it did then. His early Cubist painting *Les Demoiselles d'Avignon* was inspired not by the French town but by the Barcelona street Carrer d'Avinyó, then infamous for its brothels. After moving to Paris, Picasso returned occasionally to Barcelona until his last visit in 1934. Considering the artist's off-and-on tenure, it is remarkable that the city and Picasso should be so intertwined in the world's perception. The Picasso Museum, deservedly high on the list of the city's must-see attractions, is perhaps fourth (after the Miró, the MNAC, and the MACBA) on any connoisseur's roster of Barcelona art collections.

Iconoserveis Culturals (✉ *Av. Portal de l'Àngel 38, 4º–2ª, Born-Ribera* ☎ *93/410–1405* 🌐 *www.iconoserveis.com*) will arrange walking tours through the key spots in Picasso's Barcelona life, covering studios, galleries, family apartments, and the painter's favorite haunts and hangouts. 🎟 *Groups up to 25: €237 plus museum entrance fees.*

for: Basque pintxos; art gallery on-site; excellent Euskal Txerria confit. [$] *Average main: €23* ✉ *Placeta de Montcada 1–3, Born-Ribera* ☎ *93/310–2185* 🌐 *www.grupusagardi.com* [M] *Jaume I.*

Fismuler

$$ | **SPANISH** | The cosmopolitan crowd here doesn't come just for the stand-offish hipster waiters and stylish, stripped-down decor. Fismuler Barcelona re-creates its Madrid-based mothership's precise, market-based cooking and adds interesting local touches. **Known for:** informal atmosphere; inventive cooking; killer cheesecake. [$] *Average main: €22* ✉ *Rec Comtal 17, Born-Ribera* ☎ *93/514–0050* 🌐 *www.fismuler.com* [M] *Arc de Triomf.*

La Habana Vieja

$$ | **CUBAN** | If you have an itch for a taste of Old Havana—*ropa vieja* (shredded beef) or *moros y cristianos* (black beans and rice) with mojitos (a cocktail of rum, mint, and sugar), or a round of *plátanos a puñetazos* (punched plantains)—this is your Barcelona refuge. The upstairs tables overlooking the bar are cozy little crow's nests, and the neighborhood is filled with quirky dives and saloons for pre- and post-dinner carousing. **Known for:** Cuban specialities; post-dinner hot spot. [$] *Average main: €18* ✉ *Banys Vells 2, Born-Ribera* ☎ *93/268–2504* ⏲ *Closed Mon. No dinner Sun.* [M] *Jaume I.*

Le Cucine Mandarosso

$ | **ITALIAN** | This no-frills, big-flavor southern-Italian restaurant near the Via Laietana is a favorite with locals. Like Naples itself, it's cheap, charming, and over-full, with generous portions of lasagne, carbonara, and so on, featuring authentic ingredients from the in-store deli. **Known for:** reservations not accepted; long wait times; great homemade pastas. [$] *Average main: €12* ✉ *Verdaguer i Callís 4, Born-Ribera* ☎ *93/269–0780* 🌐 *www.lecucinemandarosso.com* 🕑 *Closed Mon.* [M] *Urquinaona.*

Llamber

$$ | **TAPAS** | It may look like one of the stylish, tourist-trap tapas restaurants that have sprung up recently, but Llamber's culinary pedigree sets it apart from the competition; chef Francisco Heras earned his chops in Spain's top restaurants. This dapper, friendly space attracts a mixed crowd with its excellent wine list and well-crafted tapas based on classic Catalan and Asturian recipes. **Known for:** well-crafted tapas; pig's trotters with rice; good late-night option. [$] *Average main: €17* ✉ *Fusina 5, Born-Ribera* ☎ *93/319–6250* 🌐 *www.llamber.com* [M] *Jaume 1.*

Mundial Bar

$$ | **TAPAS** | Opened in 1925 and still decorated with murals of old-time boxers, Mundial no longer packs the punch of years gone by when it served some of the best-value, no-frills tapas in the area. It retains its unfussy charm but inflated prices—especially for seafood—and inconsistent service suggest its best days are behind it. **Known for:** old-fashioned charm. [$] *Average main: €17* ✉ *Pl. Sant Agustí Vell 1, Born-Ribera* ☎ *93/319–9056* 🕑 *Closed Mon.* [M] *Jaume I.*

Sagardi

$$$ | **BASQUE** | An attractive wood-and-stone cider-house replica, Sagardi piles the counter with a dazzling variety of cold tapas; even better, though, are the hot offerings straight from the kitchen. The restaurant in back serves Basque delicacies like veal sweetbreads with artichokes and *txuletas de buey* (beef steaks) grilled over coals. **Known for:** multiple locations, all equally good; veal sweetbreads; charcoal grill. [$] *Average main: €23* ✉ *Argenteria 62, Born-Ribera* ☎ *93/319–9993* 🌐 *www.gruposagardi.com* [M] *Jaume I.*

Hotels

Banys Orientals

$$ | **HOTEL** | Despite its name, the "Oriental Baths" has no spa, but it does have chic high-contrast design, with dark stained wood and crisp white bedding, and is reasonably priced for the location. **Pros:** Rituals toiletries; tasteful design; steps from the port, Picasso Museum, and the Born area. **Cons:** rooms are on the small side; no room service; no terrace. [$] *Rooms from: €150* ✉ *Argenteria 37, Born-Ribera* ☎ *93/268–8460* 🌐 *www.hotelbanysorientals.com* 🛏 *43 rooms* 🍴 *No meals* [M] *L4 Jaume I.*

Hotel chic&basic Born

$ | **HOTEL** | The lobby of this hip little boutique hotel in the Born with its leather sofa and banquettes might remind you of a Starbucks, but the rooms tell a different story: the concept for chic&basic was whimsical, edgy accommodations at affordable prices, and designer Xavier Claramunt rose to the occasion. **Pros:** near upbeat Born-Ribera scene; bicycle rentals for guests; remote lets you change color of lights in room. **Cons:** no room service or minibars; no children under 12; clothing storage limited, on open racks. [$] *Rooms from: €120* ✉ *Carrer Princesa 50, Born-Ribera* ☎ *93/295–4652* 🌐 *www.chicandbasic.com* 🛏 *31 rooms* 🍴 *No meals* [M] *L4 Jaume I.*

H10 Montcada Boutique Hotel

$$$ | **HOTEL** | A short walk from the attractions of the Gothic Quarter and the Born-Ribera district, the Montcada is one of the 50 properties in the sleek H10 chain and a good choice for comfort

and convenience. **Pros:** astounding rooftop deck with Jacuzzi; great location; pleasant breakfast room. **Cons:** wardrobes a tight fit by the bed; bed lighting could improve; no pets. [$] *Rooms from: €209* ✉ *Via Laietana 24, Born-Ribera* ☎ *93/268–8570* 🌐 *www.h10hotels.com* 🛏 *80 rooms* 🍴 *No meals* [M] *Jaume I.*

★ Hotel Yurbban Trafalgar

$$ | **HOTEL** | Guests and locals alike rave about the rooftop terrace at the Yurbban Trafalgar, and with good reason: the panoramic view is hands down one of the best in the city at this hip yet sophisticated hotel. **Pros:** free cheese and wine tasting nightly (8–9 pm); bicycles free for guests; minutes from Palau de la Música. **Cons:** small rooms; room service ends at 11 pm; small shower stalls. [$] *Rooms from: €160* ✉ *Carrer Trafalgar 30, Born-Ribera* ☎ *93/268–0727* 🌐 *yurbban.com/en* 🛏 *56 rooms* 🍴 *No meals* [M] *L1/L3 Urquinaona.*

Park Hotel Barcelona

$$$ | **HOTEL** | Well situated for exploring the Born-Ribera district, Barceloneta, and the port—and in a neighborhood blessed with wine and tapas bars—this mid-priced hotel has basic rooms with espresso-color wood floors and comfortable (if generic) furnishings. **Pros:** good location; decently sized pool on rooftop terrace; room service noon to midnight. **Cons:** rooms fairly small; no pool, gym, or spa; soundproofing between rooms could improve. [$] *Rooms from: €220* ✉ *Av. Marquès de l'Argentera 11, Born-Ribera* ☎ *93/319–6000* 🌐 *www.parkhotelbarcelona.com* 🛏 *91 rooms* 🍴 *No meals* [M] *L4 Barceloneta.*

★ The Wittmore

$$$$ | **HOTEL** | Opened in 2016, the Wittmore is the adults-only romantic hideaway par excellence, tucked away in a tiny cul-de-sac in the maze of streets just north of the marina, a short walk to the Plaça Colón. **Pros:** rooms include robes and slippers; cocktail bar with fireplace; plunge pool and bar on rooftop terrace. **Cons:** no spa or gym; budget-busting rates. [$] *Rooms from: €350* ✉ *Riudares 7, Born-Ribera* ☎ *93/550–0885* 🌐 *www.thewittmore.com* 🛏 *21 rooms* 🍴 *No meals* [M] *L3 Drassanes.*

🍸 Nightlife

La Ribera, considered one of Barcelona's most posh areas during medieval times, is still home to some of the city's loveliest ancient architecture. It exudes a tranquil yet distinctive vibe, the very same atmosphere found in the select number of bars, galleries, and eateries sprinkled between patches of greenery and arched stone passageways. El Born, the most voguish part of this district, provides a more eclectic collection of bars and lounge spots specializing in everything from craft beer to organic wines.

BARS

Ale&Hop

BARS/PUBS | Ale&Hop leads the pack in the latest craft-beer-bar invasion to hit the city. A slick microbrewery with exposed brick walls, monochrome wallpaper, and indie beats, Ale&Hop serves artisanal brews on tap or directly from the bottle. A slew of eco-wines and vegetarian snacks provide a health-conscious change of pace. ✉ *Basses de Sant Pere 10, Sant Pere* ☎ *93/126–9094* [M] *Arc de Triomf.*

Bar Brutal

WINE BARS—NIGHTLIFE | Whimsically fashionable with its red tabletops, arched ceiling, and lacquered bar counter, Bar Brutal (and its adjoining bodega Can Cisa) is revered for its dedication to sustainability. The bar's entire stock of wines (300 and counting) is organically produced and much of it served straight from the barrel, without a lick of artificial additives to spoil the natural flavors. Focusing primarily on regional wines, the savvy staff is always game to suggest new vintages or the perfect food pairing. ✉ *Barra de Ferro 1, Born-Ribera* ☎ *93/295–4797* 🌐 *www.cancisa.cat* [M] *Jaume I.*

La Vinya del Senyor

WINE BARS—NIGHTLIFE | Ambitiously named "The Lord's Vineyard," this romantic wine bar directly across from the entrance to the emblematic church of Santa Maria del Mar is etched into the ground floor of an ancient building. There's an extensive wine list and bite-size edibles, and ardent aficionados order by the bottle and favor tables found up a rickety ladder on the pint-size mezzanine or, when the weather cooperates, outside on the people-watching terrace. ⊠ *Pl. de Santa Maria 5, Born-Ribera* ☎ *93/310–3379* Ⓜ *Jaume I.*

Paspartu

BARS/PUBS | Dark and inviting with just a smidgen of whimsy (check out the pop art posters and wooden crate stools), Paspartu boasts 25 gin flavors and the unspoken invitation to settle in and try each one—what else could comfy pillows, nonintrusive music, and bite-size nibbles mean? And if gin is not your bag, don't fret: the chummy bar staff is always ready to suggest the perfect combo to enhance your favorite spirit. This is a perfect unwinding spot for the young of body and at heart. ⊠ *Basses de Sant Pere 12, Barcelona* ☎ *699-546-252* Ⓜ *Arc de Triomf.*

★ Rubí Bar

BARS/PUBS | The whimsical apothecary-like spirits cabinet, exposed-stone wall, and dramatic red lighting will be the first things to catch your eye at this cozy hidden gem, tucked away in the mazelike backstreets of El Born. However, it's the friendly service, relaxed atmosphere, and inventive selection of cocktails—most notably a choice of home-brewed flavored gins tantalizingly displayed on the bar shelves in hand-labeled bottles—that brings patrons back time and again. Add to the mix an eclectic playlist of funk, soul, rock, and pop classics, tasty snacks, and inexpensive mojitos that attract locals,

expats, and the curious, ages 25–50 and beyond. ⊠ *Banys Vells 6, Born-Ribera* ☎ *671/441888* Ⓜ *Jaume I.*

THEATER

La Puntual (*Putxinel·lis de Barcelona*)

THEATER | **FAMILY** | As one of the city's pioneering puppet (in Catalan, *putxinel·li*) theaters, this beloved venue features entertaining marionette, puppet, and shadow puppet performances. Private events for schools or birthday parties can be organized in Spanish, Catalan, and English. Weekend matinee performances are major kid magnets and tend to sell out fast, so arrive early or reserve a ticket in advance online. ⊠ *Allada Vermell 15, Born-Ribera* ☎ *639/305353* ⊕ *www.lapuntual.info* Ⓜ *Jaume I.*

🛍 Shopping

The Ribera and Born neighborhoods, the old waterfront district around the Santa Maria del Mar basilica, seem to breed boutiques and shops of all kinds continuously. Interior design and clothing shops are the main draw. Check along Carrer Argenteria and Plaça de Santa Maria before zipping up Carrer Banys Vells. Two streets north of Carrer Montcada, go to Carrer Rec for designer haute couture clothing, jewelry, and knickknacks of all kinds. Carrer Vidrieria is lined with shops all the way over to Plaça de les Olles, where hometown clothing designer Custo Barcelona owns the corner across from the wildly popular tapas bar Cal Pep. Around Santa Maria del Mar basilica, the aromatic Casa Gispert on Carrer Sombrerers is not to be missed, nor is Baraka, the Moroccan goods expert on Carrer Canvis Vells. Vila Viniteca up Carrer Agullers near Via Laietana is always an interesting Bacchic browse.

CERAMICS AND GLASSWARE

Baraka

CERAMICS/GLASSWARE | Barcelona's prime purveyor of Moroccan goods, ceramics chief among them, Baraka is the city's general cultural commissar for matters relating to Spain's neighbor to the south. The pre-haggled goods here are generally cheaper (and the quality better) than you could bring back from Morocco. Other African countries are represented, such as spectacular busts covered in tiny beads from Camaroon. ⊠ *Canvis Vells 2, Born-Ribera* ☎ *93/268–4220* ⊕ *www. barakaweb.com* Ⓜ *Jaume I.*

Helena Rohner

JEWELRY/ACCESSORIES | In a small shop on a backstreet in the Born, Helena Rohner is worth seeking out for its clean lines and minimal fuss—it's reminiscent of Georg Jensen, whom she worked for in the past. Simple silver ring, earring, and pendant settings hold semiprecious stones and enamel disks in on-trend colors, conceived for accessorizing this season's wardrobe. ⊠ *L' Espasseria 13, Born-Ribera* ☎ *93/319–8879* ⊕ *www. helenarohner.com* Ⓜ *Jaume I.*

CLOTHING

Anna Povo

CLOTHING | This stylish boutique near Plaça de les Olles displays an elegant and innovative selection of relaxed knits, coats, and dresses. In general, Anna Povo's designs are sleek and minimalist and unlike many Born boutiques, there are styles suitable for older women and larger figures. Colors follow this aesthetic, with cool tones in gray and beige. The shop also stocks colorful bags in African textiles made by a local women's collective. ⊠ *Vidrieria 11, Born-Ribera* ☎ *93/319–3561* ⊕ *www.annapovo.com* Ⓜ *Jaume I.*

Coquette

CLOTHING | Coquette specializes in understated feminine beauty. The now three shops (two in the Born, one uptown) present a small, careful selection of mainly French designers, like Souur, Des Petits Hauts, and Spain's own Hoss Intrópia. Whether it's a romantic or a seductive look you're after, Coquette makes sure you'll feel both comfortable and irresistible. With an industrial-chic decor, Coquette's boutique in Carrer Bonaire (which also has men's fashion) presents the largest selection. The uptown branch is at Carrer dels Madrazo 153 (Sant Gervasi). ⊠ *Bonaire 5, Born-Ribera* ☎ *93/310–3535* ⊕ *www. coquettebcn.com/en* Ⓜ *Jaume I.*

Custo Barcelona

CLOTHING | Ever since Custo Dalmau and his brother David returned from a round-the-world motorcycle tour with visions of California surfing styles dancing in their heads, Custo Barcelona has been a runaway success with its clingy cotton tops in bright and cheery hues. Now with three branches in Barcelona (including an outlet shop at Plaça del Pi 2, in the Barri Gòtic) and many more across the globe, Custo is scoring even more acclaim by expanding into coats, dresses, and kids' wear. ⊠ *Pl. de les Olles 7, Born-Ribera* ☎ *93/268–7893* ⊕ *www.custo.com* Ⓜ *Jaume I.*

Desigual

CLOTHING | Like Custo Barcelona, Desigual's wildly appliqued and printed T-shirts and dresses, coats, and bags scream a psychedelic Mediterranean flavor that's half 1960s Ibiza and half a Daliesque dreamscape. The company's growth over the past decade has been phenomenal, with shops everywhere from Montreal to Melbourne. In a savvy move, or perhaps anticipating T-shirt overload, the company has now launched a range of hippie-chic jeans. Other branches of Desigual can be found throughout the city. ⊠ *Argenteria 65, Born-Ribera* ☎ *93/310–6944* ⊕ *www. desigual.com* Ⓜ *Jaume I.*

El Ganso

CLOTHING | Who would have thought that two Madrid-born brothers could out-Brit the Brits? One of Spain's more recent fashion success stories, El Ganso makes very appealing preppy-inspired men's, women's, and children's wear—striped blazers, pleated skirts, and tailored suits made for upper-class frolics. The label's Born shop only stocks male clothing, while its store on Rambla Catalunya (Rambla Catalunya 116) caters to men and women. ✉ *Vidrieria 7, Born-Ribera* ☎ *932/689257* ⊕ *www.elganso.com* Ⓜ *Jaume I.*

La Comercial

CLOTHING | This mini-agglomeration of boutiques spreads out over three streets, together defining El Born's penchant for the achingly à la mode. Menswear can be found at Rec 73 and 75, with the latter entirely dedicated to the natty threads of U.K. designer Paul Smith. Women can choose from predominantly French designers such as Isabel Marant and Sonia Rykiel at Rec 52. Around the corner at Bonaire 4, La Comercial aims to dress your home with a beguiling selection of objects and gadgets. After your splurge, La Comercial's outlet store, located directly opposite, will take care of any leftover change. ✉ *Rec 52–75, Carrer Rec, Born-Ribera* ☎ *93/319–3463* ⊕ *www. lacomercial.info* Ⓜ *Jaume I.*

FOOD

★ Casa Gispert

FOOD/CANDY | On the inland side of Santa Maria del Mar, this shop is one of the most aromatic and picturesque in Barcelona, bursting with teas, coffees, spices, saffron, chocolates, and nuts. The star element in this olfactory and picturesque feast is an almond-roasting stove in the back of the store—purportedly the oldest in Europe, dating from 1851 like the store itself. Don't miss the acid engravings on the office windows or the ancient wooden back door before picking up a bag of freshly roasted nuts to take with you. ✉ *Sombrerers 23, Born-Ribera* ☎ *93/319–7535* ⊕ *www. casagispert.com* Ⓜ *Jaume I.*

Demasié

FOOD/CANDY | The shop's motto, "galetes Exageradament Bones" (biscuits that are exaggeratedly good) may seem like

a bit of hype, but these rich colorful cookies are exceptionally tasty. They are best enjoyed with a cup of coffee at the bar inside, or you can have them wrapped up in a pretty duck-egg-blue box to take home with you. There is a Demasié café at Roger de Llúria 8 in the Eixample. ✉ *Princesa 28, Born-Ribera* ☎ *93/269–1180* ⊕ *www.demasie.es* Ⓜ *Jaume I.*

El Magnífico

FOOD/CANDY | Just up the street from Santa Maria del Mar, this coffee emporium is famous for its sacks of coffee beans from all over the globe. Coffee to go is also available—enjoy it on the little bench outside. ✉ *Carrer Argenteria 64, Born-Ribera* ☎ *93/319–3975* ⊕ *www. cafeselmagnifico.com* Ⓜ *Jaume I.*

La Botifarreria de Santa Maria

FOOD/CANDY | This busy emporium next to the church of Santa Maria del Mar stocks excellent cheeses, hams, pâtés, and homemade *sobrassadas* (pork pâté with paprika). Botifarra is the main item here, with a wide range of varieties, including egg sausage for meatless Lent and sausage stuffed with spinach, asparagus, cider, cinnamon, and Cabrales cheese. ✉ *Santa Maria 4, Born-Ribera* ☎ *93/319–9123* ⊕ *www.labotifarreria. com* Ⓜ *Jaume I.*

Pastelería Hofmann

FOOD/CANDY | The late Mey Hofmann, a constellation in Barcelona's gourmet galaxy for the last three decades through her restaurant and cooking courses, established this sideline dedicated exclusively to pastry. Everything from the lightest, flakiest croissants to the cakes, tarts, and ice creams are about as good they get in this sweets emporium just off the Passeig del Born. ✉ *Flassaders 44, Born-Ribera* ☎ *93/268–8221* ⊕ *www.hofmann-bcn. com* Ⓜ *Jaume I.*

★ Vila Viniteca

WINE/SPIRITS | Near Santa Maria del Mar, this is perhaps the best wine treasury in Barcelona, with a truly massive catalogue, tastings, courses, and a panoply of events, including a hugely popular street party to welcome in new-harvest wines (usually late October or early November). Under the same ownership, the tiny grocery store next door offers exquisite artisanal cheeses ranging from French goat cheese to Extremadura's famous Torta del Casar. There are a few tables inside, and, for a corkage fee, you can enjoy a bottle of wine together with a tasting platter. ✉ *Agullers 7, Born-Ribera* ☎ *93/777–7017* ⊕ *www.vilaviniteca.es* Ⓜ *Jaume I.*

GIFTS AND SOUVENIRS

Natura

GIFTS/SOUVENIRS | A gracefully decorated store in the Natura chain, this crafts specialist stocks a good selection of global trifles, including pieces from India and North Africa. Incense, clothing, tapestries, candles, shoes, gadgets, and surprises of all kinds appear in this cross-cultural craft shop. ✉ *Argenteria 78, Born-Ribera* ☎ *93/268–2525* ⊕ *www.naturaselection.com* Ⓜ *Jaume I.*

HOUSEHOLD ITEMS AND FURNITURE

Vitra

HOUSEHOLD ITEMS/FURNITURE | This dazzling two-story glass-front showroom specializes in chairs and displays all you would expect from the referential Swiss design company—swoon-worthy Eames loungers, bright Panton chairs, and many more iconic pieces from the past 50 years of mod design. ✉ *Pl. Comercial 5, Born-Ribera* ☎ *93/268–7219* ⊕ *www.vitra.com* Ⓜ *Jaume I.*

Chapter 7

LA CIUTADELLA, BARCELONETA, PORT OLÍMPIC, AND POBLENOU

7

Updated by
Elizabeth Prosser and
Steve Tallantyre

Sights	Restaurants	Hotels	Shopping	Nightlife
★★★★★	★★★★★	★★★☆☆	☆☆☆☆☆	★★★☆☆

NEIGHBORHOOD SNAPSHOT

TOP EXPERIENCES

■ **Estació de França:** Walk through this grand and elegant station, one of the most beautiful of its kind, to summon images of the bygone romance of European travel.

■ **Museu d'Història de Catalunya:** After interacting with Catalan history at this state-of-the-art museum, head to the rooftop restaurant for harbor views.

■ **Sant Miquel del Port church:** Note the controversial sculpture of Sant Miquel who is depicted as a bodybuilder as well as the facade sculptures of Sant Elm and Santa Maria de Cervelló, considered protectors of the Catalan fishing fleet.

■ **Ciutadella Park:** Join a Sunday drum fest, bring a picnic, row boats in the lake, admire the sculptures, and visit the Cascada waterfall at Barcelona's Central Park.

■ **Beachfront drinks:** Take a beachfront stroll to the luxe W Barcelona and drink in the sensational views at the Eclipse Bar on the 26th floor.

GETTING HERE

The Barceloneta stop on the metro's yellow line (L4) is the closest subway stop; there's lots to see on a walk to the beach through the Barri Gòtic from Plaça de Catalunya, but it could leave you a little footsore. For La Ciutadella, the Arc de Triomf stop on the red line (L1) is closest.

PLANNING YOUR TIME

Exploring Ciutadella Park and Barceloneta can take from three to four hours. Add at least another hour if you're stopping for lunch. Try to time your arrival in Barceloneta so you catch the local market in full swing at midday (until 3) and work your way through the neighborhood to a beachside table for paella. Can Manel la Puda serves paella until 4 pm.

QUICK BITES

■ **El Vaso de Oro.** Friendly El Vaso de Oro is a famous tapas specialist, always full of grazers, local and otherwise. Don't miss the foie gras—or the restaurant's own microbrewery beer. ⊠ *Carrer de Balboa 6, Barceloneta* ⊕ *www.vasode-oro.com* Ⓜ *Barceloneta*

■ **La Bombeta.** Excellent tapas, friendly service, a good location, and good sangria. ⊠ *Carrer de la Maquinista, Barceloneta* Ⓜ *Barceloneta*

Now Barcelona's central downtown park, La Ciutadella was originally the site of a fortress built by the conquering troops of the Bourbon monarch Felipe V after the fall of Barcelona in the 1700–1714 War of the Spanish Succession.

Barceloneta has always been a little gritty: the people who live here hang their washing out over the narrow streets; they will cheerfully direct you to the nearest tattoo parlor, or the eclectic bar around the corner that serves a great paella; they rent their flats to the rowdiest of low-budget visitors; they thumb their noses a bit at the fancy yachts in the marina across the Passeig Joan de Borbó—but like the folks in the Born, they are not immune to the recent siren song of gentrification.

Barceloneta and La Ciutadella fit together historically. In the early 18th century, some 1,000 houses in the Barrio de la Ribera, then the waterfront neighborhood around Plaça del Born, were ordered torn down, to create fields of fire for the cannon of La Ciutadella, the newly built fortress that kept watch over the rebellious Catalans. Barceloneta, then a marshy wetland, was filled in and developed almost four decades later, in 1753, to house the families who had lost homes in La Ribera.

Open water in Roman times, and gradually silted in only after the 15th-century construction of the port, it became Barcelona's fishermen's and stevedores' quarter. Originally composed of 15 longitudinal and three cross streets and 329 two-story houses, this was Europe's earliest planned urban development, built by the military engineer Juan Martin Cermeño under the command of El Marquès de la Mina, Juan Miguel de

Guzmán Dávalos Spinola (1690–1767). Barceloneta was always sort of a safety valve, a little fishing village next door where locals could go to escape the formalities and constraints of city life, for a Sunday seafood lunch on the beach and a stroll through what felt like a freer world. With its tiny original apartment blocks, and its history of seafarers and gypsies, Barceloneta even now maintains its spontaneous, carefree flavor.

◉ Sights

Arc del Triomf

MEMORIAL | This exposed-redbrick arch was built by Josep Vilaseca as the grand entrance for the 1888 Universal Exhibition. Similar in size and sense to the traditional triumphal arches of ancient Rome, this one refers to no specific military triumph anyone can recall. In fact, Catalonia's last military triumph of note may have been Jaume I el Conqueridor's 1229 conquest of the Moors in Mallorca—as suggested by the bats (always part of Jaume I's coat of arms) on either side of the arch itself. The Josep Reynés sculptures adorning the structure represent Barcelona hosting visitors to the exhibition on the western side (front), while the Josep Llimona sculptures on the eastern side depict the prizes being given to its outstanding contributors. ⊠ *Passeig de Sant Joan, La Ciutadella* Ⓜ *L1 Arc de Triomf.*

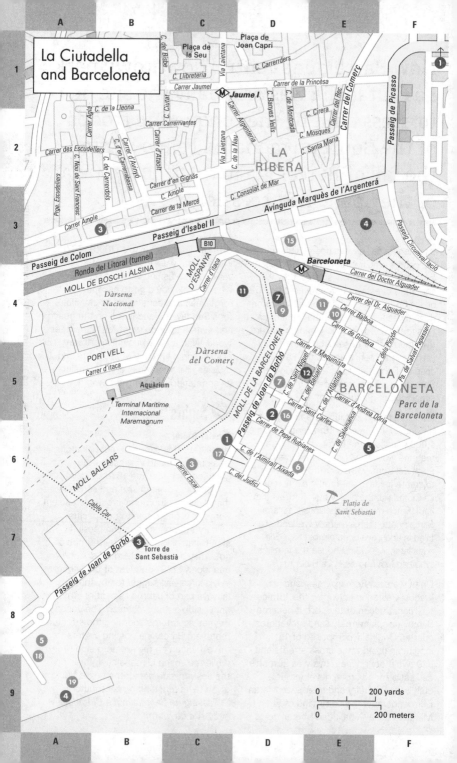

La Ciutadella and Barceloneta

A B C D E F

1

Plaça de Joan Capri
Plaça de la Seu
C. del Bisbe
C. Llibreteria
C. de les Carrerders
Carrer Jaumel
Via Laietana
Carrer de la Princesa
Carrer del Comerç
Passeig de Picasso
M Jaume I
C. d'Agià
C. de la Lleona
Carrer Aglà
Carrer Carrervantes
Carrer Argenteria
C. de Banys Vells
C. de Montcada
C. Cirera
Carrer del Rec

2

Carrer des Escudellers
C. Nou de Sant Francesc
C. de Carrerdols
Carrer d'Avinyó
Carrer d'en Carrerbassa
Carrer d'Arault
Carrer d'en Gignàs
Via Laietana
C. de la Nau
LA RIBERA
C. Mosques
C. Santa Maria
Ptge. Escudellers
C. Ample
C. de la Mercé
C. Consolat de Mar

3

Carrer Ample
Passeig d'Isabel II
B10
Avinguda Marquès de l'Argenterá
4
15
Passeig Circumval·lació

Passeig de Colom
Ronda del Litoral (tunnel)
Barceloneta
M
Carrer del Doctor Aiguader
MOLL DE BOSCH i ALSINA
MOLL D'ESPANYA

4

Dàrsena Nacional
Carrer d'itaca
11
7
9
Carrer del Dr. Aiguader
11
Carrer Balboa
10
Carrer de Ginebra
C. de la Pinzón
Pa de Salvat Papasseit

PORT VELL
Dàrsena del Comerç
Carrer la Maquinista

5

Carrer d'itaca
MOLL DE LA BARCELONETA
Passeig de Joan de Borbó
C. de Sant Niguel
7
12
C. del Baluard
C. de l'Atlàntida
Carrer d'Andrea Dòria
LA BARCELONETA
Aquàrium
2 **16**
Carrer Sant Carles
Parc de la Barceloneta
Terminal Maritime
Internacional
Maremagnum
Carrer de Pepe Rubianes
C. de Salamanca
5

6

1
17
C. de l'Almirall Aixada
6
MOLL BALEARS
Carrer Escar
3
C. del Judici

7

Cable Car
Passeig de Joan de Borbó
3 Torre de Sant Sebastià
Platja de Sant Sebastia

8

5
18

9

19
4

0 ___ 200 yards
0 ___ 200 meters

A B C D E F

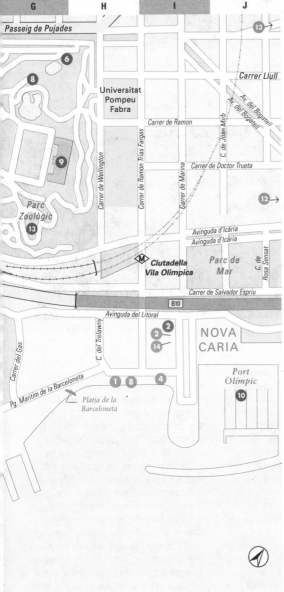

Passeig de Pujades

Carrer Llull

Universitat
Pompeu
Fabra

Carrer de Ramon

Av. del Bogatell
Av. del Bogatell

C. de Joan-Miró

Carrer de Doctor Trueta

Carrer de Ramon Trías Fargas

Carrer de Marina

Carrer de Wellington

Parc
Zoològic

Avinguda d'Icària
Avinguda d'Icària

C. de Rosa Sensat

Ⓜ Ciutadella
Vila Olímpica

Parc de
Mar

Carrer de Salvador Espriu

B10

Avinguda del Litoral

Carrer del Gas

C. del Trelawny

NOVA
CARIA

Pg. Marítim de la Barceloneta

Platja de la
Barceloneta

Port
Olímpic

7

La Ciutadella, Barceloneta, Port Olímpic, and Poblenou

KEY

1 Exploring Sights
1 Restaurants
1 Hotels
Ⓜ Metro Stops

G   H   I   J

Formerly an obsolete harbor, Port Vell is a modern yacht-basin and lively entertainment center.

Carrer Sant Carles No. 6

HOUSE | The last Barceloneta house left standing in its original 1755 two-story entirety, this low, boxlike structure was planned as a single-family dwelling with shop and storage space on the ground floor and the living space above. Overcrowding soon produced split houses and even quartered houses, with workers and their families living in tiny spaces. After nearly a century of living under Madrid-based military jurisdiction, Barceloneta homeowners were given permission to expand vertically, and houses of as many as five stories began to tower over the lowly original dwellings. The house is not open to the public. ⊠ *Carrer Sant Carles 6, Barceloneta* Ⓜ *Barceloneta.*

El Transbordador Aeri del Port

(*port cable car*)

TRANSPORTATION SITE (AIRPORT/BUS/FERRY/ TRAIN) | This hair-raising cable-car ride over the Barcelona harbor from Barceloneta to Montjuïc (with a midway stop in the port) is an adrenaline rush with a view.

The rush comes from being packed in with 18 other people (standing-room only) in a tiny gondola swaying a hundred feet or so above the Mediterranean. The cable car leaves from the tower at the end of Passeig Joan de Borbó and connects the Torre de San Sebastián on the Moll de Barceloneta, the tower of Jaume I in the port boat terminal, and the Torre de Miramar on Montjuïc. Critics maintain, not without reason, that the ride is expensive, the maintenance is so-so, and the queues can seem interminable. On the positive side, this is undoubtedly the slickest way to connect Barceloneta and Montjuïc. The Torre de Altamar restaurant in the tower at the Barceloneta end serves excellent food and wine. ⊠ *Passeig Joan de Borbó 88, Barceloneta* ☎ *93/441–4820* ⊕ *www. telefericodebarcelona.com* 🛩 *From €11* Ⓜ *L4 Barceloneta.*

Estació de França

TRANSPORTATION SITE (AIRPORT/BUS/FERRY/ TRAIN) | Barcelona's main railroad station until about 1980, and still in use, the elegant Estació de França is outside the west gate of the Ciutadella. Rebuilt in 1929 for the International Exhibition and restored in 1992 for the Olympics, this mid-19th-century building sits on Estació de Sants, the city's main intercity and international terminus. The marble and bronze, the Moderniste decorative details, and the delicate tracery of its wrought-iron roof girders make this one of the most beautiful buildings of its kind. Stop in for a sense of the bygone romance of European travel. ⊠ *Av. Marquès de l'Argentera s/n, La Ciutadella* ☎ *902/320230 RENFE office, 902/240505 ticket sales and reservations* Ⓜ *L4 Barceloneta.*

Fuente de Carmen Amaya (*Carmen Amaya Fountain*)

FOUNTAIN | Down at the eastern end of Carrer Sant Carles, where Barceloneta joins the beach, is the monument to the famous Gypsy flamenco dancer Carmen Amaya (1913–63). Amaya was born in the Gypsy settlement known as Somorrostro, part of Barceloneta until 1920 when development sent the Gypsies farther east to what is now the Fòrum grounds (from which they were again displaced in 2003). Amaya achieved universal fame in 1929 at the age of 16, when she performed at Barcelona's International Exposition. Amaya made triumphal tours of the Americas and starred in films such as *La hija de Juan Simón* (1934) and *Los Tarantos* (1962). The fountain, and its high-relief representations of cherubic children as flamenco performers (two guitarists, three dancers—in the nude, unlike real flamenco dancers), has been poorly maintained since it was placed here in 1959, but it remains an important reminder of Barceloneta's roots as a rough-and-tumble romantic enclave of free-living sailors, stevedores, Gypsies, and fishermen. This Gypsy ambience all but disappeared when the last of the *chiringuitos* (ramshackle beach restaurants specializing in fish and rice dishes)

fell to the wreckers' ball shortly after the 1992 Olympics. ⊠ *Carrer Sant Carles s/n, Barceloneta* Ⓜ *L4 Barceloneta.*

La Cascada

FOUNTAIN | The sights and sounds of Barcelona seem far away when you stand near this monumental creation by Josep Fontseré, presented as part of the 1888 Universal Exhibition. The waterfall's somewhat overwrought arrangement of rocks was the work of a young architecture student named Antoni Gaudí—his first public work, appropriately natural and organic, and certainly a hint of things to come. ⊠ *Parc de la Ciutadella, La Ciutadella* Ⓜ *L1 Arc de Triomf.*

Museu d'Història de Catalunya

MUSEUM | Established in what used to be a port warehouse, this state-of-the-art interactive museum makes you part of Catalonian history, from prehistoric times to the contemporary democratic era. After centuries of "official" Catalan history dictated from Madrid (from 1714 until the mid-19th century Renaixença, and from 1939 to 1975), this offers an opportunity to revisit Catalonia's autobiography. Explanations of the exhibits appear in Catalan, Castilian, and English. Guided tours are available Sunday at noon and 1 pm. The rooftop restaurant has excellent views over the harbor and is open to the public (whether or not you visit the museum itself) during museum hours. ⊠ *Pl. de Pau Vila 3, Barceloneta* ☎ *93/225–4700* ⊕ *www.en.mhcat.net* 🎫 *€5* 🕑 *Closed Mon.* Ⓜ *L4 Barceloneta.*

Parc de la Ciutadella (*Citadel Park*)

CITY PARK | **FAMILY** | Once a fortress designed to consolidate Madrid's military occupation of Barcelona, the Ciutadella is now the city's main downtown park. The clearing dates from shortly after the War of the Spanish Succession in the early 18th century, when Felipe V demolished some 1,000 houses in what was then the Barri de la Ribera to build a fortress and barracks for his soldiers and a *glacis* (open space) between rebellious

Barcelona and his artillery positions. The fortress walls were pulled down in 1868 and replaced by gardens laid out by Josep Fontseré. In 1888 the park was the site of the Universal Exposition that put Barcelona on the map as a truly European city; today it is home to the Castell dels Tres Dragons, built by architect Lluís Domènech i Montaner as the café and restaurant for the exposition (the only building to survive that project, now a botanical research center), the Catalan parliament, and the city zoo. ⊠ *Passeig de Picasso 21, La Ciutadella* Ⓜ *L4 Barceloneta, Ciutadella–Vila Olímpica, L1 Arc de Triomf.*

Parlament de Catalunya

BUILDING | Once the arsenal for the Ciutadella—as evidenced by the thickness of the building's walls—this is the only surviving remnant of Felipe V's fortress. For a time it housed the city's museum of modern art, before it was repurposed to house the unicameral Catalan Parliament. Under Franco, the Generalitat—the regional government—was suppressed, and the Hall of Deputies was shut fast for 37 years. Call or go online (⊕ *eed-ucativa@parlament.cat*) to book and schedule a free 45-minute guided tour of the building; the website makes it a bit complicated to register for a booking, but the grand "Salon Rose" is worth a visit in itself. ⊠ *Pl. de Joan Fiveller, Parc de la Ciutadella s/n, La Ciutadella* ☎ *93/304-6500, 93/304-6645 guided visits* ⊕ *www.parlament.cat/document/cataleg/48179.pdf* ▱ *Free* Ⓜ *L4 Ciutadella/Vila Olimpica.*

Port Olímpic

BEACH—SIGHT | Filled with yachts, restaurants, tapas bars, and mega-restaurants serving reasonably decent fare continuously from 1 pm to 1 am, the Olympic Port is 2 km (1 mile) up the beach from Barceloneta, marked by the mammoth shimmering goldfish sculpture in its net of girders by starchitect Frank Gehry. In the shadow of Barcelona's first real skyscraper, the Hotel Arts, the Olympic Port draws thousands of young people of all nationalities on Friday and Saturday nights, especially in summer, to the beach at Nova Icària, generating a buzz redolent of spring break in Cancún. ⊠ *Port Olímpic, Port Olímpic* Ⓜ *L4 Ciutadella/Vila Olímpica.*

Port Vell (*Old Port*)

MARINA | From Pla del Palau, cross to the edge of the port, where the Moll d'Espanya, the Moll de la Fusta, and the Moll de Barceloneta meet. (*Moll* means docks.) Just beyond the colorful Roy Lichtenstein sculpture in front of the post office, the modern Port Vell complex—an IMAX theater, aquarium, and Maremagnum shopping mall—stretches seaward to the right on the Moll d'Espanya. The Palau de Mar, with rows of somewhat pricey, tourist-oriented quayside terrace restaurants (try La Gavina, the Merendero de la Mari, or El Magatzem), stretches down along the Moll de Barceloneta to the left. Key points in the Maremagnum complex are the grassy hillside (popular on April 23, Sant Jordi's Day) and the *Ictineo II*, a replica of the world's first submarine created by Narcis Monturiol (1819–85), launched in the Barcelona port in 1862. ⊠ *Port Vell, Barceloneta* Ⓜ *L4 Barceloneta.*

Sant Miquel del Port

RELIGIOUS SITE | Have a close look at this baroque church with its modern (1992), pseudo-bodybuilder version of the winged archangel Michael himself, complete with sword and chain, in the alcove on the facade. (The figure is a replica; the original was destroyed in 1936.) One of the first buildings to be completed in Barceloneta, Sant Miquel del Port was begun in 1753 and finished by 1755 under the direction of architect Damià Ribes. Due to strict orders to keep Barceloneta low enough to fire La Ciutadella's cannon over, Sant Miquel del Port had no bell tower and only a small cupola until Elies Rogent added a new one in 1853. Interesting to note are the metopes:

palm-sized gilt bas-relief sculptures around the interior cornice and repeated outside at the top of the facade. These 74 Latin-inscribed allegories each allude to different attributes of St. Michael. For example, the image of a boat and the Latin inscription "iam in tuto" (finally safe), alludes to the saint's protection against the perils of the sea. To the right of Sant Miquel del Port at No. 41 Carrer de Sant Miquel is a house decorated by seven strips of floral sgraffiti and a plaque commemorating Fernando de Lesseps, the engineer who built the Suez Canal, who lived in the house while serving as French consul to Barcelona. In the square by the church, take a close look at the fountain, with its Barcelona coat of arms, and Can Ganassa, on the east side, a worthy tapas bar. ☒ *Carrer de Sant Miquel 39, Barceloneta* ☎ *93/221–6550* Ⓜ *L4 Barceloneta.*

Zoo

ZOO | FAMILY | Barcelona's zoo occupies the whole eastern end of the Parc de la Ciutadella. There's a superb reptile house and a full assortment of African animals. ☒ *Parc de la Ciutadella s/n, La Ciutadella* ☎ *93/706–5656* ⊕ *www.zoobarcelona. cat/en* ☒ *€22* Ⓜ *L4 Ciutadella–Vila Olímpica, Barceloneta; L1 Arc de Triomf.*

🔁 Beaches

Barcelona's *platges* (beaches) have improved and multiplied in number from Barceloneta north to the Fòrum site at the northeastern end of Diagonal. At Barceloneta's southwestern end is the Platja de Sant Sebastià, followed northward by the Platges de Sant Miquel, Barceloneta, Passeig Marítim, Port Olímpic, Nova Icària, Bogatell, Mar Bella, and La Nova Mar Bella (the last football-field length of which is a nudist enclave), and Llevant. The Barceloneta beach is the most popular stretch, easily accessible by several bus lines, notably the No. V15 bus (which runs all the way from Tibidàdo at the top of the city) and by the L4 metro stop at

Barceloneta, at Ciutadella–Vila Olímpica or Bogatell for Nova Icària and Bogatell beaches, and Poble Nou for the northernmost beaches such as Mar Bella. The best surfing stretch is at the northeastern end of the Barceloneta beach, and the boardwalk itself offers miles of runway for walkers, skaters, bicyclers, and joggers. Topless bathing is the norm on all beaches in and around Barcelona. There are public toilet facilities, but people often stop into a nearby bar to use the facilities. There are free showers at the edge of the beach.

Running north of Barceloneta, the first beaches are Badalona, Montgat, Ocata, Vilasar de Mar, Arenys de Mar, Canet de Mar, and Sant Pol de Mar, all accessible by train from the RENFE station in Plaça de Catalunya. Sant Pol is a good pick, with clean sand, a lovely old town, and the rustic fish restaurant Banys Lluis, which serves a flavorful paella overlooking perfect sea views. Another beach with a top-notch gastronomical opportunity is Arenys de Mar, with the famous Hispania restaurant a minute's walk from the beach across the NII road. Canet de Mar's beach extends for 10 km (6 miles), and offers rental options for surfboards or windsurfers, as well as beach restaurants such as La Roca (in summer) or El Parador (all year). The farther north you go, toward the Costa Brava, the more pristine the beaches tend to be, though this rocky coast specializes in tiny *calas* (coves or inlets) rather than lengthy strands.

Platja de la Barceloneta

BEACHES | Just to the left at the end of Passeig Joan de Borbó, this is the easiest Barcelona beach to get to, hence the most crowded and the most fun for people-watching—though itinerant beach vendors can be a nuisance. Along with swimming, there are windsurfing and kitesurfing rentals to be found just up behind the beach at the edge of La Barceloneta. Rebecca Horn's sculpture L'Estel

Ferit, a rusting stack of cubes, expresses nostalgia for the beach-shack restaurants that lined the beach here until 1992. Surfers trying to catch a wave wait just off the breakwater in front of the excellent beachfront Agua restaurant. **Amenities:** food and drink; lifeguards; showers; toilets; water sports. **Best for:** partiers; surfing; swimming; walking; windsurfing. ⊠ *Passeig Marítim de la Barceloneta s/n, Barceloneta* Ⓜ *Ciutadella/Vila Olímpica.*

Platja de la Mar Bella

BEACHES | Closest to the Poblenou metro stop near the eastern end of the beaches, this is a thriving gay enclave and the unofficial nudist beach of Barcelona (although clothed bathers are welcome, too). The water-sports center Base Nàutica de la Mar Bella rents equipment for sailing, surfing, and windsurfing. Outfitted with showers, safe drinking fountains, and a children's play area, La Mar Bella also has lifeguards who warn against swimming near the breakwater. The excellent Els Pescadors restaurant is just inland on Plaça Prim. **Amenities:** food and drink; lifeguards; showers; toilets; water sports. **Best for:** partiers; nudists; swimming; windsurfing. ⊠ *Passeig Marítim del Bogatell, Poblenou* Ⓜ *Poblenou.*

Platja de la Nova Icària

BEACHES | One of Barcelona's most popular beaches, this strand is just east of Port Olímpic, with a full range of entertainment and refreshment venues close at hand. (Xiringuito Escribà is one of the most popular restaurants overlooking neighboring Bogatell beach.) The wide beach is directly across from the neighborhood built as the residential Olympic Village for Barcelona's 1992 Olympic Games, an interesting housing project that has now become a popular residential neighborhood. Vendors prowl the sand, offering everything from sunglasses to cold drinks to massages. **Amenities:** food and drink; lifeguards; showers; toilets; water sports. **Best for:** partiers; swimming; walking; windsurfing. ⊠ *Passeig Marítim del Port Olímpic s/n, Port Olímpic* Ⓜ *Ciutadella/Vila Olímpic.*

Platja de Sant Sebastià

BEACHES | Barceloneta's most southwestern platjas (to the right at the end of Passeig Joan de Borbó), Sant Sebastià is the oldest and most historic of the city beaches; it was here that 19th-century barcelonins cavorted in bloomers and bathing costumes. Neglected (and a bit disreputable) during the Franco years, it's had a rebirth of popularity since the pre-Olympic redesign of the city's waterfront. Between the beach and the Torre Sant Sebastia cable car terminus is the Club Natació Atlètic de Barcelona; the Hotel W Barcelona is at the far south end. **Amenities:** food and drink; lifeguards; showers; toilets. **Best for:** partiers; swimming. ⊠ *Passeig Maritim de la Barceloneta s/n, Barceloneta* Ⓜ *L4, Barceloneta.*

🍴 Restaurants

Barceloneta and the Port Olímpic (Olympic Port) have little in common beyond their seaside location. Port Olímpic offers a somewhat massive-scaled and modern environment with a crazed disco strip, while Barceloneta has retained its traditional character as a blue-collar neighborhood, even if few fishermen live here now. Traditional family restaurants and tourist traps can look similar from the street; a telltale sign of unreliable establishments is the presence of hard-selling waiters outside, aggressively courting passing customers.

East of the Eixample and extending to the sea just beyond Port Olímpic, Poblenou's formerly rough-around-the-edges neighborhood with a historical heart has lately seen an influx of edgy art studios, design shops, and even a few hip restaurants—many of these spaces are installed in converted warehouses and industrial concerns.

Agua

$$ | **MEDITERRANEAN** | Hit Agua's terrace on warm summer nights and sunny winter days, or just catch rays inside the immense windows. Either way you'll have a prime spot for beachside people-watching. **Known for:** fresh seafood; must reserve in advance; popular tourist spot. [$] *Average main: €19* ✉ *Passeig Marítim de la Barceloneta 30, Port Olímpic* ☎ *93/225–1272* 🌐 *www.grupotragaluz.com* [M] *Ciutadella–Vila Olímpica.*

Arola

$$$ | **TAPAS** | Top-class tapas on a terrace are surprisingly hard to find, which is why sophisticated snack-seekers head for the eponymous restaurant of Michelin-starred chef Sergi Arola in the Hotel Arts. DJs provide a chilled-out evening atmosphere where diners can sip cocktails and enjoy views of Frank Gehry's Mediterranean-facing *Fish* statue. **Known for:** signature patatas bravas; novel presentation of dishes; superior quality. [$] *Average main: €28* ✉ *Marina 19–21, Port Olímpic* ✥ *Entrance is via lift near street-level entrance to Hotel Arts* ☎ *93/483–8090* 🌐 *www.hotelarts-barcelona.com* ⏲ *Closed Tues. and Wed.* [M] *Ciutadella/Vila Olimpica.*

Barceloneta

$$$ | **SEAFOOD** | This restaurant in an enormous riverboat-like building at the end of the yacht marina in Barceloneta is definitely geared up for high-volume business. The food—paellas and grilled fish dishes are the specialties—is delicious, the service impeccable, and the hundreds of fellow diners make the place feel like a cheerful New Year's Eve celebration. **Known for:** lively waterside spot; excellent salads, rice, and fish dishes; free valet parking. [$] *Average main: €25* ✉ *Escar 22, Barceloneta* ☎ *93/221–2111* 🌐 *www.restaurantbarceloneta.com* [M] *Barceloneta.*

Bestial

$$ | **MEDITERRANEAN** | Sea views from a multilevel terrace are Bestial's most obvious attraction, but its luxury location beneath Frank Gehry's *Fish* statue is in no way diminished by the food. On the menu, spicy clams and seasonal soups lead up to a star dish of roasted wild fish on a bed of waxy potatoes. **Known for:** beachfront terrace; fresh seafood; pre-club crowd. [$] *Average main: €20* ✉ *Ramon Trias Fargas 2–4, Port Olímpic* ☎ *93/224–0407* 🌐 *www.grupotragaluz.com* ⏲ *No dinner Sun.–Wed.* [M] *Ciutadella-Vila Olimpica.*

★ **Blue Spot**

$$ | **MEDITERRANEAN** | An architect-designed dining room with jaw-dropping views (up and down the coast, in this case) is all too often a predictor of humdrum cooking, at least in Barcelona. Blue Spot—on the eighth floor of a building at the southernmost tip of Barceloneta's beach—breaks this mold with some assured and original Mediterranean-inspired dishes. **Known for:** stunning views; charcoal-grilled food; fashionable crowd. [$] *Average main: €21* ✉ *Edifici Ocean, Passeig Joan de Borbó 101, Barceloneta* ☎ *93/144–7866* 🌐 *www.encompaniadelobos.com* [M] *Barceloneta.*

Can Majó

$$$ | **SEAFOOD** | **FAMILY** | One of Barcelona's best-known seafood restaurants sits by the beach in Barceloneta and specializes in such house favorites as *caldero de bogavante* (a cross between paella and lobster bouillabaisse) and *suquet* (fish stewed in its own juices), but the full range of typical Spanish rice and seafood dishes are also available. Can Majó doesn't consistently reach the standards that once made it famous, but the cooking is still a notch above most of the touristy haunts nearby. **Known for:** terrace overlooking the Mediterranean; Spanish rice and fish dishes; excellent paella. [$] *Average main: €25* ✉ *Almirall Aixada*

23, Barceloneta ☎ *93/221–5455* 🌐 *www.canmajo.es* ⏲ *Closed Mon. No dinner Sun.* [M] *Barceloneta.*

★ Can Solé

$$$ | **SEAFOOD** | With no sea views or touts outside to draw in diners, Can Solé has to rely on its reputation as one of Barceloneta's best options for seafood for more than 100 years. Faded photos of half-forgotten local celebrities line its walls, but there's nothing out-of-date about the food. **Known for:** open kitchen; fresh fish daily; traditional Spanish rice dishes. [$] *Average main: €27* ✉ *Sant Carles 4, Barceloneta* ☎ *93/221–5012* 🌐 *restaurantcansole.com* ⏲ *Closed Mon. and 2 wks in Aug. No dinner Sun.* [M] *Barceloneta.*

CDLC

$$$ | **ECLECTIC** | Carpe Diem Lounge Club is a combination restaurant, chill crash pad, and nightclub, with spectacular views over the beach and a continuously open kitchen from 1 pm until 1 am every day of the year. The cuisine is a hit-and-miss jumble of Asian fusion, with everything from sushi to Kobe beef from Japan to fiery Indian curry. **Known for:** lively atmosphere; Asian fusion cuisine. [$] *Average main: €27* ✉ *Passeig Marítim 32, Barceloneta* ☎ *93/224–0470* 🌐 *www.cdlcbarcelona.com* [M] *Ciutadella-Port Olímpic.*

1881 Per Sagardi

$$ | **BASQUE** | Views of yachts sailing out into the glittering Mediterranean sea and the aroma of a wood-fired grill that turns out classic Basque cuisine are a compelling combination here. The Sagardi group's most stylish establishment is perched atop a handsomely renovated former warehouse, which now houses the Catalan History Museum. **Known for:** pleasant terrace; all-day kitchen; sea views. [$] *Average main: €22* ✉ *Pl. de Pau Vila 3, Barceloneta* ☎ *93/221–0050* 🌐 *www.gruposagardi.com* [M] *Barceloneta.*

El Nou Ramonet

$$ | **CATALAN** | **FAMILY** | This spin-off restaurant has finally stepped out of Can Ramonet's shadow thanks to the input of Manairó's chef Jordi Herrera. He's built on the Barceloneta blueprint of classic tapas and added his signature creativity to dishes such as fresh sardines blowtorched tableside and garlicky salt-cod fritters, served in a jaunty, nautical environment. **Known for:** good value set lunch; creative twists on traditional tapas and seafood; good stop on the way from the beach. [$] *Average main: €19* ✉ *Carbonell 5, Barceloneta* ☎ *93/268–3313* 🌐 *www.grupramonet.com* [M] *Barceloneta.*

★ El Vaso de Oro

$ | **TAPAS** | A favorite with gourmands, this often overcrowded little counter serves some of the best beer and tapas in town. The house-brewed artisanal draft beer—named after the Fort family who own and run the bar—is drawn and served with loving care by veteran epauletted waiters who have it down to a fine art. **Known for:** old-school service; stand-up dining; beef fillet is a favorite. [$] *Average main: €15* ✉ *Balboa 6, Barceloneta* ☎ *93/319–3098* 🌐 *www.vasodeoro.com* ⏲ *Closed 1st 3 wks of Sept.* [M] *Barceloneta.*

Els Pescadors

$$$ | **SEAFOOD** | **FAMILY** | Northeast of the Port Olímpic, in the newly fashionable Poblenou neighborhood, this handsome late-19th-century dining room has a lovely terrace on a little square shaded by immense ombú trees. Kids can play safely in the traffic-free square while their parents feast on well-prepared seafood specialties such as paella, fresh fish, *fideuà* (a paella-like noodle dish), and the succulent suquet. **Known for:** village-square atmosphere; standard-setting rice and fish dishes; pretty terrace. [$] *Average main: €27* ✉ *Pl. de Prim 1, Port Olímpic* ☎ *93/225–2018* 🌐 *www.elspescadors.com* [M] *Poblenou.*

Els Tres Porquets

$$ | TAPAS | Somewhat off the beaten path (though just a 15-minute stroll from the Auditori and the Teatre Nacional de Catalunya), Els Tres Porquets (The Three Little Pigs) packs in foodies and bon vivants with a wide range of tapas and small dishes. The interesting wine list includes lesser-known but noteworthy selections from Spain and around the world. **Known for:** Iberian specialties; delicious cheeses; interesting wine list. $ *Average main: €18* ⊠ *Rambla del Poblenou 165, Poblenou* ☎ *93/300–8750* ⊕ *www.elstresporquets.es* ⊙ *Closed Sun. and 2 wks in Aug.* Ⓜ *Glòries, Clot.*

Enoteca

$$$$ | CATALAN | Located in the Hotel Arts, Enoteca is the Barcelona outlet for the talents of five—Michelin star chef Paco Pérez, two of which he has earned here. His creative and technically accomplished cooking uses peerless Mediterranean and Pyrenean products, transforming them into astonishing dishes that are both surprising and satisfying. **Known for:** superstar chef; extensive wine list; two Michelin stars. $ *Average main: €40* ⊠ *Hotel Arts, Marina 19, Port Olímpic* ☎ *93/483–8108* ⊕ *enotecapacoperez.com/en* ⊙ *Closed Sun., Mon., 2 wks in Mar., and 2 wks at Christmas. No dinner Tues.–Fri.* Ⓜ *Ciutadella–Vila Olímpica.*

Green Spot

$$ | VEGETARIAN | To call somewhere one of Barcelona's best vegan and vegetarian restaurants can be to damn it with faint praise—this is very much a city of omnivores. But Green Spot's pale oak paneling elegantly frames an open kitchen and airy dining room serving fun, fresh fusion food that everyone will like. **Known for:** delicious black pizza with activated charcoal; craft beer; stylish space. $ *Average main: €16* ⊠ *Reina Cristina 12, Barceloneta* ☎ *93/802–5565* ⊕ *www.encompaniadelobos.com* Ⓜ *Barceloneta.*

★ La Cova Fumada

$ | TAPAS | There's no glitz, no glamour, and not even a sign on the wall, but the battered wooden doors of this old, family-owned tavern hide a tapas bar to be treasured. Loyal customers queue for the market-fresh seafood, served hot from the furiously busy kitchen. **Known for:** impromptu live music; the original "bomba" fried potato croquette; erratic opening times. $ *Average main: €10* ⊠ *Baluard 56, Barceloneta* ☎ *93/221–4061* ⊙ *Closed Sun. No dinner Mon.–Wed. and Sat.* Ⓜ *Barceloneta.*

★ La Mar Salada

$$ | SEAFOOD | This restaurant stands out on a street of seafood specialists by offering creative twists on classic dishes at rock-bottom prices. Traditional favorites such as paella, black rice, and fideuà (a paella-like pasta dish) are reinvigorated, and freshness is assured as ingredients come directly from the lonja fish quay across the street, a lively auction where Barcelona's small fishing fleet sells its wares. **Known for:** fresh in-season ingredients; excellent-value seafood; creative desserts. $ *Average main: €19* ⊠ *Passeig Joan de Borbó 58, Barceloneta* ☎ *93/221–2127* ⊕ *www.lamarsalada.cat* ⊙ *Closed Tues.* Ⓜ *Barceloneta.*

Mana 75°

$$ | MEDITERRANEAN | FAMILY | Catalan fashion firm Desigual, whose offices sit above Mana 75°, has added fabrics and flair to the restaurant's beautifully airy interior, which evokes a sophisticated sea shack. Service is friendly and the high-tech open kitchen fires out precisely perfect rice dishes such as paella, but portion sizes are on the ungenerous side. **Known for:** superb paellas and rice dishes; open kitchen; free parking. $ *Average main: €19* ⊠ *Passeig de Joan de Borbó 101, Barceloneta* ☎ *93/832–6415* ⊕ *www.mana75.es* ⊙ *Closed Mon. No dinner Sun. and Tues.–Thurs.* Ⓜ *Barceloneta.*

Pez Vela

$$ | **SPANISH** | **FAMILY** | The quality of beach-side dining in Barcelona has surged in recent years, and this pseudo- *chiringuito* (beach bar) beneath the towering W Hotel is as good a place as any to combine paella with a perfect view of the sea. Rice dishes are better than at many better-known seafood specialists. **Known for:** Galician-style octopus; zingy lemon pie; beachside location and views. $ *Average main: €19* ✉ *Passeig del Mare Nostrum 19–21, Barceloneta* ☎ *93/221–6317* ⊕ *www.grupotragaluz.com* Ⓜ *Barceloneta*.

Hotels

★ Hotel Arts Barcelona

$$$$ | **HOTEL** | This luxurious Ritz-Carlton-owned, 44-story skyscraper overlooks Barcelona from the Port Olímpic, providing stunning views of the Mediterranean, the city, the Sagrada Família, and the mountains beyond. **Pros:** excellent tapas restaurant on-site; fine art throughout hotel; free cava served on club floors daily. **Cons:** a 20-minute hike or more from central Barcelona; very pricey. $ *Rooms from: €355* ✉ *Carrer de la Marina 19–21, Port Olímpic* ☎ *93/221–1000* ⊕ *www.hotelartsbarcelona.com* 🛏 *483 rooms* �’⊘ *No meals* Ⓜ *L4 Ciutadella–Vila Olímpica*.

Hotel 54 Barceloneta

$$ | **HOTEL** | Just a few minutes' walk from the beach, this 2007 addition to the Barcelona hotel scene has much to offer in location, comfort, and economy. **Pros:** rooftop terrace with great views of the marina and the Old Port; competent multilingual staff; pleasant rustic breakfast room. **Cons:** noisy around the clock on Passeig Joan de Borbó; bathrooms lack space and privacy. $ *Rooms from: €150* ✉ *Passeig Joan de Borbó 54, Barceloneta* ☎ *93/225–0054* ⊕ *www.hotel54barceloneta.es* 🛏 *28 rooms* �’⊘ *No meals* Ⓜ *L4 Barceloneta*.

La Barceloneta, Land of Paella

Paella is Valencian, not Catalan, but Sunday paella in La Barceloneta is a classic Barcelona family outing. *Paella marinera* is a seafood rice boiled in fish stock and seasoned with clams, mussels, prawns, and jumbo shrimp, while the more traditional paella valenciana omits seafood but includes chicken, rice, and snails. *Arròs negre* (black rice) is rice cooked in squid ink, and *arròs caldòs* is a soupier dish that often includes lobster. *Fideuá* is made with vermicelli noodles mixed with the standard ingredients. Paella is for a minimum of two diners—it's usually enough for three.

Soho House Barcelona

$$$$ | **HOTEL** | Not a hotel in the usual sense, Soho House is one of a group of private members' clubs for people professionally involved in one way or another in the arts; the concept originated in London in 1995 and now involves facilities worldwide. **Pros:** vibrant atmosphere; "Sunday Feast" brunch in the glassed-in atrium restaurant; well located for exploring the port, Barceloneta, and the Born-Ribera quarter. **Cons:** hard on the budget; some lounge areas and facilities are members-only; feels a bit exclusive. $ *Rooms from: €340* ✉ *Plaça del Duc de Medinaceli 4, Port Olímpic* ☎ *93/220–4600* ⊕ *www.sohohouse.com* 🛏 *57 rooms* �’⊘ *No meals* Ⓜ *L4 Barceloneta, L3 Drassanes*.

★ W Barcelona

$$$$ | **HOTEL** | This towering sail-shaped monolith dominates the skyline on the Barcelona waterfront; architect Ricardo Bofill's W, now part of the Marriott International chain, is a stunner inside and out, from the six-story atrium lobby with black ceramic tile floors, suspended

basket chairs, and glitter walls, to the adjacent bar-lounge with direct access to the "WET" lounge deck, chill-out divans, and pool. **Pros:** unrivaled views; excellent restaurants on-site; transfer service to/from airport and cruise dock. **Cons:** extra amenities can get pricey; far from public transportation (20-minute hike); loud music in public areas. [$] *Rooms from: €280* ✉ *Pl. de la Rosa del Vents 1, Moll de Llevant, Barceloneta* ☎ *93/295–2800* 🌐 *www.w-barcelona.com* 🛏 *473 rooms* 🍴 *No meals* [M] *L4 Barceloneta.*

Nightlife

Once a dingy industrial port, the stretch of seaside between Port Vell and Port Olímpic was dramatically beautified for the 1992 Summer Olympics. Today, the scenic area is bursting with Barceloneta's trendy chiringuitos (beach shacks), laid-back bars, and terraced seafood restaurants. In sharp contrast, Port Olímpic's posh nightclub scene caters to the city's fashionable glitterati, aged 21 and over. Both areas are just a short walking distance from each other, so whatever mood strikes you, dress accordingly.

Once the city's central industrial hub, Poblenou's contrasting faces—a quaint tree-lined rambla surrounded by vast warehouse spaces and ultramodern edifices—are the main reason for its recent metamorphosis into Barcelona's hippest enclave. Once-abandoned spaces have been renovated into chic artists' lofts and work spaces while vintage shops and nondescript restos are now enjoying new lives as retro-fab bars and lounges oozing with charm. Far enough from the hustle and bustle of the city's main attractions, locals in the know have turned Poblenou into paradise.

BARS

★ Balius Bar

BARS/PUBS | Named after the historic hardware store that once stood here, Balius Bar has retro-chic decor, a snazzy playlist (don't miss the live jazz sessions on Sunday), and a puckish "no standing" policy that attract hepcats aged 30 and above looking to kick back with a good cocktail and a side of nostalgia. Afternoons are reserved for vermouth and all the fixings or a chilled cava cocktail paired with fresh, often eco-conscious, bites. In the evenings, creative cocktails are the main draw; try a Cusco Maki, a tangy mixture of pisco, elderflower, and red berries with a splash of lemon. If you're lucky, you might also get a Lindy lesson or two. ✉ *Pujades 196, Poblenou* ☎ *93/315–8650* 🌐 *baliusbar.com* [M] *Poblenou.*

★ Eclipse Bar

BARS/PUBS | The sensational shoreline views from the 26th floor of the seaside W Hotel are undoubtedly a major part of Eclipse's attraction. Add to the mix an ultraslick interior design, an impressive roster of international DJs spinning themed parties every day of the week, and deluxe cocktails decadently paired with sushi, and it's little wonder that this is a favorite spot for glitterati to be seen and heard. ✉ *Pl. de la Rosa dels Vents 1, Barceloneta* ☎ *93/295–2800* 🌐 *www.eclipse-barcelona.com* [M] *Drassanes.*

La Cervecita Nuestra de Cada Día

BARS/PUBS | For craft beer lovers, this modern high-ceilinged bar and shop is must. Filled to the brim with more than 300 international craft brands plus several local artisanal beers on tap, the venue solidifies its devotion to everything cerveza with organized tastings, pairings, and courses. Claim your spot early as regulars routinely dominate the seating at the long bar or the cozy corner tables up front. ✉ *Llull 184, Poblenou* ☎ *93/486–9271* [M] *Llacuna.*

Madame George

BARS/PUBS | Everything about this stylish bar is a happy contradiction: the chandeliered space has large gilded mirrors and polished chocolate brown stools that curiously complement the rickety antiques and quirky touches (check out the bathtub sofa in the back room). The eclectic song list (jazz, rock, pop, and everything in between) alternates along with a monthly lineup of DJs and drag queen bingo sessions. And then there are the drinks: cocktails run the full gamut from classic to creative (the piscopolitan, a perfect marriage of Peruvian pisco and the classic cosmo cocktail, is a triumph) and are enjoyed by locals and expats aged 25 to young-at-heart. ⊠ *Pujades 179, Poblenou* ☎ *93/500–5151* ⊕ *www. madamegeorgebar.com* Ⓜ *Poble Nou.*

Megataverna L'Ovella Negra

BARS/PUBS | The ultimate hangout for expat students and sports fanatics, this huge (41,500 square feet) former warehouse (a follow-up to the original, smaller L'Ovella Negra, C/Sitges 5) accommodates rambunctious groups in a cavernous space with high ceilings, sturdy wooden tables, and quirky decorative touches on a brick-wall interior. The space is a one-stop shop for foosball, billiards, eating, cheap drinks (5-liter pitchers of beer and sangria are the norm), big-screen TVs, and themed live music till 3 am on most weekends. ⊠ *Zamora 78, La Rambla* ☎ *93/309–5938* ⊕ *www.ovellane-grabcn.net* Ⓜ *Catalunya.*

Més de Vi

BARS/PUBS | The brainchild of two Catalan sommeliers, Més de Vi is a chic wine bar with a purpose: to educate visitors on the art of Spanish wines, with a particular focus on regional vintages. Shelves of up-to-the-moment wine bottles are the dominant decorative flourish/functional display. Depending on mood and company, there are plenty of seating options: a tasting table for serious aficionados, romantic tête-à-tête tables for a memorable night out, and a bar area for socializing. Sold by the bottle or by the glass, the regularly updated wine selections are paired with sample-size artisanal tapas, cheese, and salads. ⊠ *Marià Aguiló 123, Poblenou* ☎ *93/007–9151* ⊕ *www.mesdvi.cat* Ⓜ *Poble Nou.*

CASINOS

Casino de Barcelona

CASINOS | Situated on the shore underneath the Hotel Arts, Barcelona's modern casino has everything from slot machines to roulette, plus restaurants, a bar, and a dance club. The casino regularly hosts Texas Hold'em poker tournaments, which add an air of Vegas-style excitement. ⊠ *Marina 19–21, Port Olímpic* ☎ *900/354354* ⊕ *www.casinobarcelona. com/en* Ⓜ *Ciutadella–Vila Olímpica.*

DANCE CLUBS

CDLC

DANCE CLUBS | Among the glitziest of Barcelona's waterfront clubs, the CDLC (Carpe Diem Lounge Club) embraces all the clichés of Ibizan over-the-top decor. The music is electronic; cocktails are exotic—and pricey. If there are celebrities in town, sooner or later they show up here. ⊠ *Passeig Marítim 32, Marina Beach, Port Olímpic* ☎ *93/224–0470, 647/779999 VIP services* ⊕ *www.cdlcbarcelona.com* Ⓜ *Ciutadella–Vila Olímpica.*

Opium Mar

DANCE CLUBS | Bordering on ostentatious, this cavernous nightspot, open until 6 am, is where most die-hard revelers end up after neighboring clubs have called it a night. Opium, flashy in every sense of the word, is a maze of split-level dance areas, pristine white lounge seating awash with dramatic pinkish-blue lighting, and scantily clad go-go dancers at every turn. All this excess culminates in the quasi-pretentious VIP area that offers patrons a privileged 360-degree view of the action. A strict door policy means style-conscious divas and debonair gents abound. ⊠ *Passeig Marítim 34, Port Olímpic* ☎ *902/267486* ⊕ *www. opiumbarcelona.com* Ⓜ *Ciutadella–Vila Olímpica.*

Pacha

DANCE CLUBS | Celebrated cherry-logoed nightlife brand Pacha is back in Barcelona after a multiyear absence. This latest reincarnation boasts an envied beachfront spot and a pricey restaurant catering mostly to summer tourists familiar with the name. After the sun goes down, however, the glitzy, floor-to-ceiling white interior transforms into a pulsating Ibiza-style showcase for local and international house and electronic acts as well as the spot for regularly changing weekday parties for the city's large community of Erasmus and under-25 partygoers. ⊠ *Passeig Marítim 38, Port Olímpic* ☎ *647/835751* ⊕ *www.pachabarcelona.es* Ⓜ *Ciutadella–Vila Olímpica.*

Shôko

DANCE CLUBS | With tony design touches and Eastern fusion cuisine, Shoko brings its own particular brand of cool to the Barcelona seaside. Located just below Frank Gehry's famous *Fish* sculpture, the swanky restaurant and lounge morphs into a party paradise featuring theme nights with international DJs ready to spin until dawn. ⊠ *Passeig Marítim de la Barceloneta 36, Port Olímpic* ☎ *93/225–9200* ⊕ *www.shoko.biz/en* Ⓜ *Ciutadella–Vila Olímpica.*

MUSIC CLUBS

Sala Razzmatazz

MUSIC CLUBS | This mega industrial warehouse turned dance club and concert hall features five distinct clubs in one: Razz Club plays indie rock; The Loft and Lo·li·ta are all about techno and electronica; and smaller, more relaxed venues Pop Bar and Rex Bar focus on experimental electro pop and indie electro, respectively. Resident DJs play nightly and live acts run from local bands to huge international names in rock and pop. Despite a casual dress code and a party scene seldom pumping before 3 am, expect long lines to get in on the weekends. ⊠ *Almogàvers 122, Poblenou* ☎ *93/320–8200* ⊕ *www.salarazzmatazz.com* Ⓜ *Marina, Bogatell.*

 Performing Arts

CONCERTS

Fabra i Coats–Fàbrica de Creació

ARTS CENTERS | This self-proclaimed artist social club—remodeled from an old textile factory on the outer limits of the Poblenou district—is a great place for emerging young visual artists to find their footing. Part of the complex accommodates work spaces for resident artists and creatives; live performances and festivals are hosted here as well. ⊠ *Sant Adrià 20, Sant Andreu* ☎ *93/256–6150* ⊕ *fabraicoats.bcn.cat* Ⓜ *Sant Andreu.*

 Shopping

While mom-and-pop shops gather dust along Rambla de Poblenou, brave new businesses selling cutting-edge design and housewares are starting to brighten up the district.

HOUSEHOLD ITEMS AND FURNITURE

BD

HOUSEHOLD ITEMS/FURNITURE | Barcelona Design, a spare, cutting-edge furniture and home-accessories store, has moved into a former industrial building near the sea. BD cofounder Oscar Tusquets Blanca, master designer and architect, gives contemporary-design star Jaime Hayon plenty of space here. The works of past giants, such as Gaudí's Casa Calvet chair, or Salvador Dalí's Gala loveseat, are also available—if your pockets are deep enough. It's not open on weekends. ⊠ *Ramón Turró 126, Poblenou* ☎ *93/458–6909* ⊕ *bdbarcelona.com* Ⓜ *Llacuna, Bogatell.*

Noak Room

HOUSEHOLD ITEMS/FURNITURE | The sleek style of Scandinavian design has truly taken hold in Barcelona, as seen in the cafés and restaurants of the Born and Eixample. Started by a couple who are passionate about retro and vintage pieces from northern Europe, this large, loftlike locale stocks a large selection of upcycled and renovated lamps, sofas, chairs, and mirrors from the 1950s to the '70s. International shipping can be arranged. ✉ *Rec Boronat 69, Poblenou* ☎ *93/309–5300* ⊕ *www.noakroom.com* Ⓜ *Llacuna.*

MARKETS

Palo Alto Market

OUTDOOR/FLEA/GREEN MARKETS | This old factory complex in the Poblenou district was one of the first to be become a creative space. Nineteen designers have studios here, including the legendary Javier Mariscal. With 19th-century industrial architecture (the "palo alto" refers to a towering chimney) and a verdant garden, it is something of an island in this newly developed district. On the first weekend of every month, the Palo Alto Market invites the public to view this urban oddity with live music and DJs, street food trucks, and dozens of stalls selling goods. Check their website for dates and get there around 11 am, as queues to get in can often snake around the block. ✉ *Pellaires 30, Poblenou* ☎ *93/159–6670* ⊕ *www.palomarketfest.com/en* Ⓜ *Selva del Mar.*

 Activities

BIKING

Barcelona By Bike

BICYCLING | Gather at the meeting point next to the main entrance of the Barcelona Casino for a three-hour guided bike tour (€24 with a complimentary drink en route) of the Old City, Gaudí architecture, and the port. ✉ *Calle Marina s/n, Port Olímpic* ☎ *671/307325* ⊕ *www.barcelonabybike.com* Ⓜ *Ciutadella/Vila Olímpica.*

Chapter 8

THE EIXAMPLE

8

Updated by
Elizabeth Prosser and
Steve Tallantyre

⊙ Sights	🍴 Restaurants	🛏 Hotels	🛍 Shopping	🍸 Nightlife
★★★★★	★★★★★	★★★★★	★★★★★	★★★★★

NEIGHBORHOOD SNAPSHOT

TOP EXPERIENCES

■ **Casa Milà:** Visit the wavy, curving stone rooftop of one of Gaudí's most celebrated designs on a night tour which includes a spectacular son et lumière projection.

■ **Temple Expiatori de la Sagrada Família:** Reserve timed tickets in advance for Barcelona's most emblematic architectural icon. Choose the "Top Views" ticket for access to the bell towers, and bring binoculars to zoom in on incredible details.

■ **Consell de Cent:** The best art galleries in Barcelona are gathered around a few blocks on Consell de Cent.

■ **La Rambla de Catalunya:** Stroll the leafy promenade of one of Barcelona's trendiest streets.

GETTING HERE

The metro stops at Plaça de Catalunya and Provença nicely bracket this quintessential Barcelona neighborhood; the Diagonal and Passeig de Gràcia stations are right in the center.

Barcelona's unnumbered Eixample (Expansion), the post-1860 grid, is a perfect place to get lost, but fear not: the Eixample is vertebrate. Carrer Balmes divides the working-class *Esquerra* (left, looking uphill) from its bourgeois *Dreta* (right). Even the blocks are divided by flats *davant* (front) or *darrera* (behind). The sides of the streets are either *mar* (seaward) or *muntanya* (facing the mountain).

PLANNING YOUR TIME

Exploring the Eixample can take days, but three hours will be enough to cover the most important sites. Add another two or three hours (including the wait in line) for the Sagrada Família. Look for the *passatges* (passageways) through some of the Eixample blocks; Passatge Permanyer, Passatge de la Concepció, and Passatge Mendez Vigo are three of the best. Beware of the tapas emporia on Passeig de Gràcia; almost all of them microwave previously prepared bits and are not the best.

QUICK BITES

■ **La Bodegueta.** If you're near Rambla Catalunya, don't hesitate to report in to the semi-subterranean La Bodegueta for some *pa amb tomaquet* (bread with olive oil and tomatoes) and bits of cheese or ham. Weather permitting, enjoy your tapas at one of the restaurant's parasol-shaded tables on the promenade. ✉ *Rambla de Catalunya 100, Eixample* ⊕ *www.labodegueta.cat* Ⓜ *Provença (FGC)*

■ **Eixampeling.** A charming all-day brunch spot with pretty presentation, good coffee, and better Bloody Marys. ✉ *Calle Diputación 158, Eixample* ⊕ *eixampeling.com* Ⓜ *Urgell*

Barcelona's most famous neighborhood, this late-19th-century urban development is known for its dazzling Art Nouveau architecture. Called the "Expansion" in Catalan, the district appears on the map as a geometric grid laid out north above the Plaça de Catalunya. The upscale shops, the art galleries, the facades of the Moderniste town houses, and the venues for some of the city's finest cuisine are the main attractions here.

The Eixample (ay-shompla) is an open-air Moderniste museum. Designed as a grid, in the best Cartesian tradition, the Eixample is oddly difficult to find your way around in; the builders seldom numbered the buildings and declined to alphabetize the streets, and even Barcelona residents can get lost in it. The easiest orientation to grasp is the basic division between the well-to-do Dreta, to the right of Rambla Catalunya looking inland, and the more working-class Ezquerra to the left. Eixample locations are also either *mar* (on the ocean side of the street) or *muntanya* (facing the mountains).

The name of Eixample's most famous block of houses, Manzana de la Discordia, is a pun on the Spanish word *manzana,* which means both "apple" and "city block," alluding to the three-way architectural counterpoint on this street and to the classical myth of the Apple of Discord, which played a part in that legendary tale about the Judgment of Paris

and the subsequent Trojan War. The houses here are spectacular and encompass three monuments of Modernisme—Casa Lleó Morera, Casa Amatller, and Casa Batlló—in significantly different styles.

The Eixample was created when the Ciutat Vella's city walls were demolished in 1860, and Barcelona embarked on a vast expansion, financed by the return of rich colonials from the Americas, aristocrats who had sold their country estates, and the city's industrial magnates. They expected their investment to trumpet not only their own wealth and influence, but also the resurgence of Barcelona itself and its unique cultural heritage—not Spanish, but Catalan, and modern European. The grid was the work of engineer Ildefons Cerdà, and much of the construction was done in the peak years of the Moderniste movement by a who's who of Art Nouveau architects, starring Gaudí, Domènech i Montaner, and Puig i Cadafalch; rising above it all is Gaudí's Sagrada Família church. The Eixample's principal thoroughfares are La Rambla de Catalunya and the Passeig de Gràcia, where many of the city's most elegant shops occupy the ground floors of the most interesting Art Nouveau buildings.

Sights

Casa Amatller

BUILDING | The neo-Gothic Casa Amatller was built by Josep Puig i Cadafalch in 1900, when the architect was 33 years old. Eighteen years younger than Domènech i Montaner and 15 years younger than Gaudí, Puig i Cadafalch was one of the leading statesmen of his generation, once the mayor of Barcelona, and in 1917, president of Catalonia's first home-rule government since 1714. Puig i Cadafalch's architectural historicism sought to recover Catalonia's proud past, in combination with eclectic elements from Flemish and Dutch architectural motifs. Note the Eusebi Arnau sculptures—especially his St. George and the Dragon, and the figures of a drummer with his dancing bear. The flowing-haired "Princesa" is thought to be Amatller's daughter; the animals above the motif are depicted pouring chocolate, a reference to the source of the Amatller family fortune. The first-floor apartment, where the Amatller family lived, is a museum, with original furniture and decor; guided tours are offered in English daily at 11 am. A quick visit will give you a sense of what the rest of the building is like and a chance to buy some chocolate *de la casa* at the boutique. ⊠ *Passeig de Gràcia 41, Eixample* ☎ *93/461–7460 tour info and ticket sales* ⊕ *amatller.org/en/* ⊠ *Tours from €19* Ⓜ *L2/L3/L5 Passeig de Gràcia, FGC Provença.*

Casa Batlló

BUILDING | FAMILY | Gaudí at his most spectacular, the Casa Batlló is actually a makeover: it was originally built in 1877 by one of Gaudí's teachers, Emili Sala Cortés, and acquired by the Batlló family in 1900. Batlló wanted to tear down the undistinguished Sala building and start over, but Gaudí persuaded him to remodel the facade and the interior, and the result is astonishing. The facade—with its rainbow of colored glass and *trencadís* (polychromatic tile fragments) and the toothy masks of the wrought-iron balconies projecting outward toward the street—is an irresistible photo op. Nationalist symbolism is at work here: the scaly roof line represents the Dragon of Evil impaled on St. George's cross, and the skulls and bones on the balconies are the dragon's victims, allusions to medieval Catalonia's code of chivalry and religious piety. Gaudí is said to have directed the composition of the facade from the middle of Passeig de Gràcia, calling instructions to workmen on the scaffolding. Inside, the translucent windows on the landings of the central staircase light up the maritime motif and the details of the building; as everywhere in his oeuvre, Gaudí opted for natural shapes and rejected straight lines. On summer evenings, you can listen to a concert (starts at 8 pm) and enjoy a drink on the terrace, as part of the "Magic Night" program.

Budget-conscious visitors can take in the view from outside the Casa Batlló; the admission fee is ridiculously high (there are discounts for booking in advance online), and you won't see much inside that you can't also see in the Casa Milà, up the Passeig de Gràcia on the opposite side. ⊠ *Passeig de Gràcia 43, Eixample* ☎ *93/216–0306* ⊕ *www.casabatllo. es* ⊠ *From €25* Ⓜ *L2/L3/L4 Passeig de Gràcia, FGC Provença.*

Casa Calvet

HOUSE | This exquisite but more conventional town house (for Gaudí, anyway) was the architect's first commission in the Eixample (the second was the dragon-like Casa Batlló, and the third, and last—he was never asked to do another—was the stone quarry–esque

Casa Milà). Peaked with baroque scroll gables over the unadorned (no ceramics, no color, no sculpted ripples) Montjuïc sandstone facade, Casa Calvet compensates for its structural conservatism with its Art Nouveau details, from the door handles to the benches, chairs, vestibule, and spectacular glass-and-wood elevator. Built in 1900 for the textile baron Pere Calvet, the house includes symbolic elements on the facade, ranging from the owner's stylized letter "C" over the door to the cypress, symbol of hospitality, above. The wild mushrooms on the main (second) floor reflect Pere Calvet's (and perhaps Gaudí's) passion for mycology, while the busts at the top of the facade represent St. Peter, the owner's patron saint, and St. Genis of Arles and St. Genis of Rome, patron saints of Vilassar, the Calvet family's hometown in the coastal Maresme north of Barcelona. The only part of the building accessible to visitors is the ground-floor **Casa Calvet** restaurant, originally the suite of offices for Calvet's textile company, with its exuberant Moderniste decor. ⊠ *Carrer Casp 48, Eixample ⊕ www.casacalvet.es (restaurant)* Ⓜ *L1/L4 Urquinaona.*

Casa de les Punxes (*House of the Spikes*)
BUILDING | Also known as Casa Terrades for the family that owned the house and commissioned Puig i Cadafalch to build it, this extraordinary cluster of six conical towers ending in impossibly sharp needles is another of Puig i Cadafalch's inspirations, this one rooted in the Gothic architecture of northern European countries. One of the few freestanding Eixample buildings, visible from 360 degrees, this ersatz Bavarian or Danish castle in downtown Barcelona is composed entirely of private apartments, some of them built into the conical towers themselves on three circular levels, connected by spiral stairways. The ground floor, first level, terrace, and towers are now open to the public; check the website for the schedule of guided tours in English. ⊠ *Av. Diagonal 416–420,*

Eixample ☎ *93/018–5242* ⊕ *casade-lespunxes.com* 🍴 *From €13* Ⓜ *L4/L5 Verdaguer, L3/L5 Diagonal.*

Casa Domènech i Estapà
BUILDING | This less radical example of Eixample Art Nouveau architecture, now an apartment building, is interesting for its balconies and curved lines on the facade, for its handsome doors and vestibule, and for the lovely etched designs on the glass of the entryway. Built by and for the architect Domènech i Estapà in 1908–09, eight years before his death, this building represents a more conservative interpretation of the aesthetic canons of the epoch, revealing the architect's hostility to the Art Nouveau movement. Domènech i Estapà built more civil projects than any other architect of his time (Reial Acadèmia de Cièncias y Artes, Palacio de Justicia, Sociedad Catalana de Gas y Electricidad, Hospital Clínico, Observatorio Fabra) and was the creator of the Carcel Modelo (Model Prison), considered a state-of-the-art example of penitentiary design when it was built in 1913. ⊠ *Carrer Valencia 241, Eixample* Ⓜ *L2/L3/L4 Passeig de Gràcia.*

Casa Golferichs (*Golferichs Civic Center*)
ARTS VENUE | Gaudí disciple Joan Rubió i Bellver built this extraordinary house, known as El Xalet (The Chalet), for the Golferichs family when he was not yet 30. The rambling wooden eaves and gables of the exterior enclose a cozy and comfortable dark-wood-lined interior with a pronounced verticality. The top floor, with its rich wood beams and cerulean walls, is often used for intimate concerts; the ground floor exhibits paintings and photographs. The building serves now as the quarters of the Golferichs Centre Civic, which offers local residents a range of conferences and discussions, exhibitions and adult education courses, and organizes various thematic walking tours of the city. ⊠ *Gran Via 491, Eixample* ☎ *93/323–7790* ⊕ *www.golferichs.org* ☉ *Closed Sun.* Ⓜ *L1 Rocafort, Urgell.*

The Eixample

Casa Macaya (*Palau Macaya*)

HOUSE | This graceful Puig i Cadafalch building constructed in 1901 was the former seat of the Obra Social "la Caixa," a deep-pocketed, far-reaching cultural and social welfare organization funded by Spain's major (and most civic-minded) savings bank. It now houses the foundation's Espai Caixa cultural center, organizing a range of conferences, discussion forums, and presentations on current social and political issues. Look for the Eusebi Arnau sculptures over the door depicting, somewhat cryptically, a man mounted on a donkey and another on a bicycle, reminiscent of the similar Arnau sculptures on the facade of Puig i Cadafalch's Casa Amatller on Passeig de Gràcia. ⊠ *Passeig de Sant Joan 108, Eixample* ☎ *93/457–9531* ⊕ *obrasociallacaixa.org* ☽ *Closed weekends* Ⓜ *L4/L5 Verdaguer.*

★ **Casa Milà**

BUILDING | Usually referred to as "La Pedrera" (the Stone Quarry), this building, with its wavy, curving stone facade undulating around the corner of the block, is one of Gaudí's most celebrated yet initially reviled designs. Topped by chimneys so eerie they were nicknamed *espantabruxes* (witch scarers), the Casa Milà was unveiled in 1910 to the horror of local residents. The exterior has no straight lines; the curlicues and wrought-iron foliage of the balconies, sculpted by Josep Maria Jujol, and the rippling, undressed stone, made you feel, as one critic put it, "as though you are on board a ship in an angry sea."

Gaudí's rooftop chimney park, alternately interpreted as veiled Saharan women or helmeted warriors, is as spectacular as anything in Barcelona, especially in late afternoon when the sunlight slants over the city into the Mediterranean. Inside, the handsome **Espai Gaudí** (Gaudí Space) in the attic has excellent critical displays of Gaudí's works from all over Spain, as well as explanations of his theories and techniques. The **Pis de la Pedrera** apartment is an interesting look into the life of a family that lived in La Pedrera in the early 20th century. People still occupy the other apartments.

In the summer, lines of visitors waiting to see the Pedrera can stretch a block or more; sign up for the "Gaudí's Pedrera: The Origins" tour of the building by night, with a spectacular son et lumière projection. Check the website for tour times and book online. Bookings are essential. On *Nits d'Estiu* (Friday and Saturday summer nights) the Espai Gaudí and the roof terrace are open for drinks and jazz concerts; the doors open at 8:30 pm and concerts begin at 9. ⊠ *Passeig de Gràcia 92, Eixample* ☎ *93/214–2576* ⊕ *www. lapedrera.com/en/home* ☞ *From €22* Ⓜ *L2/L3/L5 Diagonal, FGC Provença.*

Casa Montaner i Simó–Fundació Tàpies

BUILDING | Built in 1880, this former publishing house, and the city's first building to incorporate iron supports, has been handsomely converted to hold the work of preeminent contemporary Catalan painter Antoni Tàpies, and a collection of works by many important modern artists that he acquired over his lifetime. Tàpies, who died in 2012, was an abstract painter, but was also influenced by surrealism, which accounts for the *Núvol i Cadira* (*Cloud and Chair*) sculpture atop the structure. The modern airy split-level gallery also has a bookstore that's strong on Tàpies, Asian art, and Barcelona art and architecture. ⊠ *Carrer Aragó 255, Eixample* ☎ *93/487–0315* ⊕ *www.fundaciotapies.org* ☞ *€7* ☽ *Closed Mon.* Ⓜ *L2/ L3/L4 Passeig de Gràcia.*

Museu del Modernisme de Barcelona (*Museum of Catalan Modernism: MMBCN*)

MUSEUM | Unjustly bypassed in favor of rival displays in the Casa Milà, Casa Batlló, and the DHUB Design Museum in Plaça de les Glòries, this museum houses a small but rich collection of Moderniste furnishings, paintings and posters, sculpture (including works by Josep Limona), and decorative arts. Don't miss the section devoted to Gaudí-designed furniture. ✉ *Carrer Balmes 48, Eixample* ☎ *93/272–2896* ⊕ *www.mmbcn.cat* ✇ *€10* ⊗ *Closed Mon.* Ⓜ *L1/L2 Universitat.*

Palau Baró de Quadras

COLLEGE | The neo-Gothic and plateresque (intricately carved in silversmith-like detail) facade of this house built for textile magnate Baron Manuel de Quadras and remodeled (1902–05) by Moderniste starchitect Puig i Cadafalch, has one of the most spectacular collections of Eusebi Arnau sculptures in town (other Arnau sites include the Palau de la Música Catalana, Quatre Gats–Casa Martí, and Casa Amatller). Look for the theme of St. George slaying the dragon once again, this one in a spectacularly vertiginous rush of movement down the facade. Don't miss the intimate-looking row of alpine chalet–like windows across the top floor. The Palau currently houses the Institut Ramon Llull, a nonprofit organization dedicated to spreading the knowledge of Catalan culture worldwide. ✉ *Av. Diagonal 373, Eixample* ☎ *93/467–8000* ⊕ *www.llull.cat* ✇ *Group guided tours €10/person* Ⓜ *L2/L3/L5 Diagonal.*

Passatge Permanyer

NEIGHBORHOOD | Cutting through the middle of the block bordered by Pau Claris, Roger de Llúria, Consell de Cent, and Diputació, this charming, leafy mid-Eixample sanctuary is one of 46 passatges (alleys or passageways) that cut through the blocks of this gridlike area. Inspired by John Nash's neoclassical Regent's Park terraces in London (with their formal and separate town houses), Ildefons Cerdà originally envisioned many more of these utopian mid-block gardens, but Barcelona never endorsed his vision. Once an aristocratic enclave and hideaway for pianist Carles Vidiella and poet, musician, and illustrator Apel·les Mestre, Passatge Permanyer is, along with the nearby Passatge Méndez Vigo, the best of these through-the-looking-glass downtown Barcelona alleyways. ✉ *Passatge Permanyer, Eixample* Ⓜ *L2/L3/L4 Passeig de Gràcia.*

Plaça de Catalunya

PLAZA | Barcelona's main bus-and-metro hub is the frontier between the Old City and the post-1860 Eixample. Fountains and statuary, along with pigeons and backpackers in roughly equal numbers, make the Plaça de Catalunya an open space to scurry across on your way to somewhere quieter, shadier, and gentler on the senses. Across the street on the west side is **Café Zurich,** the classic Barcelona rendezvous point at the top of La Rambla, by the steps down to the metro. The block behind the Zurich, known as El Triangle, houses a collection of megastores, chief among them FNAC (for electronics, books, and music) and Massimo Dutti (for designer garb). Corte Inglés, the department store on the northeast side of the square, offers quality goods at decent prices—if you can get the attention of one of their famously indifferent salespeople. ✉ *Pl. de Catalunya, Eixample* Ⓜ *Pl. Catalunya.*

★ Recinte Modernista de Sant Pau

BUILDING | Among the more recent tourist attractions in Barcelona, the Recinte Modernista (Modernist Complex) is set in what was surely one of the most beautiful public projects in the world: the Hospital de Sant Pau. A UNESCO World Heritage site, the complex is extraordinary in its setting and style. The story behind it as fascinating as the site itself: architect Lluís Domènech i Montaner believed that trees, flowers, and fresh air were likely to help people recover from what ailed them more than anything doctors could do in emotionally sterile surroundings. The hospital wards were set among gardens, their brick facades topped with polychrome ceramic tile roofs in extravagant shapes and details. Domènech also believed in the therapeutic properties of form and color, and decorated the hospital with Pau Gargallo sculptures and colorful mosaics, replete with motifs of hope and healing and healthy growth. Begun in 1900, this monumental production won Domènech i Montaner his third Barcelona "Best Building" award in 1912. (His previous two prizes were for the Palau de la Música Catalana and Casa Lleó Morera.)

No longer a functioning hospital (the new Sant Pau—comparatively soulless but fully functional and state-of-the-art—is uphill from the complex), many of the buildings have been taken over for other purposes. The Sant Manuel Pavillion, for example, now houses the **Casa Àsia,** a comprehensive resource for cultural and business-related research on all the countries of Asia, with library holdings of books, films, and music from each of them. Guided tours are offered in English daily at 10:30. ✉ *Carrer Sant Antoni Maria Claret 167, Eixample* ☎ *93/553–7801* ⊕ *www.santpaubarcelona.org/en* ✆ *From €14; free 1st Sun. of month* Ⓜ *L5 Sant Pau/Dos de Maig.*

★ **Temple Expiatori de la Sagrada Família**
BUILDING | Barcelona's most emblematic architectural icon, Antoni Gaudí's Sagrada Família, is still under construction some 135 years after it was begun. This striking and surreal creation was conceived as nothing short of a Bible in stone, a gigantic representation of the entire history of Christianity, and it continues to cause responses from surprise to consternation to wonder. Plan to spend at least a few hours here to take it all in. However long your visit, it's a good idea to bring binoculars.

Looming over Barcelona like a magical mid-city massif of needles and peaks, the Sagrada Família can at first seem like piles of caves and grottoes heaped on a labyrinth of stalactites, stalagmites, and flora and fauna of every stripe and sort. The sheer immensity of the site and the energy flowing from it are staggering.

The scale alone is daunting: the current lateral facades will one day be dwarfed by the main Glory facade and central spire—the **Torre del Salvador** (Tower of the Savior), which will be crowned by an illuminated polychrome ceramic cross and soar to a final height 1 yard shorter than Montjuïc (564 feet) guarding the entrance to the port (Gaudí felt it improper for the work of man to surpass that of God). You can take an elevator skyward to the top of the bell towers for some spectacular views (choose the "Top Views" ticket). Back on the ground, visit the museum, which displays Gaudí's scale models, photographs showing the progress of construction, and images of the vast outpouring at Gaudí's funeral; the architect is buried under the basilica, to the left of the altar in the crypt.

Soaring skyward in intricately detailed and twisted carvings and sculptures, part of the Nativity facade is made of stone from Montserrat, Barcelona's cherished mountain sanctuary and home of Catalonia's patron saint, La Moreneta, the Black Virgin of Montserrat. Gaudí himself was fond of comparing the Sagrada Família to the shapes of the sawtooth massif 50 km (30 miles) west of the city; a plaque in one of Montserrat's caverns reads *"Lloc d'inspiració de Gaudí"* ("Place of inspiration for Gaudí").

History of Construction and Design. "My client is not in a hurry," Gaudí was fond of replying to anyone curious about the timetable for the completion of his mammoth project. The Sagrada Família was begun in 1882 under architect Francesc Villar, passed on in 1891 to Gaudí (who worked on the project until his death in 1926). After the church's neo-Gothic beginnings, Gaudí added Art Nouveau touches to the crypt (the floral capitals) and in 1893 went on to begin the Nativity facade of a new and vastly ambitious project. At the time of his death in 1926, however, only one tower of the Nativity facade had been completed.

Gaudí's plans called for three immense facades, the Nativity and Passion facades on the northeast and southwest sides of the church, and the even larger Glory facade designed as the building's main entry, facing east over Carrer de Mallorca. The four bell towers over each facade would together represent the 12 apostles. The first bell tower, in honor of Barnabas and the only one Gaudí lived to see, was completed in 1921. Presently there are eight towers standing: Barnabas, Simon, Judas, and Matthias (from left to right) over the Nativity facade and James, Bartholomew, Thomas, and Phillip over the Passion facade. The four larger towers around the central Tower of the Savior will represent the evangelists Mark, Matthew, John, and Luke. Between the central tower and the reredos at the northwestern end of the nave will rise the 18th and second-highest tower, crowned with a star, in honor of the Virgin Mary. The naves are not supported by buttresses but by treelike helicoidal (spiraling) columns.

Meaning and Iconography. Reading the existing facades is a challenging course in Bible studies. The three doors on the **Nativity facade** are named for Charity in the center, Faith on the right, and Hope on the left. (Gaudí often described the symbolism of his work to visitors, but because he never wrote any of it down much of the interpretation owes to oral tradition.) In the Nativity facade Gaudí addresses nothing less than the fundamental mystery of Christianity: why does God the Creator become, through Jesus Christ, a mortal creature? The answer, as Gaudí explained it in stone, is that God did this to free man from the slavery of selfishness, symbolized by the iron fence around the serpent of evil at the base of the central column of the **Portal of Charity.** The column is covered with the genealogy of Christ going back to Abraham. Above the central column is a portrayal of the birth of Christ; above that, the Annunciation is flanked by a

grotto-like arch of water. Overhead are the constellations in the Christmas sky at Bethlehem.

To the right, the **Portal of Faith** chronicles scenes of Christ's youth: Jesus preaching at the age of 13, and Zacharias prophetically writing the name of John. Higher up are grapes and wheat, symbols of the Eucharist, and a sculpture of a hand and an eye, symbols of divine providence.

The left-hand **Portal of Hope** begins at the bottom with flora and fauna from the Nile; the slaughter of the innocents; the flight of the Holy Family into Egypt; Joseph surrounded by his carpenter's tools, contemplating his son; and the marriage of Joseph and Mary. Above this is a sculpted boat with an anchor, representing the Church, piloted by St. Joseph assisted by the Holy Spirit in the form of a dove.

Gaudí planned these slender towers to house a system of tubular bells (still to be created and installed) capable of playing more complete and complex music than standard bell-ringing changes had previously been able to perform. At a height of one-third of the bell tower are the seated figures of the apostles.

The **Passion facade** on the Sagrada Família's southwestern side, over Carrer Sardenya and the Plaça de la Sagrada Família, is a dramatic contrast to the Nativity facade. In 1986, sculptor Josep Maria Subirachs was chosen by project director Jordi Bonet to finish the Passion facade. Subirachs was picked for his starkly realistic, almost geometrical sculptural style, which many visitors and devotees of Gaudí find gratingly off the mark. Subirachs pays double homage to the great Moderniste master in the Passion facade: Gaudí himself appears over the left side of the main entry, making notes or drawings, while the Roman soldiers farther out and above are modeled on Gaudí's helmeted warriors from the roof of La Pedrera. Art critic Robert Hughes calls the homage "sincere in the way that only the worst art can be: which is to say, utterly so."

Following an S-shape path across the Passion facade, the scenes represented begin at the lower left with the Last Supper. The faces of the disciples are contorted in confusion and dismay, especially that of Judas, clutching his bag of money behind his back. The next sculptural group to the right represents the prayer in the Garden of Gethsemane and Peter awakening, followed by the kiss of Judas.

In the center, Jesus is lashed to a pillar during his flagellation. Note the column's top stone is out of kilter, reminder of the stone soon to be removed from Christ's sepulcher. To the right of the door is a rooster, as well as Peter, who is lamenting his third denial of Christ: "ere the cock crows." Farther to the right are Pilate and Jesus with the crown of thorns, while just above, starting back to the left, Simon of Cyrene helps Jesus with the cross after his first fall.

Over the center is the representation of Jesus consoling the women of Jerusalem and a faceless St. Veronica (because her story is considered legendary, not historical fact), with the veil she gave Christ to wipe his face with on the way to Calvary. To the left is the likeness of Gaudí taking notes, and farther to the left is the equestrian figure of a centurion piercing the side of the church with his spear, the church representing the body of Christ. Above are the soldiers rolling dice for Christ's clothing and the naked, crucified Christ at the center. To to the right are Peter and Mary at the sepulcher. At Christ's feet is a figure with a furrowed brow, thought to be a self-portrait of Subirachs, characterized by the sculptor's giant hand and an "S" on his right arm.

Over the door will be the church's 16 prophets and patriarchs under the cross of salvation. Apostles James, Bartholomew, Thomas, and Phillip appear at a height of 148 feet on their respective bell towers. Thomas, the apostle who demanded proof of Christ's resurrection (hence the expression "doubting Thomas"), is visible pointing to the palm of his hand, asking to inspect Christ's wounds. Bartholomew, on the left, is turning his face upward toward the culminating element in the Passion facade, the 26-foot-tall gold metallic representation of the resurrected Christ on a bridge between the four bell towers at a height of 198 feet.

Future of the project. The apse of the basilica, consecrated by Pope Benedict XVI in November 2010, has space for 15,000 people and a choir loft for 1,500. The towers still to be completed over the apse include those dedicated to the four evangelists—Matthew, Mark, Luke, and John—the Virgin Mary, and the highest of all, dedicated to Christ the Savior. By 2022, the 170th anniversary of the birth of Gaudí, the great central tower and dome, resting on four immense columns of Iranian porphyry, considered the hardest of all stones, will soar to a height of 564 feet, making the Sagrada Família Barcelona's tallest building. By 2026, the 100th anniversary of Gaudí's death, after 144 years of construction, the Sagrada Família may be complete enough to be called finished. ■TIP→ **Lines to enter the church can stretch around the block. Buy your tickets online, with a reserved time of entry, and jump the queue.** ⊠ *Pl. de la Sagrada Família, Carrer Mallorca 401, Eixample* ☎ *93/207–3031, 93/208–0414 visitor info* ⊕ *www.sagradafamilia.cat* ⊠ *From €15* Ⓜ *L2/L5 Sagrada Família.*

Continued on page 177

TEMPLE EXPIATORI DE LA
SAGRADA FAMÍLIA

Antoni Gaudí's striking and surreal masterpiece was conceived as nothing short of a Bible in stone, an arresting representation of the history of Christianity. Today this Roman Catholic church is Barcelona's most emblematic architectural icon. Looming over Barcelona like a mid-city massif of grottoes and peaks, the Sagrada Família strains skyward in piles of stalagmites. Construction is ongoing and continues to stretch toward the heavens.

CONSTRUCTION, PAST AND PRESENT

"My client is not in a hurry," was Gaudí's reply to anyone curious about his project's timetable . . . good thing, too, because the Sagrada Família was begun in 1882 under architect Francesc Villar, passed on in 1891 to Gaudí, and is still thought to be more than a decade from completion. Gaudí added Art Nouveau touches to the crypt and in 1893 started the Nativity facade. Conceived as a symbolic construct encompassing the complete story and scope of the Christian faith, the church was intended by Gaudí to impress the viewer with the full sweep and force of the Gospel. At the time of his death in 1926 only one tower of the Nativity facade had been completed.

By 2026, the 100th anniversary of Gaudí's death, after 144 years of construction in the tradition of the great medieval and Renaissance cathedrals of Europe, the Sagrada Família may well be complete enough to call finished. Architect Jordi Bonet continues in the footsteps of his father, architect Lluís Bonet, to make Gaudí's vision complete as he has since the 1980s.

(left) Sagrada Família interior. (top) Shepherds gather to witness the birth of Christ in the Nativity facade.

BIBLE STUDIES IN STONE: THE FACADES

Gaudí's plans called for three immense facades. The northeast-facing **Nativity facade** and the southwest-facing **Passion facade** are complete. The much larger southeast-facing **Glory facade,** the building's main entry, is still under construction. The final church will have eighteen towers: The four **bell towers** over each facade represent the twelve apostles; the four **larger towers** represent the evangelists Mark, Matthew, John, and Luke; the **second-highest tower** in the reredos behind the altar honors the Virgin Mary; and in the center the **Torre del Salvador** (Tower of the Savior) will soar to a height of 564 feet.

THE NATIVITY FACADE

Built during Gaudí's lifetime, this facade displays his vision and sculptural style, the organic or so-called "melting wax" look that has become his signature. The facade is crowned by **four bell towers,** representing the apostles Barnabas, Jude, Simon, and Matthew and divided into three sections around the doors of **Charity** in the center, **Faith** on the right, and **Hope** on the left.

(left) The ornamental Nativity facade. (above, top right) A figure in the Portal of Faith. (above, center right) The spiraling staircase. (above, bottom right) A decorative cross.

The focal point in the Nativity facade: Joseph and Mary presenting the infant Jesus.

Over the central Portal of Charity is the birth of Christ, with a representation of the Annunciation overhead in an ice grotto, another natural element. Above that are the signs of the zodiac for the Christmas sky at Bethlehem, with two babies representing the Gemini, and the horns of a bull for Taurus. The evergreen cypress tree rising above symbolizes eternity, with the white doves as souls seeking life everlasting.

The **Portal of Faith** on the right shows Christ preaching as a youth. Higher up are the Eucharistic symbols of grapes and wheat, and a hand and eye, symbols of divine Providence.

The **Portal of Hope** on the left shows a series of biblical scenes including the slaughter of the innocents, the flight into Egypt, Joseph surrounded by his carpenter's tools looking down at his infant son, and the marriage of Joseph and Mary with Mary's parents, Joaquin and Anna, looking on. Above is a boat, representing the Church, piloted by Joseph, with the Holy Spirit represented as a dove.

THE PASSION FACADE

On the **Passion facade**, Gaudí intended to dramatize the abyss between the birth of a child and the death of a man. In 1986 Josep Maria Subirachs, an artist known for his atheism and his hard-edged and geometrical sculptural style, was commissioned to finish the Passion facade. The contrast is sharp, in content and in sculptural style, between this facade and the Nativity facade. Framed by leaning columns of tibia-like bones, the Passion facade illustrates the last days of Christ and his Resurrection. The scenes are laid out chronologically in an S-shape path beginning at the bottom left and ending at the upper right.

At bottom left is the **Last Supper**, the disciples' faces contorted in confusion and anguish, most of all Judas clutching his bag of money behind his back over a reclining hound, the contrasting symbol of fidelity. To the right is the Garden of Gethsemane and Peter awakening, followed by the **Kiss of Judas**.

Judas kissing Jesus while a cryptogram behind contains a numerical combination adding up to 33, the age of Christ's death.

The stark, geometric Passion facade.

To the right of the door is **Peter's Third Denial** of Christ "ere the cock crows." Farther to the right are **Pontius Pilate and Jesus** with the crown of thorns.

Above on the second tier are the **Three Marys** and Simon helping Jesus lift the cross. Over the center, **Jesus carries the cross.** To the left, Gaudí himself is portrayed, pencil in hand, the evangelist in stone, while farther left a **mounted centurion** pierces the side of the church with his spear, the church representing the body of Christ. At the top left, **soldiers gamble for Christ's clothing** while at the top center is the **crucifixion**, featuring Subirachs's controversial (in 1971 when it was unveiled) naked and anatomically complete Christ. Finally to the right, Peter and Mary grieve at **Christ's entombment**, an egg overhead symbolizing rebirth and the resurrection. At a height of 148 feet are the four Apostles on their bell towers. Bartholomew, on the left, looks upward toward the 26-foot risen Christ between the four bell towers at a height of 198 feet.

THE GLORY FACADE

The Glory facade, still under construction, will have a wide stairway and esplanade or porch leading up to three portals dedicated, as in the other facades, to Charity, Faith, and Hope. The doors are inscribed with the Lord's Prayer in bronze in fifty different languages with the Catalan version in the center in relief. Carrer Mallorca will be routed underground and the entire city block across the street will be razed to make space for the esplanade and park. Present predictions are between 2026 and 2030 for the completion of this phase.

A new element in the Sagrada Família: the bronze doorway of the Glory facade.

THE INTERIOR: "TEMPLE OF HARMONIOUS LIGHT"

(top) Above the altar, supporting columns form a canopy of light. (below) Towering columns and stained-glass windows keep the interior bright.

Until 2010, The Sagrada Família was able to be adequately appreciated without going inside. But since the interior was completed for the Papal consecration, it's become Barcelona's most stunning space, comparable to the breathtaking upsweep of the finest soaring Gothic architecture but higher, brighter, and carved in a dazzling fusion of hard-edged Subirachs over organic Gaudí.

DESIGN

The floor plan for the church is laid out in the form of a **Latin cross** with five longitudinal naves intersected by three transepts. The **apse** has space for 15,000 people, a choir loft for 1,500, and is large enough to encompass the entire Santa Maria del Mar basilica. From the Glory Façade, the Baptistry Chapel is to the left and the Chapel of the Sacrament and Penitence is to the right. The Chapel of the Assumption is at the back of the apse. Over the main altar is the figure of the crucified Christ, suspended in mid-air under a diaphanous canopy.

LIGHT

The main nave and the apse of the basilica create an immense and immaculate space culminated by the highest point: the hyperboloid skylight over the main altar 75 meters (247.5 ft) above the floor. The vaulting is perforated with 288 skylights admitting abundant light. The sharp-edged, tree-like leaning columns shape the interior spaces and will support the six towers being built above them. Vaults are decorated with green and gold Venetian mosaics that diffuse the light as if they were leaves in a forest, making the basilica, in the words of Gaudí, "the temple of harmonious light."

DETAILS TO DISCOVER: THE EXTERIOR

GAUDÍ IN THE PASSION FACADE

Subirachs pays double homage to the great Moderniste master in the Passion facade: Gaudí himself appears over the left side of the main entry making notes or drawings, the evangelist in stone, while the Roman soldiers are modeled on Gaudí's helmeted, Star Wars–like warriors from the roof of La Pedrera.

Gaudí in the Passion facade

TOWER TOPS

Break out the binoculars and have a close look at the pinnacles and peaks of the Sagrada Família's towers. Sculpted by Japanese artist Etsuro Sotoo, these clusters of grapes and different kinds of fruit are symbols of fertility, of rebirth, and of the Resurrection of Christ.

Sotoo's ornamental fruit

SUBIRACHS IN THE PASSION FACADE

At Christ's feet in the entombment sculpture is a blocky figure with a furrowed brow, thought to be a portrayal of the agnostic's anguished search for certainty. This figure is generally taken as a self-portrait of Subirachs, characterized by the sculptor's giant hand and an "S" on his massive right arm.

DONKEY ON THE NATIVITY FACADE

On the left side of the Nativity facade over the Portal of Hope is a *burro*, a small donkey, known to have been modeled from a donkey that Gaudí saw near the work site. The *ruc català* (Catalan donkey) is a beloved and iconic symbol of Catalonia, often displayed on Catalonian bumpers as a response to the Spanish fighting bull.

The donkey in the Nativity facade

THE ROSE TREE DOOR

The richly sculpted Rose Tree Door, between the Nativity facade and the cloisters, portrays Our Lady of the Rose Tree with the infant Jesus in her arms, St. Dominic and St. Catherine of Siena in prayer, with three angels dancing overhead. The sculptural group on the wall known as "The Death of the Just" portrays the Virgin and child comforting a moribund old man, the Spanish prayer "Jesús, José, y María, asistidme en mi última agonía" (Jesus, Joseph, and María, help me in my final agony). The accompanying inscriptions in English, "Pray for us sinners now and at the hour of our death, Amen" are the final words of the Ave María prayer.

The heavily embelished Rose door

COLUMN FROM THE PORTAL OF CHARITY

The column, dead center in the Portal of Charity, is covered with the genealogy of Christ going back through the House of David to Abraham. At the bottom of the column is the snake of evil, complete with the apple of temptation in his mouth, closed in behind an iron grate, symbolic of Christianity's mission of neutralizing the sin of selfishness.

The column in the Portal of Charity

FACELESS ST. VERONICA

Because her story is considered legendary, not historical fact, St. Veronica appears faceless in the Passion facade. Also shown is the veil she gave Christ to wipe his face with on the way to Calvary that was said to be miraculously imprinted with his likeness. The veil is torn in two overhead and covers a mosaic that Subirachs allegedly disliked and elected to conceal.

St. Veronica with the veil

STAINED-GLASS WINDOWS

The stained-glass windows of the Sagrada Família are work of Joan Vila-Grau. The windows in the west central part of the nave represent the light of Jesus and a bubbling fountain in a bright chromatic patchwork of shades of blue with green and yellow reflections. The main window on the Passion facade represents the Resurrection. Gaudí left express instructions that the windows of the central nave have no color, so as not to alter the colors of the tiles and trencadis (mosaics of broken tile) in green and gold representing palm leaves. These windows will be clear or translucent, as a symbol of purity and to admit as much light as possible.

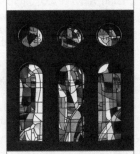

Stained-glass windows

TORTOISES AND TURTLES

Nature lover Gaudí used as many elements of the natural world as he could in his stone Bible. The sea tortoise beneath the column on the Mediterranean side of the Portal of Hope and the land turtle supporting the inland Portal of Faith symbolize the slow and steady stability of the cosmos and of the church.

SAINT THOMAS IN THE BELL TOWER

Above the Passion facade, St. Thomas demanding proof of Christ's resurrection (thus the expression "doubting Thomas") and perched on the bell tower is pointing to the palm of his hand asking to inspect Christ's wounds.

CHRIST RESURRECTED ABOVE PASSION FACADE

High above the Passion facade, a gilded Christ sits resurrected, perched between two towers.

Christ resurrected

MAKING THE MOST OF YOUR TRIP

The Nativity facade

WHEN TO VISIT

To avoid crowds, come first thing in the morning. Or, plan to visit during mid-morning and mid to late-afternoon when golden light streams through the stained glass windows.

WHAT TO WEAR AND BRING

Visitors are encouraged not to wear shors and to cover bare shoulders. It's a good idea to bring binoculars to absorb details all the way up.

TIMING

If you're just walking around the exterior, an hour or two is plenty of time. If you'd like to go inside to the crypt, visit the museum, visit the towers, and walk down the spiraling stairway, you'll need three to four hours.

BONUS FEATURES

The **museum** displays Gaudí's scale models and shows photographs of the construction. The **crypt** holds Gaudí's remains. The excellent gift shop has a wide selection of Gaudi-related articles including, sculptures, jewelry, miniature churches, and beautiful books.

PLAN AHEAD

Advance reservations (available up to two months in advance) are essential to avoid disappointment. Also, book a private tour for context and more time: it's worth it here, especially in peak season."

VISITOR INFORMATION

✉ Pl. de la Sagrada Família, Eixample
☎ 93/207–3031 ⊕ www.sagradafamilia.org
🎫 €17, with towers, €32, with audio guides €25
🕐 Oct.–Mar., daily 9–6; Apr.–Sept., daily 9–8
Ⓜ Sagrada Família.

WHICH TOWER?

We do not recommend visiting the towers while construction is ongoing but if you must, choose the Nativity Façade. These are the oldest of the Sagrada Familia's towers and the only ones that Gaudí worked on. Also, there's a small bridge which affords better views and a close-up of parts of the façade.

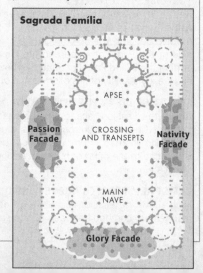

Sagrada Família

APSE

Passion Facade

CROSSING AND TRANSEPTS

Nativity Facade

MAIN NAVE

Glory Facade

🍴 Restaurants

The sprawling blocks of the Eixample contain Barcelona's finest selection of restaurants, from upscale and elegant traditional cuisine in Moderniste houses to high-concept fare in sleek minimalist-experimental spaces. Many chefs with experience in multi-star kitchens have started their own businesses here, leading to the so-called "bistronomic" movement of tiny restaurants offering limited menus of humble ingredients cooked to exacting standards. These stellar experiences at budget prices are as close as you can still get to a bargain in Barcelona.

The Alchemix

$$ | ASIAN | Traditionalists tempted to run screaming from The Alchemix's blend of creative cocktails and Asian-influenced, avant-garde gastonomy should think again. Against the odds, this strange brew is a transformative triumph. **Known for:** original cocktails; imaginitive cuisine; expert bar staff. $ *Average main: €18* ✉ *València 212, Eixample* ☎ *93/833–7678* ⊕ *www.thealchemix.com* ⊗ *Closed Sun. and Wed. No lunch Mon., Tues., and Fri.* Ⓜ *Universitat.*

Angle

$$$$ | CATALAN | ABaC may hog the spotlight, but chef Jordi Cruz's second restaurant, the relatively humble Angle, is an oft-overlooked star in its own right. Eschewing the gonzo creativity of the mothership, it instead focuses on a greatest hits menu of Cruz's dishes that have proven their appeal over the years. **Known for:** value fixed lunch; Bloody Mary appetizer; celebrity chef. $ *Average main: €85* ✉ *Aragó 214, Eixample* ☎ *93/216–7777* ⊕ *www.anglebarcelona.com* Ⓜ *Universitat.*

★ Au Port de la Lune

$ | FRENCH | The stereotypical decor of this French bistro (think Serge Gainsbourg photos) verges on parody, but the authentic food is no joke. "There's no ketchup. There's no Coca-Cola. And there never will be," reads Guy Monrepos's sign that sets the tone for a no-compromise showcase of Gallic gastronomy. **Known for:** classic French bistro food including cassoulet; no substitutions; outrageously boozy sorbet. $ *Average main: €12* ✉ *Pau Claris 103, Eixample* ☎ *93/412–2224* ⊗ *Closed Sun.* Ⓜ *Passeig de Gràcia.*

Bar Mut

$$$ | CATALAN | Just above Diagonal, this elegant retro space serves first-rate products ranging from wild sea bass to the best Ibérico hams. Crowded, noisy, chaotic, delicious—it's everything a great tapas bar or restaurant should be. **Known for:** upmarket tapas; great wine list; snacks at nearby spin-off Entrepanes Diaz. $ *Average main: €28* ✉ *Pau Claris 192, Eixample* ☎ *93/217–4338* ⊕ *www.barmut.com* Ⓜ *Diagonal.*

Bar Paris

$ | CAFÉ | Always a popular place to hang out and watch barcelonins kill some time, this lively café has hosted everyone from local poets to King Felipe. The tapas are nothing special but the sandwiches are excellent and the beer is cold. **Known for:** open every day of the year; superior sandwiches; old-fashioned bar. $ *Average main: €10* ✉ *París 187, Eixample* ☎ *93/209–8530* ▭ *No credit cards* Ⓜ *Diagonal.*

★ Bardeni

$$ | TAPAS | This "meat bar" doesn't take reservations; instead it offers a walk-in-and-graze tapas menu of items like steak tartare and aged filet mignon in a tiled, industrially chic dining room that doesn't invite lingering but is rarely empty—arrive early for a table. Former Catalan Chef of the Year Dani Lechuga throws in the occasional fine-dining dish to lighten things up. **Known for:** mouthwatering steak tartare; great aged filet mignon; award-winning chef. $ *Average main: €22* ✉ *València 454, Eixample* ☎ *93/232–5811* ⊕ *www.caldeni.com/bardeni* ⊗ *Closed Sun. and Mon.* Ⓜ *Sagrada Família.*

Blanc

$$$ | CATALAN | Overseen by feted chef Carme Ruscalleda, Blanc's menu couples traditional Catalan cuisine with her love of Asian cuisine, resulting in combinations such as suckling pig and cardamom or Galician tenderloin with sweet potato and daikon. The dining room is in a bright, white atrium at the heart of the Mandarin Oriental and feels lively at almost any time of day, right from when the first bleary hotel guests crawl in for the (excellent) breakfast. **Known for:** Catalan fused with Asian touches; superb Sunday brunch; airy atrium setting. $ *Average main: €23* ✉ *Passeig de Gràcia 38–40, Eixample* ⌖ *Entrance via Hotel Mandarin Oriental* ☎ *93/151–8783* ⊕ *www.mandarinoriental.com/barcelona/fine-dining/bars/blanc* Ⓜ *Passeig de Gràcia.*

Blau BCN

$ | CATALAN | Despite its name, there's nothing about Marc Roca's restaurant that will give you the blues; its stylish interior featuring black-and-white photos sets an elegant stage for jazzed-up versions of rustic Catalan dishes that attract discerning local diners. Slow-cooked beef cheeks, a salad of tomatoes picked the same day, and wild-mushroom-studded cannelloni all impress, but the menu is ruled by a mighty alpha-cheesecake that combines an iron fist of Roquefort in a velvet Brie glove. **Known for:** delightful wild-mushroom-studded cannelloni; tasty slow-cooked beef cheeks; killer cheesecake. $ *Average main: €15* ✉ *Londres 89, Eixample* ☎ *93/419–3032* ⊕ *blaubcn.com* ☾ *Closed Sun.* Ⓜ *Hospital Clínic.*

Boca Grande

$$$ | MEDITERRANEAN | This three-floor design triumph by Spain's hottest interior decorator, Lázaro Rosa Violán, makes up for in sheer panache what it lacks in consistency. Don't plan on a quick visit: the fresh seafood and rice dishes on offer here can take a while to reach your table. **Known for:** innovative interior design; glamorous terrace; Boca Chica bar. $ *Average main: €25* ✉ *Passatge de la Concepció 12, Eixample* ☎ *93/467–5149* ⊕ *www.bocagrande.cat* Ⓜ *Diagonal.*

Cervecería Catalana

$$ | TAPAS | FAMILY | A bright and booming tapas bar with a few tables outside, this spot is always packed for a reason: good food at reasonable prices. Try the small *solomillos* (filets mignons), mini-morsels that will take the edge off your carnivorous appetite without undue damage to your wallet, or the jumbo shrimp brochettes. **Known for:** affordable tapas; perfect jumbo shrimp brochettes; lively atmosphere. $ *Average main: €16* ✉ *Mallorca 236, Eixample* ☎ *93/216–0368* Ⓜ *Diagonal, Provença (FGC).*

★ Cinc Sentits

$$$$ | CATALAN | Obsessively local, scrupulously sourced, and masterfully cooked, the dishes of Catalan-Canadian chef Jordi Artal put the spotlight on the region's finest ingredients in an intimate, sophisticated setting. It's hard to believe that this garlanded restaurant is Jordi's first, but there's no arguing with the evidence of your *cinc sentits* (five senses). **Known for:** excellent chef; cutting-edge techniques; tasting menu only. $ *Average main: €99* ✉ *Entença 60, Eixample* ☎ *93/323–9490* ⊕ *cincsentits.com* ☾ *Closed Sun. and Mon.* Ⓜ *Provença.*

Ciudad Condal

$$ | TAPAS | At the bottom of Ramba Catalunya, this scaled-up tapas bar draws a throng of mostly international clients and has tables outside on the sidewalk virtually year-round. The solomillo (miniature beef fillet) is a winner here, as is the *broqueta d'escamarlans* (brochette of jumbo shrimp). **Known for:** long wait times; great location; reliable quality. $ *Average main: €18* ✉ *Rambla de Catalunya 18, Eixample* ☎ *93/318–1997* Ⓜ *Passeig de Gràcia, Catalunya.*

Dining with Children?

Barceloneta's beachfront paella specialists are great favorites for Sunday lunches, with children free to get up and run, skate, cycle, or generally race up and down the boardwalk while their parents linger over brandies and coffee. **Els Pescadors** (⌧ *Pl. de Prim 1, Port Olímpic, Poblenou* ☎ *93/225–2018*), a seafood restaurant, has a lovely terrace opening onto a little square that is handy for children letting off steam.

The miniature scale and finger-food aspect of tapas usually appeals, and children will happily munch on a variety of commonly found dishes, including croquettes, cured meats, toasted almonds, and fried squid rings.

Every café, bar, and terrace in town can whip up sandwiches on the go, served on fresh bread—an inexpensive and respectable snack—or the Catalan staple pa amb tomaquet. And for dessert, Barcelona's ubiquitous ice-cream parlors and vendors are another favorite. Try **Cremeria Toscana** (⌧ *Carrer Muntaner 161 or Carrer Princesa 26*) for some of the city's best *gelat*.

8

The Eixample

★ Disfrutar

$$$$ | ECLECTIC | Three former head chefs from the now-closed "World's Best Restaurant" elBulli have combined their considerable talents to create this roller-coaster ride of culinary fun. Sun streams into the gorgeous interior through skylights, spotlighting tasting menus of dazzling inventiveness and good taste. **Known for:** otherwordly desserts; tasting menus only; excellent beetroot meringues. $ *Average main: €150* ⌧ *Villarroel 163, Eixample* ☎ *93/348–6896* ⊕ *www.disfrutarbarcelona.com* ۞ *Closed weekends and 2 wks in Mar.* Ⓜ *Hospital Clínic.*

Embat

$$ | CATALAN | An *embat* is a puff of wind in Catalan, and this little bistro is a breath of fresh air in the sometimes stuffy Eixample. The highly affordable market cuisine is always impeccably fresh and freshly conceived, from flavorful brunches to a bargain lunch selection and a more elaborate evening menu. **Known for:** modern, unfussy fare; stylish minimalist interior; delicious cod. $ *Average main: €16* ⌧ *Mallorca 304, Eixample* ☎ *93/458–0855* ⊕ *embatrestaurant.*

com/ ۞ *Closed Sun. No dinner Mon.– Wed.* Ⓜ *Verdaguer.*

Etapes

$$ | SPANISH | By concentrating on sophisticated execution rather than groundbreaking creativity, the family-run Etapes provides a reliably satisfying dining experience that suits a wide range of palates. Take a seat on the pleasant terrace or in the narrow, cave-like interior and enjoy elegant interpretations of classic Catalan dishes. **Known for:** delectable roast suckling pig with calçot; homemade desserts by the co-owners' grandmother; bargain set lunch. $ *Average main: €21* ⌧ *Enric Granados 10, Eixample* ☎ *93/323–6914* ⊕ *www.etapes.cat* ۞ *No lunch weekends* Ⓜ *Universitat.*

★ Gresca

$$$$ | CATALAN | Chef-owner Rafa Peña applies the skills he honed in the world's most celebrated kitchens in this phenomenally good-value restaurant and its adjacent wine-tapas bar. He cranks out inventive dishes based on humble ingredients to a fervently loyal customer base of local foodies. **Known for:** tapas of the day; adjacent wine-tapas bar; great,

affordable cuisine. $ *Average main: €45* ✉ *Provença 230, Eixample* ☎ *93/451–6193* 🕒 *Closed weekends and 1 wk in Aug.* [M] *Provença (FGC).*

Igueldo

$$$ | **BASQUE** | Basque dishes are competently updated and delivered with a dash of style at this smart, white-walled Eixample establishment. A fiery grill turns out excellent regional meat specialties, but don't overlook fish dishes such as baby squid with cured ham and caramelized onions. **Known for:** Basque cuisine; excellent service; great wine pairings. $ *Average main: €24* ✉ *Rosselló 186, Eixample* ☎ *93/452–2555* 🕒 *Closed Sun. and 1 wk in Aug.* [M] *Diagonal.*

La Bodegueta

$ | **TAPAS** | If you can find this dive (literally: it's a short drop below sidewalk level), you'll encounter a warm and cluttered space with a dozen small tables and a few spots at the marble counter. Try the excellent pa amb tomàquet and Manchego cheese, Iberian cured ham, or *tortilla de patatas* (potato and onion omelet). **Known for:** traditional tapas; hard-to-spot dive; very local feeling. $ *Average main: €10* ✉ *Rambla de Catalunya 100, Eixample* ☎ *93/215–4894* 🌐 *www.rambla.labodegueta.cat* 🕒 *No breakfast or lunch Sun.* [M] *Provença.*

La Flauta

$ | **TAPAS** | The name of this boisterous restaurant refers to the staple flutelike baguettes used for sandwiches here. There is also an infinite number of tapas and small portions of everything from wild mushrooms in season to wild asparagus or *xipirones* (baby cuttlefish) served in this tightly packed space. **Known for:** infinite tapas list; wonderful flautas (thin sandwiches); delicious in-season vegetables. $ *Average main: €14* ✉ *Aribau 23, Eixample* ☎ *93/323–7038* 🕒 *Closed Sun. and 3 wks in Aug.* [M] *Diagonal.*

★ **La Pastisseria**

$ | **BAKERY** | This stylish *pastisseria* looks more like a designer jewelry store than a bakery. Rows of world-class cakes and pastries gleam temptingly in glass cases, ready to be taken away or enjoyed in-store with coffee or a glass of cava. **Known for:** award-winning cakes; handmade delicacies; high-quality ingredients. $ *Average main: €9* ✉ *Aragó 228, Eixample* ☎ *93/451–8401* 🌐 *www.lapastisseriabarcelona.com* 🕒 *Closed Sun. evening* [M] *Passeig de Gràcia.*

La Taverna Del Clínic

$$ | **SPANISH** | The Simoes brothers have earned a solid reputation with discerning and deep-pocketed locals for serving creative and contemporary tapas. Their bar spills out onto a sunny street-side terrace where customers can enjoy truffle cannelloni and an award-winning variation on patatas bravas, paired with selections from the excellent wine list. **Known for:** contemporary tapas; award-winning patatas bravas; superb cheese selection. $ *Average main: €20* ✉ *Rosselló 155, Eixample* ☎ *93/410–4221* 🌐 *www.latavernadelclinic.com* 🕒 *Closed Sun.* [M] *Hospital Clínic.*

La Yaya Amelia

$$ | **CATALAN** | Just two blocks uphill from Gaudí's Sagrada Família church, this kitchen serves lovingly prepared and clued-in dishes ranging from warm goat-cheese salad to foie (duck or goose liver) to *chuletón de buey a la sal* (beef cooked in salt). Decidedly old-school, the interior is largely unchanged since the restaurant opened in 1976. **Known for:** old-fashioned charm; great value; medley of Basque and Catalan cuisine. $ *Average main: €16* ✉ *Sardenya 364, Eixample* ☎ *678–355162* [M] *Sagrada Família.*

Laie

$ | **CAFÉ** | **FAMILY** | More than a bookstore, the café and restaurant here serves an all-day buffet until 9 pm. Readings, concerts, and book presentations round out an ample program of events. **Known** for: covered roof terrace; readings and children's events; all-day buffet. $ *Average main: €14* ⊠ *Pau Claris 85, Eixample* ☎ *93/318–1739* ⊕ *www.laie.es* ⊘ *Closed Sun.* Ⓜ *Passeig de Gràcia.*

★ Lasarte

$$$$ | BASQUE | Martin Berasategui, one of San Sebastián's corps of master chefs, placed his Barcelona kitchen in the capable hands of Paolo Casagrande in 2006, and it has been a culinary triumph ever since. It's now widely considered Barcelona's best restaurant. **Known for:** inventive cuisine at one of the best restaurants in Barcelona; magnificent tasting menu; heavenly grilled pigeon. $ *Average main: €59* ⊠ *Mallorca 259, Eixample* ☎ *93/445–3242* ⊕ *www.restaurantlasarte.com* ⊘ *Closed Sun., Mon., 2 wks in Jan., 1 wk at Easter, and 3 wks in Aug./Sept.* Ⓜ *Diagonal, Passeig de Gràcia, Provença (FGC).*

L'Olivé

$$ | CATALAN | Streamlined but traditional Catalan cooking means this busy and attractive spot is always packed. The crowd may be boisterous, but the dining room is seriously elegant, with crisp white tablecloths, leather chairs, and a loft-like wall of windows. **Known for:** traditional Catalan cuisine; always packed; best pa amb tomàquet in town. $ *Average main: €22* ⊠ *Balmes 47, Eixample* ☎ *93/452–1990* ⊕ *www.restaurantlolive.com* Ⓜ *Universitat, Passeig de Gràcia.*

★ Manairó

$$$ | CATALAN | A *manairó* is a mysterious Pyrenean elf, and Jordi Herrera may be the culinary version; his ingenious meat-cooking methods—such as filet mignon *al faquir* (heated from within on red-hot spikes) or blowtorched on a homemade centrifuge—may seem eccentric but produce diabolically good results. Melt-in-your-mouth meat dishes form the centerpiece of Manairó's menus, but they are ably supported by a bonanza of bold and confident creations that aren't frightened of big flavors.

Known for: innovative contemporary cuisine; delicious meat dishes; sculptures and artworks by the chef. $ *Average main: €26* ⊠ *Diputació 424, Eixample* ☎ *93/231–0057* ⊕ *www.jordiherrera.es/manairo* ⊘ *Closed Sun. and 1st wk of Jan.* Ⓜ *Monumental.*

★ Moments

$$$$ | CATALAN | Inside the ultrasleek Hotel Mandarin Oriental Barcelona, this restaurant continues the glamour with mod white chairs and glinting goldleaf on the ceiling. The food by Raül Balam and his mother—the legendary Carme Ruscalleda—lives up to its stellar pedigree, with original preparations that draw on deep wells of Catalan culinary traditions. **Known for:** chef's table; elaborate tasting menus; outstanding wine list. $ *Average main: €56* ⊠ *Passeig de Gràcia 38–40, Eixample* ☎ *93/151–8781* ⊕ *www.mandarinoriental.com* ⊘ *Closed Sun., Mon., and 2 wks in Jan.* Ⓜ *Passeig de Gràcia.*

★ Mont Bar

$$$ | CATALAN | FAMILY | Mont Bar's cramped interior belies the size of the flavors delivered from its kitchen. Star-quality morsels such as a sea cucumber carbonara and mochis stuffed with Mallorcan sobrassada are complemented by an immense wine list. **Known for:** upmarket bistro atmosphere; friendly service; mix of fine-dining dishes and barroom snacks. $ *Average main: €24* ⊠ *Diputació 220, Eixample* ☎ *93/323–9590* ⊕ *www.montbar.com* Ⓜ *Universitat.*

Mordisco

$$ | MEDITERRANEAN | The columns and skylights of this former high-class jewelers now frame a Mediterranean restaurant that emphasizes wholesome and flavorsome fare. Market-fresh produce is available to buy in the deli-like entrance, and makes its way into dishes such as artichoke hearts and hot veal carpaccios that come sizzling from the charcoal grill. **Known for:** enclosed patio; late-night cocktails at upstairs bar Thursday–Saturday; hot veal carpaccios. $ *Average main: €16*

✉ *Passatge de la Concepció 10, Eixample* ☎ *93/487–9656* ⊕ *www.grupotragaluz. com* Ⓜ *Diagonal.*

Paco Meralgo

$$ | TAPAS | The name, a pun on *para comer algo* ("to eat something" with an Andalusian accent), may be only marginally amusing, but the tapas here are no joke at all, from the classical *calamares fritos* (fried cuttlefish rings) to the *pimientos de Padrón* (green peppers, some fiery, from the Galician town of Padrón). Whether *à table,* at the counter, or in the private dining room upstairs, this modern space does traditional tapas that reliably hit the spot. **Known for:** traditional tapas; excellent wine list; montaditos (baguette slices with varied toppings). Ⓢ *Average main: €16* ✉ *Muntaner 171, Eixample* ☎ *93/430–9027* ⊕ *www.restaurant-pacomeralgo.com* Ⓜ *Hospital Clínic, Provença (FGC).*

Piratas

$ | TAPAS | Named for Roman Polanski's film of the same name, this extraordinary little spot just a block away from the Auditori de Barcelona and the new Encants market is an excellent choice for a pre- or post-concert taste of chef Lluis Ortega's improvisational cuisine, all prepared behind the bar on a single salamander. Hams, potatoes, foies, caviars, olives, anchovies, and tuna, as well as carefully selected wines and cavas, flow freely here. **Known for:** cozy space; superb cheeses; reservations essential. Ⓢ *Average main: €14* ✉ *Ausiàs Marc 157, Eixample* ☎ *93/245–7642* ⊗ *Closed Mon.–Wed. and Aug.* Ⓜ *Marina.*

Sense Pressa

$$$ | MEDITERRANEAN | *Sense pressa* means "without hurry" or "no rush" in Catalan, and if you can score one of the coveted half-dozen tables here at the corner of Carrer Córsega, you will want to linger as long as possible to enjoy this miniscule winner. *Risotto de ceps* (wild mushroom risotto), *garbanzos con espardenyes y huevos fritos* (chickpeas with sea cucumbers and fried eggs), or filet mignon of Girona beef cooked to perfection are all good choices. **Known for:** intimate tavern atmosphere; fresh local produce; toothsome risotto de ceps. Ⓢ *Average main: €24* ✉ *Enric Granados 96, Eixample* ☎ *93/218–1544* ⊕ *www.sensepressarestaurant.com* ⊗ *Closed Sun. and 2 wks in Aug. No dinner Mon.* Ⓜ *Diagonal.*

★ Sergi de Meià

$ | CATALAN | Sergi takes sourcing seriously, serving only ingredients foraged, caught, reared, or grown by people he knows personally. The result is a menu full of wild game, free-range and organic meat, seasonal vegetables, and sustainable fish, raised a notch by the skilled chef. **Known for:** family run; breakfast and brunch; always packed. Ⓢ *Average main: €15* ✉ *Aribau 106, Eixample* ☎ *93/125–5710* ⊕ *www.restaurantsergidemeia.cat* ⊗ *Closed Sun. and Mon.* Ⓜ *Universitat.*

Taktika Berri

$$ | BASQUE | Specializing in San Sebastián's favorite dishes, this Basque restaurant has only one drawback: a table is hard to score unless you call weeks in advance (an idea to consider before you travel). Your backup plan? The tapas served over the first-come, first-served bar. **Known for:** Basque pintxos; convivial tavern atmosphere; hospitable service. Ⓢ *Average main: €18* ✉ *València 169, Eixample* ☎ *93/453–4759* ⊗ *Closed Sun., 2 wks in Jan., 2 wks at Easter, and 3 wks in Aug. No dinner Sat.* Ⓜ *Hospital Clinic, Provença (FGC).*

Tapas 24

$$$ | TAPAS | The tapas emporium of celebrity chef Carles Abellán shows us how much he admires traditional Catalan and Spanish bar food, from patatas bravas to *croquetes de pollastre rostit* (roast chicken croquettes). The counter and terrace are constantly crowded, but the slightly pricey food is worth elbowing your way through the crowd for. **Known for:** traditional tapas with a twist; all-day

kitchen; bikini Carles Abellán (ham-and-cheese toastie with truffle oil). $ *Average main: €24* ⊠ *Diputació 269, Eixample* ☎ *93/488–0977* ⊕ *www.carlesabellan.com/mis-restaurantes/tapas-24* Ⓜ *Passeig de Gràcia.*

Tragaluz

$$$ | **MEDITERRANEAN** | *Tragaluz* means "skylight" (the sliding roof opens to the stars in good weather), and this is an excellent choice if you're still on a design high from shopping on Passeig de Gràcia or visiting Gaudí's Pedrera. The Mediterranean cuisine is traditional yet light and will please most palates, and it's a popular lunch spot. **Known for:** open-air dining; coffee or postdinner drink upstairs; entrance is through Japanese tavern. $ *Average main: €25* ⊠ *Passatge de la Concepció 5, Eixample* ☎ *93/487–0621* ⊕ *grupotragaluz.com* Ⓜ *Diagonal.*

Woki Organic Market

$ | **ECLECTIC** | Just off Plaça de Catalunya, this combination eco-market and restaurant serves organic ingredients prepared via healthy techniques and traditions. The beef is ecologically produced, the pastas are all made with ecologically pure flours, while the wines and vegetables are locally grown and carefully identified. **Known for:** great vegetarian and vegan dishes; sustainable food and decor; pastas made with pure flour. $ *Average main: €11* ⊠ *Ronda Universitat 20, Eixample* ☎ *93/302–5206* ⊕ *www.tribuwoki.com* Ⓜ *Catalunya.*

Xerta

$$$$ | **CATALAN** | The restaurant of the new Ohla Eixample hotel won a Michelin star in its first year. Much of Xerta's menu is the expected swanky fine-dining fare, but it stands out for its unique produce from the deltas and rivers of the Terres de l'Ebre region, such as sweet miniature *canyuts* (razor clams). **Known for:** produce from Terres de l'Ebre region; outstanding seafood and rice dishes; sweet miniature canyuts (razor clams). $ *Average main: €30* ⊠ *Còrsega 289, Eixample* ☎ *93/737–9080* ⊕ *www.xertarestaurant.com* ⊘ *Closed Sun. and Mon.* Ⓜ *Provença.*

Hotels

Alexandra Barcelona Doubletree by Hilton

$$$ | **HOTEL** | Compared with the pure mid-Eixample Moderniste buildings around it, the facade of the Alexandra can feel a bit featureless; the best of the hotel lies within this dependable lodging option (part of the Hilton group). **Pros:** excellent location; great steak restaurant Solomillo on-site; pool open daily 10 am–8 pm. **Cons:** no connecting rooms; rooms are narrow; black corridor walls on guest room floors can be overpowering. $ *Rooms from: €220* ⊠ *Carrer Mallorca 251, Eixample* ☎ *93/467–7166* ⊕ *www.hotel-alexandra.com* ⇥ *118 rooms* ⊙ *No meals* Ⓜ *Provença (FGC).*

★ Alma Hotel Barcelona

$$$$ | **HOTEL** | Only the facade is left to recall the Moderniste origins of the building; the inside spaces were completely redesigned in 2011, and the Alma emerged as Barcelona's sleekest mid-Eixample hotel. **Pros:** British afternoon tea served daily (open to the public); gorgeous garden with sushi bar; complementary minibar. **Cons:** budget-stretching room rates; pricey buffet breakfast. $ *Rooms from: €300* ⊠ *Carrer Mallorca 271, Eixample* ☎ *93/216–4490* ⊕ *www.almahotels.com* ⇥ *72 rooms* ⊙ *No meals* Ⓜ *L3/L5 Diagonal, L4 Girona, FGC Provença.*

★ Almanac Barcelona

$$$$ | **HOTEL | FAMILY** | Occupying a prime position on Barcelona's Gran Via de les Corts Catalanes, a stone's throw from Gaudí's modernist buildings on Passeig de Gràcia, this is a boutique-style hotel wrapped up in supreme luxury. **Pros:** superb location one block from Passeig de Gràcia; unbeatable rooftop views; top-quality service. **Cons:** hard on the wallet; additional charge for the spa; no

Barcelona's Must-Eat

Top priorities for a trip to Barcelona might just read: see great art and architecture, enjoy the nightlife, eat ham. In all seriousness, you shouldn't pass up the opportunity to eat Spain's exquisite artisanal ham—known in Catalan as *pernil* and in Spanish as *jamón*—made from acorn-fed native black pigs whose meat is salt-cured and then air-dried for two to four years. The best kind, *jamón ibérico de bellota*, comes from carefully managed and exercised pigs fed only acorns. This lengthy process results in a silky, slightly sweet and nutty meat that is contradictorily both light and intensely rich.

You can casually approach the quest for this delicacy at nearly any bar or restaurant across Barcelona, feasting on different qualities of hams, including jamón ibérico's lesser but still stellar cousin, *jamón serrano*.

Catalonia's love affair with cured pork isn't restricted to jamón. Sausages and other pork derivatives, known as *embutits* (*embutidos* in Spanish), are equally common sandwich-fillers, and are regularly served as starters in even high-end restaurants. For an authentic experience, try some with a cold glass of vermut and a side of potato chips, ideally as a light snack on a terrace before a full lunch.

Chorizo is, of course, the best-known and most ubiquitous sausage in Spain. Pork and paprika are the two key ingredients, but styles and quality vary widely, ranging from cheap, mass-produced batons for stews to handmade *chorizo ibérico*, best savored in wafer-thin slices.

Local Catalan favorites include the chewy but tasty *llonganissa* (cured sausages), and *fuet*. The latter can be almost too tough to eat or wonderfully delicious, depending on the quality, so don't rush to judgment after your first experience. *Bull* (pronounced, more or less, "boo-eey") comes in *blanc* (white) and *negre* (black) varieties—the latter is made with blood. Served cold in thin slices, bull is often served with salads.

Botifarra sausages are important components of Catalan cuisine. Most are served hot, typically with *mongetes* (white haricot beans), but cold *botifarra blanc* and negre are also common. A third variety, *botifarra d'ou*, includes eggs and has an unusual yellow hue. For a truly Catalan taste experience, look for *botifarra dolça*—this decidedly odd dessert sausage incorporates lemon and sugar.

pets. $ *Rooms from: €350* ⊠ *Gran Via de les Corts Catalanes 619-621, Eixample* ☎ *93/018–7000* ⊕ *www.almanachotels. com* 🛏 *91 rooms* ⊙ *No meals* Ⓜ *L2/L3/ L4 Passeig de Gràcia.*

Casa Bonay

$$ | **HOTEL** | Fueled by a team of locally based creators and designers, lighting companies, furniture makers, chefs, and even coffee experts, this independent boutique hotel, located in a beautifully renovated neoclassical town house from 1869, channels a distinctly neighborhood vibe. **Pros:** a Barcelona hub; fans in rooms; natural light in all rooms except Passage Tiny. **Cons:** courtyard room terraces are overlooked by other apartments; passage rooms have no view; breakfast not served in room. $ *Rooms from: €160* ⊠ *Gran Via de les Corts Catalanes 700, Eixample* ☎ *93/545–8070* ⊕ *www.casabonay.com* 🛏 *67 rooms* ⊙ *No meals* Ⓜ *L2 Tetuan; L1 Arc de Triomf.*

Condes de Barcelona

$$$ | **HOTEL** | One of Barcelona's most popular hotels, the Condes de Barcelona is perfectly placed for exploring the sights (and shops) of the city's most fashionable quarter, and—for the privileged location—offers exceptional value. **Pros:** elegant building with subdued contemporary furnishings; prime spot in the middle of the Eixample; excellent value. **Cons:** no spa; no pets; rooftop plunge pool is small. [$] *Rooms from: €190* ✉ *Passeig de Gràcia 73, Eixample* ☎ *93/467–4780* 🌐 *www.condesdebarcelona.com* 🛏 *126 rooms* 🍴 *No meals* [M] *L3/L5 Diagonal, Provença (FGC).*

★ **Continental Palacete**

$$ | **HOTEL** | **FAMILY** | This former palatial family home, or *palacete*, provides a splendid drawing room, a location nearly dead-center for Barcelona's main attractions, views over leafy Rambla de Catalunya, and a 24-hour free buffet. **Pros:** ornate design; attentive staff; ideal location. **Cons:** room decor is relentlessly pink and overdraped; bathrooms are a bit cramped; some street noise. [$] *Rooms from: €153* ✉ *Rambla de Calatunya 30, at Diputació, Eixample* ☎ *93/445–7657* 🌐 *www.hotelcontinental.com* 🛏 *22 rooms* 🍴 *Free Breakfast* [M] *L2/L3/L4 Passeig de Gràcia, Plaça Catalunya.*

The Corner Hotel

$$$ | **HOTEL** | This hip addition to the city's boutique hotel scene, positioned (yep, you guessed it) on a corner, has been fashioned from a handsome, turn-of-the-century building in Barcelona's stylish Eixample district, within a few blocks walking distance of Gaudí's key sights on Passeig de Gràcia. **Pros:** walking distance to Passeig de Gràcia; rooms include complimentary bottle of water plus coffee and tea; popular Sunday brunch. **Cons:** far from the old town; interior-facing rooms lack natural light; extra charge for parking. [$] *Rooms from: €190* ✉ *Mallorca, 178, Eixample* ☎ *93/554–2400* 🌐 *www.thecornerhotel-barcelona.com* 🛏 *72 rooms* 🍴 *No meals* [M] *FGC Provença; L5 Hospital Clinic.*

Calçots from Heaven

Since the late 19th century, *calçots*, long-stemmed, twice-planted white onions cooked over grapevine clippings, have provided a favorite outing from Barcelona to the Collserola hills or on the beaches of Gavá and Casteldefells from November to April. Some in-town restaurants also serve calçots, always consumed with romescu sauce and accompanied by lamb chops, botifarra sausage, and copious quantities of young red wine poured from a long-spouted *porró* held overhead.

★ **Cotton House Hotel**

$$$$ | **HOTEL** | First a sumptuous family home, this 1879 property was bought in 1961 by the city's Cotton Producers Guild and then became a hotel in 2015; it's now part of Marriott's boutique Autograph Collection and has been redesigned by Lázaro Rosa-Violán with scrupulous respect for the original features of the building: coffered ceilings, geometric parquet floors, and Frank Lloyd Wright–like touches of modernism. **Pros:** spot-on professional, friendly service; restaurant Batuar (€25) open 7 am–midnight; huge terrace off the bar with original fountains. **Cons:** bed size leaves little room to maneuver in basic rooms; some rooms with vanities outside the shower room; fairly pricey. [$] *Rooms from: €320* ✉ *Gran Vía de les Corts Catalanes 670, Eixample* ☎ *93/450–5045* 🌐 *www.hotelcottonhouse.com* 🛏 *88 rooms* 🍴 *No meals* [M] *L2/L3/L4 Passeig de Gràcia.*

El Avenida Palace

$$$$ | **HOTEL** | A minute's walk from Plaça Catalunya and the Passeig de Gràcia, this 1952 hotel earns top marks for location—and for nostalgia. **Pros:** prime location; excellent soundproofing; "Beatles suite" (the band stayed here in 1965). **Cons:** not for fans of minimalism or cutting-edge design; service can be snooty; low ceilings on guest room floors. [$] *Rooms from: €250* ✉ *Gran Via 605–607, Eixample* ☎ *93/301–9600* 🌐 *www.avenidapalace.com* 🛏 *151 rooms* 🍴 *No meals* [M] *L2/L3/L4 Passeig de Gràcia, Pl. Catalunya.*

Gallery Hotel

$$ | **HOTEL** | In the upper part of the Eixample below the Diagonal, this contemporary hotel offers impeccable service and a superb central location for exploring, with the city's prime art-gallery district just a few blocks away on Consell de Cent. **Pros:** two large rooftop terraces with year-round pools; DJ or live music on summer weekends; recently renovated. **Cons:** small closet space; rooftop deck does not offer great views. [$] *Rooms from: €165* ✉ *Roselló 249, Eixample* ☎ *93/415–9911* 🌐 *www.galleryhotel.com* 🛏 *105 rooms* 🍴 *No meals* [M] *L3/L5 Diagonal, Provença (FGC).*

Hotel Astoria

$$ | **HOTEL** | Three blocks west of Rambla Catalunya, near the upper middle of the Eixample, this renovated classic property, part of the cutting-edge Derby Hotels Collection group of brilliant artistic restorations, is a trove for the budget-minded. **Pros:** prime location; excellent value for price; free entrance to the Egyptian Museum of Barcelona. **Cons:** gym has only three machines; rooms on lower floors on the street side can be noisy; rooftop terrace pool is small. [$] *Rooms from: €140* ✉ *Carrer Paris 203, Eixample* ☎ *93/209–8311* 🌐 *www.hotelastoria-barcelona.com* 🛏 *117 rooms* 🍴 *No meals* [M] *Provença (FGC), L3/L5 Diagonal.*

Hotel Axel

$$$ | **HOTEL** | In the heart of the more fashionable Esquerra (west or "left" side) of the Eixample, this recently expanded and renovated hotel caters primarily to gay travelers in an area dubbed by locals the "Gayxample." The spacious rooms are soundproof and well lighted, with comfortable contemporary furniture and decor in white-on-white punctuated by hints of black, red, and chrome; most have queen-size beds. **Pros:** great location; exceptionally well-equipped gym; rooftop deck with pool, bar, cascade, and Jacuzzi (April–October). **Cons:** uninviting lobby; extra €2 charge for faster Wi-Fi; standard rooms have limited storage space. [$] *Rooms from: €177* ✉ *Carrer Aribau 33, Eixample* ☎ *93/323–9393* 🌐 *www.axelhotels.com* 🛏 *96 rooms* 🍴 *No meals* [M] *L1/L2 Universitat.*

★ **Hotel Claris Grand Luxe Barcelona**

$$$$ | **HOTEL** | Acclaimed as one of Barcelona's best hotels, the Claris is an icon of design, tradition, and connoisseurship. **Pros:** first-rate restaurant La Terraza; Mayan Secret Spa with temazcal and pure chocolate skin treatment; rooms in a variety of styles. **Cons:** basic ("Superior") rooms small for the price; rooftop terrace noise at night can reach down into sixth-floor rooms; capacity bookings can sometimes overwhelm the staff. [$] *Rooms from: €270* ✉ *Carrer Pau Claris 150, Eixample* ☎ *93/487–6262* 🌐 *www.hotelclaris.com* 🛏 *124 rooms* 🍴 *No meals* [M] *L2/L3/L4 Passeig de Gràcia.*

Hotel Constanza

$$ | **HOTEL** | A few minutes' walk from the heart of the city at Plaça Catalunya, this moderately priced boutique hotel has guest rooms restfully decorated in lush coffee and chocolate tones, offset with leather and wood textures. **Pros:** excellent value for price; friendly, professional staff; good grazing at restaurant Bruc 33 Tapas. **Cons:** no views; no room service. [$] *Rooms from: €174* ✉ *Carrer Bruc 33, Eixample* ☎ *93/270–1910* 🌐 *www.*

hotelconstanza.com ⤴ 46 rooms ⦿ No meals Ⓜ L1/L4 Urquinaona, L2/L3/L4 Pl. Catalunya.

★ Hotel Cram

$$ | HOTEL | A short walk from La Rambla, this Eixample design hotel offers impeccable midcity accommodations with cheerful avant-garde decor and luxurious details. **Pros:** Jordi Cruz's Angle restaurant on-site; great location; dolly slides under the bed for suitcase storage. **Cons:** Aribau is a major uptown artery, noisy at all hours; rooms are a bit small, with quirky shapes; no gym or spa. Ⓢ *Rooms from: €160* ⌧ *Carrer Aribau 54, Eixample* ☎ *93/216–7700* ⊕ *www.hotelcram.com* ⤴ *67 rooms* ⦿ *No meals* Ⓜ *L1/L2 Universitat, Provença (FGC).*

★ Hotel El Palace Barcelona

$$$$ | HOTEL | Founded in 1919 by Caesar Ritz, the original Ritz (the grande dame of Barcelona hotels) was renamed in 2005 but kept its lavish Old European style intact, from the liveried doorman in top hat and tails to the lobby's ormolu clocks and massive crystal chandelier. **Pros:** equidistant from Barri Gòtic and central Eixample; L'Éclair features live jazz and more; Mayan-style sauna in the award-winning spa. **Cons:** €30-per-night surcharge for small pets; painfully pricey; formal atmosphere. Ⓢ *Rooms from: €360* ⌧ *Gran Vía de les Corts Catalanes 668, Eixample* ☎ *93/510–1130* ⊕ *www.hotelpalacebarcelona.com* ⤴ *120 rooms* ⦿ *No meals* Ⓜ *L2/L3/L4 Passeig de Gràcia.*

Hotel Eurostars BCN Design

$$$ | HOTEL | This quirky property is what happens when design is allowed to triumph over tradition. **Pros:** friendly, helpful staff; good breakfast; in-room massage service; room service 24 hours; free late checkout to 1 pm. **Cons:** wardrobes have no drawers; washbasins and toiletry shelves poorly placed; no pets; no pool. Ⓢ *Rooms from: €220* ⌧ *Passeig de Gràcia 29–31, Eixample* ☎ *93/344–4555* ⊕ *www.eurostarsbcndesign.com/en* ⤴ *70 rooms* ⦿ *No meals* Ⓜ *Passeig de Gràcia.*

Hotel Gran Derby Suite 4*

$$$ | HOTEL | Clubby and comfortable, this Eixample hotel, made up entirely of suites and duplexes with living rooms, is ideal for groups and families. **Pros:** rooms and suites are spacious and tastefully hip; on a quiet side street; free entrance to the Egyptian Museum of Barcelona. **Cons:** far from the city's main attractions. Ⓢ *Rooms from: €190* ⌧ *Carrer Loreto 28, Eixample* ☎ *93/445–2544* ⊕ *www.hotelgranderby.com* ⤴ *43 suites* ⦿ *No meals* Ⓜ *T1/T2/T3 Tram, L5 Hospital Clinic.*

★ Hotel Granados 83

$$$ | HOTEL | Designed in the style of a New York City loft and seated on a tree-shaded street in the heart of the Eixample, this hotel blends exposed brick, steel, and glass with Greek and Italian marble and Indonesian tamarind wood to achieve downtown cool. **Pros:** luxurious duplexes with private terraces and semi-private pools; wide variety of good casual restaurants nearby; free entrance to the Egyptian Museum of Barcelona. **Cons:** rooftop terrace pool quite small; standard rooms need more storage space; Wi-Fi can be patchy. Ⓢ *Rooms from: €195* ⌧ *Carrer Enric Granados 83, Eixample* ☎ *93/492–9670* ⊕ *www.hotelgranados83.com* ⤴ *84 rooms* ⦿ *No meals* Ⓜ *Provença (FGC).*

★ Hotel Granvía

$$ | HOTEL | A 19th-century palatial home (built for the owner of the Bank of Barcelona), the Granvía opened as a hotel in 1935, and reopened in 2013 after a lengthy renovation, with its original features still intact: an art deco cupola in the entrance, coffered ceilings, pillared arches, and a marble grand staircase. **Pros:** historical setting; pleasant terrace; British-style high tea served in the salon daily 5–7 pm. **Cons:** no pool, gym, or spa; most standard rooms have twin beds yoked together rather than doubles; bathrooms a bit cramped; few amenities. Ⓢ *Rooms from: €170* ⌧ *Gran Vía de les Corts Catalanes 642, Eixample*

☎ 93/318–1900 🌐 www.hotelgranvia.com 🛏 58 rooms 🍴 Free Breakfast [M] L2/L3/ L4 Passeig de Gràcia.

Hotel H10 Casanova

$$ | HOTEL | FAMILY | A chic postmodern addition to Barcelona's lodging options is hidden behind this traditional facade, a 15-minute walk from the top of La Rambla; public spaces have a nightclub feel, with leather chairs, pillar candles, and backlit neon-green Plexiglas panels at reception and the bar. **Pros:** good combination of comfort and style; hotel has its own parking; bicycles for guests to rent. **Cons:** must walk through busy artery to get to Plaça Catalunya; room lighting could be better; breakfasts must be booked in advance for the duration of your stay. *[$] Rooms from: €149 ✉ Gran Via de les Corts Catalanes 559, Eixample ☎ 93/396–4800 🌐 www.h10hotels.com 🛏 124 rooms 🍴 No meals [M] L1 Urgell, L2 Universitat.*

Hotel Jazz

$$ | HOTEL | Bright colors, clean lines, and contemporary artwork give this hotel (dead center in the heart of Barcelona) a hip, fashionable feel. **Pros:** elevators work only on room keys, for added security; central location; rooftop bar serves pizza and tapas. **Cons:** no pets; a bit pricey. *[$] Rooms from: €170 ✉ Carrer Pelai 3, Eixample ☎ 93/552–9696 🌐 www.hoteljazz.com 🛏 108 rooms 🍴 No meals [M] L1/L2 Universitat, Catalunya.*

★ Hotel Omm

$$$$ | HOTEL | FAMILY | The lobby of this postmodern architectural stunner tells you what to expect throughout: perfect comfort, cutting-edge design, and meticulous attention to every detail. **Pros:** perfect location for the upper Eixample; fireplace in lounge; superb spa. **Cons:** small plunge pools; restaurant is pricey and a little precious; parking is expensive. *[$] Rooms from: €275 ✉ Roselló 265, Eixample ☎ 93/445–4000 🌐 www.hotelomm.com 🛏 91 rooms 🍴 No meals [M] L3/L5 Diagonal, Provença (FGC).*

Hotel Praktik Garden

$ | HOTEL | If you've ever dreamed about running away with the circus, this quirky little boutique hotel, where the walls are covered with gaily colored circus posters, is just for you. **Pros:** free coffee service in the garden; close to Passeig de Gràcia; pleasant terrace/lounge. **Cons:** pipe racks instead of closets; minimal amenities; no breakfast room. *[$] Rooms from: €107 ✉ Carrer Diputacio 325, Eixample ☎ 93/467–5279 🌐 www.hotelpraktikgarden.com 🛏 59 rooms 🍴 No meals [M] L4 Girona.*

Hotel Pulitzer

$$$ | HOTEL | Built squarely over the metro's central hub and within walking distance of everything in town, this breezy clubhouse-hotel could not be better situated. **Pros:** rooftop terrace has live music or DJ on weekends; bicycle rentals for guests; breakfast room bright and cheery. **Cons:** narrow standard rooms; no pool or gym (but privileges at nearby fitness center); pricey surcharge for pets (dogs only). *[$] Rooms from: €180 ✉ Bergara 8, Eixample ☎ 93/481–6767 🌐 www.hotelpulitzer.es 🛏 91 rooms 🍴 No meals [M] Catalunya.*

Hotel Regina

$$$ | HOTEL | FAMILY | What it lacks in bells and whistles, this family-friendly little hotel makes up for in its unparalleled location—on a side street just steps from Plaça Catalunya—and its relaxed contemporary feel. **Pros:** just steps from Plaça Catalunya; charming breakfast room has excellent buffet; live sessions in the piano bar Tuesdays at 9 pm. **Cons:** no pool or gym (but privileges at nearby fitness center); bathrooms in some superior rooms are really small; no pets. *[$] Rooms from: €180 ✉ Calle Bergara 4, Eixample ☎ 93/301–3232 🌐 www.reginahotel.com/en 🛏 99 rooms 🍴 No meals [M] Catalunya.*

★ Majestic Hotel & Spa

$$$$ | HOTEL | With an unbeatable location on Barcelona's most stylish boulevard, steps from Gaudí's La Pedrera and near the area's swankiest shops, a leafy rooftop terrace with killer views of the city's landmarks including the Sagrada Familia, this hotel is a near-perfect place to stay. **Pros:** excellent restaurant and spa; beloved city landmark with interesting history; art (including Miró prints) from owner's private collection. **Cons:** some standard rooms a bit small for the price; pricey (but award-winning) buffet breakfast. $ *Rooms from: €325* ⊠ *Passeig de Gràcia 68, Eixample* ☎ *93/488–1717* ⊕ *www.hotelmajestic.es* ⇌ *275 rooms* ⎮◎⎮ *No meals* Ⓜ *L2/L3/L4 Passeig de Gràcia, Provença (FGC).*

Mandarin Oriental Barcelona
$$$$ | **HOTEL** | **FAMILY** | A carpeted ramp leading from the elegant Passeig de Gràcia (flanked by Tiffany and Brioni boutiques) lends this hotel the air of a privileged—and pricey—inner sanctum. **Pros:** outstanding Moments restaurant; babysitters and parties for the kids, on request; Mimosa interior garden great for drinks. **Cons:** rooms relatively small for a five-star accommodation; Wi-Fi free in rooms only if booked online; lighting a bit dim. $ *Rooms from: €575* ⊠ *Passeig de Gràcia 38–40, Eixample* ☎ *93/151–8888* ⊕ *www.mandarinoriental.com/barcelona* ⇌ *120 rooms* ⎮◎⎮ *No meals* Ⓜ *L2/L3/L4 Passeig de Gràcia, L3/L5 Diagonal, Provença (FGC).*

Meliá Barcelona Sky
$$ | **HOTEL** | At a bit of a remove from the major tourist attractions, east along Diagonal from Plaça de les Glòries, the Meliá hotel group's Barcelona Sky gets much of its business from professional and trade conference organizers, but wins high marks as well from recreational visitors for its luxurious appointments and lively design. **Pros:** handy to Sagrada Família, beach, and Poble Nou nightlife scene; great views from rooftop deck; 24-hour free drinks and snacks on terrace. **Cons:** inconvenient to Eixample and Gothic Quarter; high-rise glass-and-concrete slab architecture; "open concept" bedroom/bathroom layout lacks privacy. $ *Rooms from: €160* ⊠ *Carrer Pere IV 272–286, Eixample* ☎ *902/144440* ⊕ *www.melia.com* ⇌ *258 rooms* ⎮◎⎮ *No meals* Ⓜ *L4 Poble Nou.*

★ Monument Hotel
$$$$ | **HOTEL** | Originally the home of Enric Battló, a brother of the textile magnate who commissioned Gaudí to redesign the Moderniste masterpiece Casa Battló, and a minute's walk away on the Passeig de Gràcia, the historic 1898 building that houses the Monument went through several incarnations before architect Oscar Tusquets and his project team transformed it into the elegant upmarket hotel it is today. **Pros:** helpful, professional multilingual staff; ideal mid-Eixample location; under-floor heating in the bathrooms. **Cons:** hard on the budget; most "junior suites" are in effect large doubles with seating areas; pricey American breakfast. $ *Rooms from: €300* ⊠ *Passeig de Gràcia 73, Eixample* ☎ *93/548–2000* ⊕ *www.monument-hotel.com* ⇌ *158 rooms* ⎮◎⎮ *No meals* Ⓜ *L3/L5 Diagonal, Provença (FGC).*

★ Murmuri Barcelona
$$$ | **HOTEL** | **FAMILY** | British designer Kelly Hoppen took this 19th-century town house on La Rambla de Catalunya and transformed it into a chic, intimate urban retreat, with room decor in velvety brown, beige, and black, with big mirrors, dramatic bed lighting, and arresting photography. **Pros:** private terraces in Privilege doubles; strategic Eixample location; exclusive rooftop terrace open year-round. **Cons:** no pool, gym, or spa (though guest privileges at the nearby affiliated Majestic hotel); no pets, except in the apartments; Design doubles a bit small. $ *Rooms from: €185* ⊠ *Rambla de Catalunya 104, Eixample* ☎ *93/550–0600* ⊕ *www.murmuri.com* ⇌ *61 rooms* ⎮◎⎮ *No meals* Ⓜ *L3/L5 Diagonal, Provença (FGC).*

8

The Eixample

The One Hotel
$$$$ | **HOTEL** | **FAMILY** | This highly rated H10 hotel chain property with smart, elegant interiors (courtesy of Barcelona-based design studio, Jaime Beriestain) occupies a prime position one block from Gaudí's Casa Milà. **Pros:** prime position for Gaudí sights and shopping; wonderful city views from the rooftop; generous sized rooms. **Cons:** no private on-site parking (additional cost); charge for pets; restaurant in the lobby feels a little generic. [$] *Rooms from: €300* ✉ *C/ Provença 277, Eixample* ☎ *93/214–2070* 🌐 *www.h10hotels.com* 🛏 *88 rooms* 🍴 *No meals* [M] *L5/L3 Diagonal.*

Room Mate Emma
$$ | **HOTEL** | While the hotel's slogan, "Do You Want To Sleep With Me?" is a bit gimmicky, the Emma itself is a comfortable, centrally positioned billet at an affordable price. **Pros:** pivotal location; futuristic design; bike rentals for guests at €10/four hours, €15 full day. **Cons:** rooms on lower floors can be noisy; no pool, spa, or gym; no room service. [$] *Rooms from: €150* ✉ *Carrer Rosselló 205, Eixample* ☎ *93/238–5606* 🌐 *www.room-matehotels.com* 🛏 *56 rooms* 🍴 *No meals* [M] *Provença (FGC).*

Silken Gran Hotel Havana
$$$ | **HOTEL** | Popular with cruise ship passengers who extend their vacations to savor the city, the Havana is about equidistant from the Moderniste sights of the Eixample and the Gothic Quarter. **Pros:** bright, lively public spaces; helpful, English-speaking staff; in-room massage service. **Cons:** on a major crosstown artery, where traffic is heavy night and day; not well situated for views; room service shuts down at 10:30 pm. [$] *Rooms from: €180* ✉ *Gran Via 647, Eixample* ☎ *93/341–7000* 🌐 *www.granhotelhavana.com* 🛏 *145 rooms* 🍴 *No meals* [M] *L2/L3/L4 Passeig de Gràcia, L4 Girona, L2 Tetuan.*

SixtyTwo Hotel
$$$$ | **HOTEL** | Across from Gaudí's Casa Batlló and just down Passeig de Gràcia from his Casa Milà (La Pedrera), this sleek boutique hotel, which opened in 2009, is surrounded by Barcelona's top shopping addresses and leading restaurants. **Pros:** ideal location; free coffee, tea, and snacks in the lounge, 24/7; complimentary cava every evening at 6. **Cons:** some rooms a bit small; no pool, gym, or spa; room service ends at 10 pm. [$] *Rooms from: €250* ✉ *Passeig de Gràcia 62, Eixample* ☎ *93/272–4180* 🌐 *www.sixtytwohotel.com* 🛏 *44 rooms* 🍴 *No meals* [M] *L2/L3/L4 Passeig de Gràcia.*

the5rooms
$$ | **B&B/INN** | **FAMILY** | This charming little boutique B&B in the heart of the city has been expanded into a complex of nine spacious guest rooms and three suites, with two full residential apartments next door. **Pros:** a sense of home away from home; comfortable contemporary design; honesty bar in the common area. **Cons:** no bar or restaurant; Pau Claris a busy and noisy artery; no reception after 9 pm. [$] *Rooms from: €155* ✉ *Carrer Pau Claris 72, Eixample* ☎ *93/342–7880* 🌐 *www.the5rooms.com* 🛏 *12 rooms, 2 apartments* 🍴 *Breakfast* [M] *L1/L4 Urquinaona, L2/L3/L4 Passeig de Gràcia.*

Villa Emilia
$$ | **HOTEL** | The stylish, comfortable Villa Emilia is a bit removed from the tourist attractions of the Eixample and the Old City, but a mere five minutes' walk to the Fira de Barcelona exposition grounds, Las Arenas shopping center, and the airport shuttle bus stop in Plaça Espanya. **Pros:** excellent wines at on-site bistro; barbecue and drinks on the opulent rooftop terrace (May–October). **Cons:** no pool; staff struggles a bit in English; no gym or spa. [$] *Rooms from: €170* ✉ *Carrer Calàbria 115–117, Eixample* ☎ *93/252–5285* 🌐 *www.hotelvillaemilia.com* 🛏 *53 rooms* 🍴 *No meals* [M] *L1 Rocafort.*

ⓨ Nightlife

Home to a magnificent array of Modernist architectural wonders, including Gaudí masterpieces Casa Milà, Casa Batlló, and La Sagrada Família, Barcelona's modish L'Eixample district is at once the largest and most diverse nightlife destination in town. With truly something for all tastes, on any given night you can find expat students blowing off steam at themed pubs and dance clubs catering to their likes, the LGBTQ community partying in the fashionable area affectionately known as "Gaixample," and the posh set rushing from high-end restaurants and chandeliered hotel bars to find a place at VIP tables in the city's swankiest clubs and lounges.

BARS

★ Banker's Bar

BARS/PUBS | With allusions to its past life as a bank (like the safety deposit boxes on the wall), the swank cocktail bar of the 5* Mandarin Oriental Hotel lounge is perfect for an opulent night out. DJs play relaxing jazz, swing, and blues tunes on weekends. Wednesday night is reserved for live musical performances. Oversize brown leather chairs and taupe-color detailing surround the black lacquer bar manned by barmaids dressed in matching Asian-inspired qipaos serving fare from a biannually changing "East meets West" menu that includes classic cocktail favorites alongside signature creations paired with light, bicontinental bites. ⊠ *Hotel Mandarin Oriental, Passeig de Gràcia 38–40, Eixample* ☏ *93/151–8782* ⊕ *www.mandarinoriental.es/barcelona* Ⓜ *Passeig de Gràcia.*

★ Dry Martini

BARS/PUBS | An homage to the traditional English martini bar of decades past, this stately spot is paradise for cocktail aficionados seeking the most expertly mixed drinks in town (martinis even have their own prep section). From the wood-paneled fixtures of the mirrored bar featuring a vintage brass register, to the knowledgeable barmen dressed in impeccable white coats and ties, to the wall of vintage spirit bottles overlooking plush and regal turquoise and red leather seating, each detail aims to transport the loyal clientele back to an era of inspired excellence. ⊠ *Aribau 162, Eixample* ☏ *93/217–5072* ⊕ *www.drymartiniorg.com* Ⓜ *Provença.*

La Vinoteca Torres

WINE BARS—NIGHTLIFE | In a space ideally located on Barcelona's exclusive shopping avenue, Passeig de Gràcia, the acclaimed Torres wine dynasty offers an ample selection of their international wines and spirits to accompany delectable Mediterranean fish or meat dishes such as the signature oxtail in Sangre de Toro red wine sauce. The dark, ultramodern space is adorned with walls of stacked wine bottles, and strategic lighting illuminates the natural wood tables. For an extra-special treat, book the private back room that seats up to 14. When the weather is nice, stop by for a quick glass of wine and tapas on the parasol-covered terrace. ⊠ *Passeig de Gràcia 78, Eixample* ☏ *93/272–6625* ⊕ *www.lavinotecatorres.com* Ⓜ *Passeig de Gràcia, Diagonal.*

Les Gens que J'aime

BARS/PUBS | Bohemia meets the Moulin Rouge at this intimate, below-street-level bordello-inspired pub with turn-of-the-20th-century memorabilia, including fringed lampshades, faded period portraits, stacked blue light chandelier, and comfy wicker sofas cushioned with lush red velvet. First opened in 1967, this jazz-playing dark and dusty spot offers attentive yet laid-back service, allowing guests to linger for a cocktail (whiskey sours are popular), a telling tarot card reading, or a romantic tête-à-tête by Tiffany lamplight. ⊠ *València 286, bajos, Eixample* ☏ *93/215–6879* ⊕ *www.lesgensquejaime.com* Ⓜ *Passeig de Gràcia.*

Milano

BARS/PUBS | For more than a decade, this "secret" basement bar, located in an area otherwise dominated by student pubs and tourist traps, has had a rotating lineup of international acts including blues, soul, jazz, flamenco, swing, and pop. In a space resembling a 1940s cabaret, you'll find paneled oak, a brass bar, spotlit photo prints of previous acts, and red banquette-style seating alongside matching armchairs and tables. The stage is complete with moody lighting and a curtain backdrop. Milano is open from noon for tapas lunch with cocktails (classic and creative), and shows run nightly at 9 pm and 11 pm. ✉ Ronda Universitat 35, Eixample ☎ 93/112–7150 ⊕ www.camparimilano. com/en Ⓜ Catalunya, Universitat.

★ Monvínic

WINE BARS—NIGHTLIFE | Conceptualized to celebrate wine culture at its finest, this spectacular space, aptly called "Wineworld" in Catalan, features a ritzy wine bar complete with tablet wine lists, a cavernous culinary space, a reference library, a vertical garden, and the pièce de résistance: a vast cellar housing a mind-blowing 3,500 vintages from around the world. Small plates of regional jamón and inventive riffs on classical Catalan cuisine complement the vino. Wine tastings, both traditional and creative, are held regularly for groups or individuals looking to become oenophiles. ✉ Diputació 249, Eixample ☎ 93/272–6187 ⊕ www.monvinic.com Ⓜ Passeig de Gràcia.

Morro Fi

BARS/PUBS | Tiny and unpretentious yet decidedly on trend, this untraditional vermuteria is reintroducing classic vermouth to the masses. Opened by a trio of vermouth aficionados, Morro Fi (loosely translates as "refined palate") was originally a foodie blog that morphed into a bar determined to educate visitors about enjoying vermouth (they even produce their own brand) with select tapas. The result? Locals and the odd expat routinely spilling out into the streets, drink in hand while indie music blares. ✉ Consell de Cent 171, Eixample ⊕ www.morrofi.cat Ⓜ Urgell.

Senyor Vermut

BARS/PUBS | This snazzy, high-ceilinged vermuteria has guests lining up to sample a generous selection of more than 40 vermuts served with traditional tapas. From bitter to earthy or aged in a barrel, this classic aperitif is clearly the star attraction despite other offerings including wine, beer, juices, and hot beverages. Located on a quiet corner free of the tourist-baiting menus that abound in the neighborhood, Senyor Vermut serves its legion of loyal customers an uninterrupted array of food and drink daily, either inside, or outside on the year-round terrace. ✉ Carrer de Provença 85, Eixample ☎ 93/532–8865 Ⓜ Entença.

★ Solange Cocktails and Luxury Spirits

BARS/PUBS | The latest venture from the Pernia brothers—the trio whose Tandem Cocktail Bar (Aribau 86) pioneered Barcelona's emerging cocktail scene back in the '80s—is a sleek, golden-hued, luxurious lounge space aptly named after Solange Dimitrios, 007's original Bond girl. Smartly dressed mixologists cater to well-heeled 30-plus professionals at the stunning long bar or on posh lounge divans so extravagant in look and feel that one expects the debonair spy to walk in at any moment. The homage continues with signature cocktails that reference Bond films, characters, and even a "secret mission" concoction for the more daring. ✉ Carrer Aribau 143, Eixample ☎ 93/164–3625 Ⓜ Hospital Clínic, Diagonal.

DANCE CLUBS

Antilla Salsa Barcelona (Antilla Salsa Barcelona)

DANCE CLUBS | You'll find this exuberant Caribbean spot sizzling with salsa, son cubano, and merengue from the moment you step in the door. From 10 to 11 on Wednesday, enthusiastic dance instructors teach bachata for free. After that, the dancing begins and the dancers rarely stop to draw breath. This self-proclaimed "Caribbean cultural center" cranks out every variation of salsa ever invented. There are regular live concerts, and on Friday and Saturday, the mike gives way to animated Latin DJs. ✉ Aragó 141, Eixample ☎ 610/900588 ⊕ www.antillasalsa.com Ⓜ Urgell, Hospital Clínic.

Bikini Barcelona

DANCE CLUBS | This sleek megaclub, which was reborn as part of L'Illa shopping center, boasts the best sound system in Barcelona. A smaller space puts on concerts of emerging and cult artists—the Nigerian singer-songwriter Asa, local soulsters The Pepper Pots, and Gil Scott-Heron in one of his final performances are just some of the noteworthy events here. When gigs finish around midnight, the walls roll back and the space ingeniously turns into a sweaty nightclub. ✉ Diagonal 547, Eixample ☎ 93/322–0800 ⊕ www.bikinibcn.com Ⓜ Maria Cristina.

Boyberry

BARS/PUBS | This gay hub combines a wide range of resources, from films and darkrooms to Internet connections, and a lounge. ✉ Calàbria 96, Eixample ☎ 93/426–2312 ⊕ www.boyberry.com Ⓜ Rocafort.

City Hall

DANCE CLUBS | Nightly parties starring electro house music and guest DJs from neighboring clubs guarantee dancing till you drop at this raging mid-city favorite, set in a gorgeously revamped turn-of-the-20th-century theater. ✉ Rambla Catalunya 2–4, Eixample ☎ 93/233–3333 ⊕ cityhallbarcelona.com Ⓜ Catalunya.

Luz de Gas

DANCE CLUBS | Luz de Gas, an ornate 19th-century theater, offers everything from live performances (mostly world music and Latin) to wild late-night

dancing (expect soul and standards). ✉ Muntaner 246, Eixample ☎ 93/209–7711 ⊕ www.luzdegas.com Ⓜ Muntaner, Diagonal.

Otto Zutz

DANCE CLUBS | Just off Vía Augusta above Diagonal, this nightclub and disco (dating back to 1985) is a perennial Barcelona favorite that keeps attracting a glitzy mix of Barcelona movers and shakers, models, ex-models, wannabe models, and the hoping-to-get-lucky mob that predictably follows this sort of pulchritude. Hip-hop, house, and Latin make up the standard soundtrack on the dance floor, with more mellow notes upstairs and in the coveted Altos Club Privé (or "VIP section," to the rest of us). ✉ Lincoln 15, Eixample ☎ 93/238–0722 office ⊕ www.ottozutz. com Ⓜ Sant Gervasi, Gràcia.

Punto BCN

BARS/PUBS | A musical LGBTQ bar with billiards tables, this mid-Eixample hub is a clearinghouse for all persuasions and tastes, with women often outnumbering the men, pool tables or not. ✉ Carrer Muntaner 63–65, Eixample ☎ 93/487–8342 ⊕ www.grupoarena.com Ⓜ Universitat.

Sala B

DANCE CLUBS | Music described as "humana" (suggesting no teeth-rattling techno) keeps Sala B filled with the mid-twenties and thirtysomething set until 5 in the morning on Friday and Saturday. Just above the Diagonal near Luz de Gas, this veteran nightspot is an offshoot of the parent club as evidenced by the shared website. Concerts and DJ music for dancing alternate at this comfortable club designed for semicivilized nightlife. ✉ Muntaner 244, Eixample ☎ 93/209–.7711 ⊕ www.luzdegas.com Ⓜ Provença.

The Sutton Club

DANCE CLUBS | If there's anywhere you should dress up to get past the door, it's here. If the international see-and-be-seen crowd converges around the seaside clubs below Hotel Arts, their local equivalent come to Sutton. The club is segregated into several bars and dancing areas, playing R&B, hip-hop, house, and the occasional live performance. Not as happening as in its mid-2000s heyday, it still merits a visit, if anything to enjoy the festive atmosphere. Sutton is like a Vegas club in Barcelona: it may not be classy, but it's always entertaining. ⊠ *Tuset 13, Eixample* ☎ *667/432759* ⊕ *www.thesuttonclub.com* Ⓜ *Diagonal.*

 Performing Arts

ART GALLERIES

Fundació Antoni Tàpies

ARTS CENTERS | This foundation created in 1984 by Catalonia's then-most important living artist continues to promote the work of important Catalan artists and writers, particularly that of the late Antoni Tàpies, whose passion for art and literature still echos in the halls of this enchanting Modernist building by esteemed architect Domènech i Montaner. It hosts thought-provoking temporary exhibitions, a comprehensive lecture series, and film screenings, and houses an excellent library specializing in contemporary art. ⊠ *Aragó 255, Eixample* ☎ *93/487–0315* ⊕ *www.fundaciotapies.org* Ⓜ *Passeig de Gràcia.*

CONCERTS

L'Auditori de Barcelona

CONCERTS | Functional, sleek, and minimalist, the Rafael Moneo–designed Auditori has a full calendar of classical music performances—with regular forays into jazz, flamenco, and pop—near Plaça de les Glòries. Orchestras that perform here include the Orquestra Simfònica de Barcelona i Nacional de Catalunya (OBC) and the Orquestra Nacional de Cambra de Andorra. The excellent Museu de la Música is on the first floor. ⊠ *Lepant 150, Eixample* ☎ *93/247–9300* ⊕ *www.auditori.cat* Ⓜ *Marina, Monumental, Glòries.*

FLAMENCO

Palacio del Flamenco

DANCE | This Eixample music hall showcases some of the city's best flamenco. Prices start at €45 for a drink and a show, up to €110. (Save money by purchasing tickets online in advance.) Late shows are slightly cheaper. ⊠ *Balmes 139, Eixample* ☎ *93/218–7237* ⊕ *www.palaciodelflamenco.com* Ⓜ *Provença, Diagonal.*

THEATER

Teatre Nacional de Catalunya

THEATER | Near Glòries, the area with the highest concentration of development in recent years at the eastern end of the Diagonal, this grandiose glass-enclosed classical temple was designed by Ricardo Bofill, architect of Barcelona's airport. Programs cover everything from Shakespeare to avant-garde theater. Most productions, as the name suggests, are in Catalan but beautiful to witness all the same. ⊠ *Pl. de les Arts 1, Eixample* ☎ *93/306–5700* ⊕ *www.tnc.cat* Ⓜ *Glòries, Monumental.*

Teatre Tívoli

DANCE | One of the city's most beloved traditional theater and dance venues, the Tívoli has staged timeless classics and has hosted everyone from the Ballet Nacional de Cuba to flamenco and teeny-bopper treats. ⊠ *Casp 8, Eixample* ☎ *93/215–9570* ⊕ *www.grupbalana.com* Ⓜ *Catalunya.*

Shopping

Beginning with the Triangle d'Or at the top of La Rambla and up Passeig de Gràcia, now rightly considered one of the world's greatest shopping streets, the Eixample is a compendium of design and fashion stores that could take years to fully explore. Eixample means "Expansion" (from the Catalan verb *eixamplar*) and, indeed, not only is this neighborhood immensely wide, stretching from Plaça de les Glòries all the way out to

Plaça Francesc Macià, but it can cut a wide swath through your bank statement before you know it.

Passeig de Gràcia, with reportedly the most expensive retail floor space in Spain, accommodates a lengthy and luxurious list of fashionista showcases, such as Prada, Stella McCartney, and Loewe, with more down-to-earthling brands such as Zara and Mango situated at the southern end. Also in the Eixample, Moderniste grocery stores such as Queviures Murria dazzle foodies. Other targets of opportunity include Rambla de Catalunya (which runs parallel to Passeig de Gràcia and is less uptight) and Carrer Enric Granados. But this is just the tip of the shopping iceberg: turn yourself loose and discover the factory outlet stores along Carrer Girona, or wander into the Bermuda Triangle of antiques shopping in Bulevard dels Antiquaris at Passeig de Gràcia 55–57.

ANTIQUES AND COLLECTIBLES

Acanto

ANTIQUES/COLLECTIBLES | This shop, in the pivotal Bulevard dels Antiquaris, is a major clearinghouse for buying and selling a wide range of items from paintings, furniture, silver, sculpture, and bronzes to wood carvings, marble, clocks, watches, tapestries, porcelain, and ceramics. ⊠ *Passeig de Gràcia 55–57, Eixample* ☎ *93/215–3297* Ⓜ *Passeig de Gràcia.*

Bulevard dels Antiquaris

ANTIQUES/COLLECTIBLES | Look carefully for the stairway leading one flight up to this 73-store antiques arcade off Passeig de Gràcia. You never know what you might find: dolls, icons, Roman or Visigothic objects, paintings, furniture, cricket kits, fly rods, or toys from a century ago. Haggling is common practice—but Catalan antiques dealers are tough nuts to crack. ⊠ *Passeig de Gràcia 55, Eixample* ☎ *93/215–4499* ⊕ *www.bulevarddelsantiquaris.com* Ⓜ *Passeig de Gràcia.*

El Recibidor

ANTIQUES/COLLECTIBLES | Like a scene from *Mad Men*, El Recibidor oozes mid-century modern elegance. This large split-level showroom deals in furniture and objects, mainly of European provenance, from the art deco period onward. From small ceramic figurines to dining tables, table lamps, and vintage TVs, each item has been curated and restored with a deep understanding of the period's aesthetic and value. ⊠ *Carrer de Calàbria 85, Eixample* ☎ *93/530–4221* ⊕ *www.elrecibidor.com* Ⓜ *Sant Antoni.*

Novecento

ANTIQUES/COLLECTIBLES | A standout primarily for being so out of place among all the design emporiums and fashion denizens on this great white way of high commerce, Novecento is an antique jewelry store with abundant items from all epochs and movements from Victorian to Art Nouveau to Belle Époque. ⊠ *Passeig de Gràcia 75, Eixample* ☎ *93/215–1183* Ⓜ *Passeig de Gràcia.*

ART GALLERIES

Galeria Joan Prats

ART GALLERIES |"La Prats" has been one of the city's top galleries since the 1920s, showing international painters and sculptors from Henry Moore to Antoni Tàpies. Barcelona painter Joan Miró was a prime force in the founding of the gallery when he became friends with Joan Prats. The motifs of bonnets and derbies on the gallery's facade are callbacks to the trade of Prats's father. José Maria Sicilia and Juan Ugalde have shown here, while Erick Beltrán, Hannah Collins, and Eulàlia Valldosera are among the regular artists on display. ⊠ *Balmes 54, Eixample* ☎ *93/216–0290* ⊕ *www.galeriajoanprats.com* Ⓜ *Passeig de Gràcia.*

Galeria Toni Tàpies

ART GALLERIES | After the prolific Catalan painter Antoni Tàpies died in 2012, his son Toni decided to change the direction of his successful gallery and, as a touching homage, only show his late father's work, which is now on show permanently. This is complemented by periodic smaller shows and events from other leading artists, sometimes of one single piece, which have been chosen to create a "dialogue" with the Tàpies oeuvre. ✉ Consell de Cent 282, Eixample ☎ 93/487–6402 ⊕ www.tonitapies.com Ⓜ Catalunya, Passeig de Gràcia.

Marlborough

ART GALLERIES | This international giant occupies an important position in Barcelona's art-gallery galaxy with exhibits of major contemporary artists from around the world, as well as local stars. Recent shows featured the hyperrealist collages of Antonio López García and the contemporary designer and painter Alberto Corazón. ✉ Enric Granados 68, Eixample ☎ 93/467–4454 ⊕ www.galeriamarlborough.com Ⓜ Passeig de Gràcia.

N2

ART GALLERIES | Since it opened, the Galería N2 has established its position as a beacon at the crossroads of tradition and modernity, of high- and low-brow art. The vanguard but careful selection of artists featured in six annual solo shows includes the street artist Sixeart and the Argentine surrealist Mauricio Vergara. Since N2 specializes in up-and-coming and mid-career artists, works are generally affordable yet safe to invest in, and browsing here makes for a lighthearted change from the Eixample's more serious art houses. ✉ Enric Granados 61, Eixample ☎ 93/452–0592 ⊕ www.n2galeria.com.

Projecte SD

ART GALLERIES | This gallery, located in one of the Eixample's most beautiful little passages, doesn't go easy on its visitors. No show at Projecte SD can be grasped without the explanatory booklet; no piece of art can be fully appreciated in isolation. The pieces exhibited and sold here are complex, philosophical, challenging, and bleedingly conceptual—anything but simply decorative. Projecte SD is really more of a museum than a gallery. That makes every visit an experience and every purchase an audacious act of faith. ✉ Passatge Mercader 8, Baixos 1, Eixample ☎ 93/488–1360 ⊕ www.projectesd.com Ⓜ Diagonal, Provença.

Sala Dalmau

ART GALLERIES | An old-timer in the established Consell de Cent gallery scene, Sala Dalmau shows an interesting and heterodox range of Catalan and international artists. ✉ Consell de Cent 349, Eixample ☎ 93/215–4592 ⊕ www.saladalmau.com Ⓜ Passeig de Gràcia.

BOOKS AND STATIONERY

Altaïr

BOOKS/STATIONERY | Barcelona's premier travel and adventure bookstore stocks many titles in English. Book presentations and events scheduled here feature a wide range of notable authors from Alpinists to Africanists. ✉ Gran Via 616, Eixample ☎ 93/342–7171 ⊕ www.altair.es Ⓜ Catalunya.

Casa del Llibre

BOOKS/STATIONERY | On Barcelona's most important shopping street, Casa del Llibre is a major book feast with a wide variety of English titles. ✉ Passeig de Gràcia 62, Eixample ☎ 902/026407 ⊕ www.casadellibro.com Ⓜ Passeig de Gràcia.

FNAC

BOOKS/STATIONERY | For musical recordings and the latest book publications, this is one of Barcelona's most dependable and happening addresses. Regular concerts, presentations of new recordings, and art exhibits take place in FNAC, both here at the branch in the Triangle Shopping Center on Plaça Catalunya and one on Diagonal in the L'Illa shopping center. Much more than a bookstore, it's an important cultural resource. ✉ Centro Comercial El Triangle, Pl. Catalunya 4, Eixample ☎ 902/100632 ⊕ www.fnac.es Ⓜ Maria Cristina, Les Corts.

Laie

BOOKS/STATIONERY | Not overly stocked with English-language titles, this bookstore boasts a very pleasant café-restaurant upstairs; the space is often used for readings and other and cultural events. Other branches of Laie are located around Barcelona, including major museums such as the Museu Picasso and Cosmocaixa. ⊠ *Pau Claris 85, Eixample* ☎ *93/318–1739* ⊕ *www. laie.es* Ⓜ *Catalunya*.

Pepa Paper

BOOKS/STATIONERY | Barcelona's most famous paper and stationery store, Pepa Paper (Pepa is a nickname for Josefina and Paper, Catalan for—you guessed it—paper), carries a gorgeous selection of stationery and more. In addition to the Balmes location, the chain has two other downtown shops including one on Avenida Diagonal and another on Avenida Paris. ⊠ *Carrer de Balmes 50, Eixample* ☎ *93/505–4510* ⊕ *pepapaper.com/shop* Ⓜ *Hospital Clínic/Provença*.

CERAMICS AND GLASSWARE

★ Lladró

CERAMICS/GLASSWARE | This Valencia company is famed worldwide for the beauty and quality of its figures. Barcelona's only Lladró factory store, this location has exclusive pieces of work, custom-designed luxury items of gold and porcelain, and classic and original works. Look for the cheeky figurines by Jaime Hayon, a Spanish designer, and the spectacular chandeliers by Bodo Sperlein. ⊠ *Passeig de Gràcia 101, Eixample* ☎ *93/270–1253* ⊕ *www.lladro.com* Ⓜ *Diagonal*.

CLOTHING

Adolfo Domínguez

CLOTHING | One of Barcelona's longtime fashion giants, this is one of Spain's leading clothing designers, with many locations around town. Famed as the creator of the Iberia Airlines uniforms, Adolfo Domínguez has been in the not-too-radical mainstream of Spanish couture for the past quarter century. ⊠ *Passeig de Gràcia 32, Eixample* ☎ *93/487–4170* ⊕ *www.adolfodominguez.com* Ⓜ *Passeig de Gràcia*.

Aílanto

CLOTHING | Twin brothers Iñaki and Aitor Muñoz are the creative and business force behind Aílanto, an avant-garde fashion brand renowned for sculptural silhouettes and daring prints. Winners of various accolades and regulars at Madrid's Fashion Week, their Barcelona shop is as drama-filled as their collections, with flowering metallic lamps dangling from double-height ceilings and dressing rooms swathed in fringes and velvet. Oversized coats, heavily textured fabrics, and patterns inspired by major artistic movements have become the brand's signatures. ⊠ *C/ Enric Granados 46, Eixample* ☎ *93/451–3106* ⊕ *www. ailanto.com* Ⓜ *Provença*.

The Avant

CLOTHING | Under her own label, Silvia Garcia Presas—the creator of El Avant—offers quietly elegant and effortlessly chic clothing for women in her simple boutique at the top end of Enric Granados. Fabrics are 100% natural (organic cotton, alpaca wool, etc.), and the generous and easy cuts are transgenerational and flattering. A small room at the back displays handmade soaps, ceramic wares, home textiles, and other gifty bits sourced from across Asia and the Americas. El Avant has also has a smaller boutique in La Ribera district at Esparteria 13. ⊠ *Enric Granados 106, Eixample* ☎ *93/300–7673* ⊕ *www.theavant.com* Ⓜ *Diagonal*.

Carolina Herrera

CLOTHING | Originally from Venezuela but professionally based in New York, Carolina Herrera and her international CH logo have become Barcelona mainstays. (Daughter Carolina Herrera Jr. is a Spain resident and married to former bullfighter Miguel Báez.) Fragrances for men and women and clothes with a simple, elegant line—a white blouse is the CH icon—are the staples here. Herrera's light ruffled dresses and edgy urban footwear add feminine flourishes. ✉ *Passeig de Gràcia 87, Eixample* ☎ *93/272–1584* ⊕ *www.carolinaherrera.com* Ⓜ *Diagonal.*

★ Cortana

CLOTHING | A sleek and breezy Balearic Islands look for women is what this designer from Mallorca brings to the fashion scene of urban Barcelona in a whitewashed shop reminiscent of an art gallery. Her dresses transmit a casual, minimalistic elegance and have graced many a red carpet all over Spain. ✉ *Provença 290, Eixample* ☎ *93/487– 2070* ⊕ *www.cortana.es* Ⓜ *Provença.*

Erre de Raso

CLOTHING | Popular with the uptown crowd, Erre de Raso makes clothes in bright and breezy shades and patterns. With colors ranging from electric fuchsias to bright indigo blues and materials ranging from satin (raso) to cottons and silks, the objective is to outfit stylish women in chameleonic outfits that look equally appropriate picking up the kids from school, dropping by an art gallery opening, and hitting a cocktail party in the same sortie. ✉ *València 419, Eixample* ☎ *93/487–9595* Ⓜ *Girona.*

Furest

CLOTHING | This centenary menswear star, with four stores in town and another at the airport, markets selections from Armani Jeans, Scotch & Soda, Hugo Boss, and Blackstone, as well as its own collection of dapper suits, shirts, and gentlemen's accessories. ✉ *Passeig de Gràcia 12–14, Eixample* ☎ *93/301–2000* ⊕ *www.furest.com* Ⓜ *Catalunya.*

Loewe

CLOTHING | Occupying the ground floor of Lluís Domènech i Montaner's Casa Lleó Morera, Loewe is Spain's answer to Hermès, a classical clothing and leather emporium for men's and women's fashions and luxurious handbags that whisper status (at eye-popping prices). ✉ *Passeig de Gràcia 35, Eixample* ☎ *93/216–0400* ⊕ *www.loewe.com* Ⓜ *Passeig de Gràcia.*

Purificación García

CLOTHING | Known as a gifted fabric expert whose creations are invariably based on the qualities and characteristics of her raw materials, Galicia-born Purificación García enjoys solid prestige in Barcelona. Understated hues and subtle combinations of colors and shapes place this contemporary designer squarely in the camp of the less-is-more school, and, although her women's range is larger and more diverse, she understands men's tailoring. ✉ *Provença 292, Eixample* ☎ *93/496–1336* ⊕ *www.purificaciongarcia.com* Ⓜ *Diagonal.*

Santa Eulalia

CLOTHING | The history of this luxury fashion superstore, which moved into its 2,000-square-meter premises designed by William Sofield in 2011, goes back to 1843. That year Domingo Taberner Prims opened the first shop, which would soon evolve into one of the city's first and foremost haute couture tailoring houses. Today it's run by the fourth generation of the founding family and features one of the best luxury brand selections in the country. It also regularly teams up with designers and design schools to present special collections or awards. When you're done browsing everything from Agent Provocateur to Vera Wang, refresh with some tea and cake at the fabulous café-terrace on the first floor, or head to the basement to see the in-house tailors at work on bespoke suits and men's shirts. ✉ *Passeig de Gràcia 93, Eixample* ☎ *93/215–0674* ⊕ *www.santaeulalia.com* Ⓜ *Diagonal.*

Sita Murt

CLOTHING | The local Catalan designer Sita Murt produces smart, grown-up women's wear under her own label in this minimalist space in the Eixample. Colorful chiffon dresses and light, gauzy tops and knits characterize this line of clothing popular with professional women and wedding goers. ✉ *Mallorca 242, Eixample* ☎ *93/215–2231* ⊕ *www.sitamurt.com* Ⓜ *Passeig de Gràcia, Diagonal.*

Teresa Helbig

CLOTHING | A regular at Madrid Fashion Week, Teresa Helbig designs feminine and elegant pret-a-porter women's collections. Yet she is better known, and worth visiting, for her bespoke bridal wear and evening gowns, timeless haute couture she concocts for her well-heeled clients at her Barcelona studio-showroom. It may not come cheap, but you'll be able to hand it down through generations. ✉ *Mallorca 184, Loft, Eixample* ☎ *93/451–5544* ⊕ *www.teresahelbig.com.*

DEPARTMENT STORES AND MALLS

El Corte Inglés

DEPARTMENT STORES | Iconic and ubiquitous, this Spanish department store has its main Barcelona branch on Plaça de Catalunya, with one annex close by in Porta de l'Àngel for younger fashion and sporting goods. You can find just about anything here—clothing, shoes, perfumes, electronics—and there is a wonderful supermarket and food mall on the lower-ground floor. With branches in all major cities, El Corte Inglés is Spain's only large department store and has leagues of heritage fans. Service is inconsistent, but the sale season in August is worth fighting the crowds for. ✉ *Pl. de Catalunya 14, Eixample* ☎ *93/306–3800* ⊕ *www.elcorteingles.es* Ⓜ *Catalunya* ✉ *Portal de l'Àngel 19, Barri Gòtic* ☎ *93/306–3800* ⊕ *elcorteingles.es* Ⓜ *Catalunya* ✉ *Av. Diagonal 471, Pl. Francesc Macia, Eixample* ☎ *93/493–4800* Ⓜ *Hospital Clinic* ✉ *Av. Diagonal 617, Diagonal Mar* ☎ *93/366–7100* Ⓜ *Maria Cristina.*

L'Illa Diagonal

DEPARTMENT STORES | This rangy complex buzzes with shoppers swarming through more than 100 stores and shops, including food specialists, Decathlon

Custo Gusto

Only Barcelona could come up with Custo, an idiosyncratic fashion line created by a couple of motorcycling brothers. Since they started the business in the 1980s, Custo and David Dalmau have parlayed their passion for colorful and original tops into an empire that now includes footwear, denim, handbags, knits, and more. With stores scattered around Barcelona and the world, Custo's quirky embroidery and metallic graphic prints have become nearly as iconic as Gaudí's organic stalagmites or Miró's colorful asteroids.

sports gear, and Imaginarium toys, plus FNAC, Zara, Benetton, and all the usual High Street suspects. ✉ *Av. Diagonal 557, Eixample* ☎ *93/444–0000* ⊕ *www.lilla.com* Ⓜ *Maria Cristina.*

FOOD

Cacao Sampaka

FOOD/CANDY | This centrally located shop is perfect for chocolate addicts. While it's perfectly possible to dash in and fill your bags with boxes of Cacao Sampaka's exquisite cocoa creations to take home with you (or nibble on the way back to your hotel), consider setting aside 30 minutes to sit down in the pleasant in-store café and order an "Azteca" hot chocolate drink. Quite possibly the best hot chocolate in Spain, a sip of this thick, rich, heaven-in-a-cup is the highlight of any Barcelona shopping spree. ✉ *Carrer del Consell de Cent 292, Eixample* ☎ *93/272–0833* ⊕ *www.cacaosampaka.com* Ⓜ *Passeig de Gràcia.*

Oriol Balaguer

FOOD/CANDY | Owner Balaguer is surely running out of room to store all the "Spain's Best…" trophies he's collected over the years. He's a consultant to some of the world's most famous restaurants, and the heart of his empire is this little shop of chocolate-making magic. Bring your credit card and prepare to have your mind blown. Some of the confectionery creations are so beautiful you'll feel bad about biting into them—at least until you taste them. Balaguer has a second equally stunning boutique at Travessera de les Corts 340, which also sells bread and pastries. ⊠ Pl. de Sant Gregori Taumaturg 2, Eixample ☎ 93/201–1846 ⊕ www. oriolbalaguer.com Ⓜ La Bonanova.

Queviures Murria

FOOD/CANDY | Founded in 1890, this historic Moderniste shop, its windows decorated with Ramón Casas paintings and posters, has a superb selection of some 200 cheeses, sausages, wines, and conserves from Spain, Catalunya, and beyond. The ceramic Casas reproductions lining the interior walls are eye candy, as are all the details in this work of art–cum–grocery store (queviures means foodstuffs, literally, "things to keep you alive"). ⊠ Roger de Llúria 85, Eixample ✛ Near metro Passeig de Gràcia ☎ 93/215–5789 ⊕ www.murria.cat Ⓜ Passeig de Gràcia.

Reserva Ibérica

FOOD/CANDY | Purveyor of fine hams in Spain and abroad for more than 30 years, Reserva Ibérica has a shop in the Eixample where it not only sells a selection of its best, all-acorn-fed products, but also offers the opportunity for customers to taste the hams, accompanied by a glass of wine. ⊠ Rambla de Catalunya 61, Eixample ☎ 93/215–5230 ⊕ www.reservaiberica.com Ⓜ Passeig de Gràcia.

GIFTS AND SOUVENIRS

Servei Estació

HOUSEHOLD ITEMS/FURNITURE | It's a hardware store, yes, but one like you've never seen before. Servei Estació is situated in a rationalist-style landmark building dating from 1962. For decades it served the city's builders and handymen with tools and materials, but more recently the huge inventory has expanded to modern design and housewares, and sells everything from ropes of string to designer shopping carts. ⊠ Aragó 270-272, Eixample ☎ 93/393–2410 ⊕ www. serveiestacio.com Ⓜ Passeig de Gràcia.

HOUSEHOLD ITEMS AND FURNITURE

Fins de Siècles

HOUSEHOLD ITEMS/FURNITURE | The third of the Fins de Siècles shops is, like its siblings in Brussels and Isle sur Sorgue, the product of the undying passion of its Belgian owners to rescue as much European design heritage from the 20th century as they can. Their particular fascination is with the art deco period ranging from the 1930s through the '50s, which they buy all over Europe and have restored and newly upholstered respecting traditional methods. Desks, sofas, vanities, and tables are shipped all over the world, but they also stock smaller (and more affordable) items like lamps, vases, rugs, and silverware. ⊠ Enric Granados 70, Eixample ☎ 93/511–7606 ⊕ www.finsdesiecles-artdeco.com Ⓜ Provença.

Jaime Beriestain Concept Store

GIFTS/SOUVENIRS | The concept store of one of the city's hottest interior designers provides mere mortals the chance to appreciate the Beriestain groove. Reflecting his hotel and restaurant projects, the shop offers an exciting mixture of mid-century modern classics and new design pieces, peppered with freshly cut flowers (also for sale), French candles, handmade stationery, and the latest international design and architecture magazines to dress up your coffee table. ⊠ Pau Claris 167, Eixample ☎ 93/515–0779 ⊕ www. beriestain.com Ⓜ Diagonal.

Mar de Cava

HOUSEHOLD ITEMS/FURNITURE | This Aladdin's Cave of design, housewares, furniture, clothing, and accessories bursts with creativity and color. The carefully curated collection includes everything from vases by cult ceramics maker

Apparatu, cabinets rendered in Technicolor lacquers, African bead necklaces, and tables covered in antique tiles. The emphasis is more on craftsmanship than the latest trends—just about every item has an intriguing backstory. ⊠ *Valencia 293, Eixample* ☎ *93/458–5333* ⊕ *www.mardecava.com* Ⓜ *Girona.*

Nanimarquina
HOUSEHOLD ITEMS/FURNITURE | A lover of both traditional methods and exuberant design, Nani Marquina makes textural rugs that look just as good on a wall as they do on the floor. Some of her rugs re-create ancient Persian or Hindu styles; others are trendy compositions by designers like Sybilla or the Bouroullec brothers. Half of this large showroom—an ingenious conversion from an old private garage—accommodates Doméstico, a colorful emporium of designer objects and furniture. ⊠ *Rosselló 256/Av. Diagonal, Eixample* ☎ *93/487–1606* ⊕ *www.nanimarquina.com* Ⓜ *Diagonal.*

JEWELRY
Bagués Masriera
JEWELRY/ACCESSORIES | The Bagués dynasty has bejeweled barcelonins since 1839. While they stock much that glitters, the Lluís Masriera line of original Art Nouveau pieces is truly unique; intricate flying nymphs, lifelike golden insects, and other easily recognizable motifs from the period take on a new depth of beauty when executed in the translucent enameling process that Masriera himself developed. The location in Moderniste architect Puig i Cadafalch's Casa Amatller in the famous Mansana de la Discòrdia on Passeig de Gràcia is worth the visit alone, although sadly, the interior of the shop bears little of the building's exuberance. ⊠ *Passeig de Gràcia 41, Eixample* ☎ *93/216–0174* ⊕ *www.masriera.es* Ⓜ *Catalunya, Passeig de Gràcia.*

Zapata Joyeros
JEWELRY/ACCESSORIES | The Zapata family, with five stores around town, has been prominent in Barcelona jewelry design

and retail for the last half century. With original designs of their own and a savvy selection of the most important Swiss and international watch designers, this family business is now in its second generation and makes a point of taking good care of clients with large or small jewelry needs. Their L'Illa store, for example, specializes in jewelry accessible to the budgets of younger clients. In addition to their central shop on Avenida Diagonal, they have two stores in the neighborhood of Gràcia and two in the L'illa Diagonal mall. ⊠ *Buenos Aires 60, Eixample* ☎ *93/430–6238* ⊕ *www.zapatajoyeros.com* Ⓜ *Provença.*

MARKETS
Els Encants Vells
OUTDOOR/FLEA/GREEN MARKETS | One of Europe's oldest flea markets, Els Encants has a new home—a stunning, glittering metal canopy that protects the rag-and-bone merchants (and their keen customers) from the elements. Stalls, and a handful of stand-up bars, have become a bit more upmarket, too, although you'll still find plenty of oddities to barter over in the central plaza. Saturday is the busiest day—try going on the weekdays that it's open for a more relaxed rummage around this fascinating slice of urban history. ⊠ *Av. Meridiana 69, Pl. de Les Glóries Catalans, Eixample* ☎ *93/246–3030* ⊕ *encantsbcn.com/en* Ⓜ *Glóries.*

SHOES
Camper
SHOES/LUGGAGE/LEATHER GOODS | This internationally famous Spanish shoe emporium, which in Barcelona also comprises a 25-room boutique hotel of the same name and numerous branches, offers a comprehensive line of funky boots, heels, and shoes of all kinds. Both men's and women's shoes, all in line with the company's organic outdoor philosophy, are displayed against an undulating chrome-and-wood backdrop designed by architect Benedetta Tagliabue. ⊠ *Passeig de Gràcia 2–4, Eixample* ☎ *93/521–6250* ⊕ *www.camper.com* Ⓜ *Catalunya.*

Castañer

SHOES/LUGGAGE/LEATHER GOODS | The rope-soled sandal, or *alpargata*, has come a long way. What started as humble farmers' treads turned to military footwear and then accessory favored by Yves Saint Laurent. Founded in 1927, the Castañer clan has seen all the chapters. Mixing tradition, craftsmanship, and modernity, the brand has elevated the espadrille to fashion must-have. Wedge-heels, booties, and flats for both men and women are on sale in this citrus-toned boutique, designed by noted architect Benedetta Tagliabue. ✉ *Rosselló 230, Eixample* ☎ *93/414–2428* ⊕ *www.castaner.com* Ⓜ *Diagonal.*

★ Norman Vilalta

SHOES/LUGGAGE/LEATHER GOODS | Norman Vilalta was a lawyer in Buenos Aires before he decided to move to Florence, Italy, and do something rather unusual: learn the trade of a traditional cobbler. Today he is one of a handful of people in the world who produce artisanal bespoke shoes, which take three months to make. The shoes come complete with a video showing the entire making of, and will set you back somewhere between €2,500 and €5,000. However, you will also join the ranks of the chef Ferran Adrià, the architect Oscar Tusquets, and members of the Spanish royal family as owner of a pair of Norman Vilalta shoes. And since they fit like no other and last a lifetime, you might consider it a worthy investment. For a more affordable option, Vilalta's ready-to-wear footwear is available at the high-fashion emporium Santa Eulalia on the Passeig de Gràcia. ✉ *Enric Granados 5, Eixample* ☎ *93/323–4014* ⊕ *www.normanvilalta.com* Ⓜ *Universitat.*

★ The Outpost

SHOES/LUGGAGE/LEATHER GOODS | A shop dedicated exclusively to men's accessories of the finest kind, the Outpost was created by a former Prada buyer who considers it his mission to bring stylishness to Barcelona men with this oasis of avant-garde fashion. The constantly changing window displays are works of art, providing a first taste of what's to be found inside: Robert Clergerie shoes, Albert Thurston suspenders, Roland Pineau belts, Yves Andrieux hats, Balenciaga ties. You enter the Outpost as a mere mortal, but leave it as a gentleman—provided you carry the necessary cash. ✉ *Rosselló 281, bis, Eixample* ☎ *93/457–7137* ⊕ *www.theoutpostbcn. com* Ⓜ *Diagonal, Verdaguer.*

Tascón

SHOES/LUGGAGE/LEATHER GOODS | International footwear designers and domestic shoemakers alike fill these stores with trendy urban footwear from brands such as Camper, United Nude, and Audley, as well as more sturdy models from Timberland and the like. Models designed in-house and made locally offer high style at reasonable prices. You will find other branches of Tascón in strategic shopping hubs. ✉ *Passeig de Gràcia 64, Eixample* ☎ *93/487–9084* ⊕ *www.tascon.es* Ⓜ *Passeig de Gràcia.*

Chapter 9

GRÀCIA

Updated by
Elizabeth Prosser and
Steve Tallantyre

👁 **Sights**
★★★☆☆

🍴 **Restaurants**
★★★★☆

🛏 **Hotels**
★★☆☆☆

🛍 **Shopping**
★★☆☆☆

🍸 **Nightlife**
★★★★☆

NEIGHBORHOOD SNAPSHOT

TOP EXPERIENCES

■ **Gran de Gràcia:** Stroll Gràcia's central artery, lined with buildings of great artistic and architectural interest.

■ **Mercat de la Llibertat:** This great little market, and occasional venue for folk music concerts, is a joy to visit and graze.

■ **Park Güell:** Walk down through Gràcia from Park Güell, one of the most impressive public parks in the world

■ **Plaça de la Vila de Gràcia:** Linger at a sidewalk café in this historic square in the heart of the Gràcia neighborhood.

■ **Late-night supper:** Wander the maze-like back alleyways and side streets of the neighborhood to hop between upscale wine bars, '50s-style gin joints, and traditional tapas spots.

GETTING HERE

By metro, the Gràcia stop on the FGC (Ferrocarril de la Generalitat de Catalunya) trains that connect Sarrià, Sabadell, Terrassa, and Sant Cugat with Plaça de Catalunya is your best option. The metro's green line (L3) stations at Fontana and Lesseps put you in the heart of Gràcia and in hiking distance of Park Güell, respectively. The yellow line (L4) stop at Joanic is a short walk from Gràcia's northeast side.

PLANNING YOUR TIME

Exploring Gràcia is at least a several-hours outing, or an entire day if you want to get the full feel of the neighborhood. Evening sessions at the popular Verdi cinema (showing films in their original languages) usually get out just in time for a late-night supper in any of a number of bars and restaurants, including Botafumeiro, which closes at 1 am. Park Güell is best in the afternoon, when the sun spotlights the view east over the Mediterranean. Exploring Gràcia when the Llibertat and Revolució markets are closed would be a major loss, so plan to get here before 2 pm.

QUICK BITES

■ **Botafumeria.** For an upscale treat, Botafumeiro never disappoints; the counter is the place to be for icy Albariño white wine and *pop a feira* (octopus on potato slices with smoked paprika), a Galician favorite. ✉ *Carrer Gran de Gràcia 81, Gràcia* ⊕ *botafumeiro.es/en* Ⓜ *Gràcia (FGC), Fontana*

■ **Nou Candanchú.** A refreshing stop, this bar runs tables inside and out until early morning, serving a variety of tapas, sandwiches, salads, and seafood dishes. Weather permitting, take a table out on the square and order a paella. ✉ *Pl. de la Vila de Gràcia 9, Gràcia* Ⓜ *Gràcia (FGC)*

Gràcia is a state of mind. More than a neighborhood, it is a village republic that has periodically risen in armed rebellion against city, state, and country; its jumble of streets have names (Llibertat, Fraternitat, Progrès) that invoke the ideological history of this fierce little progressive, working-class enclave.

The site of Barcelona's first factory collectives, it was fertile ground for all sorts of radical reform movements, as workers organized and developed into groups ranging from anarchists to feminists to Esperantists. Once an independent village that joined the municipality of Barcelona only under duress, Gràcia attempted to secede from the Spanish state in 1856, 1870, 1873, and 1909.

Lying above the Diagonal from Carrer de Còrsega all the way up to Park Güell, Gràcia is bound by Via Augusta and Carrer Balmes to the west and Carrer de l'Escorial and Passeig de Sant Joan to the east. Today the area is filled with hip little bars and trendy restaurants, movie theaters, outdoor cafés, gourmet shops and designer boutiques, and the studios of struggling artists: this is where Barcelona's young cohort want to live, and come to party. Mercé Rodoreda's novel *La Plaça del Diamant* (translated by the late David Rosenthal as *The Time of the Doves*) begins and ends in Gràcia during the August Festa Major, a festival that fills the streets with the rank-and-file residents of this always lively, intimate little pocket of general resistance to Organized Life.

 Sights

Casa Comalat

HOUSE | At the bottom of Gràcia between the Diagonal and Carrer Còrsega, this often overlooked Moderniste house (not open to the public) built in 1911 is worth stopping by to view the exterior. For a look at the best side of this lower Gràcia Art Nouveau gem, cut down past Casa Fuster at the bottom of Gran de Gràcia, take a left on Bonavista, then a right on Santa Teresa down to Casa Comalat just across Carrer Còrsega. This Salvador Valeri i Pupurull creation is one of Barcelona's most interesting Moderniste houses, with its undulating polychrome ceramic balconies and its Gaudí-on-steroids columned arches on the ground level. Look for the curious wooden galleries, and the turret on the Carrer Corsega side of the building, clad in green ceramic tiles. Don't miss a look into the excellent Bar Mut at Pau Claris 192 just across the street. ✉ *Av. Diagonal 442, Gràcia* ☎ *93/285–3834* Ⓜ *L3/L5 Diagonal.*

Casa-Museu Gaudí

HOUSE | Up the steps of **Park Güell** and to the right is the whimsical Alice-in-Wonderland-esque house where Gaudí lived with his niece from 1906 to his death in 1926. Now a small museum, exhibits

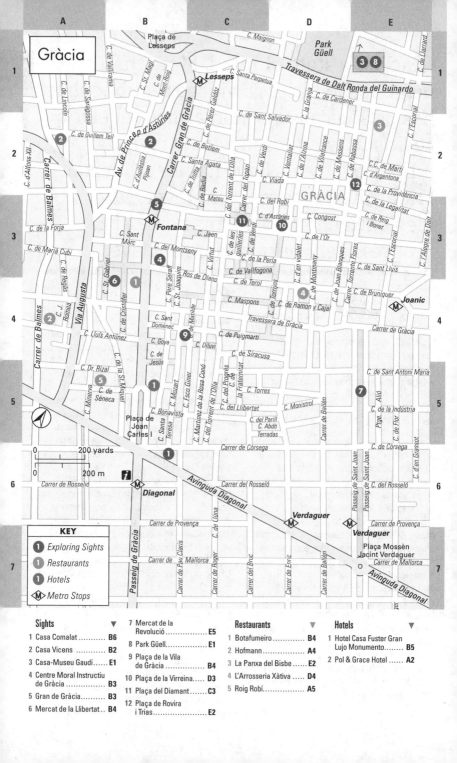

Gràcia

KEY

- 1 *Exploring Sights*
- 1 *Restaurants*
- 1 *Hotels*
- Ⓜ *Metro Stops*

0 — 200 yards
0 — 200 m

include Gaudí-designed furniture and decorations, drawings, and portraits and busts of the architect. Stop by if you are in the area, but the museum is not worth traveling far for. ⊠ *Park Güell, Carretera del Carmel 23A, Gràcia* ☏ *93/219–3811* ⊕ *www.casamuseugaudi.org* ⊑ *€5.50* Ⓜ *L3 Lesseps, Vallcarca.*

★ Casa Vicens

HOUSE | Antoni Gaudí's first important commission as a young architect began in 1883 and finished in 1889. For this house Gaudí still used his traditional architect's tools, particularly the T square. The historical eclecticism (that is, borrowing freely from past architectural styles around the world) of the early Art Nouveau movement is evident in the Orientalist themes and Mudejar (Moorish-inspired) motifs lavished throughout the design. The client, Don Manuel Vicens Montaner, owned a brick and tile factory—which explains the lavish use of the green and yellow ceramic tiles, in checkerboard and floral patterns, that animate the facade. (Casa Vicens was in fact the first polychromatic facade to appear in Barcelona.) The chemaro palm leaves decorating the gate and surrounding fence are thought to be the work of Gaudí's assistant Francesc Berenguer; the comic iron lizards and bats oozing off the facade are Gaudí's playful version of the Gothic gargoyle.

In 1900 the house was sold to Antonio Jover, a prominent local doctor, and remained in the family until 2014, when it was sold to the Andorra-based MoraBank; the bank established a foundation to preserve this remarkable historic property, and opened it to the public in 2017. The interior is even more surprising than the outside, with its trompe-l'oeil birds painted on the walls and intricately carved ceilings; the phantasmic Moorish design and cupola in the little smoking alcove on the main floor is enough to make you wonder what folks back then were putting in their pipes. In any case, it is a must-visit.

Gaudí's second commission, built in 1885, was in the little town of Comillas in Santander, for the Marquès de Comillas, Antonio López y López, a shipping magnate and the most powerful man of his time. Not surprisingly, the two houses bear a striking resemblance to each other. ⊠ *Carrer de les Carolines 24–26, Gràcia* ⊕ *www.casavicens.org* Ⓜ *L3 Fontana, Lesseps.*

Centre Moral Instructiu de Gràcia

ARTS VENUE | Another creation by Gaudí's assistant Francesc Berenguer (Gràcia is Berenguer country), the Centre Moral Instructiu was built in 1904 and still functions as a cultural institution; its wide range of programs—founded, it would seem, on the premise that recreation and sport are morally uplifting—includes chess and table tennis tournaments, craft workshops, language courses, and children's theater performances. The Centre even has its own resident repertory theater company. Berenguer himself was its president at one time. ⊠ *Carrer de Ros de Olano 9, Gràcia* ☏ *93/218–1964* ⊕ *www. elcentregracia.cat* Ⓜ *Gràcia (FGC).*

Gran de Gràcia

NEIGHBORHOOD | This highly trafficked central artery up through Gràcia is lined with buildings of great artistic and architectural interest, beginning with the hotel **Can Fuster**. Built between 1908 and 1911 by Palau de la Música Catalana architect Lluís Domènech i Montaner in collaboration with his son Pere Domènech i Roure, the building shows a clear move away from the chromatically effusive heights of Art Nouveau. More powerful, and somehow less superficial, than much of that style of architecture, it uses the winged supports under the balconies and the floral base under the corner tower as important structural elements instead of as pure ornamentation, as Domènech i Montaner the elder might have. As you move up Gran de Gràcia, probable Francesc Berenguer buildings can be identified at No. 15; No. 23, with

Plaça d'Anna Frank

Near Plaça del Diamant is a small square honoring Anne Frank, the young woman whose diary was published several years after she perished in the Bergen-Belsen concentration camp in 1945. As you leave Plaça del Diamant on Carrer de l'Or, a left on Torrent de l'Olla and an immediate right on Carrer de Jaén lead down some stairs and into a small space where you will see, lying over the edge of the roof of the CAT (Centre Artesá Tradicionàrius),

the bronze figure of a young girl, by Catalan sculptress Sara Pons Arnal, pen and journal in hand, head cocked pensively, her foot raised idly, playfully, behind her. The inscription in the open bronze book on the wall reads "While even the names of her executioners are gone, she lives on. But may never return the long shadow and the river of blood and tears and mud and mourning that snuffed out so much beauty, the symbol of which was a young girl in bloom."

its scrolled cornice; and Nos. 35, 49, 51, 61, and 77. Officially attributed to a series of architects—Berenguer lacked a formal degree, having left architecture school to become Gaudí's "right hand"—these Moderniste masterworks have long inspired debate over Berenguer's role. ✉ *Gran de Gràcia, Gràcia* Ⓜ *L3 Fontana, Lesseps; FGC Gràcia.*

Mercat de la Llibertat

MARKET | This uptown version of the Rambla's Boqueria market is one of Gràcia's coziest spaces, a food market big enough to roam in and small enough to make you feel at home. Built by Francesc Berenguer between 1888 and 1893, the Llibertat market reflects, in its name alone, the revolutionary and democratic sentiment strong in Gràcia's traditionally blue-collar residents. Look for Berenguer's decorative swans swimming along the roof line and the snails surrounding Gràcia's coat of arms. ✉ *Pl. Llibertat 27, Gràcia* 🕿 *93/217–0995* ⊕ *www.bcn.es/mercats-municipals* ⊙ *Closed Sun.* Ⓜ *FGC Gràcia.*

Mercat de la Revolució

MARKET | Officially the Abaceria Central, the market got its early name from the nearby Plaça de la Revolució de

Setembre de 1868 just a block away up Carrer dels Desamparats. Browse your way through, and consider having something delicious such as a plate of wild mushrooms or a *tortilla de patatas* (potato omelet) at the bar and restaurant at the far corner on the lower east side. ✉ *Travessera de Gràcia 186, Gràcia* 🕿 *93/213–6286* ⊕ *www.mercatabaceria.com* Ⓜ *L4 Joanic, FGC Gràcia.*

★ **Park Güell**

CITY PARK | FAMILY | This park is one of Gaudí's, and Barcelona's, most visited attractions. Named for and commissioned by Gaudí's steadfast patron, Count Eusebi Güell, it was originally intended as a gated residential community based on the English Garden City model. The centerpiece of the project was a public square, with a pillared marketplace beneath it. Only two of the houses were ever built, one of which was designed by Gaudí's assistant Francesc Berenguer and became Gaudí's home from 1906 to 1926. It now houses the **Casa-Museu Gaudí** museum of memorabilia. Ultimately, the Güell family turned the area over to the city as a public park for local residents, and it remains so today. Visitors must pay an entrance fee to the "monumental area," where the main attractions are located; the rest of the park remains free to enter. You can purchase tickets online, at the park, and at the Lesseps and Vallcarca metro stations.

An Art Nouveau extravaganza with gingerbread gatehouses, Park Güell is a perfect place to visit on a sunny afternoon, when the blue of the Mediterranean is best illuminated by the western sun. The gatehouse on the right, topped with a rendition in ceramic tile of the hallucinogenic red-and-white fly amanita wild mushroom (rumored to have been a Gaudí favorite) houses the Park Güell Interpretation Center. The center has plans, scale models, photos, and suggested routes analyzing the park in detail. Atop the gatehouse on the left sits the *phallus impudicus* (no translation necessary). Other Gaudí highlights include the Room of a Hundred Columns—a covered market supported by tilted Doric-style columns and mosaic medallions—the double set of stairs, and the iconic lizard guarding the fountain between them. There's also the fabulous serpentine, polychrome bench enclosing the square. The bench is one of Gaudí assistant Josep Maria Jujol's most memorable creations, and one of Barcelona's best examples of the trencadís technique (mosaics of broken tile fragments: recycling as high art). From the metro at Plaça de Lesseps, or the Bus Turístic stop on Travessera de Dalt, take Bus No. 24 to the park entrance, or make the steep 10-minute climb uphill on Carrer de Lallard. ✉ *Carrer d'Olot s/n, Gràcia* ☎ *93/409–1831* ⊕ *www.parkguell.cat/en* 🎟 *From €9* Ⓜ *L3 Lesseps, Vallcarca.*

Plaça de la Vila de Gràcia

PLAZA | Originally named (until 2009) for the memorable Gràcia mayor Francesc Rius i Taulet, this is the town's most emblematic and historic square, marked by the handsome clock tower in its center. The tower, built in 1862, is just over 110 feet tall. It has water fountains around its base, royal Bourbon crests over the fountains, and an iron balustrade atop the octagonal brick shaft stretching up to the clock and belfry. The symbol of Gràcia, the clock tower was bombarded by federal troops when Gràcia attempted to secede from the Spanish state during the 1870s. Always a workers' neighborhood and prone to social solidarity, Gràcia was mobilized by mothers who refused to send their sons off as conscripts to fight for the crumbling Spanish Imperial forces during the late 19th century, thus requiring a full-scale assault by Spanish troops to reestablish law and order. Today sidewalk cafés prosper under the leafy canopy here. The Gràcia Casa de la Vila (town hall) at the lower end of the square is yet another Francesc Berenguer opus. ✉ *Pl. de la Vila de Gràcia, Gràcia* Ⓜ *L3 Fontana, Gràcia (FGC).*

Plaça de la Virreina

PLAZA | The much-damaged and oft-restored church of Sant Joan de Gràcia in this square stands where the Palau de la Virreina once stood, the mansion of the same *virreina* (wife, or in this case, widow of a viceroy) whose 18th-century palace, the Pallau de la Virreina, stands on the Rambla. (The Palau is now a prominent municipal museum and art gallery.) The story of La Virreina, a young noblewoman widowed at an early age by the death of the elderly viceroy of Peru, is symbolized in the bronze sculpture in the center of the square: it portrays Ruth of the Old Testament, represented carrying the sheaves of wheat she was gathering when she learned of the death of her husband, Boaz. Ruth is the Old Testament paradigm of wifely fidelity to her husband's clan, a parallel to La Virreina—who spent her life doing good deeds with her husband's fortune.

The rectorial residence at the back of the church is the work of Gaudí's perennial assistant and right-hand man Francesc Berenguer. Just across the street, the

Berenguer: Gaudí's Right Hand

Francesc Berenguer's role in Gaudí's work and the Moderniste movement, despite his leaving architecture school prematurely to work for Gaudí, was significant (if not decisive), and has been much debated by architects and Art Nouveau scholars. If Barcelona was Gaudí's grand canvas, Gràcia was Berenguer's. Though he was not legally licensed to sign his projects, Berenguer is known to have designed nearly every major building in Gràcia, including the Mercat de la Llibertat. The house at Carrer de l'Or 44 remains one of his greatest achievements, a vertical tour de force with pinnacles at the stress lines over rich stacks of wrought-iron balconies. The Gràcia Town Hall in Plaça Rius i Taulet and the Centre Moral Instructiu de Gràcia at Carrer Ros de Olano 9 are confirmed as his; the buildings on Carrer Gran de Gràcia at Nos. 15, 23, 35, 49, 51, 61, 77, and 81 are all either confirmed or suspected Berenguer designs. Even Gaudí's first domestic commission, Casa Vicens, owes its palm-leaf iron fence to Berenguer. When Berenguer died young in 1914, at the age of 47, Gaudí said he had "lost his right hand." Indeed, in his last 12 years, Gaudí worked on nothing but the Sagrada Família and, in fact, made little progress there.

house at Carrer de l'Or 44 was built in 1909, also by Berenguer. Giddily vertical and tightly packed into its narrow slot, it demonstrates one of his best tricks: putting up town houses that share walls with adjacent buildings. ⊠ *Pl. de la Virreina, Gràcia* Ⓜ *L3 Fontana.*

Plaça del Diamant

PLAZA | This little square is of enormous sentimental importance in Barcelona as the site of the opening and closing scenes of 20th-century Catalan writer Mercé Rodoreda's famous 1962 novel *La Plaça del Diamant.* Translated by the late American poet David Rosenthal as *The Time of the Doves,* it is the most widely translated and published Catalan novel of all time: a tender yet brutal story of a young woman devoured by the Spanish Civil War and, in a larger sense, by life itself. An angular and oddly disturbing steel and bronze statue in the square, by Xavier Medina-Campeny, portrays Colometa, the novel's protagonist, caught in the middle of her climactic scream. The bronze birds represent the pigeons that Colometa spent her life obsessively breeding; the male figure on the left pierced by bolts of steel is Quimet, her first love and husband, whom she met at a dance in this square and later lost in the war. Most of the people taking their ease at the cafés in the square will be unaware that some 40 feet below them is one of the largest air-raid shelters in Barcelona, hacked out by the residents of Gràcia during the bombardments of the civil war. ⊠ *Pl. del Diamant, Barcelona* Ⓜ *L3 Fontana.*

Plaça Rovira i Trias

PLAZA | This charming little square and the story of Antoni Rovira i Trias shed much light on the true nature of Barcelona's eternal struggle with Madrid and Spanish central authority. Take a careful look at the map of Barcelona positioned at the feet of the bronze effigy of the architect and urban planners near the center of the square and you will see a vision of what the city might have looked like if Madrid's (and the Spanish army's) candidate for the design of the Eixample in 1860, Ildefons Cerdà, had not been imposed over the plan devised by Rovira i Trias, initial and legitimate winner of the open competition for the commission. Rovira i

Trias's plan shows an astral design radiating out from a central Eixample square that military minds saw as avenues of approach; Cerdà's design, on the other hand, made the Diagonal into a natural barrier. ✉ *Pl. Rovira i Trias, Gràcia* [M] *L3 Lesseps, L4 Joanic.*

🍴 Restaurants

This lively and intimate neighborhood is home to many of Barcelona's artists, musicians, and actors. The bohemian atmosphere is reflected in an eclectic collection of restaurants encompassing everything from street food and affordable ethnic cuisine to thoroughly sophisticated dining.

Botafumeiro

$$$$ | **SEAFOOD** | On Gràcia's main thoroughfare, Barcelona's best-known Galician restaurant has maritime motifs, snowy tablecloths, wood paneling, and fleets of waiters in spotless white outfits steering diners toward the more expensive end of the menu. The bank-breaking *mariscada Botafumeiro* is a seafood medley from shellfish to fin fish to cuttlefish to caviar. **Known for:** outstanding seafood; all-day opening; pricey. [$] *Average main: €35* ✉ *Gran de Gràcia 81, Gràcia* ☎ *93/218–4230* 🌐 *www.botafumeiro.es* [M] *Metro: Fontana.*

Hofmann

$$$$ | **MEDITERRANEAN** | The late Mey Hofmann, German-born and Catalonia-trained, was revered for decades for her creative Mediterranean and international cuisine based on carefully selected raw materials prepared with unrelenting quality. Her team carries on her legacy at her locale, a graceful designer space with a glassed-in kitchen as center stage. **Known for:** sardine tartare; foie gras in puff pastry; prawn risotto. [$] *Average main: €35* ✉ *La Granada del Penedès 14–16, Gràcia* ☎ *93/218–7165* 🌐 *www.hofmann-bcn.com* ⏲ *Closed Sun. and Aug. No lunch Sat.* [M] *Gràcia, Diagonal.*

La Panxa del Bisbe

$ | **MEDITERRANEAN** | "The Bishop's Belly" achieves a rare feat: putting modern international twists on Mediterranean cuisine without ruining it. La Panxa is off the beaten path and thrives on a steady stream of repeat customers, who file into its bare-brick dining room for tapas and small dishes such as veal cheeks with beetroot gnocchi. **Known for:** good stop on way back from Park Güell; value set lunch; great tapas. [$] *Average main: €15* ✉ *Torrent de les Flors 158, Gràcia* ☎ *93/213–7049* ⏲ *Closed Sun. and Mon.* [M] *Lesseps or Joanic.*

L'Arrosseria Xàtiva

$$ | **SPANISH** | This rustic dining room in Gràcia, a spin-off from the original in Les Corts, evokes the rice paddies and lowlands of Valencia. Low lighting imparts a warm glow over exposed brick walls, wood-beam ceilings, and bentwood chairs, and it's a great spot to savor some of Barcelona's finest paellas and rice dishes. **Known for:** traditional paella; lovingly prepared food; all-day kitchen on weekends. [$] *Average main: €20* ✉ *Torrent d'en Vidalet 26, Gràcia* ☎ *93/284–8502* 🌐 *www.grupxativa.com* [M] *Joanic.*

Roig Robí

$$$ | **CATALAN** | Rattan chairs and a garden terrace characterize this polished dining spot in the bottom corner of Gràcia just above the Diagonal (near Vía Augusta). Rustic and relaxed, Roig Robí (ruby red in Catalan, as in the color of certain wines) maintains a high level of culinary excellence, serving traditional Catalan market cuisine with original touches directed by chef Mercé Navarro. **Known for:** top-notch guinea-fowl canelón; seasonal specials; helmed by excellent chef. [$] *Average main: €26* ✉ *Sèneca 20, Gràcia* ☎ *93/218–9222* 🌐 *www.roigrobi.com* ⏲ *Closed Sun., and 2 wks in Aug. No lunch Sat.* [M] *Diagonal, Gràcia (FGC).*

Park Güell was originally built to be a private garden community. One of the houses built here became Gaudí's residence from 1906 to 1926.

Hotels

★Hotel Casa Fuster Gran Lujo Monumento
$$$$ | HOTEL | This hotel offers one of two chances (the other is the Hotel España) to stay in an Art Nouveau building designed by Lluís Domènech i Montaner, architect of the sumptuous Palau de la Música Catalana. **Pros:** well situated for exploring both Gràcia and the Eixample; ample rooms with luxury-level amenities; all the Moderniste details you could want. **Cons:** rooms facing Passeig de Gràcia could use better soundproofing; no pets; service can be a bit stiff. *[$] Rooms from: €290 ✉ Passeig de Gràcia 132, Gràcia ☎ 93/255–3000 🌐 www.hotelcasafuster.com 🛏 105 rooms 🍴 No meals [M] L3/L5 Diagonal.*

Pol & Grace Hotel
$$ | HOTEL | Renovated and reopened in 2015 under new ownership—the hip young enthusiastic pair renamed the hotel after themselves—the Pol & Grace is strategically located for exploring Gràcia, a short walk to Gaudí's Casa Vicens, and well connected by FGC train to the head of the Rambla. **Pros:** fun and laid-back atmosphere; children under 10 stay free; book exchange and DVD collection in the lobby. **Cons:** no restaurant on-site; building of no particular architectural interest; no gym or pool. *[$] Rooms from: €130 ✉ Guillem Tell 49, Gràcia ☎ 93/415–4000 🌐 www.polgracehotel.es 🛏 64 rooms 🍴 No meals [M] Sant Gervasi, Pl. Molina (FGC).*

Nightlife

With a bohemian look and feel more akin to a small village than an urban landscape, Gràcia welcomes revelers of all stripes looking for easygoing pleasures. On any given night, hordes of visitors pour into the district's ancient squares to sample freshly made tapas paired with beer or wine. But for the slightly more adventurous, exploring the graffiti-filled, maze-like back alleyways and side streets usually provides ample rewards: gourmet eateries, upscale wine bars, and contempo *coctelerias*

Ground Rules for Coffee

Coffee culture in Barcelona continues to focus on simplicity, in defiance of the near-infinite choices offered by certain barista-fronted international chains now moving into the city. A normal espresso, black coffee, is simply *un cafè*—a *café solo* in the rest of Spain. Add some extra water and it's a *cafè Americá*. In summer add ice for a *cafè amb gel*, and in winter add a dash of rum or brandy to make a *cigaló* (*carajillo* in Spanish). A *tallat*, from the Catalan verb *tallar* (to cut), is coffee with just a little milk (*café cortado* in Spanish), while *cafè amb llet* is Catalan

for *café con leche*, or coffee mixed more evenly with milk. That's about as far as coffee menus stretch, but if you really want to see the waiter's eyes glaze over, order a *café descafeinado de maquina con leche desnatada natural* (decaffeinated coffee made in the espresso machine with skim milk applied at room temperature).

Finally, a word of warning to those who prefer their java to go: coffee is still, for the most part, a sit-down or belly-up-to-the-bar affair; take time to stop and smell the fresh roast.

that coexist in perfect harmony with the neighborhood dives.

BARS

★ Elephanta

BARS/PUBS | Diminutive in size but huge in personality and warmth, Elephanta is that rare neighborhood spot that offers a little something for everyone. Patrons enjoy an extensive menu (printed on authentic vinyl album covers) of quality gins and seasonal fruity cocktails in a dimly lighted retro space peppered with comfy mismatched furnishings and India-inspired decor. Music varies though the ambience is always chill; perfect for laptop lounging or hosted cultural screenings. ✉ *Torrent d'en Vidalet 37, Gràcia* ☎ *93/237–6906* ⊕ *elephanta.cat* Ⓜ *Joanic.*

Ítaca

BARS/PUBS | This contemporary *cervecería* resembles many of the cool offerings routinely sprouting up in Gràcia, one of the city's most popular neighborhoods. Patrons can top off drinks with self-service pours from local brewer Estrella Damm. Local craft favorites such as Brew Dog Punk IPA and classic cocktails are also on offer. Enjoy a drink with nachos, burgers, and tapas while

listening to local tunes around the tiny, natural-wood bar. ✉ *Santa Rosa 14, Gràcia* ☎ *93/129–8095* ⊕ *www.grupitaca. cat* Ⓜ *Fontana.*

L'Entresòl

BARS/PUBS | Come for the laid-back vibe and retro furnishings, stay for the large selection of premium gin (35-plus and counting), and guest DJs playing the grooviest indie, funk, and soul on weekends. Perfect for pre-club gintonics with friends or dates. ✉ *Carrer del Planeta 39, Gràcia* ☎ *685/533941* Ⓜ *Fontana.*

★ Old Fashioned

BARS/PUBS | Reminiscent of a '50s-style gin joint—black and white with red quilted booths and framed prints—this small-but-swanky bar regularly draws in the crowds due in large part to entertaining master mixologists (nattily dressed in suspenders and ties) and their out-of-this-world experimental takes on cocktail classics. Try a Fashionista, the house special prepared with bourbon, sherry, and hazelnuts, among other ingredients, and flambéed with a blowtorch. Other playfully named concoctions include Anything Goes and Run to Your Mama. ✉ *Santa Teresa 1, Gràcia* ☎ *93/368–5277* Ⓜ *Diagonal.*

★ Viblioteca

WINE BARS—NIGHTLIFE | Adding a little uptown pizzazz to boho-chic enclave Gràcia, this diminutive, minimalist, white-walled wine bar and eatery is the local "it" vintage. Wines sourced and served with engaging backstories can be sampled at the seven-seater bar or at a table, accompanied by a large assortment of cured meats, cheeses, and salads or with a few choice liquors. Advance booking is highly recommended. ⊠ *Vallfogona 12, Gràcia* ☎ *93/284–4202* ⊕ *www.viblioteca. com* Ⓜ *Fontana.*

Shopping

The onetime outlying village of Gràcia is has become a shopping destination in its own right with a host of creatively conceived, owner-run design and fashion stores, art and design galleries, and crafts studios. Major High Street brands sit cheek by jowl along Gran de Gràcia, the neighborhood's main drag. Venture farther to Carrer Verdi, Carrer Torrijos, and around the Mercat de la Llibertat, Plaça del Sol, and Plaça Rius i Taulet, all which abound in fashion and jewelry shops, along with arty cafés, taverns, and gourmet food boutiques. Along Carrer d'Asturiés there are dozens of shops selling clothing and food adhering to the organic, alternative lifestyle principles Gràcia's residents are famous for.

BEAUTY

Herbolari del Cel

SPA/BEAUTY | Gràcia's "Herbolarium from Heaven" is widely considered among the best in Barcelona for herbal remedies, teas, spices, oils, natural cures and treatments, and cosmetics of all kinds. A mere deep breath of air here will probably cure whatever ails you. ⊠ *Travessera de Gràcia 120, Gràcia* ☎ *93/218–7331* ⊕ *www.herbolaridelcel.com* Ⓜ *Fontana.*

FOOD

Planeta Te

FOOD/CANDY | With more than 1,000 products on offer, this must be widest variety of teas and infusions available in Barcelona. Planeta Te sell herbs and blends by weight from pretty tin boxes and drawers that line the walls. You will also find organic tea bags, a colorful range of teapots and other tea-making paraphernalia, and a seductive aroma as soon as you enter this sweet old-fashioned shop. ⊠ *Asturies 50, Gràcia* ☎ *93/210–3922* Ⓜ *Fontana.*

Tea Shop

FOOD/CANDY | Earl Grey, black, white, red, green: every kind of tea you've ever heard of and many you probably haven't are available at this encyclopedic tea repository on Gràcia's main drag. The Taller de Cata (Tasting Workshop) held periodically will stimulate your tea culture in the event that you are interested in learning how to distinguish a Pai Mu Tan (white tea) from a Lung Ching (green tea) or how to correctly prepare and serve different varieties of this universal world brew and beverage. ⊠ *Gran de Gràcia 91, Gràcia* ☎ *93/217–4923* ⊕ *www.teashop. com/en* Ⓜ *Passeig de Gràcia.*

SHOES

BBB

SHOES/LUGGAGE/LEATHER GOODS | Any shoe store that satisfies the legendary three B requirements—*bueno, bonito,* and *barato* (good, beautiful, and cheap)—is not to be missed. Shoes in many styles from sandals to stilettos pack this popular Gràcia shoe emporium. ⊠ *Gran de Gràcia 233, Gràcia* ☎ *93/237–3514* Ⓜ *Fontana.*

TOYS

Bateau Lune

TOYS | **FAMILY** | Crafts, disguises, puzzles, games, and a thousand things to make you want to be a kid again are on display in this creative child-oriented gift shop on one of Gràcia's most emblematic squares. ⊠ *Pl. de la Virreina 7, Gràcia* ☎ *93/218–6907* ⊕ *www.bateaulune.com* Ⓜ *Fontana.*

Chapter 10

UPPER
BARCELONA

Updated by
Elizabeth Prosser and
Steve Tallantyre

◉ Sights	🍴 Restaurants	🛏 Hotels	🛍 Shopping	🍸 Nightlife
★★★☆☆	★★★★☆	★★★☆☆	★★★☆☆	★★☆☆☆

NEIGHBORHOOD SNAPSHOT

TOP EXPERIENCES

■ **Monestir de Pedralbes:** Meditate in the three-story cloister surrounding a lush garden in this convent founded in 1326 then check out the treasures in the nuns' dormitory.

■ **Torre Bellesguard:** Walk up to one of Gaudi's lesser known, and less-trafficked masterpieces, for a fascinating architectural gem and incredible views. A guided tour really enhances the experience so book ahead.

■ **Bar Tomás** Fill up on *patatas bravas* and *patatas bravas y salsa con allioli* (as well as other traditional tapas) widely considered the best in Barcelona.

■ **Tibidabo:** take the funicular up to this mountain overlooking Barcelona and check out the neo-Gothic church and amusement park.

GETTING HERE

Sarrià is best reached on the FGC (Ferrocarril de la Generalitat de Catalunya) line, which is integrated with the city metro system, though a cut above. From Plaça de Catalunya, all the FGC trains (except those bound for Tibidabo) stop at Sarrià; only local trains branch off from there to the terminus at Reina Elisenda. The trip uptown takes about 15 minutes. By bus, you can take the V7, which runs from Plaça d'Espanya to Sarrià, or the No. 64, which takes a somewhat roundabout route from Barceloneta to Pedralbes, with a stop at Plaça Sarrià.

PLANNING YOUR TIME

An exploration of Sarrià and Pedralbes is a three- to four-hour jaunt, including at least an hour in the monastery. Count four or five with lunch included. Plan to visit the monastery in the morning. Bar Tomás serves its famous potatoes with *allioli* (spicy garlic mayonnaise) 1–4 pm and 7–10 pm, another key timing consideration, while the Foix de Sarrià pastry emporium is open until 9 pm.

QUICK BITES

■ **Bar Tomas.** On the corner of Mayor de Sarrià and Carrer Jaume Piquet, Bar Tomás is a Barcelona institution, home of the finest *patatas bravas* (fried potatoes) in town—a cynosure so prosperous it can afford to shut for the night at 10 pm. Order the famous *doble mixta* of potatoes with *allioli* and hot sauce, and a draft beer (ask for a *caña*) to sluice them down ⊠ *Major de Sarrià 49, Sarrià* Ⓜ *Sarrià (FCG)*

■ **Foix de Sarria.** A must visit in Sarrià and arguably the best patisserie in Barcelona. Sip a hot chocolate or coffee while you sample an array of exquisite cakes and sweets. ⊠ *Pl. de Sarrià 12-13, Sarrià* ⊕ *www.foixdesarria. com* Ⓜ *Sarrià (FCG)*

Sarrià was originally a country village, overlooking Barcelona from the foothills of the Collserola. Eventually absorbed by the westward-expanding city, the village, 15 minutes by FGC commuter train from Plaça de Catalunya, has become a unique neighborhood made up of old-timers, who speak only Catalan; writers, artists, and other creatives; gourmet shops and upscale restaurants; and expats, who prize the neighborhood for its proximity to the international schools.

J. V. Foix, the famous Catalan poet, was a native son of Sarrià; his father founded what is arguably the best patisserie in Barcelona, and his descendants still run the quintessential Sarrià family business. On Sunday, barcelonins come to the village from all over town; Sunday just wouldn't be Sunday without a cake from Foix to take to grandma's. Cross Avinguda Foix from Sarrià and you're in Pedralbes—the wealthiest residential neighborhood in the city. (Fútbol superstar Leo Messi has his multimillion-euro home here, and the exclusive Real Club de Tenis de Barcelona is close by.) The centerpiece of this district is the 14th-century Monestir (Monastery) de Pedralbes; other points of interest include Gaudí's Pavellons de la Finca Güell on Avinguda de Pedralbes, and the gardens of the Palau Reial de Pedralbes, a 20-minute walk downhill from the monastery. The Futbol Club at Barcelona's Camp Nou stadium and the museum are another 20 minutes' walk, down below the Diagonal.

 Sights

Col·legi de les Teresianes

COLLEGE | Built in 1889 for the Reverend Mothers of St. Theresa, when Gaudí was still occasionally using straight lines, the upper floors of this former operating school are reminiscent of those in Berenguer's apartment at Carrer de l'Or 44, with its steep peaks and verticality. Hired to take over for another architect, Gaudí found his freedom of movement somewhat limited in this project. The dominant theme here is the architect's use of steep, narrow catenary arches and Mudejar exposed-brick pillars. The most striking effects are on the second floor, where two rows of a dozen catenary arches run the width of the building, each of them unique; as

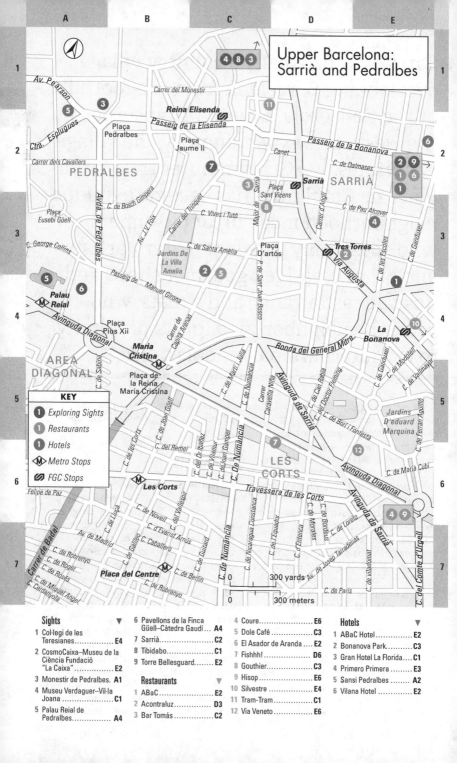

Upper Barcelona: Sarrià and Pedralbes

KEY

- 1 Exploring Sights
- 1 Restaurants
- 1 Hotels
- Ⓜ Metro Stops
- Ⓕ FGC Stops

Gaudí explained, no two things in nature are identical. The brick columns are crowned with T-shaped brick capitals (for St. Theresa). Look down at the marble doorstep for the inscription by mystic writer and poet Santa Teresa de Avila (1515–82), the much-quoted "todo se pasa" (all things pass). The Col·legi is a private secondary school, and normally not open to visitors, but the sisters may organize guided group visits on request. ⊠ Ganduxer 85, Sant Gervasi ☎ 93/212–3354 ⊕ ganduxer.escolateresiana.com Ⓜ La Bonanova, Les Tres Torres (FGC).

CosmoCaixa–Museu de la Ciència Fundació "La Caixa"

MUSEUM | FAMILY | Young scientific minds work overtime in this interactive science museum, just below Tibidabo. Among the many displays designed for children seven and up are the Geological Wall, a history of rocks and rock formations; the digital Planetarium; and the Underwater Forest, showcasing a slice of the Amazonian rain forest in a large greenhouse. ⊠ Carrer Isaac Newton 26, Sant Gervasi ☎ 93/212–6050 ⊕ obrasociallacaixa.org/es/ciencia/cosmocaixa/el-museo 🎟 €4 (plus €4 per interactive activity inside); accompanied children under 16 free ⊗ Closed Mon. Ⓜ FGC line L7 to Av. de Tibidabo and Tramvía Blau.

★ Monestir de Pedralbes

MUSEUM | This marvel of a monastery, named for its original white stones (pedres albes), is really a convent, founded in 1326 for the Franciscan order of Poor Clares by Reina (Queen) Elisenda. The three-story Gothic cloister, one of the finest in Europe, surrounds a lush garden. The day cells, where the nuns spend their mornings praying, sewing, and studying, circle the arcaded courtyard. The queen's own cell, the Capella de Sant Miquel, just to the right of the entrance, has murals painted in 1346 by Catalan master Ferrer Bassa. Look for the letters spelling out Joan no m'oblides ("John, do not forget me") scratched

between the figures of St. Francis and St. Clare (with book and quill), written by a brokenhearted novice. The nuns' upstairs dormitory contains the convent's treasures: paintings, liturgical objects, and seven centuries of artistic and cultural patrimony. Temporary exhibits are displayed in this space. The refectory where the Poor Clares dined in silence has a pulpit used for readings, while wall inscriptions exhort Silentium ("Silence"), Audi tacens ("Listening makes you wise"), and Considera morientem ("Consider, we are dying"). Notice the fading mural in the corner, and the paving tiles broken by heavy cannon positioned here during the 1809 Napoleonic occupation. ⊠ Baixada del Monestir 9, Pedralbes ☎ 93/256–3434 ⊕ monestirpedralbes. bcn.cat/en 🎟 €5; free Sun. after 3 pm, and 1st Sun. of every month ⊗ Closed Mon. Ⓜ Reina Elisenda (FGC).

Museu Verdaguer–Vil·la Joana

HOUSE | Catalonian poet Jacint Verdaguer died in this house in 1902. The story of Verdaguer's reinvention of Catalan nationalism in the late 19th century, and his ultimate death in disgrace, defrocked and impoverished, is a fascinating saga. Considered the national poet of Catalonia and the most revered and beloved voice of the Catalan "Renaixença" of the 19th century, Verdaguer—universally known as Mossèn Cinto (Mossèn is Catalan for priest; Cinto is from Jacinto, Spanish for Jacint)—finally succumbed to tuberculosis and a general collapse triggered by economic, existential, and doctrinal religious troubles. Priest, poet, mystic, student, hiker, and lover of the Pyrenees, he was seen as a virtual saint, and wrote works of great religious and patriotic fervor such as Idilis and Cants mistichs, as well his famous long masterpiece, Canigó (1886). In La Atlàntida (1877), eventually to become a Manuel de Falla opera-oratorio, he wrote about prehistoric myths of the Iberian Peninsula and the Pyrenees. Verdaguer's death provoked massive mourning. His popularity was so

A Good Tour

The L7 trains on the FGC (Ferrocarrils de la Generalitat de Catalunya, a separate system from the city-administered Metro) run from Plaça Catalunya to the Avinguda Tibidabo station in Plaça Kennedy, at the top of Carrer de Balmes. The first building on the right as you start up Avinguda del Tibidabo is known as La Rotonda, notable for its Art Nouveau ceramic ornamentation on the upper part of the facade. The Tramvía Blau (Blue Trolley) sets out from just above La Rotonda and, passing the imposing white **Casa Roviralta–El Frare Blanc**, drops you at Plaça del Doctor Andreu, where the funicular climbs up to the heights of **Tibidabo**. Plaça del Doctor Andreu has several restaurants, the best of which is La Venta. From Tibidabo the road to the **Torre de Collserola** continues another 2 km (1 mile) over to **Vallvidrera**, where there are several good restaurants (such as Can Trampa in Plaça de Vallvidrera). From Vallvidrera, return to Barcelona via the funicular or on foot. The other way to approach is via the Baixador de Vallvidrera stop on the FGC Generalitat railway line to San Cugat, Sabadell, or Terrassa. A five-minute walk up to the **Museu Verdaguer** at Vil·la Joana will put you on well-marked trails through the Parc de Collserola. There are also trail markings to Vil·la Joana from the Torre de Collserola. The Barcelona train from the Baixador de Vallvidrera will drop you back in Plaça de Catalunya in 20 minutes.

enormous that violently anticlerical Barcelona anarchists in mid-uprising ceased fighting and stormed the churches to ring the bells on hearing the news of his death. The funeral was one of the most heavily attended events in Barcelona history, comparable only to Gaudí's in spontaneity and emotion.

Lines from his patriotic poem *Enyorança* (*Yearning*) are slowly and sonorously recited at Vil·la Joana every June 10 on the anniversary of his death. ✉ *Vil.la Joana, Ctra. de l'Església 104, Vallvidrera* ☎ *93/256–2122* ⊕ *www.museuhistoria. bcn.cat/es/muhba-villa-joana* ⚑ *Free* Ⓜ *Baixador de Vallvidrera (FGC).*

Palau Reial de Pedralbes (*Royal Palace of Pedralbes*)
CASTLE/PALACE | Built in the 1920s as the palatial estate of Count Eusebi Güell—one of Gaudí's most important patrons—this mansion was transformed into a royal palace by architect Eusebi Bona i Puig and completed in 1929. King Alfonso XIII, grandfather of Spanish king Juan Carlos I, visited the palace in the mid-1920s before its completion. In 1931, during the Second Spanish Republic, the palace became the property of the municipal government, and it was converted to a decorative arts museum in 1932. (The museum is now part of the Disseny Hub complex in Plaça de les Glòries Catalanes.) In 1936 the rambling, elegant country-manor-house palace was used as the official residence of Manuel Azaña, last president of the Spanish Republic. The gardens and grounds are open to the public; the buildings are not. ✉ *Av. Diagonal 686, Pedralbes* Ⓜ *L3 Palau Reial.*

Pavellons de la Finca Güell–Càtedra Gaudí
BUILDING | Work on the Finca began in 1883 as an extension of Count Eusebi Güell's family estate. Gaudí, the count's architect of choice, was commissioned to do the gardens and the two entrance pavilions (1884–87); the rest of the project was never finished. The Pavellons

(pavilions) now belong to the University of Barcelona; the one on the right houses the Càtedra Gaudí, a Gaudí library and study center. The fierce wrought-iron dragon gate is Gaudí's reference to the Garden of the Hesperides, as described by national poet Jacint Verdaguer's epic poem *L'Atlàntida* (1877)—the *Iliad* of Catalonia's historic-mythic origins. The property is open for guided tours in English on weekends at 10:15 and 12:15. Admission is limited to 25 visitors: call ahead, or book on the Ruta del Modernisme website. The Ruta is a walking tour covering 120 masterworks of the Moderniste period, including those by Gaudí, Domènech i Montaner, and Puig i Cadafalch. Pick up a guide—which includes a map, suggested short and longer itineraries, and a book of discount vouchers for admission to many of the sites—here at the Pavellons. ⊠ *Av. Pedralbes 7, Pedralbes* ☎ *93/256–2504 guided tours* ⊕ *www.rutadelmodernisme.com* ✉ *Tours €5* Ⓜ *L3 Palau Reial.*

Sarrià

LOCAL INTEREST | The village of Sarrià was originally a cluster of farms and country houses overlooking Barcelona from the hills. Once dismissively described as nothing but "winds, brooks, and convents," this quiet enclave is now a prime residential neighborhood at the upper edge of the city. Start an exploration at the square—the locus, at various times, of antique and bric-a-brac markets, book fairs, artisanal food and wine fairs, sardana dances (Sunday morning), concerts, and Christmas pageants. The 10th-century Romanesque **Church of Sant Vicenç** dominates the main square, the Plaça de Sarrià; the bell tower, illuminated on weekend nights, is truly impressive. Across Passeig de la Reina Elisenda from the church (50 yards to the left) is the 100-year-old Moderniste **Mercat de Sarrià.**

From the square, cut through the Placeta del Roser to the left of the church to the elegant **Town Hall** (1896) in the Plaça de la Vila; note the buxom bronze sculpture of **Pomona,** goddess of fruit, by famed Sarrià sculptor Josep Clarà (1878–1958). Follow the tiny Carrer dels Paletes, to the left of the Town Hall (the saint enshrined in the niche is Sant Antoni, patron saint of *paletes,* or bricklayers), and right on Major de Sarrià, the High Street of the village. For lunch, try Casa Raphael, on the right as you walk down—in business (and virtually unchanged) since 1873. Farther on, turn left into **Carrer Canet.** The two-story row houses on the right were first built for workers on the village estates, now converted to other uses (including a pre-school); these, and the houses opposite at Nos. 15, 21, and 23, are among the few remaining original village homes in Sarrià. Turn right at the first corner on Carrer Cornet i Mas and walk two blocks down to Carrer Jaume Piquet.

On the left is No. 30, Barcelona's most perfect small-format **Moderniste house,** thought to be the work of architect Domènech i Montaner, complete with faux-medieval upper windows, wrought-iron grillwork, floral and fruited ornamentation, and organically curved and carved wooden doors either by or inspired by Gaudí himself. The next stop down Cornet i Mas is Sarrià's prettiest square, **Plaça Sant Vicens,** a leafy space ringed by old Sarrià houses and centered on a statue of Sarrià's patron St. Vicenç, portrayed (as always) beside the millstone used to sink him to the bottom of the Mediterranean after he was martyred in Valencia in AD 302. **Can Pau,** the café on the lower corner with Carrer Mañé i Flaquer, is the local hangout, once a haven for authors Gabriel García Marquez and Mario Vargas Llosa, who lived in Sarrià in the late 1960s and early 1970s.

Other Sarrià landmarks to look for include the two **Foix** pastry shops, one at Plaça Sarrià 9–10 and the other at Major de Sarrià 57, above Bar Tomás. The late J. V. Foix (1893–1987), son of the shop's founder,

A quiet space for reflection: the courtyard of the Monestir de Pedralbes

was one of the great Catalan poets of the 20th century, a key player in keeping the Catalan language alive during the 40-year Franco regime. The shop on Major de Sarrià has a bronze plaque identifying the house as the poet's birthplace and inscribed with one of his most memorable verses, translated as, "Every love is latent in the other love / every language is the juice of a common tongue / every country touches the fatherland of all / every faith will be the lifeblood of a higher faith." ⊠ *Sarrià* Ⓜ *Sarrià (FGC Line L6)*.

Tibidabo. One of Barcelona's two promontories, this hill bears a distinctive name, generally translated as "To Thee I Will Give." It refers to the Catalan legend that this was the spot from which Satan tempted Christ with all the riches of the earth below (namely, Barcelona). On a clear day, the views from this 1,789-foot peak are legendary. Tibidabo's skyline is marked by a neo-Gothic church, the work of Enric Sagnier in 1902, and—off to one side, near the village of Vallvidrera—the 854-foot communications tower,

the **Torre de Collserola,** designed by Sir Norman Foster. If you're with kids, take the San Francisco–style Tramvía Blau (Blue Trolley) from Plaça Kennedy to the overlook at the top, and transfer to the funicular to the 100-year-old **amusement park** at the summit. ⊠ *Pl. Tibidabo 3–4, Tibidabo* ☎ *93/211–7942 amusement park* ⊕ *www.tibidabo.cat* ⊠ *Amusement park €29* Ⓜ *FGC L7 Tibidabo, then Tramvía Blau.*

★ Torre Bellesguard

HOUSE | For an extraordinary Gaudí experience, climb up above Plaça de la Bonanova to this private residence built between 1900 and 1909 over the ruins of the summer palace of the last of the sovereign count-kings of the Catalan-Aragonese realm, Martí I l'Humà (Martin I the Humane), whose reign ended in 1410. In homage to this medieval history, Gaudí endowed the house with a tower, gargoyles, and crenellated battlements; the rest—the catenary arches, the trencadís in the facade, the stained-glass windows—are pure Art Nouveau. Look for the red and gold Catalan senyera (banner) on the tower, topped by the four-armed Greek cross Gaudí often used. Over the front door is the inscription *"Sens pecat fou concebuda"* ("Without sin was she conceived"), referring to the Immaculate Conception of the Virgin Mary; on either side of the front door are benches with trencadís of playful fish bearing the crimson *quatre barres* (four bars) of the Catalan flag as well as the Corona d'Aragó (Crown of Aragón). The visit includes access to the roof, which Gaudí designed to resemble a dragon, along with the gardens, patio, and stables. **■ TIP→ Reservations required for the highly recommended guided tour (reserva@bellesguardgaudi.com).** ✉ *Calle Bellesguard 16–20, Sant Gervasi* ☎ *93/250–4093* 🌐 *www.bellesguardgaudi.com* 🎫 *From €9* 🕒 *Closed Mon.* [M] *Av. Tibidabo (FGC).*

Vallvidrera

This perched village is a quiet respite from Barcelona's headlong race. Oddly, there's nothing exclusive or upmarket—for now—about Vallvidrera, as most well-off barcelonins prefer to be closer to the center. From **Plaça Pep Ventura**, in front of the Moderniste funicular station, there are superb views over the Vallvidrera houses and the Montserrat. Vallvidrera can be reached from the Peu Funicular train stop and the Vallvidrera funicular, by road, or on foot from Tibidabo or Vil·la Joana. The cozy Can Trampa at the center of town in Plaça de Vallvidrera, and Can Martí down below are fine spots for a meal.

🍴 Restaurants

Take an excursion to the upper reaches of town for an excellent selection of bars, cafés, and restaurants, along with cool summer evening breezes and a sense of well-heeled village life.

ABaC

$$$$ | **CATALAN** | Jordi Cruz is a culinary phenomenon in Spain. The only choice here is between the two tasting menus, and you can trust this chef to give you the best he has; the hypercreative sampling varies wildly from season to season, but no expense or effort is ever spared. **Known for:** celebrity chef; creative in-season dishes; elegant setting in elegant boutique hotel. [$] *Average main: €180* ✉ *Av. del Tibidabo 1–7, Tibidabo* ☎ *93/319–6600* 🌐 *www.abacbarcelona.com* [M] *Tibidabo.*

Acontraluz

$$ | **CATALAN** | A stylish covered terrace in the leafy upper-Barcelona neighborhood of Tres Torres, Acontraluz has a strenuously varied market-based menu ranging from game in season, such as *rable de liebre* (stewed hare) with chutney, to the more northern *pochas con almejas* (beans with clams). All dishes are prepared with care and talent, and the lunch menu is a relative bargain. **Known for:** stylish dining room with a retractable roof; bargain lunch menu; excellent stewed hare. [$] *Average main: €20* ✉ *Milanesat 19, Tres Torres* ☎ *93/203–0658* 🌐 *acontraluz.com* 🕒 *No dinner Sun. Closed 2 wks in Aug.* [M] *Les Tres Torres.*

Bar Tomás

$ | **TAPAS** | Famous for its *patatas bravas amb allioli* (potatoes with fiery hot sauce and allioli, an emulsion of crushed garlic and olive oil), accompanied by freezing mugs of San Miguel beer, this old-fashioned Sarrià classic is worth seeking out as a contrast to the bland designer tapas bars that are ubiquitous in Barcelona. You'll have to elbow your way to a tiny table and shout to be heard over the hubbub, but you'll get an authentic taste of local bar life. **Known for:** excellent patatas bravas; traditional tavern atmosphere; San Miguel beer in frozen mugs. [$] *Average main: €8* ✉ *Major de Sarrià 49, Sarrià*

☎ *93/203–1077* 🌐 *www.eltomasdesarria.com* 💳 *No credit cards* ⏲ *Closed Wed. and Sun. Closed Aug.* [M] *Sarrià.*

★ Coure

$$$ | MEDITERRANEAN | *Cuina d'autor* is Catalan for creative or original cooking, and that is exactly what you get in this smart subterranean space on the intimate and restaurant-centric Passatge Marimón, just above the Diagonal thoroughfare. The upstairs bar gets busy with a post-work crowd of food-loving locals, but downstairs is a cool, minimalist restaurant. **Known for:** interesting wine list; great local fish; seasonal mushrooms. [$] *Average main: €24* ✉ *Passatge Marimón 20, Sant Gervasi* ☎ *93/200–7532* ⏲ *Closed Sun. and Mon. Closed 3 wks in Aug.* [M] *Diagonal.*

Dole Café

$ | CAFÉ | Little more than a slender slot on the corner of Capità Arenas and Manuel de Falla, this famous upper Barcelona café is absolutely vital to the Sarrià and Capità Arenas neighborhoods. Sandwiches and pastries here are uncannily well made and tasty. **Known for:** top-notch sandwiches and pastries; popeye sandwich is a favorite; often packed. [$] *Average main: €10* ✉ *Manuel de Falla 16–18, Sarrià* ☎ *93/204–1120* ⏲ *Closed Sun. No dinner Mon.–Sat.* [M] *Metro: Maria Cristina, FGC: Sarrià.*

★ El Asador de Aranda

$$$ | SPANISH | FAMILY | It's a hike to get to this immense palace a few minutes' walk above the Avenida Tibidabo train station—but it's worth it. The kitchen, featuring a vast, wood-fired clay oven, specializes in Castilian cooking, with *cordero lechal* (roast suckling lamb), *morcilla* (black sausage), and pimientos de piquillo as star players. **Known for:** beautiful Art Nouveau setting; excellent roasted lamb; spectacular city views from terrace. [$] *Average main: €25* ✉ *Av. del Tibidabo 31, Tibidabo* ☎ *93/417–0115* 🌐 *www.asadordearanda.net* [M] *Tibidabo (FGC).*

Fishhh!

$$ | SEAFOOD | Housed inside the L'Illa Diagonal shopping mall, you can combine retail therapy with a seafood feast at Fishhh!, a first-rate oyster bar and fish restaurant. Owner Lluís de Buen is long a major seafood supplier of Barcelona's top restaurants (check out his seafood-central command post off the back left corner of the Boqueria market) and his staff have put together a lively and popular dining space that exudes Boqueria market–style excitement in the midst of a busy shopping venue. **Known for:** oysters and Champagne; seafood specialties; king crab served table-side. [$] *Average main: €15* ✉ *Av. Diagonal 557, Sant Gervasi, Les Corts* ☎ *93/444–1139* 🌐 *fishhh.net* ⏲ *Closed Sun.* [M] *Les Corts.*

Gouthier

$$ | SEAFOOD | This Paris-style oyster bar spills out onto a pretty square in the former village of Sarrià. Pristine oysters of all kinds are shucked and served fresh alongside rye bread and creamy pats of French butter. **Known for:** supplies oysters to leading restaurants; quiet location; pleasant terrace. [$] *Average main: €18* ✉ *Mañé i Flaquer 8, Sarrià* ✥ *Located on the Pl. Vicenç de Sarrià* ☎ *93/205–9969* 🌐 *www.gouthier.es* ⏲ *Closed Sun. and Mon.* [M] *Sarrià.*

★ Hisop

$$$ | CATALAN | The minimalist interior design of Oriol Ivern's small restaurant is undistinguished, but his cooking is stellar. This is budget-conscious fine dining that avoids exotic ingredients but lifts local dishes to exciting new heights. **Known for:** great-value cuisine; Michelin star; delicious cod with morel sauce. [$] *Average main: €25* ✉ *Passatge de Marimón 9, Sant Gervasi* ☎ *93/241–3233* 🌐 *www.hisop.com* ⏲ *Closed Sun., and 1st wk of Jan. No lunch Sat.* [M] *Diagonal.*

Continued on page 232

Vineyard in Rioja.

THE WINES OF SPAIN

After years of being in the shadows of other European wines, Spanish wines are finally gunning for the spotlight—and what has taken place is nothing short of a revolution. The wines of Spain, like its cuisine, are currently experiencing a firecracker explosion of both quality and variety that has brought a new level of interest, awareness, and recognition throughout the world, propelling them to superstar status. A generation of young, ambitious winemakers has jolted dormant areas awake and even the most established regions have undergone makeovers in order to compete in the global market. And it's paid off: 2016 figures show Spain as the world's biggest wine producer by land area, surpassing France and Italy.

THE ROAD TO GREAT WINE

Frank Gehry designed the visitor center for the Marqués de Riscal winery in Rioja.

Spain has a long wine history dating back to the time when the Phoenicians introduced viticulture, over 3,000 years ago. Some of the country's wines achieved fame in Roman times, and the Visigoths enacted early wine laws. But in the regions under Muslim rule, winemaking slowed down for centuries. Starting in the 16th century, wine trade expanded along with the Spanish Empire, and by the 18th and 19th centuries the Sherry region *bodegas* (wineries) were already established.

In the middle of the 19th century, seeds of change blossomed throughout the Spanish wine industry. In 1846, the estate that was to become Vega Sicilia, Spain's most revered winery, was set up in Castile. Three years later the famous Tío Pepe brand was established to produce the excellent dry fino wines. Marqués de Murrieta and the Marqués de Riscal wineries opened in the 1860s creating the modern Rioja region and clearing the way for many centenary wineries. *Cava*—Spain's white or pink sparkling wine—was created the following decade in Catalonia.

After this flurry of activity, Spanish wines languished for almost a century. Vines were hit hard by phylloxera, and then a civil war and a long dictatorship left the country stagnant and isolated. Just 30 short years ago, Spain's wines were split between the same dominant trio of Sherry, Rioja, and cava, and loads of cheap, watered-down wines made by local cooperatives with little gumption to improve and even less expertise.

Starting in the 1970s, however, a wave of innovation crashed through Rioja and emergent regions like Ribera del Duero and Penedés. In the 1990s, it turned into a revolution that spread all over the landscape—and is still going strong. Today, Spain is the largest wine producer in the world in terms of land area and volume. Europe's debt crisis means domestic wine consumption is down and vintners are doubling their effort to appeal to export markets.

SPANISH WINE CATEGORIES BY AGE

A unique feature of Spanish wines is their indication of aging process on wine labels. DO wines (see "A Vino Primer" on following page) show this on mandatory back panels. Aging requirements are longer for reds, but also apply to white, rosé, and sparkling wines. For reds, the rules are as follows:

Vino Joven
A young wine that may or may not have spent some time aging in oak barrels before it was bottled. Some winemakers have begun to shun traditional regulations to produce cutting-edge wines

in this category. An elevated price distinguishes the ambitious new reds from the easy-drinking *jóvenes*.

Crianza
A wine aged for at least 24 months, six of which are in barrels (12 in Rioja, Ri-

bera del Duero, and Navarra). A great bargain in top vintages from the most reliable wineries and regions.

Reserva
A wine aged for a minimum of 36 months, at least 12 of which are in oak.

Gran Reserva
Traditionally the top of the Spanish wine hierarchy, and the pride of the historic Rioja wineries. A red wine aged for at least 24 months in oak, followed by 36 months in the bottle before release.

Joven or Cosecha		Crianza	Reserva		Gran Reserva
Minimum Aging Period in Months	24	36	48	60	

READING LABELS LIKE A PRO

Term meaning that the wine was bottled at the property

Name of the wine

For some prestigious wines, each bottle is numbered

Alcohol content

Name of the winery

Aging category

Means the wine was made from vines on a single plot of land

Name of the appellation (look for the expression "Denominación de Origen" displayed in small print just below the appellation's name)

Town where the winery is located

Vintage year

ESTATE BOTTLED   PRODUCE OF SPAIN

SINGLE VINEYARD

CONTINO
RIOJA
DENOMINACIÓN DE ORIGEN CALIFICADA

De esta cosecha se han embotellado
117.139 botellas de Reserva

13,5% Vol.   BOT.   75 cl. ℮
R.E.
N°
5212 VI
Embotellado en la propiedad
VIÑEDOS DEL CONTINO, S. A.
LAGUARDIA · LASERNA · ESPAÑA

RESERVA 2002

A VINO PRIMER

Spain offers a daunting assortment of wine styles, regions, and varietals. But don't worry: a few pointers will help you understand unfamiliar names and terms. Most of Spain's quality wines come from designated regions called *Denominaciones de Origen* (Appellations of Origin), often abbreviated as DO. Spain has more than 69 of these areas, which are tightly regulated to protect the integrity and characteristics of the wines produced there.

Beyond international varieties like Cabernet Sauvignon and Chardonnay, the country is home to several high-quality varietals, both indigenous and imported. Reds include Tempranillo, an early-ripening grape that blends and ages well, and Garnacha (the Spanish name for France's Grenache), a spicy, full-bodied red wine. The most popular white wines are the light, aromatic Albariño or Ruedas, and the full-bodied Verdejo.

Rioja wines

GENTES DE FORASTE
RIOJA

❶ The green and more humid areas of the Northwest deliver crisp, floral white albariños in Galicia's Rías Biaxas. In the Bierzo DO, the Mencía grape distills the essence of the schist slopes, where it grows into minerally infused red wines.

❷ Moving east, in the iron-rich riverbanks of the Duero, Tempranillo grapes, here called "Tinto Fino," produce complex and age-worthy Ribera del Duero reds and hefty Toro wines. Close by, the Rueda DO adds aromatic and grassy whites from local Verdejo and adopted Sauvignon Blanc.

❸ The Rioja region is a winemaker's paradise. Here a mild, nearly perfect vine-growing climate marries limestone and clay soils with Tempranillo, Spain's most noble grape, to deliver wines that possess the two main features of every great region: personality and quality. Tempranillo-based Riojas evolve from a young cherry color and aromas of strawberries and red fruits, to a brick hue, infused with scents of tobacco and leather. Whether medium or full-bodied, tannic or velvety, these reds are some of the most versatile and food-friendly wines, and have set the standard for the country for over a century.

Nearby, Navarra and three small DO's in Aragón deliver great wines made with the local Garnacha, Tempranillo, and international grape varieties.

❹ Southwest of Barcelona is the region of Catalonia, which encompasses the areas of Penedès and Priorat. Catalonia is best known as the heartland of cava, the typically dry, sparkling wine

Chardonnay vines in Navarra.

Grapes harvested for Sherry

Bay of Biscay

Santiago de O A Coruña
Campostela

Rías Baixas

① Bierzo

Leon

Bilbao

Pamplona

FRANCE

Navarra

Rioja

Campo de Borja

Zaragoza

② Toro

Ribera del Duero

③

Priorat

④ Catalonia

Barcelona

Rueda

Segovia

Cariñena

Penedès

Calatayud

★ MADRID

Toledo

⑥ La Mancha

⑤ Valencia

Valencia

MAJORCA

IBIZA

Jumilla

Córdoba

Sevilla

Montilla-Moriles

Granada

BALEARIC ISLANDS

Mediterranean Sea

⑦ Andalusia

Jerez/Sherry

Cádiz

STRAIT OF GIBRALTAR

Atlantic Ocean

PORTUGAL

Ebro R.

Duero R.

made from three indigenous Spanish varietals: Parellada, Xarel-lo, and Macabeo. The climatically varied Penedès—just an hour south of Barcelona—produces full-bodied reds like Garnacha on coastal plains, and cool-climate varietals like Riesling and Sauvignon Blanc in the mountains. Priorat is a region that has emerged into the international spotlight during the past decade, as innovative winemakers have transformed winemaking practices there. Now, traditional grapes like Garnacha and Cariñena are blended with Cabernet Sauvignon and Syrah to produce rich, concentrated reds with powerful tannins.

⑤ The region of Valencia is south of Catalonia on the Mediterranean coast. The wines of this area have improved markedly in recent years, with red wines from Jumilla and other appellations finding their way onto the international market. Tempranillo and Monastrell (France's Mourvèdre) are the most common reds. A local specialty of the area is Moscatel de Valencia, a highly aromatic sweet white wine.

⑥ In the central plateau south of Madrid, rapid investment, modernization, and replanting is resulting in medium bodied, easy drinking, and fairly priced wines made with Tempranillo (here called

"Cencíbel"), Cabernet, Syrah, and even Petit Verdot, that are opening the doors to more ambitious endeavors.

⑦ In sun-drenched Andalusia, where the white albariza limestone soils reflect the powerful sunlight while trapping the scant humidity, the fortified Jerez (Sherry) and Montilla emerge. In all their different incarnations, from dry finos, Manzanillas, amontillados, palo cortados, and olorosos, to sweet creams and Pedro Ximénez, they are the most original wines of Spain.

JUST OFF THE VINE: NEW WINE DEVELOPMENTS

Beyond Tempranillo:
The current wine revolution has recovered many native varieties. Albariño, Godello, and Verdejo among the whites, and Callet, Cariñena, Garnacha, Graciano, Mandó, Manto Negro, Mencía, and Monastrell among the reds, are gaining momentum and will likely become more recognized.

Vinos de Pagos:
Pago, a word meaning plot or vineyard, is the legal term chosen to create Spain's equivalent of a *Grand Cru* hierarchy, by protecting quality oriented wine producers that make wine from their own estates.

Petit Verdot: Winemakers in Spain are discovering that Petit Verdot, the "little green" grape of Bordeaux, ripens much easier in warmer climates than in its birthplace. This is contributing to the rise of Petit Verdot in red blends, and even to the production of single varietal wines.

Andalusia's New Wines:
For centuries, scorching southern Andalusia has offered world-class Sherry and Montilla wines. Now trailblazing winemakers are making serious inroads in the production of quality white, red, and new dessert wines, something deemed impossible a few years back.

Cult Wines: For most of the past century, Vega Sicilia Unico was the only true cult wine from Spain. The current explosion has greatly expanded the roster: L'Ermita, Pingus, Clos Erasmus, Artadi, Cirsion, Terreus, and Termanthia are the leading names in a list that grows every year.

V.O.S. and V.O.R.S: Sherry's most dramatic change in over a century is the creation of the "Very Old Sherry" designation for wines over 20 years of age, and the addition of "Rare" for those over 30, to easier distinguish the best, oldest, and most complex wines.

Innovative New Blends:
A few wine regions have strict regulations concerning the varieties used in their wines, but most allow for experimentation. All over the country, *bodegas* are crafting wines with creative blends that involve local varieties, Tempranillo, and famous international grapes.

Island Wines: In both the Balearic and Canary Islands the strong tourist industry helped to revive local winemaking. Although hard to find, the best Callet and Manto Negro based red wines of Majorca, and the sweet *malvasías* of Lanzarote will reward the adventurous drinker.

SPAIN'S SUPERSTAR WINEMAKERS

Mariano García ·   Peter Sisseck   Alvaro Palacios   Josep Lluís Pérez

The current wine revolution has made superstars out of a group of dynamic, innovative, and visionary winemakers. Here are some of the top names:

Mariano García. His 30 years as winemaker of Vega Sicilia made him a legend. Now García displays his deft touch in the Ribera del Duero and Bierzo through his four wineries: Aalto, Mauro, San Román, and Paixar.

Peter Sisseck. A Dane educated in Bordeaux, Sisseck found his calling in the old Ribera del Duero vineyards, where he crafted Pingus, Spain's most coveted cult wine.

Alvaro Palacios. In Priorat, Palacios created L'Ermita, a Garnacha wine that is one of Spain's most remarkable bottlings. Palacios also is a champion of the Bierzo region, where he produces wines from the ancient Mencía varietal, known for their vibrant berry flavors and stony minerality.

Josep Lluís Pérez. From his base in Priorat and through his work as a winemaker, researcher, teacher, and consultant, Pérez (along with his daughter Sara Pérez) has become the main driving force in shaping the modern Mediterranean wines of Spain.

MATCHMAKING KNOW-HOW

A pairing of wine with jamón and Spanish olives.

Spain has a great array of regional products and cuisines, and its avant-garde chefs are culinary world leaders. As a general rule, you should match local food with local wines—but Spanish wines can be matched very well with some of the most unexpected dishes.

Albariños and the white wines of Galicia are ideal partners for seafood and fish. Dry sherries complement Serrano and Iberico hams, *lomo, chorizo,* and *salchichón* (white dry saugage), as well as olives and nuts. Pale, light, and dry finos and Manzanillas are the perfect aperitif wines, and the ideal companion for fried fish. Fuller bodied amontillados, palo cortados, and olorosos go well with hearty soups. Ribera del Duero reds are the perfect match for the outstanding local lamb. Try Priorat and other Mediterranean reds with strong cheeses and barbecue meats. Traditional Rioja harmonizes well with fowl and game. But also take an adventure off the beaten path: manzanilla and fino are great with sushi and sashimi; Rioja *reserva* fit tuna steaks; and cream sherry will not be out of place with chocolate. *¡Salud!*

Silvestre

$$ | **CATALAN** | A graceful and easygoing mainstay in Barcelona's culinary landscape, this restaurant serves modern market cuisine to discerning diners. Look for fresh produce lovingly prepared in dishes such as tuna tartare, noodles and shrimp, or wood pigeon with duck liver. **Known for:** semisecret house wines; cozy setting; half portions available. [$] *Average main: €20* ✉ *Santaló 101, Sant Gervasi* ☎ *93/241–4031* 🌐 *www.restaurante-silvestre.com* 🕒 *Closed Sun., and 3 wks in Aug. No lunch Sat.* [M] *Muntaner.*

★ **Tram-Tram**

$$$ | **CATALAN** | At the end of the old tram line above the village of Sarrià, this restaurant offers one of Barcelona's finest culinary stops, with Isidre Soler and his wife, Reyes, at the helm. Perfectly sized portions and an airy white space within this traditional Sarrià house add to the experience. **Known for:** menú de degustació (tasting menu); pleasant interior garden patio; refined Catalan cuisine. [$] *Average main: €24* ✉ *Major de Sarrià 121, Sarrià* ☎ *93/204–8518* 🌐 *tram-tram.com* 🕒 *Closed Mon., and 2 wks in Aug. No dinner Sun. and Tues.* [M] *Sarrià.*

★ **Via Veneto**

$$$$ | **CATALAN** | Open since 1967, this family-owned temple of fine Catalan dining offers a contemporary menu punctuated by old-school classics. Service from the veteran waiters is impeccable, and diners can safely place themselves in the hands of the expert sommelier to guide them through a daunting 10,000-bottle-strong wine list. **Known for:** favorite of Salvador Dalí and now sports stars; incredible roast duck; smoking room for postprandial cigars. [$] *Average main: €37* ✉ *Ganduxer 10, Sant Gervasi* ☎ *93/200–7244* 🌐 *www.viavenetobarcelona.com* 🕒 *Closed Sun. and Aug. No lunch Sat.* [M] *La Bonanova (FGC), Maria Cristina.*

🛏 Hotels

ABaC Hotel

$$$$ | **HOTEL** | This classy boutique hotel with a Michelin-starred restaurant is located in the environs of Gràcia, at the base of Avenida Tibidado, and provides a complete respite from the bustle of the city—and the busy thoroughfare on which it is placed. **Pros:** oasis-style rooms, completely soundproofed; the best restaurant in town; walk through the kitchen whenever you choose. **Cons:** far from the old town and beaches; only 15 rooms, so it's easily booked up; layout of hotel can be disorientating. [$] *Rooms from: €310* ✉ *Av. Tibidabo 1, Sant Gervasi* ☎ *93/319–6600* 🌐 *www.abacbarcelona.com/en* 🛏 *15 rooms* 🍴 *No meals* [M] *FGC L7 Avinida Tibidabo.*

Bonanova Park

$$ | **HOTEL** | **FAMILY** | In upper Barcelona near Sarrià, this no-frills hotel offers an escape from busy downtown at a moderate cost. **Pros:** close to great restaurants and metro stops; bargain breakfast; short walk to the Camp Nou stadium. **Cons:** soundproofing and bed lighting could be improved; no pool or spa; reception service can be hit-or-miss. [$] *Rooms from: €125* ✉ *Carrer Capità Arenas 51, Sarrià* ☎ *93/204–0900* 🌐 *www.hotelbonanovapark.com* 🛏 *63 rooms* 🍴 *No meals* [M] *Sarrià (FGC), L3 Maria Cristina.*

Gran Hotel la Florida

$$$$ | **HOTEL** | **FAMILY** | Peace, privacy, and a stunning panoramic view set this luxurious mountaintop retreat apart. **Pros:** first-rate spa, fitness center, and sauna; friendly and attentive front staff; decor by celebrity designers. **Cons:** pricey food and beverage add-ons; pets accepted with an €80 surcharge; isolated location, with infrequent shuttle service to city center. [$] *Rooms from: €240* ✉ *Ctra. Vallvidrera al Tibidabo 83–93, Tibidabo* ☎ *93/259–3000* 🌐 *www.hotellaflorida.com* 🛏 *70 rooms* 🍴 *No meals* [M] *Tibidabo (FGC).*

★ Primero Primera

$$$$ | **HOTEL** | **FAMILY** | The Perez family converted their apartment building on a leafy side street in the quiet, upscale, residential neighborhood of Tres Torres and opened it as an exquisitely designed, homey boutique hotel in 2011. **Pros:** retro-modern ambience; 24-hour free snack bar; electric bicycle rentals for guests. **Cons:** bit of a distance from downtown; very small pool; service can be uneven. [$] *Rooms from: €230* ✉ *Doctor Carulla 25–29, Sant Gervasi* ☎ *93/417–5600* 🌐 *www.primeroprimera.com* 🛏 *30 rooms* 🍴 *Free Breakfast* [M] *Tres Torres (FGC).*

Sansi Pedralbes

$$ | **HOTEL** | A contemporary polished-marble-and-black-glass box, with Japanese overtones, a stone's throw from the gardens of the Monestir de Pedralbes, this hotel may be a bit removed from the action downtown, but there's a stop on the Bus Turistic just across the street, and the views up into the Collserola Hills above Barcelona are splendid. **Pros:** small and intimate; close to Carretera de les Aigües, Barcelona's best running track; quiet area near the Güell Pavilions. **Cons:** the nearest subway stations are 15–20 minutes away on foot; no pets; pricey breakfast. [$] *Rooms from: €150* ✉ *Av. Pearson 1–3, Pedralbes* ☎ *93/206–3880* 🌐 *www.sansihotels.com* 🛏 *60 rooms* 🍴 *No meals* [M] *Reina Elisenda (FGC), L3 Maria Cristina.*

Vilana Hotel

$$ | **HOTEL** | In an upscale residential neighborhood above Passeig de la Bonanova, this boutique accommodation can ease some of the budgetary strains of coming to a prime tourist destination. **Pros:** quiet surroundings; large, sunlit rooms; pleasant, attentive English-speaking staff. **Cons:** 30 minutes to center of town; no pool or spa; room service closes at 10:30. [$] *Rooms from: €135* ✉ *Vilana 7, Sant Gervasi* ☎ *93/434–0363* 🌐 *vilanahotel.com* 🛏 *22 rooms* 🍴 *No meals* [M] *Sarrià (FGC).*

El Barça: More Than a Club

El Barça: més qu'un club is the motto for this soccer superpower out to win every championship. Basketball, roller-skate hockey, and team handball have all won national and European titles, while the club's soccer team has conquered dozens of Spanish Leagues and European championships. "More than a club" refers to FC Barcelona's place in the Catalan sense of national identity. With teams at all levels, el Barça is financed by 500,000 season-ticket holders, generating an annual operating capital of more than €100 million.

Shopping

Just like its residents, shops in Sarrià are smart and well-heeled. Most are along the Major de Sarrià, the main drag, and on the elegant Plaça de Sarrià. The emphasis is on kitchen gadgets and gourmet food, like what you'll find at the legendary Foix de Sarrià and a lively local fresh produce market.

BEAUTY

JC Apotecari

GIFTS/SOUVENIRS | Downtown beauty junkies happily make the trip uptown for the hard-to-source cult products that fill the lab-like shelves of JC Apotecari. Skin and hair brands such as Australian botanical Aesop products and Dr. Jackson's are offered alongside perfumed candles from Diptyque and Tweezerman tweezers. ✉ *Major de Sarrià 96, Sarrià* ☎ *93/205–8734* 🌐 *www.jcapotecari.com* [M] *Sarrià.*

CERAMICS
Neo Cerámica
CERAMICS/GLASSWARE | This is the store to visit if you need an order of handsome tiles for your kitchen back home. With some truly striking patterns and the shipping system to get them to you in one piece (each tile, that is), you can trust the Vidal-Quadras clan for care and quality. ✉ *Mandri 43, Sarrià* ☎ *93/211–8958* ⊕ *www.neoceramica.es* Ⓜ *Sarrià, El Putxet.*

FOOD
Foix de Sarrià
FOOD/CANDY | Pastry and poetry under the same roof merit a stop. The verses of J. V. Foix, a major Catalan poet who managed to survive the Franco regime with his art intact, are engraved in bronze on the outside wall of the Major de Sarrià location, where he was born. Excellent pastries, breads, wines, cheeses, and cavas, all available on Sunday, have made Foix de Sarrià a Barcelona landmark. There is a smaller branch nearby at Major de Sarrià 57. ✉ *Pl. Sarrià 12–13, Sarrià* ☎ *93/203–0473* ⊕ *www.foixdesarria.com* Ⓜ *Sarrià.*

Ískia
FOOD/CANDY | Good wine advice and a perennially changing selection of bottles make Iskia one of upper Barcelona's best wine emporiums. The proprietors speak English and are glad to talk about latest wine trends or explain their products at length. ✉ *Major de Sarrià 132, Sarrià* ☎ *93/205–0070* ⊕ *www.iskiavins.com* Ⓜ *Sarrià.*

MARKETS
Sarrià
FOOD/CANDY | A small Tuesday antiques markets in Sarrià's town square provides another good reason to explore this charming once-outlying village in the upper part of the city. On other days, the nearby produce market, a mini-Boqueria, is the place for picnic fare before or after a hike over to the Monestir de Pedralbes. ✉ *Pl. de Sarrià, Sarrià* Ⓜ *Sarrià, Reina Elisenda.*

Activities

SOCCER
Futbol Club Barcelona
SOCCER | Founded in 1899, FC Barcelona won its third European Championship in 2009, the Liga championship, and its 27th Copa del Rey (King's Cup)—Spain's first-ever *triplete*—and did it again in 2015. Even more impressive was its razzle-dazzle style of soccer, rarely seen in the age of cynical defensive lockdowns and muscular British-style play. Barça, as the club is known, is Real Madrid's nemesis (and vice versa) and a sociological and historical phenomenon of deep significance in Catalonia. Ticket windows at Access 14 to the Camp Nou stadium are open Monday–Thursday 9–5, Friday 9–2:30, and Saturday 9–1:30 (if there's a match at home). You can also buy tickets online through the FC Barcelona website, or from Ticketmaster (*www.ticketmaster.es*) or Entradas (*www.entradas.es*). Tours of the stadium and museum can also be organized through the FC Barcelona website. ✉ *Camp Nou, Aristides Maillol 12, Les Corts* ☎ *902/189900* ⊕ *www.fcbarcelona.com* Ⓜ *Collblanc, Palau Reial.*

Chapter 11

MONTJUÏC AND POBLE SEC

Updated by
Elizabeth Prosser and
Steve Tallantyre

⊙ Sights   🍴 Restaurants   🛏 Hotels   🛍 Shopping   🍸 Nightlife
★★★★★   ★★★☆☆   ☆☆☆☆☆   ★★★☆☆   ★★★☆☆

NEIGHBORHOOD SNAPSHOT

TOP EXPERIENCES

■ **The Museu Nacional d'Art de Catalunya:** MNAC contains what is considered the world's best collection of Romanesque frescoes, removed for restoration from Pyrenean chapels in the 1930s and ingeniously restored with their original contours. Definitely worth some time and contemplation, as is the sunset from the top of the stairs here.

■ **Mies van der Rohe Pavilion:** Set high on Montjuïc, on a plinth of travertine, Mies van der Rohe's sleek and elegant Pavilion separates itself from the bustling streets of the city and is considered one of the most influential modernist buildings of the 20th century.

■ **CaixaForum:** Attend a concert or show at one of the most dynamic cultural venues in the city.

■ **Poble Espanyol:** Shop for traditional crafts and wander the boutiques, cafés, workshops, and studios of this Spanish Village.

■ **Fundació Miró:** Explore one of Barcelona's most exciting showcases of modern and contemporary art.

GETTING HERE

The most dramatic approach to Montjuïc is the cross-harbor cable car (Transbordador Aeri) from Barceloneta or from the mid-station in the port. You can also take a taxi or Bus No. 61 (or walk) from Plaça d'Espanya; yet another option is the funicular from the Paral·lel (Paral·lel metro stop, L3). The Telefèric de Montjuïc from the funicular stop to the Castell de Montjuïc is the final leg to the top.

PLANNING YOUR TIME

With unhurried visits to the Miró Foundation and any or all of the Museu Nacional d'Art de Catalunya collections in the Palau Nacional, this is a four- to five-hour excursion, if not a full day. Have lunch afterward in the Poble Espanyol, just up from Mies van der Rohe's Barcelona Pavilion or in the cafeteria-restaurant at the Fundació Miró.

QUICK BITES

■ **Quimet & Quimet.** Come before 1:30 pm or 7:30 pm if you want to try to get a table at this hugely popular family-run tapas spot with great, local wines. ⊠ *Poeta Cabanyes 25, Poble Sec* Ⓜ *Paral.lel*

■ **Cactus Cafe.** This cute and cool café is the spot for breakfast and brunch in the area ⊠ *Carrer de Blasco de Garay 10, Poble Sec* Ⓜ *Poble Sec*

A bit remote from the hustle and bustle of Barcelona street life, Montjuïc more than justifies a day or two of exploring. The Miró Foundation, the Museu Nacional d'Art de Catalunya, the minimalist Mies van der Rohe Pavilion, the lush Jardins de Mossèn Cinto Verdaguer, and the gallery and auditorium of the CaixaForum (the former Casaramona textile factory) are all among Barcelona's must-see sights.

Other Montjuïc attractions include the fortress, the Olympic stadium, the Palau Sant Jordi, and the Poble Espanyol. There are buses within Montjuïc that visitors can take from sight to sight.

This hill overlooking the south side of the port is said to have originally been named Mont Juif for the Jewish cemetery once on its slopes, though a 3rd-century Roman document referring to the construction of a road between Mons Taber (around the cathedral) and Mons Jovis (Mount of Jove) suggests that in fact the name may derive from the Roman deity Jupiter. Either way, Montjuïc is now Barcelona's largest and lushest public space, a vast complex of museums and exhibition halls, gardens and picnic grounds, sports facilities, and even a Greek-style amphitheater.

Sights

★ **CaixaForum** (*Casaramona*)
ARTS VENUE | FAMILY | This 1911 neo-Mudejar Art Nouveau masterpiece, originally built to house a factory by Josep Puig i Cadafalch (architect of Casa de les Punxes, Casa Amatller, Casa Martí, and Casa Quadras) is a center for art exhibits, concerts, lectures, and cultural events, and well worth keeping an eye on in newspaper and magazine leisure listings for special exhibitions. The CaixaForum also regularly lays on a whole range of films, concerts, and hands-on learning activities for kids. The original brickwork is spectacular; the restoration is a brilliant example of the fusion of ultramodern design techniques with traditional (even Art Nouveau) architecture. The entryway was designed by Japanese architect Arata Isozaki, author of the nearby Palau Sant Jordi. ✉ *Av. Francesc Ferrer i Guàrdia 6–8, Montjuïc* ☎ *93/476–8600* ⊕ *www.obrasocial.lacaixa.es* 🎫 *€4* Ⓜ *L1/ L3 Pl. d'Espanya.*

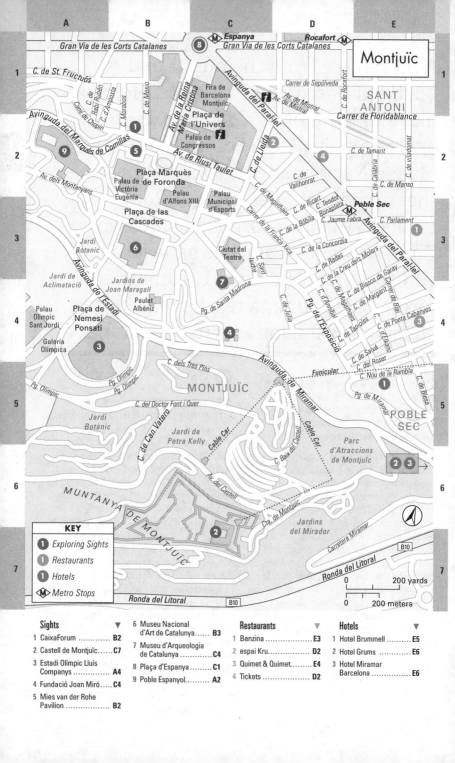

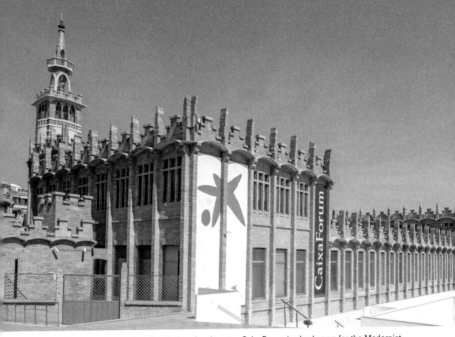

In addition to being a social, cultural and educational centre, CaixaForum is also known for the Modernist style of its building.

Castell de Montjuïc

CASTLE/PALACE | Built in 1640 by rebels against Felipe IV, the castle has had a dark history as a symbol of Barcelona's military domination by foreign powers, usually the Spanish army. The fortress was stormed several times, most famously in 1705 by Lord Peterborough for Archduke Carlos of Austria. In 1808, during the Peninsular War, it was seized by the French under General Dufresne. Later, during an 1842 civil disturbance, Barcelona was bombed from its heights by a Spanish artillery battery. After the 1936–39 civil war, the castle was used as a dungeon for political prisoners. Lluís Companys, president of the Generalitat de Catalunya during the civil war, was executed by firing squad here on October 14, 1940. In 2007 the fortress was formally ceded back to Barcelona. The present uses of the space include an Interpretation Center for Peace, a Space for Historical Memory, and a Montjuïc Interpretation Center, along with cultural and educational events and activities. A popular weekend park and picnic area, the moat contains attractive gardens, with one side given over to an archery range, and the various terraces have panoramic views over the city and out to sea. From July through the first week of August on Mondays, Wednesdays, and Fridays from 8:30 pm the castle hosts the Sala Montjuic Open Air Cinema of subtitled classic films (⊕ *www.salamontjuic.org*), with live music concerts before the showings. ✉ *Ctra. de Montjuïc 66, Montjuïc* ☎ *93/256–4440, 93/302–3553 for Sala Montjuic* ⊕ *www.bcn.cat/castelldemontjuic* 🎫 *€5 (free Sun. from 3 pm); Sala Montjuic tickets €6.50* Ⓜ *L2/L3 Paral.lel and Funicular.*

Estadi Olímpic Lluís Companys (*Olympic Stadium*)

MUSEUM | Open for visitors, the Olympic Stadium was originally built for the International Exhibition of 1929, with the idea that Barcelona would then host the 1936 Olympics (ultimately staged in Hitler's Berlin). After failing twice to win the nomination, the city celebrated the attainment of its long-cherished goal by renovating the semi-derelict stadium—preserving the original facade and shell—in time for 1992, providing seating for 70,000. The nearby **Museu Olímpic i de l'Esport,** a museum about the Olympic movement in Barcelona, shows audiovisual replays from the 1992 Olympics, and provides interactive simulations for visitors to experience the training and competition of Olympic athletes. An information center traces the history of the modern Olympics from Athens in 1896 to the present. Next door and just downhill stands the futuristic **Palau Sant Jordi Sports Palace,** designed by the noted Japanese architect Arata Isozaki. ⊠ *Av. de l'Estadi s/n, Montjuïc* ☏ *93/426–2089 Estadi Olímpic, 93/292–5379 Museu Olímpica* ⊕ *www.fundaciobarcelonaolimpica.es* ▣ *Free* ⊙ *Museum closed Mon.* Ⓜ *L1/ L3 Espanya.*

★ **Fundació Joan Miró**

MUSEUM | The Miró Foundation, a gift from the artist Joan Miró to his native city, is one of Barcelona's most exciting showcases of modern and contemporary art. The airy white building, with panoramic views north over Barcelona, was designed by the artist's close friend and collaborator Josep Lluís Sert and opened in 1975; an extension was added by Sert's pupil Jaume Freixa in 1988. Miró's playful and colorful style, filled with Mediterranean light and humor, seems a perfect match for its surroundings, and the exhibits and retrospectives that open here tend to be progressive and provocative—look for Alexander Calder's fountain of moving mercury. Miró himself rests in the cemetery on Montjuïc's southern slopes. ⊠ *Av. Miramar 71–75, Parc de Montjuïc, Montjuïc* ☏ *93/443–9470* ⊕ *www.fmirobcn. org* ▣ *€12* ⊙ *Closed Mon.* Ⓜ *L1/L3 Pl. Espanya; L3 Paral.lel, then Funicular de Montjuïc.*

Mies van der Rohe Pavilion

BUILDING | One of the masterpieces of the Bauhaus School, the legendary Pavelló Mies van der Rohe—the German contribution to the 1929 International Exhibition, reassembled between 1983 and 1986—remains a stunning "less is more" study in interlocking planes of white marble, green onyx, and glass. In effect, it is Barcelona's aesthetic antonym (in company with Richard Meier's Museu d'Art Contemporani and Rafael Moneo's Auditori) to the flamboyant Art Nouveau—the city's signature Modernisme—of Gaudí and his contemporaries. Note the mirror play of the black carpet inside the pavilion with the reflecting pool outside, or the iconic Barcelona chair designed by Ludwig Mies van der Rohe (1886–1969); reproductions have graced modern interiors around the world for decades. ⊠ *Av. Francesc Ferrer i Guàrdia 7, Montjuïc* ☏ *93/423–4016, 93/215–1011* ⊕ *miesbcn.com* ▣ *€5* Ⓜ *L1/ L3 Pl. Espanya.*

Museu d'Arqueologia de Catalunya

MUSEUM | Just downhill to the right of the Palau Nacional, the Museum of Archaeology holds important finds from the Greek ruins at Empúries, on the Costa Brava. These are shown alongside fascinating objects from, and explanations of, megalithic Spain. ⊠ *Passeig Santa Madrona 39–41, Montjuïc* ☏ *93/423–2149* ⊕ *www. mac.cat/eng* ▣ *€4.50; last Tues. of month; free Oct.–June* ⊙ *Closed Mon.* Ⓜ *L1/L3 Pl. Espanya.*

★ **Museu Nacional d'Art de Catalunya** (*Catalonian National Museum of Art, MNAC*) MUSEUM | Housed in the imposingly domed, towered, frescoed, and columned **Palau Nacional,** built in 1929 as the centerpiece of the International Exposition, this superb museum was renovated in 1995 by Gae Aulenti, architect of the Musée d'Orsay in Paris. In 2004 the museum's three holdings (Romanesque, Gothic, and the Cambó

Collection—an eclectic trove, including a Goya, donated by Francesc Cambó) were joined by the 19th- and 20th-century collection of Catalan impressionist and Moderniste painters. Also now on display is the Thyssen-Bornemisza collection of early masters, with works by Zurbarán, Rubens, Tintoretto, Velázquez, and others. With this influx of artistic treasure, the MNAC has become Catalonia's grand central museum. Pride of place goes to the Romanesque exhibition, the world's finest collection of Romanesque frescoes, altarpieces, and wood carvings, most of them rescued from chapels in the Pyrenees during the 1920s to save them from deterioration, theft, and art dealers. Many, such as the famous *Cristo de Taüll* fresco (from the church of Sant Climent de Taüll in Taüll), have been painstakingly removed from crumbling walls of abandoned sites and remounted on ingenious frames that exactly reproduce the contours of their original settings. The stunning central hall of the museum contains an enormous pillared and frescoed cupola. ⊠ *Palau Nacional, Parc de Montjuïc s/n, Montjuïc* ☎ *93/622–0360* ⊕ *www.museunacional.cat* 🎟 *From €12 (valid for day of purchase and 1 other day in same month); free Sat. after 3 pm and 1st Sun. of month* ⊙ *Closed Mon.* Ⓜ *L1/L3 Pl. Espanya.*

Plaça d'Espanya

CONVENTION CENTER | This busy circle is a good place to avoid, but sooner or later you'll probably need to cross it to go to the convention center or to the Palau Nacional. It's dominated by the so-called Venetian Towers (they're actually Tuscan) built in 1927 as the grand entrance to the 1929 International Exposition. The towers flank the lower end of the Avinguda Maria Cristina (the buildings on both sides are important venues for the trade fairs and industrial expositions that regularly descend on Barcelona);

at the far end is the Font Màgica (the Magic Fountain, which has a spectacular nighttime display of lights and music) below the National Museum of Catalan Art in the Palau Nacional on Montjuïc. The fountain is the work of Josep Maria Jujol, the Gaudí collaborator who designed the curvy and colorful benches in Park Güell. The sculptures are by Miquel Blay, one of the master artists and craftsmen who put together the Palau de la Música. To the right of the Towers, the neo-Mudejar bullring, Les Arenes, is now a multilevel shopping mall. On the corner of Carrer Llançà, just down to the right looking at the bullring, you can just get a glimpse of the huge polychromatic butterfly atop the Art Nouveau building known popularly as the "Casa de la Papallona" (House of the Butterfly). From the plaza, you can take the metro or Bus 38 back to the Plaça de Catalunya. ⊠ *Pl. Espanya, Sants* Ⓜ *L1/L3 Pl. Espanya.*

★ Poble Espanyol (*Spanish Village*)

BUILDING | FAMILY | Created for the 1929 International Exhibition, the Spanish Village is a sort of open-air architectural museum, with faithful replicas to scale of building styles, from an Aragonese Gothic-Mudejar bell tower to the tower walls of Ávila, drawn from all over Spain; the ground-floor spaces are devoted to boutiques, cafés and restaurants, workshops, and studios. The liveliest time to come is at night, and a reservation at one of the half dozen restaurants gets you in for free, as does the purchase of a ticket for either of the two discos or the Tablao del Carmen flamenco club. ⊠ *Av. Francesc Ferrer i Guàrdia 13, Montjuïc* ☎ *93/508–6300* ⊕ *www.poble-espanyol.com* 🎟 *€14 (€12.60 online); after 8 pm €7 (€6.30 online)* Ⓜ *L1/L3 Pl. Espanya.*

🍴 Restaurants

Benzina

$$ | ITALIAN | Named in homage to the gas station that once sat here, Benzina blends industrial elements with splashes of color, supremely comfortable chairs, and excellent music (on vinyl, naturally) to create a hip but cozy Italian restaurant that would not look out of place in New York. The food is center stage, however; the freshly made pasta—combined with classic sauces or the chef's whims—is among the best in the city. **Known for:** chic decor; fresh house-made pastas; new twists on traditional dishes. 💲 *Average main: €17* ⌧ *Passatge Pere Calders 6, Born-Ribera* 🕿 *93/659–5583* ⊕ *www.benzina.es* 🕙 *No lunch weekdays* Ⓜ *Poble Sec.*

★ espai Kru

$$$ | ECLECTIC | What happens when one of Barcelona's most venerable seafood restaurants joins the creative cooking revolution? The answers can be found at espai Kru, upstairs from the eye-wateringly expensive Rías de Galicia, where the finest ingredients from the deep are given a more modestly priced makeover in contemporary surroundings. **Known for:** fresh seafood; oyster bar; light-as-air lobster sandwiches. 💲 *Average main: €26* ⌧ *Lleida 7, Poble Sec* 🕿 *93/424–8152* ⊕ *www.espaikru.com* 🕙 *Closed Mon. No dinner Tues.–Sat. No lunch Sun.* Ⓜ *Pl. Espanya/Poble Sec.*

Quimet & Quimet

$ | TAPAS | A foodie haunt, this tiny tapas place is hugely popular with locals and in-the-know visitors alike; if you show up too late, you might not be able to get in—come before 1:30 pm or 7:30 pm, however, and you might snag a stand-up table. Fourth-generation chef-owner Quim and his family improvise ingenious canapés. **Known for:** local wines; family-run; intimate space (long wait times). 💲 *Average main: €15* ⌧ *Poeta Cabanyes 25, Poble Sec* 🕿 *93/442–3142* 🕙 *Closed Sun. and Aug. No dinner Sat.* Ⓜ *Paral.lel.*

Tickets

$$$ | TAPAS | Ferran and Albert Adrià of former "World's Best Restaurant" elBulli fame are the ringleaders behind this circus-themed big top of creative tapas. Tickets offers tapas twists you've never dreamed of, like strawberry-bearing trees (complete with pruning scissors) with pistachio acorns, and a round-the-world ride of oysters. **Known for:** off-the-wall creativity; online reservations only; enthusiastic and knowledgeable waitstaff. 💲 *Average main: €25* ⌧ *Av. Paral.lel 164, Poble Sec* ⊕ *www.ticketsbar.es/en* 🕙 *Closed Sun. and Mon., 2 wks in Aug., and 1 wk at Christmas. No lunch Tues.–Fri.* Ⓜ *Poble Sec.*

🛏 Hotels

Hotel Brummell

$$$ | HOTEL | Opened in 2015, the Brummell is among the more recent of the stylish new ventures now starting to give the once-scruffy neighborhood of Poble Sec a different buzz. **Pros:** young, friendly international staff; smart TVs; excellent brunch. **Cons:** no room service; storage is limited; vending machines in lieu of in-room minibars. 💲 *Rooms from: €180* ⌧ *Nou de la Rambla 174, Poble Sec* 🕿 *93/125–8622* ⊕ *www.hotelbrummell.com* ⟿ *20 rooms* ⦿ *No meals* Ⓜ *L3 Para.lel.*

Hotel Grums

$$$ | HOTEL | FAMILY | Tucked off on a side street in Poble Sec, on the far side of El Raval, this pleasant little boutique hotel lies within easy walking distance to the port and La Rambla—an especially convenient bivouac for cruise ship visitors, and with easy access to the museums and gardens of Montjuïc. **Pros:** quiet location; good for families; each room has its own character. **Cons:**

Find replicas of buildings from all over Spain and see craftspeople at work in the Spanish village, at the foot of Montjuïc.

bed lighting could be better; far from the attractions of the Eixample; charge for the spa. $ *Rooms from: €177* ✉ *Carrer Palaudaries 26, Poble Sec* ☎ *93/442066* ⊕ *www.hotelgrumsbarcelona.com* ⟿ *78 rooms* |◯| *No meals* Ⓜ *L2/L3 Paral.lel.*

★ Hotel Miramar Barcelona
$$$ | HOTEL | FAMILY | Only the facade remains of this imposing "palace," built in 1929 for Barcelona's second Universal Expositionas and later acquired by a TV network as its studio headquarters, then abandoned from 1983 until 2006, when it was gutted and transformed by architect Oscar Tusquets into an elegant, romantic hillside resort. **Pros:** complimentary glass of cava on check-in; easy access to beach and Barceloneta by cable car; parking free if booked online (otherwise €12 outside, €18 inside). **Cons:** no shuttle service; pricey breakfast. $ *Rooms from: €220* ✉ *Pl. Carlos Ibáñez 3, Montjuïc* ☎ *93/281–1600* ⊕ *www.hotelmiramarbarcelona.com* ⟿ *66 doubles, 8 suites* |◯| *No meals* Ⓜ *L3 Drassanes.*

▼ Nightlife

Facing each other from opposite sides of the historic theater strip Avenida Paral·lel, the two contrasting areas, Poble Sec and Sant Antoni, are often overlooked by night birds. Sant Antoni's after-dark offerings may seem quiet in comparison to other iconic neighbors, but bars and bodegas here exude a genuine and welcoming quality only found in tourist-free zones. Poble Sec, on the other hand, is a stone's throw away from the huge L'Eixample district and routinely vies for a little attention with its eclectic collection of fashionable cafés, bars, and eateries.

BARS
Bodega 1900
BARS/PUBS | Celebrated chef Albert Adrià (Tickets, at Avenida del Paral·lel 164, is just across the street) pays homage to time-honored traditional *vermuterias* by combining his creative culinary wizardry with conventional products, resulting in elevated versions

of turn-of-the-20th-century dishes and drinks. Sleekly decorated in white and aged wood, this contemporary eatery resembles a dreamy but traditional vermouth bar with steep prices. ⊠ *Tamarit 91, Poble Sec* ☎ *93/325–2659* ⊕ *www.bodega1900.com* Ⓜ *Poble Sec.*

Celler Cal Marino
BARS/PUBS | Rustic and charming with an arched, brick-walled center, barrel tables, and rows of multicolor *sifón* fizzy-water bottles, this homey venue serves wine by the glass or liter (for takeaway) from the wine cellar, artisanal beers, and vermouth paired with homemade tapas. Tuesday through Friday the special is three drinks matched with three tapas, while Sunday is often dedicated to live jazz concerts and vermouth aperitifs. ⊠ *Margarit 54, Poble Sec* ☎ *93/329–4592* ⊕ *www.calmarino.com* Ⓜ *Poble Sec, Paral.lel.*

Dòmino Bar
BARS/PUBS | On a quiet street, just steps from the buzzing Avenida Paral·lel, this little brick-walled bunker of inventive fruity concoctions effectively paired with artsy pizzas is a welcome sight. The space is diminutive but with just enough kitschy touches (domino seat cushions!) to give it oomph. Tunes range from jazz to soul to funky electronic, and the vibe transforms from tame to animated, attracting wandering souls in the mood for a chill night. ⊠ *Flors 16, Poble Sec* ☎ *696/461725* ⊕ *www.dominobar.com.*

El Rouge
BARS/PUBS | El Rouge has a bohemian vibe, complete with a selection of mismatched, threadbare furniture, posters of impressionist paintings tacked to the wall, and the low light created by red pashmina shawls draped over lampshades. Here you'll find an excellent mixologist and tasteful lounge music playing in the background. ⊠ *Poeta Cabanyes 21, Poble Sec* ☎ *634/127581* ☾ *Closed Wed. and Sun.* Ⓜ *Paral.lel.*

★ Jonny Aldana
BARS/PUBS | This cheery technicolor bar-resto, featuring a tiled facade and open-window bar with stools inside and out, is bursting with 1950s iconography and blackboards that demand your attention. Wines are sold by the glass, beer is served from the tap, but it's the superb vermouths and cocktails combined with veggie and vegan tapas that reel in patrons. Local DJs spin on certain nights. ⊠ *Aldana 9, Poble Sec* ☎ *93/174–2083* Ⓜ *Paral·lel.*

★ Xixbar
BARS/PUBS | The interior of this Alice in Wonderland–like venue of checkered half walls, a marble bar, and contempo objets d'art rarely seen on ceilings is the first clue that you've landed somewhere special. Beyond that, with 50-plus flavors of gins and infusions on offer—ranging from spicy ginger to tarty chocolate—an ultra-knowledgeable bar staff, and a lounge-friendly 3 am curfew on weekends, Xix turns conventional cocktail drinkers into card-carrying gin lovers. ⊠ *Carrer de Rocafort 19, Poble Sec* ☎ *93/423–4314* ⊕ *www.xixbar.com* Ⓜ *Poble Sec.*

MUSIC CLUBS
Sala Apolo
DANCE CLUBS | Once part of the music-hall scene along the Paral·lel, these days the beats come from an eclectic and varied program of international and local acts. Salif Keita, LCD Soundsystem, and Sharon Jones and the Dap-Kings are just a few that have taken the stage in the past, though the offerings vary wildly from jazz and swing to flamenco and hard rock. After the last encore, Sala Apolo converts to a hugely popular dance club—the Nasty Monday and Crappy Tuesday nights are particularly sinful ways to start the week. ⊠ *Nou de la Rambla 113, Poble Sec* ☎ *93/441–4001* ⊕ *www.sala-apolo.com* Ⓜ *Paral.lel.*

🎭 Performing Arts

ART GALLERIES

★ CaixaForum

ART GALLERIES—ARTS | The building itself, a restored textile factory, is well worth exploring (and is directly across from the Mies van der Rohe Pavilion on Montjuïc at the bottom of the steps up to the Palau Nacional). Temporary exhibits show the work of major artists from around the world, while the auditorium (and sometimes the outdoor area) hosts a regular program of world-music concerts, theater, and performance art. There are also regular workshops and special events for families. ⊠ *Av. Francesc Ferrer i Guàrdia 6–8, Montjuïc* ☎ *93/476–8600* ⊕ *www.caixaforum.es/ barcelona* Ⓜ *Espanya.*

Fundació Miró

ART GALLERIES—ARTS | Occasionally used for outdoor concerts in the summer months, Joan Miró's sculpture garden at his foundation on Montjuïc hill is a surrealistic and enchanting place, and the permanent collection contains some of his most stunning paintings. What makes this foundation truly stand out though are the ambitious temporary exhibitions, often organized together with international museums, that can range from a showcase of leading mural artists to a masterpiece in the evolution of British art post–World War II. ⊠ *Parc de Montjuïc, Montjuïc* ☎ *93/443–9470* ⊕ *www.fmirobcn.org.*

CONCERTS

Barts (Arts on Stage)

THEATER | This state-of-the-art theater right in the middle on the Avenida Paral·lel—remodeled from the old Artèria Music Hall—has wildly diverse programming, with everything from performance art to the latest indie bands, to musicals, magic shows, and cutting-edge theater. ⊠ *Paral·lel 62, Poble Sec* ☎ *93/324–8492* ⊕ *www.barts. cat* Ⓜ *Paral·lel.*

Palau Sant Jordi

CONCERTS | Arata Isozaki's immense domed venue, built for the 1992 Olympic Games, has hosted superstar performers such as Bruce Springsteen and Beyoncé. Also presented are Disney specials, Cirque de Soleil, occasional operas, and other musical events. ⊠ *Palau Sant Jordi, Passeig Olímpic 5–7, Montjuïc* ☎ *93/426–2089* ⊕ *www.palausantjordi. cat/en* Ⓜ *Espanya.*

DANCE

El Mercat de les Flors

DANCE | An old flower market converted into a modern performance space, theater, and dance school, the Mercat de Les Flors forms part of the Institut de Teatre and is set on lovely, expansive grounds at the foot of verdant Montjuïc. Modern dance is the Mercat's raison d'être, and it remains one of the few theaters in Spain that is exclusively dedicated to contemporary dance. The on-site café has a terrace out on the square, ideal for pre- or post-performance drinks. ⊠ *Lleida 59, Poble Sec* ☎ *93/256-2600* ⊕ *mercatflors.cat* Ⓜ *Poble Sec, Espanya.*

FLAMENCO

El Tablao de Carmen

DANCE | Large tour groups come to this venerable flamenco dinner-theater venue in the Poble Espanyol named after, and dedicated to, the legendary dancer Carmen Amaya. Die-hard flamenco aficionados might dismiss the ensembles that perform here as a tad touristy, but the dancers, singers, and guitarists are pros. Visitors can enjoy one of the two nightly performances over a drink or over their choice of a full-course, prix-fixe meal. Reservations are recommended. Dinner shows are held daily at 6 pm and 8:30 pm. ⊠ *Poble Espanyol, Av. Francesc Ferrer i Guàrdia 13, Montjuïc* ☎ *93/325–6895* ⊕ *www.tablaodecarmen.com* Ⓜ *Espanya.*

THEATER
El Molino
CABARET | For most of the 20th century, this venue was the most legendary of all the cabaret theaters on Avinguda Paral·lel. Modeled after Paris's Moulin Rouge, it closed in the late 1990s as the building was becoming dangerously run-down. After an ambitious refurbishment in 2010, El Molino reopened as one of the most stunning state-of-the-art cabaret theaters in Europe. The building now has five—instead of the original two—stories, with a bar and terrace on the third. What has remained the same, however, is its essence—a contemporary version of burlesque, but bump-and-grind all the same. You can purchase tickets online or before performances (which usually start at 9:30 pm). ⊠ *Vilà i Vilà 99, Poble Sec* ☎ *93/205–5111* ⊕ *www.elmolinobcn.com* Ⓜ *Paral.lel.*

Teatre Victòria
THEATER | This historic theater in the heart of Barcelona's show district features dramas, musicals, and dance productions, from ballet to Bollywood. ⊠ *Av. Paral·lel 67–69, Poble Sec* ☎ *93/324–9742* ⊕ *www.teatrevictoria. com* Ⓜ *Paral·lel.*

Chapter 12

CATALONIA, VALENCIA, AND THE COSTA BLANCA

12

Updated by
Elizabeth Prosser

WELCOME TO CATALONIA, VALENCIA, AND THE COSTA BLANCA

TOP REASONS TO GO

★ **Girona:** Explore a city where monuments of Christian, Jewish, and Islamic cultures have coexisted for centuries and are just steps apart.

★ **Valencia reborn:** The city has seen a transformation of the Turia River into a treasure trove of museums, concert halls, parks, and architectural wonders.

★ **Great restaurants:** Foodies argue that the fountainhead of creative gastronomy has moved from France to Spain— and in particular to the great restaurants of the Empordà and Costa Brava.

★ **Dalí's home and museum:** "Surreal" doesn't begin to describe the Teatre-Museu Dalí in Figueres or the wild coast of the artist's home at Cap de Creus.

★ **Las Fallas festival:** Valencia's Las Fallas in mid-March, a week of fireworks and solemn processions with a finale of spectacular bonfires, is one of the best festivals in Europe.

Year-round, Catalonia is the most visited of Spain's autonomous communities. The Pyrenees, which separate it from France, provide some of the country's best skiing, and the rugged Costa Brava in the north and the Costa Daurada to the south are havens for sun-seekers. Excellent rail, air, and highway connections link Catalonia to the beach resorts of Valencia, its neighbor to the south.

1 **Girona**

2 **Figueres**

3 **Besalú**

4 **Olot**

5 **Blanes**

6 **Tossa de Mar**

7 **Sant Feliu de Guixols**

8 **S'Agaró**

9 **Calella de Palafrugell and Around**

10 **Begur and Around**

11 **Cadaqués and Around**

12 **Montserrat**

13 **Sitges**

14 **Santes Creus**

15 **Santa Maria de Poblet**

16 **Tarragona**

17 **Valencia**

18 **Albufera Nature Park**

19 **Dénia**

20 **Calpe**

21 **Altea**

22 **Alicante**

FRANCE
Cap de Creus
Puigcerda
Cadaqués
CATALÒNIA 2
Ripoll 11 Figueres
Besalú 3 Empordà
Berga 4 Olot 10
Puigreig Girona 9
Vic 1
BARCELONA GIRONA 8
Manresa 5 Palafrugell
Gualada Montserrat 6 7
12 Blanes
Santes Arenys De Mar
Creus Sabadell Mataro
Montblanch 14 Barcelona
Santa Maria de Poblet
15 Valls 13
El Priorat
Reus 16 Sitges
Gandesa Tarragona
TARRAGONA
La Ametlla De Mar
Tortosa
Morella San Carlos de la Rapita
Vinaroz
CASTELLON Peniscola
DE LA PLANA
Torreblanca
Alcora Borriol
Jerica Castello de la Plana
Segorbe Burriana
Vall De Uxo
El Puerto
Burjasot 17 Valencia
18 Albufera Nature Park
VALENCIA Cullera
Tabernes De Valldigna
Almansa Gandia
Ontaniente Dénia
Alcoy 19 Cabo De La Nao
Villena 20
Yecla Altea
Pinoso 22 21
ALICANTE
Elche Alicante
Oribuela
Torrevieja

Mediterranean Sea

COSTA BRAVA
COSTA DORADA
COSTA DEL AZAHAR
COSTA BLANCA

0   20 mi
0   20 km

EATING AND DRINKING WELL IN CATALONIA, VALENCIA, AND THE COSTA BLANCA

Cuisine in both Catalonia and Valencia includes classic Mediterranean dishes, and Catalans feel right at home with paella valenciana (Valencian paella). Fish preparations are similar along the coast, though inland favorites vary from place to place.

The grassy inland meadows of Catalonia's northern Alt Empordà region put quality beef on local tables; from the Costa Brava comes fine seafood, such as anchovies from L'Escala and *gambas* (prawns) from Palamós, both deservedly famous. *Romesco*—a blend of almonds, peppers, garlic, and olive oil—is used as a vegetable, fish, and seafood sauce in Tarragona, especially during the *calçotadas* (spring onion feasts) in February. *Allioli*, garlicky mayonnaise, is another popular topping. The Ebro Delta is renowned for fresh fish, oysters, and eels, as well as *rossejat* (fried rice in a fish broth). Valencia and the Mediterranean coast are the homeland of paella valenciana. *Arròs a banda* is a variant in which the fish and rice are cooked separately.

CALÇOTS

The *calçot* is a sweet spring onion developed by a 19th-century farmer who discovered how to extend the edible portion by packing soil around the base. It is grilled on a barbecue, then peeled and dipped into romesco sauce. In January, the town of Valls holds a *calçotada* where upward of 30,000 people gather for meals of onions, sausage, lamb chops, and red wine.

RICE

Paella valenciana is one of Spain's most famous gastronomic contributions. A simple country dish dating to the early 18th century, "paella" refers to the wide frying pan with short, sturdy handles that's used to cook the rice. Anything fresh from the fields that day, along with rice and olive oil, traditionally went into the pan, but paella valenciana has particular ingredients: short-grain rice, chicken, rabbit, *garrofó* (a local legume), tomatoes, green beans, sweet peppers, olive oil, and saffron. *Paella marinera* (seafood paella) is a different story: rice, cuttlefish, squid, mussels, shrimp, prawns, lobster, clams, garlic, olive oil, sweet paprika, and saffron, all stewed in fish broth. Other paella variations include *paella negra,* a black rice dish made with squid ink; *arròs a banda* made with peeled seafood; and *fideuà,* paella made with noodles.

SEAFOOD STEWS

Sèpia amb pèsols is a vegetable and seafood *mar i muntanya* ("surf and turf") beloved on the Costa Brava: cuttlefish and peas are stewed with potatoes, garlic, onions, tomatoes, and a splash of wine. The *picadillo*—the finishing touches of flavors and textures—includes parsley, black pepper, fried bread, pine nuts, olive oil, and salt. *Es niu* ("the nest") of game fowl, cod, tripe, cuttlefish, pork, and

rabbit is another Costa Brava favorite. Stewed for a good five hours, this is a much-celebrated wintertime classic. You'll also find *suquet de peix,* the Catalan fish stew, at restaurants along the Costa Brava.

FRUITS AND VEGETABLES

Valencia and the eastern Levante region have long been famous as Spain's *huerta,* or garden. The alluvial soil of the littoral produces an abundance of everything from tomatoes to asparagus, peppers, chard, spinach, onions, artichokes, cucumbers, and the whole range of Mediterranean bounty. Catalonia's Maresme and Empordà regions are also fruit and vegetable bowls, making this coastline a true cornucopia of fresh produce.

WINES

The Penedès wine region west of Barcelona has been joined by new wine Denominations of Origin from all over Catalonia. Alt Camp, Tarragona, Priorat, Montsant, Costers del Segre, Pla de Bages, Alella, and Empordà all produce excellent reds and whites to join Catalonia's sparkling cava on local wine lists. The rich, full-bodied reds of Montsant and Priorat, especially, are among the best in Spain.

The long curve of the Mediterranean from the French border to Cabo Cervera below Alicante encompasses the two autonomous communities of Catalonia and Valencia, with the country's second- and third-largest cities (Barcelona and Valencia, respectively). Rivals in many respects, the two communities share a language, history, and culture that set them apart from the rest of Spain.

Girona is the gateway to Northern Catalonia's attractions—the Pyrenees, the volcanic region of La Garrotxa, and the beaches of rugged Costa Brava. Northern Catalonia is memorable for the soft, green hills of the Empordà farm country and the Alberes mountain range at the eastern end of the Pyrenees. Across the landscape are *masías* (farmhouses) with staggered-stone roofs and square towers that make them look like fortresses. Even the tiniest village has its church, arcaded square, and *rambla*, where villagers take their evening *paseo* (stroll).

Salvador Dalí's deep connection to the Costa Brava is enshrined in the Teatre-Museu Dalí in Figueres: he's buried in the crypt beneath it. His wife Gala is buried in his former home, a castle in Púbol. His summer home in Port Lligat Bay, north of Cadaqués, is now a museum of his life and work.

The province of Valencia was incorporated into the Kingdom of Aragón, Catalonia's medieval Mediterranean empire, when it was conquered by Jaume I in the 13th century. Along with Catalonia,

Valencia became part of the united Spanish state in the 15th century, but defenders of its separate cultural and linguistic identity still resent the centuries of Catalan domination. The Catalan language prevails in Tarragona, a city and province of Catalonia, but Valenciano—a dialect of Catalan—is spoken and used on street signs in the Valencian provinces.

The fertile, irrigated coastal plain is devoted mainly to citrus and vegetable farming, which lends color to the landscape and fragrance to the air. Arid mountains form a stark backdrop to the lush coast. Over the years these shores have entertained Phoenician, Greek, Carthaginian, and Roman visitors; the Romans stayed several centuries and left archaeological remains all the way down the coast, particularly in Tarragona, the capital of Rome's Spanish empire by 218 BC. Rome's dominion did not go uncontested, however; the most serious challenge came from the Carthaginians of North Africa. The three Punic Wars, fought over this territory between 264 and 146 BC, established the reputation of the Carthaginian general Hannibal.

The coastal farmland and beaches that attracted the ancients now call to modern-day tourists, though in parts, a number of "mass-tourism" resorts have marred the shore. Inland, however, local culture survives intact. The rugged and beautiful territory is dotted with small fortified towns, several of which bear the name of Spain's 11th-century national hero, El Cid, commemorating the battles he fought here against the Moors some 900 years ago.

MAJOR REGIONS

For many, **Northern Catalonia** is one of the top reasons reason to visit Spain. The historic center of **Girona**, its principal city, is a labyrinth of climbing cobblestone streets and staircases, with remarkable Gothic and Romanesque buildings at every turn. El Call, the Jewish Quarter, is one of the best-preserved areas of its kind in Europe, and the Gothic cathedral is an architectural masterpiece. Streets in the modern part of the city are lined with smart shops and boutiques, and the overall quality of life in Girona is considered among the best in Spain. Nearby towns **Besalú** and **Figueres** are vastly different. Figueres is an unremarkable town made exceptional by the Dalí Museum. Besalú is a picture-perfect Romanesque village on a bluff overlooking the Riu Fluvià, with one of the most prestigious restaurants in Catalonia. Lesser known are the medieval towns in and around the volcanic (now extinct) area of La Garrotxa: Vic, Rupit, and Olot boast the best produce in the region.

The Costa Brava (Wild Coast) is a nearly unbroken series of sheer rock cliffs dropping down to clear blue-green waters, punctuated by innumerable coves and tiny beaches on narrow inlets, called *calas*. It basically begins at **Blanes** and continues north along 135 km (84 miles) of coastline to the French border at Portbou. Although the area does have spots of real-estate excess, the rocky terrain of many pockets (**Tossa de Mar**, **Begur**, and **Cadaqués**) has discouraged

overbuilding. On a good day here, the luminous blue of the sea contrasts with red-brown headlands and cliffs, and the distant lights of fishing boats reflect on wine-color waters at dusk. Small stands of umbrella pine veil the footpaths to many of the secluded coves and little patches of white sand—often, the only access is by boat.

The **Southern Catalonia** area is home to **Montserrat**, home to the shrine of La Moreneta (the Black Virgin of Montserrat), the lively coastal town of **Sitges**, the Cistercian monasteries of **Santes Creus** and **Santa Maria de Poblet**, and the region's principal town of **Tarragona**, once an important outpost of the Roman Empire. Farther south lies **Valencia**, Spain's third-largest city and the capital of its region and province, equidistant from Barcelona and Madrid. For a day trip there's the **Albufera**, a scenic coastal wetland teeming with native wildlife, especially migratory birds.

The Costa Blanca (White Coast) begins at **Dénia**, south of Valencia, and stretches down roughly to Torrevieja, below Alicante. It's best known for its magical vacation combo of sand, sea, and sun, with popular beaches and more secluded coves and stretches of sand. **Alicante** itself has two long beaches, a charming old quarter, and mild weather most of the year.

Planning

When to Go

Come for the beaches in the hot summer months, but expect crowds and serious heat—in some places up to 40°C (104°F). The Mediterranean coast is more comfortable in May and September.

February and March are the peak months for skiing in the Pyrenees. Winter travel in the region has other advantages:

Valencia still has plenty of sunshine, and if you're visiting villages and wineries in the countryside, you might have the place all to yourself. Note that many restaurants and hotels outside the major towns may close on weekdays or longer in winter, so call ahead. Many museums and sites close early in winter (6 pm).

The Costa Brava and Costa Blanca beach areas get hot and crowded in summer, and accommodations are at a premium. In contrast, spring is mild and an excellent time to tour the region, particularly the rural areas, where blossoms infuse the air with pleasant fragrances and wildflowers dazzle the landscape.

Planning Your Time

Not far from Barcelona, the beautiful towns of Vic, Girona, and Cadaqués are easily reachable from the city by bus or train in a couple of hours. Figueres is a must if you want to see the Teatre-Museu Dalí. Girona makes an excellent base from which to explore La Garrotxa—for that, you'll need to rent a car. Allot a few days to explore Tarragona, easily reached from Barcelona by train or a 1½-hour drive. If you're driving, take a detour to the wineries in the Penedès region; most of Spain's cava comes from here. Explore Tarragona's Roman wonders on foot, and stop for a meal at any of the fine seafood restaurants in the Serallo fishing quarter.

Valencia is three hours by express train from Barcelona; stop in Tarragona on your way if you have time. From Tarragona, it's a comfortable hour-long train ride to Valencia; if driving, stop off for a meal or stroll in one of the coastal towns like Castellon. Historic Valencia and the Santiago Calatrava–designed City of Arts and Sciences complex can be covered in two days, but stay longer and indulge in the city's food and explore the nightlife in the Barrio del Carmen.

Travel agencies in Alicante can arrange tours of the city and bus and train tours to Guadalest, the Algar waterfalls, the Peñón de Ifach (Calpe) on the Costa Blanca, and inland to Elche.

FESTIVALS

In Valencia, **Las Fallas** fiestas begin March 1 and reach a climax between March 15 and El Día de San José (St. Joseph's Day) on March 19, Father's Day in Spain. Las Fallas originated from St. Joseph's role as patron saint of carpenters; in medieval times, carpenters' guilds celebrated the arrival of spring by cleaning out their shops and making bonfires with scraps of wood. These days it's a 19-day celebration ending with fireworks, floats, carnival processions, and bullfights. On March 19, huge wood and papier-mâché effigies of political figures and other personalities (the result of a year's work by local community groups) are torched to end the fiestas.

Getting Here and Around

AIR TRAVEL

El Prat de Llobregat in Barcelona is the main international airport for the Costa Brava; Girona is the closest airport to the region, with bus connections directly into the city and to Barcelona. Valencia has an international airport with direct flights to London, Paris, Brussels, Lisbon, Zurich, and Milan as well as regional flights from Barcelona, Madrid, Málaga, and other cities in Spain. There is a regional airport in Alicante serving the Valencian region and Murcia.

BOAT AND FERRY TRAVEL

Many short-cruise lines along the coast offer the chance to view the Costa Brava from the sea. Visit the port areas in the main towns and you'll quickly spot several tourist cruise lines. Plan to spend around €15–€27, depending on the length of the cruise. Many longer cruises include a stop en route for a swim. The glass-keel Nautilus boats for observation of the Medes Islands underwater park cost around €20 and run daily April–October and weekends November–March.

The shortest ferry connections to the Balearic Islands originate in Dénia. Balearia sails from there to Ibiza, Formentera, and Mallorca.

BOAT AND FERRY INFORMATION

Balearia. ☎ 902/160180, 865/608423 from abroad ⊕ www.balearia.com.
Nautilus. ✉ Passeig Marítim 23, L'Estartit ☎ 972/751489 ⊕ www.english.nautilus.es.

BUS TRAVEL

Private companies run buses down the coast and from Madrid to Valencia, and to Alicante. ALSA is the main bus line in this region; check local tourist offices for schedules. Sarfa operates buses from Barcelona to Blanes, Lloret, Sant Feliu de Guixols, Platja d'Aro, Palamos, Begur, Roses, L'Escala, and Cadaqués.

CONTACTS ALSA. ☎ 902/422242 ⊕ www.alsa.es. **Moventis Sarfa.** ✉ Estació del Nord, Alí Bei 80, Barcelona ☎ 902/302025 ⊕ compras.moventis.es/en-GB Ⓜ Arc de Triomf. **Sagalés.** ✉ Estació del Nord, Alí Bei 80, Barcelona ☎ 902/130014 tickets ⊕ www.sagales.com Ⓜ Arc de Triomf. **Sagalés AirportLine.** ☎ 902/130014 ⊕ www.sagalesairportline.com.

CAR TRAVEL

A car is necessary for explorations inland and convenient for reaching locations on the coast, where drives are smooth and scenic. Catalonia and Valencia have excellent roads; the only drawbacks are the high cost of fuel and the high tolls on the *autopistas* (highways, usually designated by the letters "AP"). The national roads (starting with the letter N) can get clogged, however, so you're often better off on toll roads if your time is limited.

TRAIN TRAVEL

Most of the Costa Brava is not served directly by railroad. A local line runs up the coast from Barcelona to Blanes, then turns inland and connects at Maçanet-Massanes with the main line up to France. Direct trains stop only at major connections, such as Girona, Flaçà, and Figueres. To visit one of the smaller towns in between, you can take a fast direct train from Barcelona to Girona, for instance, then get off and wait for a local to come by. The stop on the main line for the middle section of the Costa Brava is Flaçà, where you can take a bus or taxi to your final destination. Girona and Figueres are two other towns with major bus stations that feed out to the towns of the Costa Brava. The train serves the last three towns on the north end of the Costa Brava: Llançà, Colera, and Portbou.

Express intercity trains reach Valencia from all over Spain, arriving at the new Joaquin Sorolla station; from there, a shuttle bus takes you to the Estación del Norte, the terminus in the center of town, for local connections. From Barcelona there are 15 trains a day, including the fast train TALGO, which takes 3½ hours. There are 22 daily trains to Valencia from Madrid; the high-speed train takes about 1 hour 40 minutes.

For the Costa Blanca, the rail hub is Alicante; for southern Catalonia, make direct train connections to Tarragona from either Barcelona or Valencia.

CONTACTS RENFE. ☎ 912/320320 ⊕ www.renfe.com.

Tours

Hiking, cycling, and walking tours are available around Valencia and the Costa Blanca.

Riding schools in a number of towns in the region provide classes and trekking opportunities. Pick up brochures at local tourist offices.

Learn to sail in most of the major resorts. For kitesurfing or windsurfing, gear is available for rent at many of the beaches. Many companies offer scuba-diving excursions; in the smaller coastal towns it's possible to dive in the protected waters of offshore nature reserves if you book ahead.

This region is a bird-watcher's paradise, especially in the salt pans of Santa Pola and Albufera Lake. The main coastal plain is a migratory highway for thousands of birds winging their way between Europe and Africa.

CONTACTS

Abdet

EXCURSIONS | The Sierra Mariola and Sierra Aitana regions are both easily accessible from the Costa Blanca resorts. Abdet, near Guadalest, offers itineraries and traditional self-catering guesthouses amid breathtaking scenery. ⊕ *www.abdet.com* ⊠ *From €380.*

Association of Diving Centers Costa Brava Sub

ADVENTURE TOURS | For comprehensive information on diving, equipment hire, and courses in the Costa Brava region, contact the association, which includes upward of 34 associated and accredited diving centers. ☎ 972/600017 ⊕ *www. submarinismocostabrava.com/en.*

Ciclo Costa Blanca

BICYCLE TOURS | If pedal power is your thing, Ciclo Costa Blanca is a good place to start, with both guided and self-guided tours. ⊠ *Meta Bike Cafe Comercio Enara 2, Calle Vell de Altea 24, Alicante* ☎ 966/868104 ⊕ *www.ciclocostablanca. com* ⊠ *From €330.*

Mountain Walks

SPECIAL-INTEREST | Self-guided or guided bird-watching, mountain-walking, and cycling tours are customized to suit your requirements, with picturesque cottage accommodations, meals, and transportation included in the price. ⊠ *San Gregorio 4, Quatretondeta, Alicante* ☎ 965/511044 ⊕ *www.mountainwalks. com* ⊠ *From €120.*

Farmhouse Stays in Catalonia

Dotted throughout Catalonia are farmhouses (*casas rurales* in Spanish, and *cases de pagès* or *masíes* in Catalan), where you can spend a weekend or longer. Accommodations vary from small rustic homes to spacious luxurious farmhouses with fireplaces and pools. Stay in a guest room at a bed-and-breakfast, or rent an entire house and do your own cooking. Most tourist offices, including the main Catalonia Tourist Office, have information and listings. Several organizations in Spain have detailed listings and descriptions of Catalonia's farmhouses.

CONTACTS Agroturisme.org.
☎ 932/680900 ⊕ *www.agroturisme. cat.* **Cases Rurals.** ☎ 660/576834 ⊕ *www. casesrurals.com.*

Restaurants

Catalonia's eateries are deservedly famous. Girona's El Celler de Can Roca was voted Best Restaurant in the World multiple times in recent years in the annual critics' poll conducted by British magazine *Restaurant,* and a host of other first-rate establishments continue to offer inspiring fine dining in Catalonia, which began in the hinterlands at the legendary Hotel Empordà. Yet you needn't go to an internationally acclaimed restaurant to dine well. Superstar chef Ferran Adrià of the former foodie paradise elBulli dines regularly at dives in Roses, where straight-up fresh fish is the attraction. Northern Catalonia's Empordà region is known for seafood and rich assortment of inland and upland products. Beef from Girona's verdant pastureland is prized throughout Catalonia, while wild mushrooms from the Pyrenees and game from the Alberes range offer seasonal depth to menus across the region. From a simple beachside paella or *llobarro* (sea bass) at a *chiringuito* (beach shack) with tables on the sand, to the splendor of a meal at El Celler de Can Roca, playing culinary hopscotch through Catalonia is a good way to get to know the region.

Hotels

Lodgings on the Costa Brava range from the finest hotels to spartan pensions. The better accommodations have splendid views of the seascape. If you plan to visit during the high season (July and August), be sure to book reservations well in advance at almost any hotel in the area; the Costa Brava remains one of the most popular summer resort areas in Spain. Many Costa Brava hotels close down in the winter season (November–March).

Hotel reviews have been shortened. For full information, visit Fodors.com.

What It Costs in Euros			
$	$$	$$$	$$$$
RESTAURANTS			
under €12	€12–€17	€18–€22	over €22
HOTELS			
under €90	€90–€125	€126–€180	over €180

Girona

97 km (60 miles) northeast of Barcelona.

At the confluence of four rivers, Northern Catalonia's Girona (population: 97,000) keeps intact the magic of its historic past; with its brooding hilltop castle, soaring Gothic cathedral, and dreamy riverside setting, it resembles a vision from the Middle Ages. Today, as a university center, Girona combines past and vibrant present: art galleries, chic cafés, and trendy boutiques have set up shop in many of the restored buildings of the old quarter, known as the Força Vella (Old

Fortress), which is on the east side of the Riu Onyar. Built on the side of the mountain, it presents a tightly packed labyrinth of medieval buildings and monuments on narrow cobblestone streets with connecting stairways. You can still see vestiges of the Iberian and Roman walls in the cathedral square and in the patio of the old university. In the central quarter is El Call, one of Europe's best-preserved medieval (12th- to 15th-century) Jewish communities and an important center of Kabbalistic studies.

The main street of the Força Vella is Carrer de la Força, which follows the old Via Augusta, the Roman road that connected Rome with its provinces.

Explore Girona on foot to discover many of its delights. One of Girona's treasures is its setting, high above where the Onyar merges with the Ter; the latter flows from a mountain waterfall that can be glimpsed in a gorge above the town. Walk first along the west bank of the Onyar, between the train trestle and the Plaça de la Independència, to admire the classic view of the old town, with its pastel waterfront facades. Many of the windows and balconies are adorned with fretwork grilles of embossed wood or delicate iron tracery. Cross Pont de Sant Agustí over to the old quarter from under the arcades in the corner of Plaça de la Independència and find your way to the Punt de Benvinguda tourist office, to the right at Rambla Llibertat 1. Work your way up through the labyrinth of steep streets, using the cathedral's huge baroque facade as a guide. Try to be in Girona during the second week of May, when the streets of the old quarter are festooned with the flowers of spring during the Girona Festival of Flowers.

GETTING HERE AND AROUND

There are more than 20 daily trains from Barcelona to Girona (continuing on to the French border). Regional trains can take between one and two hours, and can be picked up from a number of stations

Northern Catalonia and the Costa Brava

in Barcelona, while the high-speed AVE train service is a convenient option, running from Barcelona Sants station to Girona in under 40 minutes (it's advisable to prebook the AVE). The train station is about a 20-minute walk from the old quarter; alternatively, taxis can be picked up in front of the train station on arrival. There are frequent Sagales buses to Girona Airport; they take an average of 75 minutes and cost €16 one way, €25 round-trip. The Sagales 602 and 603 buses run from Barcelona's El Prat de Llobregat airport and Estació del Nord, in the city center of Barcelona, to Girona city bus station. Getting around the city is easiest on foot or by taxi; several bridges connect the historic old quarter with the more modern town across the river.

CONTACTS Sagalés. ☎ 902/130014 ⊕ www.sagales.com.

DISCOUNTS AND DEALS

The GironaMuseus discounts admission to all the city's museums. ■**TIP→ Some are free on the first Sunday of every month.** Check the tourist office or at the Punt de Benvinguda welcome center, which can also arrange guided tours.

TOURS

Bike Breaks

BICYCLE TOURS | In recent times, Girona has developed a passion for all things bike related. Bike Breaks provides bike rentals and tours so that you can get to know the city and its surroundings on two wheels. ✉ Carrer Nou 14 E ☎ 972/205465 ⊕ www.gironacyclecentre. com ✉ Tours from €25.

VISITOR INFORMATION Girona Office of Tourism. ✉ Rambla de la Llibertat 1 ☎ 972/010001 ⊕ www.girona.cat/turisme. **Punt de Benvinguda.** ✉ Berenguer Carnicer

*3 ☎ 972/211678, 972/011669 ⊕ www.
gironawalks.com.*

Sights

Banys Arabs (*Arab Baths*)

HOT SPRINGS | A misnomer, the Banys
Arabs were actually built by Morisco
craftsmen (workers of Moorish descent)
in the late 12th century, long after Girona's
Islamic occupation (714–797) had ended.
Following the old Roman model that had
disappeared in the West, the custom of
bathing publicly may have been brought
back from the Holy Land with the
Crusaders. These baths are sectioned off
into three rooms in descending order: a
frigidarium, or cold bath, a square room
with a central octagonal pool and a skylight
with cupola held up by two stories of eight
fine columns; a *tepidarium,* or warm bath;
and a *caldarium,* or steam room, beneath
which is a chamber where a fire was
kept burning. Here the inhabitants of old
Girona came to relax, exchange gossip,
or do business. It is known from another
public bathhouse in Tortosa, Tarragona, that
the various social classes came to bathe
by sex and religion on fixed days of the
week: Christian men on one day, Christian
women on another, Jewish men on still
another, Jewish women (and prostitutes)
on a fourth, Muslims on others. ⊠ *Carrer Ferran el Catòlic s/n ☎ 972/190969
⊕ www.banysarabs.org ⊠ €2.*

Basilica of Sant Feliu

RELIGIOUS SITE | One of Girona's most
beloved churches and its first cathedral
until the 10th century, Sant Feliu was
repeatedly rebuilt and altered over four
centuries and stands today as an amal-
gam of Romanesque columns, a Gothic
nave, and a baroque facade. The vast
bulk of this structure is landmarked by
one of Girona's most distinctive belfries,
topped by eight pinnacles. The basilica
was founded over the tomb of St. Felix of
Africa, a martyr under the Roman emper-
or Diocletian. ⊠ *Pujada de Sant Feliu 29
☎ 972/201407 ⊠ From €7.*

★ Cathedral

BUILDING | At the heart of the Força Vella,
the cathedral looms above 90 steps and
is famous for its nave—at 75 feet, the
widest in the world and the epitome of
the spatial ideal of Catalan Gothic architects. Since Charlemagne founded the
original church in the 8th century, it has
been through many fires and renovations.
Take in the rococo-era facade, "eloquent
as organ music" and impressive flight of
17th-century stairs, which rises from its
own *plaça.* Inside, three smaller naves
were compressed into one gigantic hall
by the famed architect Guillermo Bofill in
1416. The change was typical of Catalan
Gothic "hall" churches, and it was done
to facilitate preaching to crowds. Note
the famous silver canopy, or *baldaquí*
(baldachin). The oldest part of the cathedral is the 11th-century Romanesque
Torre de Carlemany (Charlemagne Tower).

The cathedral's exquisite 12th-century
cloister has an obvious affinity with the
cloisters in the Roussillon area of France.
Inside the Treasury there's a variety of
precious objects. They include a 10th-cen-
tury copy of Beatus's manuscript *Commentary on the Apocalypse* (illuminated
in the dramatically primitive Mozarabic
style), the Bible of Emperor Charles V,
and the celebrated *Tapís de la Creació*
(*Tapestry of the Creation*), considered by
most experts to be the finest tapestry
surviving from the Romanesque era (and,
in fact, thought to be the needlework of
Saxons working in England). Made of
wool, with predominant colors of green,
brown, and ocher, the tapestry once
hung behind the main altar as a pictorial
Bible lesson. Representations of time
and nature circle around a central figure,
likening paradise to the eternal cosmos
presided over by Christ. The bottom band
(which appears to have been added at a
later date) contains two *iudeis,* or Jews,
dressed in the round cloaks they were
compelled to wear to set them apart
from Christians. This scene is thought to
be the earliest portrayal of a Jew (other

There's more to Girona's cathedral than the 90 steps to get to it; inside there's much to see, including the Treasury.

than biblical figures) in Christian art. ✉ *Pl. de la Catedral s/n* ☎ *972/427189* ⊕ *www. catedraldegirona.cat* ✉ *From €7.*

★ El Call

HISTORIC SITE | Girona is especially noted for its 13th-century Jewish Quarter, El Call, which branches off Carrer de la Força, south of the Plaça Catedral. The quarter is a network of lanes that criss-cross above one another, and houses built atop each other in disorderly fashion along narrow stone medieval streets. With boutique shopping, artsy cafés, and lots of atmospheric eateries and bars, there is plenty to explore.

The word *call* (pronounced "kyle" in Catalan) may come from an old Catalan word meaning "narrow way" or "passage." Others suggest that it comes from the Hebrew word *qahal,* meaning "assembly" or "meeting of the community." The earliest presence of Jews in Girona is uncertain, but the first historical mention dates from 982, when a group of 25 Jewish families moved to Girona from nearby Juïgues. Owing allegiance to the Spanish king (who exacted tribute for this distinction) and not to the city government, this once-prosperous Jewish community—one of the most flourishing in Europe during the Middle Ages—was, at its height, a leading center of learning. ✉ *Girona.*

Monestir de Sant Pere de Galligants

MUSEUM | The church of St. Peter, across the Galligants River, was finished in 1131, and is notable for its octagonal Romanesque belfry and the finely detailed capitals atop the columns in the cloister. It now houses the **Museu Arqueològic** (Museum of Archaeology), which documents the region's history since Paleolithic times and includes some artifacts from Roman times. ✉ *Carrer Santa Llúcia 8* ☎ *972/202632* ⊕ *www.macgirona.cat* ✉ *€4.50* ⊙ *Closed Mon.*

Museu d'Art

MUSEUM | The Episcopal Palace near the cathedral contains the wide-ranging collections of Girona's main art museum. On display is everything from superb Romanesque *majestats* (carved wood figures of Christ) to reliquaries from Sant Pere de Rodes, illuminated 12th-century manuscripts, and works of the 20th-century Olot school of landscape painting. ✉ *Pujada de la Catedral 12* ☎ *972/203834* 🌐 *www.museuart.com* 🎫 *€4.50* 🕓 *Closed Mon.*

Museum of Jewish History

MUSEUM | Housed in a former synagogue and dedicated to the preservation of Girona's Jewish heritage, this center organizes conferences, exhibitions, and seminars and contains 21 stone tablets, one of the finest collections in the world of medieval Jewish funerary slabs. These came from the old Jewish cemetery of Montjuïc, revealed when the railroad between Barcelona and France was laid out in the 19th century. Its exact location, about 1½ km (1 mile) north of Girona on the road to La Bisbal and known as La Tribana, is being excavated. The center also holds the **Institut d'Estudis Nahmànides,** with an extensive library of Judaica. ✉ *Carrer de la Força 8* ☎ *972/216761* 🌐 *www.girona.cat/call/eng/museu.php* 🎫 *€4.*

Passeig Arqueològic

ARCHAEOLOGICAL SITE | The landscaped gardens of this stepped archaeological walk are below the restored walls of the Força Vella (which you can walk, in parts) and enjoy superlative views of the city from belvederes and watchtowers. From there, climb through the Jardins de la Francesa to the highest ramparts for a view of the cathedral's 11th-century Torre de Carlemany. ✉ *Girona.*

🍴 Restaurants

Cal Ros

$$$ | **CATALAN** | Tucked under the arcades just behind the north end of Plaça de la Llibertat, this restaurant combines ancient stone arches with crisp, contemporary furnishings and cheerful lighting. The menu changes regularly, featuring organically raised local produce in season, and fresh fish in updated versions of traditional Catalan cuisine. **Known for:** rice dishes; tucked under the arches of the old quarter; updated traditional cuisine. [$] *Average main: €22* ✉ *Carrer Cort Reial 9* ☎ *972/219176* 🕓 *Closed Mon. and Tues. No dinner Sun.*

★ El Celler de Can Roca

$$$$ | **CONTEMPORARY** | Anointed twice (in 2013 and 2015) by an international panel of food critics and chefs as the best restaurant in the world, El Celler de Can Roca is a life-changing culinary experience. The Roca brothers—Joan, Josep, and Jordi—showcase their masterful creations in two tasting menus, at €180 and €205. **Known for:** extensive wine selection; one of the best restaurants in the world; reservations required many months or even a year ahead. [$] *Average main: €180* ✉ *Can Sunyer 48* ☎ *972/222157* 🌐 *cellercanroca.com* 🕓 *Closed Sun. and Mon., Easter wk, 1 wk in Aug., and Dec. 23–Jan. 16. No lunch Tues.*

La Fabrica

$ | **CAFÉ** | Christian, a professional cyclist, and his wife, Amber, opened this inviting space, serving brunch and superb coffee, in an old carpentry factory (La Fabrica means "the factory" in Spanish). There are raw concrete floors, exposed brick walls, high ceilings, and an abundance of bike memorabilia. **Known for:** bike-friendly stop; excellent coffee; setting in converted factory. [$] *Average main: €9* ✉ *Carrer de la Llebre 3* ☎ *972/296622* 🌐 *www.lafabricagirona.com* 🕓 *No dinner.*

Restaurante La Carnisseria

$$ | **CATALAN** | Craftsmanship, family traditions, and a lot of love combine at this restaurant dedicated to providing the best cuts of meat in town. Tucked down a slender street in Girona's ancient Call (Jewish Quarter) and habitually packed with diners on the three nights it is open, La Carnisseria is run by a family of butchers with a shared passion for meat that goes back generations. **Known for:** best cuts of meat in town; warm

With its picturesque rivers, Girona is often called the Spanish Venice.

and professional service in cozy setting; dedicated family business. $ *Average main: €15* ✉ *Puja Sant Domènec 9* ☎ *697/479784* ⊘ *No lunch. Closed Sun.–Wed.*

Rocambolesc

$ | **CAFÉ** | **FAMILY** | Couldn't get a table at El Celler de Can Roca? Keep trying, but in the meantime there's Rocambolesc, the latest of the Roca family culinary undertakings. **Known for:** ice cream and sorbet; popsicles; fun toppings. $ *Average main: €5* ✉ *Carrer Santa Clara 50* ☎ *972/416667* ⊕ *www.rocambolesc. com* ▭ *No credit cards.*

Hotels

★ Alemanys 5

$$$$ | **RENTAL** | **FAMILY** | Award-winning architect Anna Noguera and partner Juan-Manuel Ribera transformed a 16th-century house steps from the cathedral into two extraordinary apartments: one for up to five people, the other for six. **Pros:** perfect for families or small groups; ideal location; superb architectural design. **Cons:** difficult to navigate the small streets by car (hotel provides instructions); minimum stay required; needs booking in advance. $ *Rooms from: €300* ✉ *Carrer Alemanys 5* ☎ *649/885136* ⊕ *www.alemanys5.com* ⮌ *2 apartments* ⦿ *No meals.*

Bellmirall

$ | **B&B/INN** | This pretty little *hostal* (guesthouse) in the old city, on the edge of El Call, makes up in value and location what it lacks in amenities and services; when there's no staff on call, you come and go with your own key. **Pros:** steps from the important sites; charming sitting room; good value. **Cons:** bedrooms are small; some rooms have shared bathrooms; no elevator. $ *Rooms from: €88* ✉ *Carrer de Bellmirall 3* ☎ *972/204009* ⊕ *www.bellmirall.eu* ⊘ *Closed Jan.* ⮌ *7 rooms* ⦿ *Free Breakfast.*

Hotel Peninsular

$$ | **HOTEL** | In a handsomely restored early-20th-century building across the Riu Onyar, with views into Girona's historic

Força Vella, this modest but useful hotel occupies a strategic spot at the end of the Pont de Pedra (Stone Bridge), a Girona landmark in the center of the shopping district. **Pros:** good location at the hub of Girona life; near the stop for the bus from Girona airport; friendly staff. **Cons:** smallish rooms; basic decor; no frills. $ *Rooms from: €90* ⊠ *Carrer Nou 3, Av. Sant Francesc 6* ☎ *972/203800* ⊕ *www.hotelpeninsulargirona.com* 🛏 *48 rooms* ❌ *No meals.*

Nightlife

Girona is a university town, so the night scene is especially lively during the school year. In the labyrinth of small streets throughout the pedestrianized Barri Vell (Old Town), several *vermuterias* (vermouth-focused bars), wine bars, and affable taverns provide entertainment as night falls.

Nou Platea
BARS/PUBS | This nightspot, popular with students and visitors alike, has both disco and live bands in concert, depending on the day of the week. ⊠ *Carrer Jeroni Real de Fontclara 4* ☎ *972/227288.*

Sunset Jazz Club
MUSIC CLUBS | As the evening develops, drop into the Sunset Jazz Club to catch some live jazz by national and international artists in a softly lit, buzzing venue with exposed brick walls and dark furnishings. ⊠ *Calle Jaume Pons i Martí* ☎ *872/080145* ⊕ *www.sunsetjazz-club.com.*

⚪ Shopping

BOOKS
Llibreria 22
BOOKS/STATIONERY | Girona's best bookstore has a large travel-guide section and a small selection of English fiction. ⊠ *Carrer Hortes 22* ☎ *972/212395* ⊕ *www. llibreria22.net.*

FOOD, CANDY, AND WINE
Gluki
FOOD/CANDY | This chocolatier and confectioner has been in business since 1870. ⊠ *Carrer Nou 9* ☎ *972/201989* ⊕ *www. gluki.cat.*

La Simfonia
WINE/SPIRITS | At this relaxed wine shop and bar, you can be guided through a stellar range of regional wines (and cheeses)—and sample before you buy. ⊠ *Pl. de l'Oli 6* ☎ *972/411253* ⊕ *www. lasimfonia.com.*

Torrons Victoria Candela
FOOD/CANDY | Tasty nougat is the specialty here. ⊠ *Carrer Anselm Clavé 3* ☎ *972/211103* ⊕ *www.turronescandela. com.*

JEWELRY
Baobab
JEWELRY/ACCESSORIES | A lot of designer Anna Casal's original jewelry seems at first sight to be rough-hewn; it takes a second careful look to realize how sophisticated it really is. This shop doubles as her studio. ⊠ *Carrer de les Hortes 18* ☎ *972/410227.*

Figueres

37 km (23 miles) north of Girona.

Figueres is the capital of the *comarca* (county) of the Alt Empordà, the bustling county seat of this predominantly agricultural region. Local people come from the surrounding area to shop at its many stores and stock up on farm equipment and supplies. Thursday is market day, and farmers gather at the top of La Rambla to do business and gossip, taking refreshments at cafés and discreetly pulling out and pocketing large rolls of bills, the result of their morning transactions. What brings the tourists to Figueres in droves, however, has little to do with agriculture and everything to do with Salvador Dalí's jaw-droppingly

Figueres's Famous Son

With a painterly technique that rivaled that of Jan van Eyck, a flair for publicity so aggressive it would have put P. T. Barnum to shame, and a penchant for the shocking (he loved telling people Barcelona's historic Barri Gòtic should be knocked down), artist Salvador Dalí, whose most lasting image may be the melting watches in his iconic 1931 painting *The Persistence of Memory*, enters art history as one of the foremost proponents of surrealism, the movement launched in the 1920s by André Breton. The artist, who was born in Figueres and died there in 1989, decided to create a museum-monument to himself during the last two decades of his life. Dalí often frequented the Cafeteria Astòria at the top of La Rambla (still the center of social life in Figueres), signing autographs for tourists or just being Dalí: he once walked down the street with a French omelet in his breast pocket instead of a handkerchief.

surreal "theater-museum"—one of the most visited museums in Spain.

GETTING HERE AND AROUND

Figueres is one of the stops on the regular train service from Barcelona to the French border. Local buses are also frequent, especially from nearby Cadaqués, with more than eight scheduled daily. If you're driving, take the AP7 north from Girona. The town is small enough to explore on foot.

VISITOR INFORMATION

CONTACTS Figueres. ⊠ *Pl. de l'Escorxador 2* ☎ *972/503155* ⊕ *en.visitfigueres.cat.*

 Sights

Castell de Sant Ferran

CASTLE/PALACE | Just a minute's drive northwest of Figueres is this imposing 18th-century fortified castle, one of the largest in Europe—only when you start exploring can you appreciate how immense it is. The parade grounds extend for acres, and the arcaded stables can hold more than 500 horses; the perimeter is roughly 4 km (2½ miles around). This castle was the site of the last official meeting of the Republican parliament (on February 1, 1939) before it surrendered to Franco's forces. Ironically, it was here that Lieutenant Colonel Antonio Tejero was imprisoned after his failed 1981 coup d'état in Madrid. ■ **TIP→ Call ahead and arrange for the two-hour Catedral de l'Aiguas guided tour in English (€15), which includes a trip through the castle's subterranean water system by Zodiac pontoon boat.** ⊠ *Pujada del Castell s/n* ☎ *972/506094* ⊕ *www.castillosanfernando.org/en/* ⊠ *€3.50* ⊗ *Closed Mon. (except public holidays).*

Museu del Joguet de Catalunya

MUSEUM | FAMILY | Hundreds of antique dolls and toys are on display here—including collections owned by, among others, Salvador Dalí, Federico García Lorca, and Joan Miró. The museum also hosts Catalonia's only *caganer* exhibit. These playful little figures answering nature's call have long had a special spot in the Catalan *pessebre* (Nativity scene). Farmers are the most traditional figures, squatting discreetly behind the animals, but these days you'll find Barça soccer players and politicians, too. ⊠ *Carrer de Sant Pere 1* ☎ *972/504585* ⊕ *www.mjc.cat* ⊠ *€7* ⊗ *Closed Mon. Oct.–May and late Jan.–mid-Feb.*

The Dalí Museum in Figueres is itself a work of art. Note the eggs on the exterior: they're a common image in the artist's work.

★ Teatre-Museu Dalí

BUILDING | "Museum" was not a big enough word for Dalí, so he christened his monument a theater. In fact, the building was once the Força Vella theater, reduced to a ruin in the Spanish Civil War. Now topped with a glass geodesic dome and studded with Dalí's iconic egg shapes, the multilevel museum pays homage to his fertile imagination and artistic creativity. It includes gardens, ramps, and a spectacular drop cloth Dalí painted for Les Ballets de Monte Carlo. Don't look for his greatest paintings here, although there are some memorable images, including *Gala at the Mediterranean,* which takes the body of Gala (Dalí's wife) and morphs it into the image of Abraham Lincoln once you look through coin-operated viewfinders. The sideshow theme continues with other coin-operated pieces, including *Taxi Plujós* (*Rainy Taxi*), in which water gushes over the snail-covered occupants sitting in a Cadillac once owned by Al Capone, or *Sala de Mae West,*

a trompe-l'oeil vision in which a pink sofa, two fireplaces, and two paintings morph into the face of the onetime Hollywood sex symbol. Fittingly, another "exhibit" on view is Dalí's own crypt. When his friends considered what flag to lay over his coffin, they decided to cover it with an embroidered heirloom tablecloth instead. Dalí would have liked this unconventional touch if not the actual site: he wanted to be buried at his castle of Púbol next to his wife, but the then-mayor of Figueres took matters into his own hands. The summer night session (August evenings from 10 pm to 1 am) is a perfect time to browse through the world's largest surrealist museum. Entrance tickets can be purchased in advance online, or bought in person at the museum ticket office. ⊠ *Pl. Gala-Salvador Dalí 5* ☎ *972/677500* ⊕ *www.salvador-dali. org* ⊠ *€15* ⊗ *Closed Mon. Oct.–May (except public holidays).*

Dali's Castle

Castell Gala Dalí - Púbol. The third point of the Dalí triangle is the medieval castle of Púbol, where the artist's wife and perennial model, Gala, is buried in the crypt. During the 1970s this was Gala's residence, though Dalí also lived here in the early 1980s. It contains paintings and drawings, Gala's haute-couture dresses, and other objects chosen by the couple. It's also a chance to wander through another Daliesque landscape, with lush gardens, fountains decorated with masks of Richard Wagner (the couple's favorite composer), and distinctive elephants with giraffe's legs and claw feet. Púbol, a small village roughly between Girona and Figueres, is near the C66. If you are traveling by train, get off at the Flaçà station on RENFE's Barcelona–Portbou line; walk or take a taxi 4 km (2½ miles) to Púbol. The Sarfa bus company also has a stop in Flaçà and on the C66 road, some 2 km (1¼ miles) from Púbol. ✉ *Pl. Gala-Dalí s/n, Púbol* ☎ *972/488655* 🌐 *www.salvador-dali.org* 🎟 *€8* 🕒 *Closed early Jan.–mid-Mar. and Mon. mid-Mar.–mid-June and mid-Sept.–early-Jan. (except public holidays).*

🍴 Restaurants

★ **Hotel Empordà**

$$$$ | **CATALAN** | Just 1½ km (1 mile) north of town, this restaurant run by Jaume Subirós—housed within a rather nondescript, 42-room hotel—has been hailed as the birthplace of modern Catalan cuisine and has become a beacon for gourmands. The menu changes seasonally and may contain dishes such as *cordero lechal al romero, cebollitas, pera, y boniato* (suckling lamb with rosemary, onion, pear, and sweet potato) or *espárragos de Riumors, al perfume de trufa blanca y pecorino* (asparagus from Riumors, with white truffle parfum and pecorino). **Known for:** historic culinary destination; birthplace of modern Catalan cuisine; impeccable service. [$] *Average main: €30* ✉ *Av. Salvador Dalí i Domènech 170* ☎ *972/500562* 🌐 *www.hotelemporda.com.*

🛏 Hotels

Hotel Duràn

$$ | **HOTEL** | Dalí had his own private dining room in this former stagecoach relay station, though the guest rooms, refurbished in bland pale-wood tones and standard contemporary furnishings, offset the hotel's historic 19th-century exterior. **Pros:** good central location; dining room has pictures of Dalí; family-friendly. **Cons:** rooms lack character; parking inconvenient and an extra charge; no pets. [$] *Rooms from: €90* ✉ *Carrer Lasauca 5* ☎ *972/501250* 🌐 *www.hotelduran.com* 🔑 *65 rooms* 🍽 *No meals.*

Besalú

34 km (21 miles) northwest of Girona, 25 km (15 miles) west of Figueres.

Besalú, the capital of a feudal county until power was transferred to Barcelona at the beginning of the 12th century, remains one of the best-preserved medieval towns in Catalonia. Among its main sights are the 12th-century Romanesque fortified bridge over the Riu Fluvià; two churches—Sant Vicenç (set on an attractive, café-lined plaza) and Sant Pere; and the ruins of the convent of Santa Maria on the hill above town.

GETTING HERE AND AROUND

With a population of less than 2,500, the village is easily small enough to stroll through—restaurants and sights are within walking distance of each other. There is bus service to Besalú from Figueres and the surrounding Costa Brava resorts.

VISITOR INFORMATION

CONTACTS Besalú Tourist Office. ✉ *Carrer del Pont 1* ☎ *972/591240* 🌐 *www.besalu.cat.*

Sights

Església de Sant Pere

RELIGIOUS SITE | This 12th-century Romanesque church is part of a 10th-century monastery, still in an excellent state of preservation. ✉ *Pl. de Sant Pere s/n.*

Església de Sant Vicenç

BUILDING | Founded in 977, this pre-Romanesque gem contains the relics of St. Vincent as well as the tomb of its benefactor, Pere de Rovira. La Capella de la Veracreu (Chapel of the True Cross) displays a reproduction of an alleged fragment of the True Cross brought from Rome by Bernat Tallafer in 977 and stolen in 1899. ✉ *Pl. Sant Vicenç s/n.*

Jewish ritual baths

ARCHAEOLOGICAL SITE | The remains of this 13th-century *mikvah,* or Jewish ritual bath, were discovered in the 1960s; it's one of the few surviving in Spain. A stone stairway leads down into the chamber where the water was drawn from the river, but little else indicates the role that the baths played in the medieval Jewish community. Access is by guided tour only (organized through the tourist office). ✉ *Calle de Pont Vell 1* ☎ *972/591240 tourist office* 🎟 *€3* 🕒 *Admission by guided tour only.*

Pont Fortificat

BRIDGE/TUNNEL | The town's most emblematic feature is this Romanesque 11th-century fortified bridge with crenellated battlements spanning the Riu Fluvià. ✉ *Carrer del Pont.*

Restaurants

★ Els Fogons de Can Llaudes

$$$$ | CATALAN | A faithfully restored 10th-century Romanesque chapel holds proprietor Jaume Soler's outstanding restaurant—one of Catalonia's best. A typical dish could be *confitat de bou i raïm glacejat amb el seu suc* (beef confit au jus with glacé grapes), but the menu changes weekly. **Known for:** rotating fixed-price menu only; excellent decor; Romanesque chapel. [$] *Average main: €80* ✉ *Pl. de Prat de Sant Pere 6* ☎ *972/590858* 🕒 *Closed Tues., and last 2 wks of Nov.*

Olot

21 km (13 miles) west of Besalú, 55 km (34 miles) northwest of Girona.

Capital of the comarca (administrative region) of La Garrotxa, Olot is famous for its 19th-century school of landscape painters and has several excellent Art Nouveau buildings, including the Casa Solà-Morales, which has a facade by Lluís Domènech i Montaner, architect of Barcelona's Palau de la Música Catalana. The Sant Esteve church at the southeastern end of Passeig d'en Blay is famous for its El Greco painting *Christ Carrying the Cross* (1605).

The villages of Vall d'En Bas lie south of Olot, off the C153. A freeway cuts across this countryside to Vic, but you'll miss a lot by taking it. The twisting old road leads you through rich farmland past farmhouses with dark wooden balconies bedecked with bright flowers. Turn off for Sant Privat d'En Bas and Els Hostalets d'En Bas. Farther on, the picturesque medieval village of **Rupit** has excellent restaurants serving the famous *patata de Rupit,* potato stuffed with duck and beef, while the rugged Collsacabra mountains offer some of Catalonia's most pristine landscapes.

Besalú contains astonishingly well-preserved medieval buildings.

🍴 Restaurants

Ca l'Enric

$$$$ | CATALAN | Chefs Jordi and Isabel Juncà have become legends in the town of La Vall de Bianya, just north of Olot, with exquisite cuisine that's firmly rooted in local products. Dishes star game of all sorts, truffles, and wild mushrooms, and are served in a historic stone-walled 19th-century inn. **Known for:** local ingredients; rotating menu; fixed-price menus. [$] *Average main: €85* ✉ *Ctra. de Camprodon s/n, La Vall de Bianya* ✣ *Nacional 260, Km 91* ☎ *972/290015* 🌐 *www.restaurantcalenric.cat* 🕒 *Closed Mon., Dec. 27–Jan. 17, and 1st 2 wks of July (can vary). No dinner Sun.–Wed.*

Les Cols

$$$$ | CATALAN | Chef Fina Puigdevall has made this sprawling 18th-century *masia* (Catalan farmhouse) a triumph. In the restaurant, the cuisine on the prix-fixe menu (no à la carte option) is seasonal and based on locally grown products, from wild mushrooms to the extraordinarily flavorful legumes and vegetables produced by the rich, volcanic soil of La Garrotxa. **Known for:** local ingredients; seasonal fixed-price menu; incredible decor. [$] *Average main: €60* ✉ *Mas les Cols, Ctra. de la Canya s/n* ☎ *972/269209* 🌐 *www.lescols.com* 🕒 *Closed Mon., and 1st 3 wks of Jan. No dinner Sun. and Tues.*

Blanes

60 km (37 miles) northeast of Barcelona, 45 km (28 miles) south of Girona.

The Costa Brava (Wild Coast) begins at Blanes with five different beaches, running from Punta Santa Anna on the far side of the port—a tiny cove with a pebbly beach at the bottom of a chasm encircled by towering cliffs, fragrant pines, and deep blue-green waters—to the 2½-km-long (1½-mile-long) S'Abanell beach, which draws the crowds. Small boats can take you from the harbor to Cala de Sant Francesc or the double beach at Santa Cristina May–September.

The castle of Sant Joan, seated on a mountain overlooking the town, dates back to the 11th century. The watchtower on the coast was built in the 16th century to protect against Barbary pirates. Most travelers skip the working port of Blanes.

GETTING HERE AND AROUND

From Barcelona, the fastest way by car to Blanes, entry point for the Costa Brava, is to start up the inland AP7 tollway toward Girona, then take Sortida 10 (Exit 10) for Blanes. Blanes is 18½ km (11½ miles) down the coast from Tossa de Mar.

FESTIVALS

Els Focs de Blanes (*Fireworks Competition*)
FESTIVALS | FAMILY | The summer event in Blanes that everyone waits for is the fireworks competition, held every night at 11, around July 23–26 (dates vary year to year; check the website for the schedule), which coincides with the town's annual festival. The fireworks are launched over the water from a rocky outcropping in the middle of the seaside promenade known as Sa Palomera while people watch from the beach and surrounding area as more gunpowder is burned in a half hour than at the battle of Trafalgar. ⊠ *Blanes* ⊕ *www.blanes. cat/focs.*

Sights

Jardí Botànic Marimurtra (*Marimurtra Botanic Garden*)
GARDEN | Offering spectacular coastal panoramas and more than 4,000 plant species—many of which are exotic—this garden atop steep cliffs is considered one of Europe's finest. ⊠ *Passeig de Carles Faust 9* ☎ *972/330826* ⊕ *www. marimurtra.cat/en* ☜ *€7.*

Tossa de Mar

80 km (50 miles) northeast of Barcelona, 41 km (25 miles) south of Girona.

Christened "Blue Paradise" by painter Marc Chagall, who summered here for four decades, Tossa's pristine beaches are among Catalonia's best. Set around a blue buckle of a bay, Tossa de Mar is a symphony in two parts: the Vila Vella (Old Town) and the Vila Nova (New Town), the latter a lovely district open to the sea and threaded by 18th-century lanes. The Vila Vella is a knotted warren of steep cobblestone streets with many restored buildings. It sits on the Cap de Tossa promontory that juts out into the sea.

Ava Gardner filmed the 1951 British drama *Pandora and the Flying Dutchman* here (a statue dedicated to her stands on a terrace on the medieval walls). Things may have changed since those days, but this beautiful village retains much of the unspoiled magic of its past. The primary beach at Tossa de Mar is the Platja Gran (Big Beach) in front of the town beneath the walls, and just next to it is Mar Menuda (Little Sea), where the small, colorfully painted fishing boats—maybe the same ones that caught your dinner—pull up onto the beach.

The beaches and town act as a magnet for many vacationers in July and August. Out of season, it's far more sedate, but the mild temperatures make it an ideal stop for coastal strolls.

GETTING HERE AND AROUND

By car, the fastest way to Costa Brava's Tossa de Mar from Barcelona is to drive up the inland AP7 tollway toward Girona, then take Sortida 10 (Exit 10). The old national route, N11, can also get you there, but is slow, heavily traveled, and more dangerous, especially in summer. The main bus station (as well as the local tourist office inside the station) is on Plaça de les Nacions Sense Estat.

Did You Know?

In the 1950s, Tossa de Mar was famous for the arrival of Ava Gardner to film "The Flying Dutchman" with James Mason. In 1998 a bronze statue was erected within the castle walls to honor her.

For a journey back in time to the Middle Ages, take Avinguda Ferran and Avinguda Costa Brava to head down the slope to the waterfront and the Vila Vella, which you enter via the Torre de les Hores, and head to the Vila Vella's heart—the Gothic church of Sant Vicenç.

◎ Sights

Museu Municipal

MUSEUM | In a lovingly restored 14th-century house, this museum is said to be Catalonia's first dedicated to modern art. It is home to one of the only three Chagall paintings in Spain, *Celestial Violinist*. ✉ *Pl. Pintor Roig i Soler 1* ☎ *972/340709* 🖾 *€3* 🕙 *Closed Mon.*

Vila Vella and Castillo de Tossa de Mar

CASTLE/PALACE | Listed as a national artistic-historic monument in 1931, Tossa de Mar's **Vila Vella** (Old Town) is the only remaining example of a fortified medieval town in Catalonia. Set high above the town on a promontory, the Old Town is presided over by the ramparts and towers of the 13th-century **Castillo de Tossa de Mar,** and is situated on a steep yet worthy climb up from the main town, accessed from the western side of Platja Gran Tossa de Mar (Playa Grande). The cliff-top views, particularly at sunset, are remarkable, and the labyrinth of narrow, cobblestone lanes lined with ancient houses (some dating back to the 14th century) is a delight to explore at a leisurely pace. ■TIP→ **At Bar del Far del Tossa (Carrer del Far 14), near the lighthouse, you can enjoy the best views in town. Reviving post-climb drinks, snacks, and light meals are available.** ✉ *Passeig de Vila Vella 1.*

🏖 Beaches

Mar Menuda (*Little Sea*)

BEACH—SIGHT | Just north of the town center, this gentle 460-foot sandy crescent is a pleasant Blue Flag beach that's popular with local families. The sand is coarse, but the sparkling, calm, shallow waters make it ideal for children. Fishing boats bob peacefully in the water nearby after completing their morning's work. At the top of the beach there is a second cove called La Banyera de Ses Dones (the women's bathtub), which provides ideal conditions for diving, though if the sea is not calm, it is dangerous for swimmers. By day there is little natural shade, so bring adequate sunblock and an umbrella if you plan a long beach session. It gets extremely busy in high season. **Amenities:** none. **Best for:** snorkeling; sunset; swimming. ✉ *Av. Mar Menuda.*

Platja Gran (*Big Beach*)

BEACH—SIGHT | Sweeping past the Vila Vella, this well-maintained, soft-sand beach runs along the front of town to meet the base of the Cap de Tossa. One of the most photographed coastlines in this area of Spain, it is also, at the height of summer, one of the busiest. Conditions are normally fine for swimming (any warnings are announced via loudspeaker). A rising number of motorboats is impacting on the water quality, but for now it retains its Blue Flag status. Running behind the beach, there is no shortage of cafés and kiosks selling ice cream and snacks. There is no natural shade, but you can rent deck chairs and umbrellas. **Amenities:** food and drink; lifeguards; showers; toilets; water sports. **Best for:** snorkeling; sunset; swimming. ✉ *Av. de sa Palma.*

🍴 Restaurants

La Cuina de Can Simon

$$$$ | CATALAN | Elegantly rustic, this restaurant right beside Tossa de Mar's medieval walls serves a combination of classical Catalan cuisine with up-to-date, innovative touches. The menu changes with the season; two tasting menus (€68 and €135) provide more than enough to sample, and you can also order à la carte. **Known for:** top-notch service; seasonal menu; welcoming tapa and cava upon

entrance. $ *Average main: €30* ✉ *Carrer del Portal 24* ☎ *972/341269* ⊕ *www. restaurantcansimon.com* ⊘ *Closed Mon. and Tues.*

Hotels

Hotel Capri

$$ | HOTEL | FAMILY | Located on the beach, this hotel is in hailing distance of the old quarter in the medieval fortress; rooms are simple, and those with sea views have private terraces. **Pros:** family-friendly option; perfect location; good value. **Cons:** rooms are small; minimal amenities; no private parking. $ *Rooms from: €106* ✉ *Passeig del Mar 17* ☎ *972/340358* ⊕ *www.hotelcapritossa.com* ⊘ *Closed Nov.–Feb.* ⇘ *22 rooms* ⦿ *Free Breakfast.*

★ Hotel Diana

$$$$ | HOTEL | Built in 1906 by architect Antoni de Falguera i Sivilla, disciple of Antoni Gaudí, this Moderniste gem sits on the square in the heart of the Vila Vella, steps from the beach. **Pros:** attentive service; ideal location, with sea views; Moderniste touches. **Cons:** minimal amenities; room rates unpredictable; some rooms are small. $ *Rooms from: €250* ✉ *Pl. de Espanya 6* ☎ *972/341886* ⊕ *www.hotelesdante.com* ⊘ *Closed Nov.–Mar.* ⇘ *21 rooms* ⦿ *Free Breakfast.*

Hotel Sant March

$$ | HOTEL | FAMILY | This family hotel in the center of town is two minutes from the beach, with guest rooms that open onto a pleasant interior garden that serve as an oasis of tranquility in a sometimes hectic town. **Pros:** warm personal touch; good value; central location. **Cons:** no elevator; rooms a bit small; few exterior views. $ *Rooms from: €110* ✉ *Av. Pelegrí 2* ☎ *972/340078* ⊕ *www.hotelsantmarch. com* ⊘ *Closed Oct. 15–Mar.* ⇘ *29 rooms* ⦿ *Free Breakfast.*

Sant Feliu de Guixols

23 km (14 miles) northeast of Tossa de Mar.

The little fishing port of Sant Feliu de Guixols is set on a small bay; Moderniste mansions line the seafront promenade, recalling a time when the cork industry made this one of the wealthier towns on the coast. In front of them, a long crescent beach of fine white sand leads around to the fishing harbor at its north end. Behind the promenade, a well-preserved old quarter of narrow streets and squares leads to a 10th-century gateway with horseshoe arches (all that remains of a pre-Romanesque monastery); also here is a church that combines Romanesque, Gothic, and baroque styles. Nearby, the iron-structured indoor market, which dates back to the 1930s, sells the freshest and finest local produce, with colorful stalls often overflowing onto the Plaça del Mercat in front.

GETTING HERE AND AROUND
To get here, take the C65 from Tossa de Mar—though adventurous souls might prefer the harrowing hairpin curves of the G1682 coastal corniche.

Sights

Museu d'Història de Sant Feliu de Guíxols

MUSEUM | The Romanesque Benedictine monastery houses this museum, which contains interesting exhibits about the town's cork and fishing trades, and displays local archaeological finds. ✉ *Pl. del Monestir s/n* ☎ *972/821575* ⊕ *www. museu.guixols.cat* ⊒ *€2.*

 Restaurants

Can Segura

$$ | CATALAN | Half a block in from the beach at Sant Feliu de Guixols, this restaurant serves home-cooked seafood and upland specialties. The dining room is always full, with customers waiting their turn in the street, but the staff is good at finding spots at the jovially long communal tables. **Known for:** first-rate seafood specialties; communal dining; excellent rice dishes. [$] *Average main: €13* ✉ *Carrer de Sant Pere 11* ☎ *972/321009.*

El Dorado Mar

$$$ | SEAFOOD | FAMILY | Around the southern end of the beach at Sant Feliu de Guixols, perched over the entrance to the harbor, this family seafood restaurant offers superb sea views as well as fine fare at unbeatable prices. Whether straight seafood such as *lubina* (sea bass) or *dorada* (gilt-head bream) or *revuelto de setas* (eggs scrambled with wild mushrooms), everything served here is fresh and flavorful. **Known for:** affordable cuisine; knockout egg scramble; fresh seafood. [$] *Average main: €18* ✉ *Passeig President Irla 15* ☎ *972/321818* 🌐 *www.grupeldorado.com* 🕓 *No dinner Tues. Closed Wed.*

🛏 Hotels

Hostal del Sol

$$ | HOTEL | FAMILY | Once the summer home of a wealthy family, this Moderniste hotel has a grand stone stairway and medieval-style tower, as well as a garden and a lawn where you can relax by the pool. **Pros:** family-friendly option; good value; good breakfast. **Cons:** bathrooms a bit claustrophobic; far from the beach; on a busy road. [$] *Rooms from: €120* ✉ *Ctra. a Palamós 194* ☎ *972/320193* 🌐 *www.hostaldelsol.cat/en* 🕓 *Closed mid-Oct.–Easter* 🛏 *41 rooms* 🍴 *Free Breakfast.*

S'Agaró

3 km (2 miles) north of Sant Feliu.

S'Agaró is an elegant gated community on a rocky point at the north end of the cove. The 30-minute walk along the **sea wall** from Hostal de La Gavina to Sa Conca Beach is a delight, and the one-hour hike from Sant Pol Beach over to Sant Feliu de Guixols offers views of the Costa Brava at its best.

🍴 Restaurants

Villa Mas

$$$$ | CATALAN | This Moderniste villa on the coast road from Sant Feliu to S'Agaró, with a lovely turn-of-the-20th-century zinc bar, serves up typical Catalan and seasonal Mediterranean dishes like *arròs a la cassola* (deep-dish rice) with shrimp brought fresh off the boats in Palamos, just up the coast. The terrace is a popular and shady spot just across the road from the beach. **Known for:** dining on terrace; across from beach; fresh seafood catches. [$] *Average main: €28* ✉ *Passeig de Sant Pol 95, Sant Feliu de Guixols* ☎ *972/822526* 🌐 *www.restaurantvillamas.com* 🕓 *Closed Mon.; no dinner Sun. or Tues.–Thurs.*

🛏 Hotels

★ **L'Hostal de la Gavina**

$$$$ | HOTEL | Opened in 1932 by farmer-turned-entrepreneur Josep Ensesa, the original hotel grew from a cluster of country villas into a sprawling complex of buildings of extraordinary splendor that have attracted celebrity guests from Orson Welles and Ava Gardner to Sean Connery. **Pros:** in a gated community; impeccable service and amenities; sea views, including from pool and terrace. **Cons:** hard on the budget; walls are thin; expensive restaurant. [$] *Rooms from: €490* ✉ *Pl. Roserar s/n, S'Agar¿* ☎ *972/321100* 🌐 *www.lagavina.com* 🕓 *Closed Nov.–Easter* 🛏 *74 rooms* 🍴 *Free Breakfast.*

Calella de Palafrugell and Around

25 km (15½ miles) north of S'Agaró.

Up the coast from S'Agaró, the C31 brings you to Palafrugell and Begur; to the east are some of the prettiest, least developed inlets of the Costa Brava. One road leads to **Llafranc**, a small port with waterfront hotels and restaurants, and forks right to the fishing village of **Calella de Palafrugell**, known for its July habaneras festival. (The *habanera* is a form of Cuban dance music brought to Europe by Catalan sailors in the late 19th century; it still enjoys a nostalgic cachet here.) Just south is the panoramic promontory of **Cap Roig**, with views of the barren Formigues Isles.

North along the coast lie **Tamariu, Aiguablava, Fornell, Platja Fonda,** and (around the point at Cap de Begur) **Sa Tuna** and **Aiguafreda.** There's not much to do in any of these hideaways, but you can luxuriate in wonderful views, some of the Costa Brava's best beaches and coves, and the soothing quiet. Tamariu, a largely unspoiled former fishing village backed by simple whitewashed houses and a small strip of seafood restaurants that hug the shoreline, is reached by descending a vertiginous road set between mountains and pine forests. Farther north, toward Begur, the small, sheltered Aiguablava beach sets the stage for memorable sunsets. Its restaurant, Toc Al Mar, is a firm favorite with barcelonins (Barcelona residents) on weekend coastal jaunts and offers picture-perfect views.

 Restaurants

★ Pa i Raïm
$$$ | **CATALAN** | "Bread and Grapes" in Catalan, Pa i Raïm is an excellent restaurant set in writer Josep Pla's ancestral family home in Palafrugell. It has one rustic dining room as well as another in a glassed-in winter garden, plus a leafy terrace, which is the place to be in summer. **Known for:** traditional country cuisine; contemporary fare; standout prawns tempura. ⓢ *Average main: €20* ⊠ *Torres i Jonama 56, Palafrugell* ☏ *972/447278* ⊕ *www.pairaim.com* ⊙ *Closed Mon. No dinner Sun.–Thurs.*

Hotels

El Far Hotel-Restaurant
$$$$ | **B&B/INN** | **FAMILY** | Rooms in this 17th-century hermitage attached to a 15th-century watchtower have original vaulted ceilings, hardwood floors, and interiors accented with floral prints; the larger doubles and the suite can accommodate extra beds for children. **Pros:** friendly service; graceful architecture; spectacular views of bay. **Cons:** a bit of a distance from the beach; pricey for the value; need car. ⓢ *Rooms from: €235* ⊠ *Muntanya de Sant Sebastia, Carrer Uruguai s/n, Llafranc* ☏ *972/301639* ⊕ *www.elfar.net* ⊙ *Closed Jan.–early Feb.* ⇨ *9 rooms* ⓘ⊙ *Free Breakfast.*

Begur and Around

11 km (7 miles) north of Calella de Palafrugell.

From Begur, go east through the calas or take the inland route past the rose-color stone houses and ramparts of the restored medieval town of **Pals.** Nearby **Peratallada** is another medieval fortified town with an 11th-century castle, tower, and palace. The name is derived from *pedra tallada,* meaning "carved stone," and behind the town's well-preserved walls is a maze of narrow streets and ivy-covered houses built from stone that was carved from the moat, which still encircles the town. In the center, the arcaded Plaça de les Voltes is alive with restaurants, shops, and cafés. North of Pals there are signs for **Ullastret,** an

Iberian village dating to the 5th century BC. **L'Estartit** is the jumping-off point for the spectacular natural park surrounding the Medes Islands, famous for its protected marine life and consequently for diving and underwater photography.

Sights

Empúries
ARCHAEOLOGICAL SITE | The Greco-Roman ruins here are Catalonia's most important archaeological site, and this port is one of the most monumental ancient engineering feats on the Iberian Peninsula. As the Greeks' original point of arrival in Spain, Empúries was also where the Olympic Flame entered Spain for Barcelona's 1992 Olympic Games. ✉ *Puig i Cadafalch s/n* ☎ *972/770208* 🌐 *www.macempuries.cat* 🎫 *€5.50* 🕒 *Closed Mon. mid-Nov.–mid-Feb.*

Medes Islands (*Underwater Natural Park*)
NATURE PRESERVE | The marine reserve around the Medes Islands, an archipelago of several small islands, is just off the coastline of L'Estartit, and is touted as one of the best places in Spain to scuba dive. Thanks to its protected status, the marine life—eels, octopus, starfish, and grouper—is tame, and you can expect high visibility unless the weather is bad. If diving doesn't appeal, you can take one of the glass-bottomed boats that frequent the islands from the mainland and view from above. ✉ *L'Estartit.*

Restaurants

Restaurant Ibèric
$$$ | **CATALAN** | This excellent pocket of authentic Costa Brava cuisine serves everything from snails to wild boar in season. The terrace is ideal for leisurely dining. **Known for:** eclectic cuisine; high-quality seasonal fare; traditional setting. [$] *Average main: €20* ✉ *Carrer Valls 11, Ullastret* ☎ *972/757108* 🌐 *www.restaurantiberic.com* 🕒 *Closed Mon. No dinner Tues.–Thurs. and Sun.*

Hotels

El Convent Hotel and Restaurant
$$$$ | **HOTEL** | Built in 1730, this elegant former convent is a 10-minute walk to the beach at the Cala Sa Riera—the quietest and prettiest inlet north of Begur. **Pros:** outstanding architecture; quiet and private; terrace for dining. **Cons:** minimum three-night stay in summer; rooms are not soundproofed; need car. [$] *Rooms from: €240* ✉ *Ctra. de la Platja del Racó 2, Begur* ☎ *972/623091* 🌐 *www.hotelconventbegur.com* 🛏 *25 rooms* 🍴 *Free Breakfast.*

★ **Hotel Aigua Blava**
$$$$ | **HOTEL** | **FAMILY** | What began as a small hostal in the 1920s is now a sprawling luxury hotel, run by the fourth generation of the same family. **Pros:** impeccable service; gardens and pleasant patios at every turn; private playground. **Cons:** no elevator; no beach in the inlet; expensive restaurant. [$] *Rooms from: €330* ✉ *Platja de Fornells s/n, Begur* ☎ *972/622058* 🌐 *www.aiguablava.com* 🕒 *Closed Nov.–Mar.* 🛏 *85 rooms* 🍴 *Free Breakfast.*

Cadaqués and Around

70 km (43 miles) north of Begur.

Spain's easternmost town, Cadaqués, still has the whitewashed charm that transformed this fishing village into an international artists' haunt in the early 20th century. Salvador Dalí's house, now a museum, is at Port Lligat, a 15-minute walk north of town.

Sights

★ **Cap de Creus**
NATURE SITE | North of Cadaqués, Spain's easternmost point is a fundamental pilgrimage, if only for the symbolic geographical rush. The hike out to the lighthouse—through rosemary, thyme,

and the salt air of the Mediterranean—is unforgettable. The Pyrenees officially end (or rise) here. New Year's Day finds mobs of revelers awaiting the first emergence of the "new" sun from the Mediterranean. Gaze down at heart-pounding views of the craggy coast and crashing waves with a warm mug of coffee in hand or fine fare on the table at **Bar Restaurant Cap de Creus,** which sits on a rocky crag above the Cap de Creus. On a summer evening, you may be lucky and stumble upon some live music on the terrace. ⊠ *Carrer de Cadaqués al Cap de Creus.*

Casa Salvador Dalí - Portlligat

HOUSE | This was Dalí's summerhouse and a site long associated with the artist's notorious frolics with everyone from poets Federico García Lorca and Paul Eluard to filmmaker Luis Buñuel. Filled with bits of the surrealist's daily life, it's an important point in the "Dalí triangle," completed by the castle at Púbol and the Teatre-Museu Dalí in Figueres. You can get here by a 3-km (2-mile) walk north along the beach from Cadaqués. Only small groups of visitors are admitted at any given time, and reservations in advance are required. ⊠ *Portlligat s/n, Cadaqués* ☎ *972/251015* ⊕ *www.salvador-dali.org* 🖾 *€12; advance reservation required* ۞ *Closed Mon. mid-Feb.–mid.-Mar. and Nov.–Dec. Closed Jan. 7–mid Feb.*

★ Sant Pere de Rodes

RELIGIOUS SITE | The monastery of Sant Pere de Rodes, 7 km (4½ miles) by car (plus a 20-minute walk) above the pretty fishing village of El Port de la Selva, is a spectacular site. Built in the 10th and 11th centuries by Benedictine monks— and sacked and plundered repeatedly since—this restored Romanesque monolith commands a breathtaking panorama of the Pyrenees, the Empordà plain, the sweeping curve of the Bay of Roses, and Cap de Creus. (Topping off the grand trek across the Pyrenees, Cap de Creus is a spectacular six-hour walk from here on the well-marked GR11 trail.) ■**TIP**→ **In July and August, the monastery is the setting for the annual Festival Sant Pere (www.festivalsantpere.com), drawing top-tier classical musicians from all over the world.** Find event listings online (in Catalan); phone for reservations or to book a postconcert dinner in the monastery's refectory-style restaurant: ☎ *972/194233 or 610/310073.* ⊠ *Camí del Monestir s/n, El Porte de la Selva* ☎ *972/387559* ⊕ *www.festivalsantpere.com* 🖾 *€5.50* ۞ *Closed Mon.*

 Restaurants

★ Casa Anita

$$$$ | **SEAFOOD** | Simple, fresh, and generous dishes are the draw at this informal little eatery, an institution in Cadaqués. It sits on the street that leads to Port Lligat and Dalí's house. **Known for:** no menu; regional wines; famous clientele. 🖫 *Average main: €25* ⊠ *Carrer Miquel Rosset 16, Cadaqués* ☎ *972/258471* ۞ *Closed Mon., and mid-Oct.–1st wk in Dec.*

Compartir

$$$$ | **CATALAN** | The concept may be similar, but Compartir ("to share") is no tapas restaurant. This award-winning restaurant bases its menu on a small-plate sharing approach that has been taken to another level by the culinary team of Mateu Casañas, Oriol Castro, and Eduard Xatruch (all former elBulli chefs), who transform traditional recipes into an outstanding gourmet experience. **Known for:** sharing plates; creative gastronomy; beautiful courtyard setting. 🖫 *Average main: €24* ⊠ *Riera Sant Vicenç s/n, Cadaqués* ☎ *972/258482* ⊕ *www. compartircadaques.com* ۞ *Closed Mon., and Jan.–early Feb.*

🛏 Hotels

Hotel Playa Sol

$$$$ | **HOTEL** | **FAMILY** | In business for more than 50 years, this hotel on the cove of Es Pianc, just a five-minute walk from

The popular harbor of Cadaqués

the village center, is a good option for families, due to its connecting rooms, swimming pool, and bike rental. **Pros:** attentive, friendly service; family-friendly; great views. **Cons:** decor could be more colorful; rooms with balcony and sea views are harder to book; small rooms. [$] *Rooms from: €250* ✉ *Riba Es Pianc 3, Cadaqués* ☎ *972/258100* 🌐 *www.playas-ol.com* ⏲ *Closed Nov.–mid-Mar.* 🛏 *48 rooms* 🍴 *No meals.*

Llané Petit

$$$ | **HOTEL** | This intimate, typically Mediterranean bay-side hotel caters to people who want to make the most of their stay in the village and don't want to spend too much time in their hotel. **Pros:** semiprivate beach next to hotel; free Wi-Fi; good breakfast. **Cons:** small rooms; somewhat lightweight beds and furnishings; some soundproofing issues. [$] *Rooms from: €142* ✉ *Pl. Llane Petit s/n, Cadaqués* ☎ *972/251020* 🌐 *www.llanepetit.com* ⏲ *Closed Nov.–Mar.* 🛏 *37 rooms* 🍴 *Free Breakfast.*

Montserrat

50 km (31 miles) west of Barcelona.

A popular side trip from Barcelona is a visit to the dramatic, sawtooth peaks of Montserrat, where the shrine of La Moreneta (the Black Virgin of Montserrat) sits. Montserrat is as memorable for its strange topography as it is for its religious treasures. The views over the mountains that stretch all the way to the Mediterranean and, on a clear day, to the Pyrenees, are breathtaking. The rugged, boulder-strewn terrain makes for exhilarating walks and hikes.

GETTING HERE AND AROUND

By car from Barcelona, follow the A2/A7 autopista on the upper ring road (Ronda de Dalt), or from the western end of the Diagonal as far as Salida 25 to Martorell. Bypass this industrial center and follow signs to Montserrat. You can also take the FGC train from the Plaça d'Espanya metro station (hourly 7:36 am–5:41 pm, connecting with either the cable car at

Aeri Montserrat or with the rack railway (Cremallera) at Monistrol Montserrat. Both the cable car and rack railway take 15 minutes and depart every 20 minutes and 15 minutes, respectively. Once you arrive at the monastery, several funiculars can take you farther up the mountain.

Sights

★ La Moreneta

RELIGIOUS SITE | The shrine of La Moreneta, one of Catalonia's patron saints, resides in a Benedictine monastery high in the Serra de Montserrat, surrounded by—and dwarfed by the grandeur of—sheer, jagged peaks. The crests above the monastic complex bristle with chapels and hermitages. The shrine and its setting have given rise to countless legends about what happened here: St. Peter left a statue of the Virgin Mary carved by St. Luke, Parsifal found the Holy Grail, and Wagner (who wrote the opera *Parsifal*) sought musical inspiration. The shrine is world famous and one of Catalonia's spiritual sanctuaries, and not just for the monks who reside here—honeymooning couples flock here by the thousands seeking La Moreneta's blessing on their marriages, and twice a year, on April 27 and September 8, the diminutive statue of Montserrat's Black Virgin becomes the object of one of Spain's greatest pilgrimages. Only the basilica and museum are regularly open to the public. The basilica is dark and ornate, its blackness pierced by the glow of hundreds of votive lamps. Above the high altar stands the polychrome statue of the Virgin and Child, which can be viewed more closely (and respectfully) by way of a separate door. The hermitage of Sant Joan can be reached by funicular. Although a monastery has stood on the same site in Montserrat since the early Middle Ages, the present 19th-century building replaced the rubble left by Napoléon's troops in 1812. ■ TIP→ The famous Escolania de Montserrat boys'

choir sings the Salve and Virulai from the liturgy weekdays at 1 pm and Sunday at noon. ⊠ *Montserrat* ☏ *No phone* ⊕ *www. montserratvisita.com* 🖅 *€16 sanctuary, audio guide, museum, and audiovisual presentation.*

Sitges

43 km (27 miles) southwest of Barcelona.

Sitges is the prettiest and most popular resort in Barcelona's immediate environs, with an excellent beach and a whitewashed and flowery old quarter. It's also one of Europe's premier gay resorts. From April through September, the fine white sand of the Sitges beach is elbow-to-elbow with sun worshippers. On the eastern end of the strand is an alabaster statue of the 16th-century painter El Greco, usually associated with Toledo, where he spent most of his professional career. The artist Santiago Rusiñol is responsible for this surprise; he was such a Greco fan that he not only installed two of his paintings in his Museu del Cau Ferrat but also had this sculpture planted on the beach.

Sitges and the two nearby Cistercian monasteries to the west of it, Santes Creus and Santa Maria de Poblet, are a trio of attractions that can be seen in a day.

GETTING HERE AND AROUND

By car from Barcelona, head southwest along Gran Vía or Passeig Colom to the freeway that passes the airport on its way to Castelldefels. From here, the freeway and tunnels will get you to Sitges in 20–30 minutes. En route, the small village of Garraf is a worthwhile pit stop, with narrow lanes flanked by whitewashed houses that cling to a promontory looking out to sea. It has a small beach backed by colorful beach huts, providing a quieter refuge from the crowds in Sitges (although it too gets busy in high season).

A Musical Side Trip

Museu Pau Casals. The family house of renowned cellist Pau (Pablo) Casals (1876–1973) is on the beach at Sant Salvador, just east of the town of El Vendrell. Casals, who left Spain in self-imposed exile after Franco seized power in 1939, left a museum of his possessions here, including several of his cellos, original music manuscripts, paintings, and sculptures. Other exhibits describe the Casals campaign for world peace ("Pau," in Catalan, means both Paul and peace), his speech at the United Nations in 1971 (at the age of 95), and his haunting interpretation of *El Cant dels Ocells (The Song of the Birds)*, his homage to his native Catalonia. Across the street, the Auditori Pau Casals holds frequent concerts and, in July and August, a classical music festival. The museum is about 32 km (20 miles) south of Sitges, en route to Tarragona, ✉ *Av. Palfuriana 67, Sant Salvador, Tarragona* ☎ *977/684276* ⊕ *www.paucasals. org* 🎫 *€8* ⊗ *Closed Mon.*

Just over 30 minutes by train (€3.80 each way), there's regular service from all three Barcelona stations. Buses, roughly the same price, run at least hourly from Plaza Espanya and take about 45 minutes, depending how many stops they make. If you're driving head south on the C32.

 ## Sights

Bodegas Torres
WINERY/DISTILLERY | This family vineyard-winery provides tours and tastings of some excellent Penedès wines. There are also pairings on offer—wine with cheese or wine and Ibérico ham. ✉ *Finca "El Maset," Ctra. BP2121 (direction Sant Martí Sarroca), Vilafranca del Penedès* ⊹ *From Sitges, make straight for the AP–2 autopista by way of Vilafranca del Penedès* ☎ *938/177400* ⊕ *www.torres.es* 🎫 *From €12; includes tour and wine tasting.*

Museu del Cau Ferrat
MUSEUM | This is the most interesting museum in Sitges, established by the bohemian artist and cofounder of the Quatre Gats café in Barcelona, Santiago Rusiñol (1861–1931), and containing some of his own paintings together with two by El Greco. Connoisseurs of wrought iron will love the beautiful collection of *cruces terminales,* crosses that once marked town boundaries. Next door is the **Museu Maricel de Mar,** with more artistic treasures. ✉ *Carrer Fonollar 6, Sitges* ☎ *938/940364* ⊕ *www.museusdesitges.com* 🎫 *€10, includes Museu Maricel de Mar* ⊗ *Closed Mon.*

Passeig Maritim
BEACH—SIGHT | A focal point of Sitges life, this long esplanade is an iconic pedestrianized promenade that sweeps past the bay of Sitges. It's backed by upmarket villas, mountain vistas, and ocean views. ✉ *Sitges.*

Restaurants

Vivero
$$$ | **SEAFOOD** | Perched on a rocky point above the bay at Playa San Sebastián, Vivero specializes in paellas and seafood; try the *mariscada,* a meal-in-itself ensemble of lobster, mussels, and prawns. Weather permitting, the best seats in the house are on the terraces, with wonderful views of the water. **Known for:** outdoor dining; excellent mariscada; wonderful water views. $ *Average main: €22* ✉ *Passeig Balmins s/n, Playa San Sebastián, Sitges* ☎ *938/942149* ⊕ *www.elviverositges.com.*

Whitewashed buildings dominate the landscape in Sitges.

Santes Creus

95 km (59 miles) west of Barcelona.

Sitges, with its beach and its summer festivals of dance and music, film and fireworks, is anything but solemn. Head inland, however, some 45 minutes' drive west, and you discover how much the art and architecture—the very tone of Catalan culture—owes to its medieval religious heritage. Monolithic Roman-esque architecture and beautiful cloisters characterize the Cistercian monasteries at Santes Creus and Poblet.

GETTING HERE AND AROUND
It takes about 45 minutes to drive to Santes Creus from Sitges. Take the C32 west, then get onto the C51 and TP2002, or drive inland toward Vilafranca del Penedès and the AP-7 freeway, followed by the AP-2 (Lleida).

Regular trains leave Sants and Passeig de Gràcia stations for Sitges, Garraf, and Vilafranca del Penedès; the ride takes a half hour to an hour. To get to Santes Creus or Poblet from Sitges, take a Llei-da-bound train to L'Espluga de Francolí, 4 km (2½ miles) from Poblet; there's one direct train in the morning at 7:37 and four more during the day with transfers at Sant Vicenç de Calders. From L'Espluga, take a cab to the monastery.

Sights

Montblanc
TOWN | The ancient gates are too narrow for cars, and a walk through its tiny streets reveals Gothic churches with stained-glass windows, a 16th-century hospital, and medieval mansions. ⊠ *Off AP-2, Salida 9 (Exit 9).*

Santes Creus
RELIGIOUS SITE | Founded in 1157, Santes Creus is the first of the monasteries you'll come upon as the A2 branches west toward Lleida; take Exit 11 off the highway. Three austere aisles and an unu-sual 14th-century apse combine with the restored cloisters and the courtyard of

the royal palace. ⊠ *Pl. Jaume el Just s/n, Santes Creus* ☎ *977/638329* ✉ *€5.50* ☉ *Closed Mon.*

Santa Maria de Poblet

8 km (5 miles) west of Santes Creus.

This splendid Cistercian monastery, located at the foot of the Prades Mountains, is one of the great masterpieces of Spanish monastic architecture. Declared a UNESCO World Heritage site, the cloister is a stunning combination of lightness and size, and on sunny days the shadows on the yellow sandstone are extraordinary.

GETTING HERE AND AROUND

The Barcelona–Lleida train can drop you at L'Espluga de Francolí, from where it's a 4-km (2½-mile) walk to the monastery. Buses from Tarragona or Lleida will get you a little closer, with a 2¾-km (1½-mile) walk. The drive from Sitges takes about an hour, via the C32 and AP-2 (Exit 9 when coming from Sitges).

◉ Sights

★ Monasterio de Santa María de Poblet

BUILDING | Founded in 1150 by Ramón Berenguer IV in gratitude for the Christian Reconquest, the monastery first housed a dozen Cistercians from Narbonne. Later, the Crown of Aragón used Santa Maria de Poblet for religious retreats and burials. The building was damaged in an 1836 anticlerical revolt, and monks of the reformed Cistercian Order have managed the difficult task of restoration since 1940. Today, a community of monks and novices still pray before the splendid retable over the tombs of Aragonese rulers, restored to their former glory by sculptor Frederic Marès; they also sleep in the cold, barren dormitory and eat frugal meals in the stark refectory. ⊠ *Off AP-2 (Exit 9 from Barcelona, Exit 8 from Lleida), Pl. Corona de Aragón 11* ☎ *977/870089* ⊕ *www.poblet. cat* ✉ *€8.50.*

Celebrated Onions

Valls. This town, famous for its early spring *calçotada* (onion feast) held on the last Sunday of January, is 10 km (6 miles) from Santes Creus and 15 km (9 miles) from Poblet. Even if you miss the big day, calçots are served November through April at rustic farmhouses such as **Cal Ganxo** in nearby Masmolets (*Carrer de la Font F 14* ☎ *977/605960*).

Tarragona

98 km (61 miles) southwest of Barcelona, 251 km (156 miles) northeast of Valencia.

Tarragona, the principal town of southern Catalonia, today is a vibrant center of culture and art, a busy fishing and shipping port, and a natural jumping-off point for the towns and pristine beaches of Sitges and the Costa Daurada, 216 km (134 miles) of coastline north of the Costa del Azahar. However, in Roman times, Tarragona was one of the finest and most important outposts of the Roman Empire, and was famous for its wine even before that. The town's population was the first *gens togata* (literally, the toga-clad people) in Spain, which conferred on them equality with the citizens of Rome. Its vast Roman remains, chief among them the Circus Maximus, bear witness to Tarragona's grandeur, and to this the Middle Ages added wonderful city walls and citadels. Due to its Roman remains and medieval Christian monuments, Tarragona has been designated a UNESCO World Heritage site.

Though modern, Tarragona has preserved its heritage superbly. Stroll along the town's cliff-side perimeter and you'll see why the Romans set up shop here:

Tarragona is strategically positioned at the center of a broad, open bay, with an unobstructed view of the sea. As capital of the Roman province of Hispania Tarraconensis (from 218 BC), Tarraco (as it was then called) formed the empire's principal stronghold in Spain. St. Paul preached here in AD 58, and Tarragona became the seat of the Christian church in Spain until it was superseded by Toledo in the 11th century.

If you're entering the city en route from Barcelona, you'll pass the **Triumphal Arch of Berà**, dating from the 3rd century BC, 19 km (12 miles) north of Tarragona; and from the Lleida (Lérida) autopista, you can see the 1st-century **Roman aqueduct** that helped carry fresh water 32 km (20 miles) from the Gaià River. Tarragona is divided clearly into old and new by Rambla Vella; the old town and most of the Roman remains are to the north, while modern Tarragona spreads out to the south. Start your visit at acacia-lined Rambla Nova, at the end of which is a balcony overlooking the sea, the **Balcó del Mediterràni.** Then walk uphill along Passeig de les Palmeres; below it is the ancient amphitheater, the curve of which is echoed in the modern, semicircular Imperial Tarraco hotel on the promenade.

GETTING HERE AND AROUND

Tarragona is well connected by train. There are half-hourly express trains from Barcelona (1 hour 20 minutes; prices from €8.05) and regular train service from other major cities, including Madrid.

Buses are frequent between Barcelona and Tarragona—7 to 10 leave Barcelona's Estació del Nord for Tarragona every day. Connections between Tarragona and Valencia are frequent too. There are also bus connections with the main Andalusian cities, plus Alicante and Madrid.

Tours of the cathedral and archaeological sites are conducted by the tourist office, located just below the cathedral.

VISITOR INFORMATION

CONTACTS Visitor Information Tarragona. ⊠ *Carrer Major 37* ☎ *977/250795* ⊕ *www.tarragonaturisme.cat/en.*

 Sights

Amphitheater

ARCHAEOLOGICAL SITE | Tarragona, the Emperor Augustus's favorite winter resort, had arguably the finest amphitheater in Roman Iberia, built in the 2nd century AD for gladiatorial and other contests. The remains have a spectacular view of the sea. You're free to wander through the access tunnels and along the tiers of seats. In the center of the theater are the remains of two superimposed churches, the earlier of which was a Visigothic basilica built to mark the bloody martyrdom of St. Fructuós and his deacons in AD 259. ■ **TIP→ €7.40 buys a combination ticket valid for all Tarragona's Roman sites and is valid for one year.** ⊠ *Parc de l'Amphiteatre Roma s/n* ☎ *977/242579* ☑ *€4* ⊗ *Closed Mon.*

Casa Castellarnau

HOUSE | Now an art and historical museum, this Gothic *palauet* (town house) built by Tarragona nobility in the 18th century includes stunning furnishings from the 18th and 19th centuries. The last member of the Castellarnau family vacated the house in 1954. Casa Castellarnau is the headquarters of the city's **Museu d'Història** (History Museum), with plans showing the evolution of the city. The museum's highlight is the **Hippolytus Sarcophagus,** which bears a bas-relief depicting the legend of Hippolytus and Fraeda. ⊠ *Carrer dels Cavallers 14* ☎ *977/242220* ☑ *€3.15, €7.40 combination ticket with Roman Circus and Praetorium* ⊗ *Closed Mon.*

Catedral

BUILDING | Built between the 12th and 14th century on the site of a Roman temple and a mosque, this cathedral shows the transition from Romanesque to Gothic style. The initial rounded placidity of the Romanesque apse gave way to the spiky restlessness of the Gothic—the result is somewhat confusing. If no Mass is in progress, enter the cathedral through the cloister, where the Diocesan Museum houses a collection of artistic and religious treasures. The main attraction here is the 15th-century Gothic alabaster altarpiece of Sant Tecla by Pere Joan, a richly detailed depiction of the life of Tarragona's patron saint. Converted by Sant Paul and subsequently persecuted by local pagans, Sant Tecla was repeatedly saved from demise through divine intervention. ⊠ Pl. Pla de la Seu s/n ☎ 977/226935 ⊕ www.catedraldetarragona.com 🖃 €5 (cathedral and museum) ⊗ Closed Sun. in winter.

El Serrallo
MARKET | The always-entertaining fishing quarter and harbor are below the city near the bus station and the mouth of the Francolí River. Attending the afternoon fish auction is a golden opportunity to see how choice seafood starts its journey toward your table in Barcelona or Tarragona. Restaurants in the port, such as the popular El Pòsit del Serrallo (Moll des Pescadors 25), offer fresh fish in a rollicking environment. ⊠ Tarragona.

Gaudí Centre
MUSEUM | This small museum in Reus (a 20-minute drive from Tarragona) showcases the life and work of the city's most illustrious son, including copies of the models Gaudí made for his major works and a replica of his studio. His original notebook—with English translations—is filled with his thoughts on structure and ornamentation, complaints about clients, and calculations of cost-and-return on his projects. A pleasant café on the third floor overlooks the main square of the old city and the bell tower of the Church of Sant Pere. The Centre also houses the **Tourist Office**; pick up information here about visits to two of Lluís Domènech i Montaner's most important buildings,

the Casa Navàs (by appointment, €10) and the Institut Pere Mata (€6). ⊠ Pl. del Mercadal 3, Reus ☎ 977/010670 ⊕ www.gaudicentre.cat/en 🖃 €9.

Museu Nacional Arqueològic de Tarragona
MUSEUM | A 1960s neoclassical building contains this museum housing the most significant collection of Roman artifacts in Catalonia. Among the items are Roman statuary and domestic fittings such as keys, bells, and belt buckles. The beautiful mosaics include a head of Medusa, famous for its piercing stare. Don't miss the video on Tarragona's history. ⊠ Pl. del Rei 5 ☎ 977/236209 ⊕ www.mnat.cat 🖃 €4.50 combined entry ticket with the Museu Paleocristià i Necrópolis ⊗ Closed Mon.

Passeig Arqueològic
ARCHAEOLOGICAL SITE | A 1½-km (1-mile) circular path skirting the surviving section of the 3rd-century-BC Ibero-Roman ramparts, this walkway was built on even earlier walls of giant rocks. On the other side of the path is a glacis, a fortification added by English military engineers in 1707 during the War of the Spanish Succession. Look for the rusted bronze of Romulus and Remus. ⊠ Access from Via de l'Imperi Romà.

Praetorium
HOUSE | This towering building was Augustus's town house, and is reputed to be the birthplace of Pontius Pilate. Its Gothic appearance is the result of extensive alterations in the Middle Ages, when it housed the kings of Catalonia and Aragón during their visits to Tarragona. ⊠ Pl. del Rei ☎ 977/221736, 977/242220 🖃 €3.30 (includes Roman Circus) ⊗ Closed Mon.

Roman Circus
ARCHAEOLOGICAL SITE | Students have excavated the vaults of the 1st-century AD Roman arena, near the amphitheater. The plans just inside the gate show that the vaults now visible formed only a small corner of a vast space (350 yards long), where 23,000 spectators gathered

12

Catalonia, Valencia, and the Costa Blanca TARRAGONA

Tarragona's cathedral is a mix of Romanesque and Gothic styles.

to watch chariot races. As medieval Tarragona grew, the city gradually engulfed the circus. ✉ *Pl. del Rei, Rambla Vella s/n* ☎ *977/221736* 🎟 *€3.30 (includes Praetorium)* 🕒 *Closed Mon.*

🍴 Restaurants

Les Coques

$$$$ | **CATALAN** | If you have time for only one meal in the city, take it at this elegant little restaurant in the heart of historic Tarragona. The menu is bursting with both mountain and Mediterranean fare, and the prix-fixe lunch is a bargain at €18. **Known for:** mountain fare; good-value prix-fixe lunch; good wine list. [$] *Average main: €24* ✉ *Carrer Sant Llorenç 15* ☎ *977/228300* 🌐 *www.les-coques.com* 🕒 *Closed Sun.*

Les Voltes

$$ | **CATALAN** | Built into the vaults of the Roman Circus, this unique spot serves a hearty cuisine within one of the oldest sites in Europe. You'll find Tarragona specialties, mainly fish dishes, as well as international recipes, with calçots (spring onions, grilled over a charcoal fire) in winter. (For the calçots, you need to reserve a day—preferably two or more—in advance.) **Known for:** calçots (reserve a day or more in advance); Tarragona specialties; historic setting. [$] *Average main: €15* ✉ *Carrer Trinquet Vell 12* ☎ *977/230651* 🌐 *www.restaurantlesvoltes.cat* 🕒 *Closed Mon. No dinner Sun.*

🛏 Hotels

Plaça de la Font

$ | **HOTEL** | The central location and the cute rooms at this budget choice just off the Rambla Vella in the Plaça de la Font make for a practical base in downtown Tarragona. **Pros:** easy on the budget; comfortable, charming rooms; nearby public parking lot. **Cons:** rooms are on the small side; rooms with balconies can be noisy on weekends; basic facilities. [$] *Rooms from: €78* ✉ *Pl. de la Font 26* ☎ *977/240882* 🌐 *www.hotelpdelafont.com* 🛏 *20 rooms* 🍽 *No meals.*

ⓨ Nightlife

Nightlife in Tarragona takes two forms: older and quieter in the upper city, younger and more raucous down below. There are some lovely rustic bars and wine bars in the *casco antiguo*, the upper section of Old Tarragona, around Plaça del Forum and Carrer de Santa Anna. Port Esportiu, a pleasure-boat harbor separate from the working port, has another row of dining and dancing establishments; young people flock here on weekends and summer nights.

El Korxo

WINE BARS—NIGHTLIFE | This popular, cozy wine bar, with chunky wooden tables, subdued lighting, and quirky creative details, offers its clientele a taste of different wines from around Spain, as well as craft beers, charcuterie and cheeses, and other light snacks. ✉ *Santa Anna 6* ☎ *692/460018.*

Teatre Metropol

CONCERTS | Tarragona's center for music, dance, theater, and cultural events stages performances ranging from castellers (human-castle formations, usually performed in August and September) to folk dances. ✉ *Rambla Nova 46* ☎ *977/244795.*

⬤ Shopping

Carrer Major

ANTIQUES/COLLECTIBLES | You have to haggle for bargains, but Carrer Major has some exciting antiques stores. They're worth a thorough rummage, as the gems tend to be hidden. ✉ *Tarragona.*

Valencia

351 km (218 miles) southwest of Barcelona, 357 km (222 miles) southeast of Madrid.

Valencia, Spain's third-largest municipality, is a proud city with a thriving nightlife and restaurant scene, quality museums, and spectacular contemporary architecture, juxtaposed with a thoroughly charming historic quarter, making it a popular destination year in and year out. During the civil war, it was the last seat of the Republican Loyalist government (1935–36), holding out against Franco's National forces until the country fell to 40 years of dictatorship. Today it represents the essence of contemporary Spain—daring design and architecture along with experimental cuisine—but remains deeply conservative and proud of its traditions. Although it faces the Mediterranean, Valencia's history and geography have been defined most significantly by the Turia River and the fertile huerta that surrounds it.

The city has been fiercely contested ever since it was founded by the Greeks. El Cid captured Valencia from the Moors in 1094 and won his strangest victory here in 1099: he died in the battle, but his corpse was strapped into his saddle and so frightened the besieging Moors that it caused their complete defeat. In 1102 El Cid's widow, Jimena, was forced to return the city to Moorish rule; Jaume I finally drove them out in 1238. Modern Valencia was best known for its frequent disastrous floods until the Turia River was diverted to the south in the late 1950s. Since then the city has been on a steady course of urban beautification. The lovely bridges that once spanned the Turia look equally graceful spanning a wandering municipal park, and the spectacularly futuristic Ciutat de les Arts i les Ciències (City of Arts and Sciences), most of it designed by Valencia-born architect Santiago Calatrava, has at last created an exciting architectural link between this river town and the Mediterranean. If you're in Valencia, an excursion to Albufera Nature Park (which is in the area said to be the birthplace of paella) is a worthwhile day trip.

GETTING HERE AND AROUND

By car, Valencia is about 3½ hours from Madrid via the A3 motorway, and about the same from Barcelona on the AP-7 toll road. Valencia is well connected by bus and train, with regular service to and from cities throughout the country, including nine daily AVE high-speed express trains from Madrid, making the trip in 1 hour 40 minutes, and six Euromed express trains daily from Barcelona, taking about 3½ hours. Valencia's bus station is across the river from the old town; take Bus No. 8 from the Plaza del Ayuntamiento. Frequent buses make the four-hour trip from Madrid and the five-hour trip from Barcelona. Dozens of airlines, large and small, serve Valencia airport, connecting the city with dozens of cities throughout Spain and the rest of Europe.

Once you're here, the city has an efficient network of bus, tram, and metro service. For timetables and more information, stop by the local tourist office. The double-decker Valencia Bus Turístic runs daily 9:30–7:45 (until 9:15 in summer) and departs every 20–30 minutes from the Plaza de la Reina. It travels through the city, stopping at most of the main sights: 24- and 48-hour tickets (€17 and €19, respectively) let you get on and off at eight main boarding points, including the Institut Valencià d'Art Modern, the Museo de Bellas Artes, and the Ciutat de les Arts i les Ciències. The same company also offers a two-hour guided trip (€17) to Albufera Nature Park, including an excursion by boat through the wetlands, departing from the Plaza de la Reina. In summer (and sometimes during the rest of the year) Valencia's tourist office organizes tours of Albufera. You see the port area before continuing south to the lagoon itself, where you can visit a traditional *barraca* (thatch-roof farmhouse).

BUS CONTACT Valencia Bus Station. ⊠ *Carrer de Menendez Pidal 11* ☎ *963/466266.*

FESTIVALS

Gran Fira de València (Great Valencia Fair)
ARTS FESTIVALS | Valencia's monthlong festival, in July, celebrates theater, film, dance, and music. ⊠ *Valencia* ⊕ *www. granfiravalencia.com.*

★ **Las Fallas**
FESTIVALS | If you want nonstop nightlife at its frenzied best, come during the climactic days of Las Fallas, March 15–19 (the festival begins March 1), when revelers throng the streets to see the gargantuan *ninots,* effigies made of wood, paper, and plaster depicting satirical scenes and famous people. Last call at many bars and clubs isn't until the wee hours, if at all. On the last night, all the effigies but one (the winner is spared) are burned to the ground during La Crema, and it seems as though the entire city is ablaze. ⊠ *Valencia* ⊕ *www.visitvalencia.com/en/whats-on-offer-valencia/festivities/the-fallas.*

TOURS

Valencia Bus Turístic
BUS TOURS | Valencia's tourist bus allows you to hop on and hop off as you please, while audio commentary introduces the city's history and highlights. ⊠ *Pl. de la Reina s/n* ☎ *699/982514* ⊕ *www.valenciabusturistic.com* ⊞ *From €17.*

VISITOR INFORMATION

CONTACTS Valencia Tourist Office. ⊠ *Pl. del Ayuntamiento 1* ☎ *963/524908* ⊕ *www.visitvalencia.com/en.*

Sights

Casa Museo José Benlliure
HOUSE | The modern Valencian painter and sculptor José Benlliure (1858–1937) is known for his intimate portraits and massive historical and religious paintings, many of which hang in Valencia's Museo de Bellas Artes (Museum of Fine Arts). Here in his elegant house and studio are 50 of his works, including paintings, ceramics, sculptures, and drawings. Also on display are works

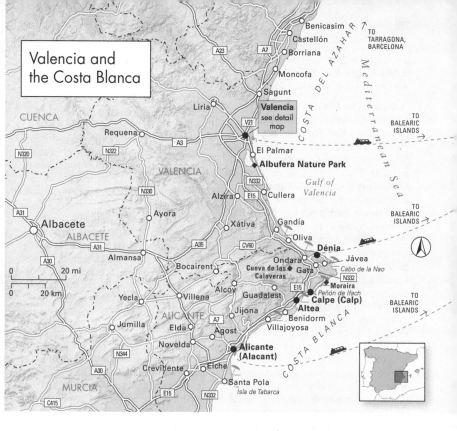

Valencia and
the Costa Blanca

by his son, Pepino, who painted in the small, flower-filled garden in the back of the house, and iconographic sculptures by Benlliure's brother, the well-known sculptor Mariano Benlliure. ✉ *Calle Blanquerías 23* 🕾 *963/911662* 💷 *€2; free Sun.* 🕾 *Closed Mon.*

★ **Catedral de Valencia**

BUILDING | Valencia's 13th- to 15th-century cathedral is the heart of the city. The building has three portals—Romanesque, Gothic, and rococo. Inside, Renaissance and baroque marble were removed to restore the original Gothic style, as is now the trend in Spanish churches. The Capilla del Santo Cáliz (Chapel of the Holy Chalice) displays a purple agate vessel purported to be the Holy Grail (Christ's cup at the Last Supper) and thought to have been brought to Spain in the 4th century. Behind

the altar is the left arm of **St. Vincent,** martyred in Valencia in 304. Stars of the cathedral **museum** are Goya's two famous paintings of St. Francis de Borja, Duke of Gandia. Left of the entrance is the octagonal tower **El Miguelete,** which you can climb (207 steps) to the top: the roofs of the old town create a kaleidoscope of orange and brown terra-cotta, with the sea in the background. It's said that you can see 300 belfries from here, many with bright-blue cupolas made of ceramic tiles from nearby Manises. The tower was built in 1381 and the final spire added in 1736. ■TIP→ **The Portal de los Apostoles, on the west side of the cathedral, is the scene every Thursday at noon of the 1,000-year-old ceremony of the Water Tribunal: the judges of this ancient court assemble here, in traditional costume, to hand down their decisions on local irrigation-rights disputes.** ✉ *Pl. de l'Almoina,* *s/n, Ciutat Vella* ☎ *963/918127* ⊕ *www. catedraldevalencia.es* 🖥 *€7, includes audio guide* 🕑 *Closed Sun. Nov.–Mar.*

★ Ciutat de les Arts i les Ciències

ARTS VENUE | FAMILY | Designed mainly by native son Santiago Calatrava, this sprawling futuristic complex is the home of Valencia's **Museu de les Ciències Príncipe Felipe** (Prince Philip Science Museum), **L'Hemisfèric** (Hemispheric Planetarium), **L'Oceanogràfic** (Oceanographic Park), and **Palau de les Arts** (Palace of the Arts, an opera house and cultural center). With resplendent buildings resembling combs and crustaceans, the Ciutat is a favorite of architecture buffs and curious kids. The Science Museum has soaring platforms filled with lasers, holograms, simulators, hands-on experiments, and a swell "zero gravity" exhibition on space exploration. The eye-shape planetarium projects 3-D virtual voyages on its huge IMAX screen. At l'Oceanogràfic (the work of architect Felix Candela), the largest marine park in Europe, you can take a submarine ride through a coastal marine habitat. Other attractions include an amphitheater, an indoor theater, and a chamber-music hall. ✉ *Av. del Profesor López Piñero 7* ☎ *961/974686* ⊕ *www. cac.es* 🖥 *Museu de les Ciències from €8, L'Oceanogràfic from €30, L'Hemisfèric from €8. Combined ticket €38.20.*

Institut Valencià d'Art Modern (IVAM)

MUSEUM | Dedicated to modern and contemporary art, this blocky, uninspired building on the edge of the old city—where the riverbed makes a loop—houses a permanent collection of 20th-century avant-garde painting, European Informalism (including the Spanish artists Antonio Saura, Antoni Tàpies, and Eduardo Chillida), pop art, and photography. ✉ *Carrer de Guillem de Castro 118, Ciutat Vella* ☎ *963/176600* ⊕ *www.ivam. es* 🖥 *€6; free Fri. 7:30 pm–9 pm, Sat. 3–7 pm, and Sun.* 🕑 *Closed Mon.*

★ Lonja de la Seda (*Silk Exchange*)

BUILDING | On the Plaza del Mercado, this 15th-century building is a product of Valencia's golden age, when the city's prosperity as one of the capitals of the Corona de Aragón made it a leading European commercial and artistic center. The Lonja was constructed as an expression of this splendor and is widely regarded as one of Spain's finest civil Gothic buildings. Its facade is decorated with ghoulish gargoyles, complemented inside by high vaulting and slender helicoidal (twisted) columns. Opposite the Lonja stands the **Iglesia de los Santos Juanes** (Church of the St. Johns), gutted during the 1936–39 Spanish Civil War, and, next door, the Moderniste **Mercado Central** (Central Market, ⇨ *see Shopping*), with its wrought-iron girders and stained-glass windows. ✉ *Lonja 2, Ciutat Vella* ☎ *962/084153* 🖥 *€2.*

★ Mercado Central (Central Market)

FOOD/CANDY | This bustling food market (at nearly 88,000 square feet, one of the largest in Europe) is open from 7 am to 3 pm, Monday through Saturday. Locals and visitors alike line up at the 1,247 colorful stalls to shop for fruit, vegetables, meat, fish, and confectionery. Hop on a stool at The Central Bar, located in the heart of the throng, and taste award-winning chef Ricard Camarena's casual yet no less tasty take on tapas and *bocadillos* (sandwiches), while enjoying front-row-seat viewing of the action. ✉ *Pl. Ciudad de Brujas s/n* ☎ *963/829100* ⊕ *www.mercadocentralvalencia.es* 🕑 *Closed Sun.*

★ Museo de Bellas Artes (*Museum of Fine Arts*)

MUSEUM | Valencia was a thriving center of artistic activity in the 15th century—one reason that the city's Museum of Fine Arts, with its lovely palm-shaded cloister, is among the best in Spain. To get here, cross the old riverbed by the Puente de la Trinidad (Trinity Bridge) to the north bank; the museum is at the edge of the **Jardines del Real** (Royal Gardens; open daily 8–dusk), with its fountains, rose gardens, tree-lined avenues, and small zoo. The permanent collection of the museum includes many of the finest paintings by Jacomart and Juan Reixach, members of the group known as the Valencian Primitives, as well as work by Hieronymus Bosch—or El Bosco, as they call him here. The ground floor has a number of brooding, 17th-century Tenebrist masterpieces by Francisco Ribalta and his pupil José Ribera, a Diego Velázquez self-portrait, and a room devoted to Goya. Upstairs, look for Joaquín Sorolla (Gallery 66), the Valencian painter of everyday Spanish life in the 19th century. ⊠ *Calle San Pío V 9, Trinitat* ☎ *963/870300* ⊕ *www. museobellasartesvalencia.gva.es* ⊠ *Free* ⊗ *Closed Mon.*

Palacio del Marqués de Dos Aguas (*Ceramics Museum*)

CASTLE/PALACE | Since 1954, this palace has housed the **Museo Nacional de Cerámica,** with a magnificent collection of local and artisanal ceramics. Look for the Valencian kitchen on the second floor. The building itself, near Plaza Patriarca, has gone through many changes over the years and now has elements of several architectural styles, including a fascinating baroque alabaster facade. Embellished with carvings of fruits and vegetables, the facade was designed in 1740 by Ignacio Vergara. It centers on the two voluptuous male figures representing the Dos Aguas (Two Waters), a reference to Valencia's two main rivers and the origin of the noble title of the Marqués de Dos Aguas. The museum's collection centers around traditional Valencian ceramics, textiles, furniture, and clothing as well as a section on antique pottery from Greek, Iberian, and Roman times through to the 20th century. ⊠ *Rinconada Federico García Sanchiz 6* ☎ *963/516392* ⊠ *Palace and museum €3; free Sat. 4–8 and Sun.* ⊗ *Closed Mon.*

Palau de la Generalitat

BUILDING | On the left side of the Plaza de la Virgen, fronted by orange trees and box hedges, is this elegant facade. The Gothic building was once the home of the Cortes Valencianas (Valencian Parliament), until it was suppressed by Felipe V for supporting the losing side during the 1700–14 War of the Spanish Succession. The two *salones* (reception rooms) in the older of the two towers have superb woodwork on the ceilings. Don't miss the Salon de los Reyes, a long corridor lined with portraits of Valencia's kings through the ages; call in advance for permission to enter it. ⊠ *Calle Caballeros 2* ☎ *963/863558* ⊗ *Closed weekends.*

Plaza del Ayuntamiento

BUILDING | With the massive baroque facades of the Ayuntamiento (City Hall) and the Correos (central Post Office) facing each other across the park, this plaza is the hub of city life. The Ayuntamiento itself houses the municipal tourist office and a museum of paleontology. ∎**TIP**→ **Pop in just for a moment to marvel at the Post Office, with its magnificent stained-glass cupola and ring of classical columns. They don't build 'em like that any more.** ⊠ *Plaza del Ayuntamiento, Casco Antiguo* ☎ *963/525478* ⊕ *www. visitvalencia.com* ⊗ *Ayuntamiento closed weekends. Post Office closed Sun.*

Real Colegio del Corpus Christi (*Iglesia del Patriarca*)

MUSEUM | This seminary, with its church, cloister, and library, is the crown jewel of Valencia's Renaissance architecture. Founded by San Juan de Ribera in the 16th century, it has a lovely Renaissance patio and an ornate church, and its museum—Museum of the Patriarch—holds artworks by Juan de Juanes, Francisco Ribalta, and El Greco. ⊠ *Calle de la Nave 1, Casco Antiguo* ☎ *963/514176* ⊕ *www.seminariocorpuschristi.org* ⊠ *€3* ⊗ *Closed Sun.*

Valencia

San Nicolás

RELIGIOUS SITE | A small plaza contains Valencia's oldest church (dating to the 13th century), once the parish of the Borgia Pope Calixtus III. The first portal you come to, with a tacked-on, rococo bas-relief of the Virgin Mary with cherubs, hints at what's inside: every inch of the originally Gothic church is covered with exuberant ornamentation. ✉ *Calle Caballeros 35, Casco Antiguo* ☎ *963/913317* 🌐 *www.sannicolasvalencia.com* 🎟 *€5* 🕒 *Closed Mon.*

Beaches

Playa las Arenas

BEACH—SIGHT | This wide (nearly 450 feet) and popular grand municipal beach stretches north from the port and the America's Cup marina more than a kilometer (½ mile), before it gives way to the even busier and livelier Platja de Malvarossa. The Paseo Marítimo promenade runs the length of the beach and is lined with restaurants and small hotels, including the **Neptuno** and the upscale **Las Arenas Balneario** resort. There's no shade anywhere, but the fine golden sand is kept pristine and the water is calm and shallow. There are three lifeguard posts and first-aid stations. Brisk off-shore winds can make this ideal for windsurfing and small-craft sailing; there's a sailing school on the beach to meet the demand. Valencia can be mild and sunny year-round, and there are excellent lunch options along the seafront even out of season. **Amenities:** food and drink; lifeguards; showers; toilets; water sports. **Best for:** sunset; swimming; walking; windsurfing. ✉ *Valencia* 🌐 *www.playadelasarenas.com/en.*

Restaurants

La Casa Montaña

$$$ | TAPAS | The walls are lined with rotund wine barrels at this welcoming bodega with a Moderniste facade, tucked down a side street in the city's old fishermen's quarter. Established in 1836, the restaurant serves a large and varied selection of tapas, from melt-in-your-mouth jamón to rustic stews and grilled seafood, all well accompanied by a superlative, regularly updated selection of wines. **Known for:** good tapas and shared plates; loads of character; quality wine list. [$] *Average main: €21* ✉ *Carrer de Josep Benlliure 69* ☎ *963/672314* 🌐 *www.emilianobodega.com* 🕒 *No dinner Sun.*

La Pepica

$$$ | SPANISH | Locals regard this bustling, informal restaurant, on the promenade at El Cabanyal beach, as the best in town for seafood paella. Founded in 1898, the walls of the establishment are covered with signed pictures of appreciative visitors, from Ernest Hemingway to King Juan Carlos and the royal family. **Known for:** locally revered seafood paella; fruit tarts; historic locale. [$] *Average main: €20* ✉ *Av. Neptuno 6* ☎ *963/710366* 🌐 *www.lapepica.com* 🕒 *Closed last 2 wks in Nov. and last 2 wks in Jan. No dinner Sun.–Thurs.*

La Riuà

$$ | SPANISH | A favorite of Valencia's well connected and well-to-do since 1982, this family-run restaurant a few steps from the Plaza de la Reina specializes in seafood dishes like *anguilas* (eels) prepared with *all i pebre* (garlic and pepper), *parrillada de pescado* (selection of freshly grilled fish), and traditional paellas. Lunch begins at 2 and not a moment before. **Known for:** specialty eel dish; award-winning dining; longtime family-run establishment. [$] *Average main: €16* ✉ *Calle del Mar 27, bajo* ☎ *963/914571* 🌐 *www.lariua.com* 🕒 *Closed Sun. No dinner Mon.*

La Sucursal

$$$$ | MEDITERRANEAN | This thoroughly modern but comfortable restaurant in the Institut Valencià d'Art Modern is likely to put a serious dent in your budget, but it's unlikely you'll sample better venison carpaccio anywhere else, or partake of any finer an *arroz caldoso de bogavante*

Valencia's L'Oceanogràfic (Ciutat de les Arts i les Ciènces) has amazing exhibits, as well as an underwater restaurant.

(soupy rice with lobster). The dinner menu is prix-fixe (€70). $ *Average main: €60* ✉ *Carrer Guillem de Castro 118, El Carmen* ☎ *963/746665* ⊕ *www.restaurantelasucursal.com.*

Sagardi

$$$ | **BASQUE** | The upstairs dining room at this popular Basque restaurant is dominated by two huge wooden cider barrels, long rustic tables for 10—they're geared to groups and big families, but tables can pull apart as needed—and half-moon windows overlooking San Vicente Mártir, the busy street between the plazas of the City Hall and the cathedral. Indulge here in market-fresh fish, charcoal-grilled *a la donostiarra* (oven-baked, San Sebastian–style, with garlic, cayenne pepper, and apple cider vinegar); or *mollejas* (sweetbreads) of beef with artichokes. **Known for:** market-fresh fish; good for groups; downstairs tapas bar. $ *Average main: €22* ✉ *Calle San Vicente Mártir 6, Ciutat Vella* ☎ *963/910668* ⊕ *www.gruposagardi.com/restaurante/sagardi-cocineros-vascos/valencia.*

 ## Hotels

Ad Hoc Monumental

$$ | **HOTEL** | This nicely designed 19th-century town house sits on a quiet street at the edge of the old city, a minute's walk from the Plaza Almoina and the cathedral in one direction, and steps from the Turia gardens in the other. **Pros:** close to sights but quiet; courteous, helpful staff; great value. **Cons:** parking can be a nightmare; not especially family-oriented; small rooms. $ *Rooms from: €90* ✉ *Carrer Boix 4, Ciutat Vella* ☎ *963/919140* ⊕ *www.adhochoteles.com* ⤷ *28 rooms* ⎮⎮ *No meals.*

★ Antigua Morellana

$ | **B&B/INN** | Run by four convivial sisters, this 18th-century town house provides the ultimate no-frills accommodation in the heart of the old city. **Pros:** friendly service; excellent location; complimentary tea in the lounge. **Cons:** no parking; simple amenities; small rooms. $ *Rooms from: €70* ✉ *Carrer d´En Bou 2, Ciutat Vella* ☎ *963/915773* ⊕ *www.hostalam.com* ⤷ *18 rooms* ⎮⎮ *No meals.*

⭐ Caro Hotel

$$$$ | HOTEL | A triumph of design, opened in 2012, this elegant modern hotel is seamlessly wedded to an important historical property: a 14th-century Gothic palace, built on the 12th-century Arabic wall and over the Roman Circus, fragments of which are on show. **Pros:** good location, a few minutes' walk from the cathedral; spot-on, attentive service; oasis of quiet. **Cons:** the two top-floor rooms have low, slanted ceilings; valet parking is rather pricey; decidedly not family-friendly. *$ Rooms from: €200 ⊠ Carrer Almirante 14 ☎ 963/059000 ⊕ www.carohotel.com ⤴ 26 rooms ❘⊙❘ No meals.*

Neptuno Hotel

$$$$ | HOTEL | FAMILY | This beachfront hotel is a slick, modern addition to the city's accommodations options. **Pros:** superb restaurant; great location for families; hydromassage baths and showers. **Cons:** extremely long walk to the historic center; gets booked up early in the summer; erratic service. *$ Rooms from: €184 ⊠ Paseo de Neptuno 2 ☎ 963/567777 ⊕ www.hotelneptunovalencia.com ⤴ 50 rooms ❘⊙❘ Free Breakfast.*

Palau de la Mar

$$$$ | HOTEL | In a restored 19th-century palace, this boutique hotel looks out at the Porta de La Mar, which marked the entry to the old walled quarter of Valencia. **Pros:** big bathrooms with double sinks; great location near the sights and shops; courtyard and garden. **Cons:** top-floor rooms have low, slanted ceilings; rooms overlooking road can be noisy; small gym. *$ Rooms from: €240 ⊠ Av. Navarro Reverter 14, Ciutat Vella ☎ 963/162884 ⊕ www.hospes.com/en/palau-mar ⤴ 66 rooms ❘⊙❘ Free Breakfast.*

Westin Valencia

$$$$ | HOTEL | Built in 1917 as a cotton mill, with successive recyclings as a fire station and a stable for the mounted National Police Corps, this classic property was transformed in 2006 into a luxury hotel. **Pros:** attentive, professional, multilingual staff; location steps from the metro that connects directly to the airport; pet-friendly. **Cons:** rates rise to astronomical during special events; some rooms could use refreshing; patchy Wi-Fi. *$ Rooms from: €200 ⊠ Av. Amadeo de Saboya 16, Pl. del Reial ☎ 963/625900 ⊕ www.westinvalencia.com ⤴ 135 rooms ❘⊙❘ No meals.*

🍸 Nightlife

Valencianos have perfected the art of doing without sleep. Nightlife in the old town centers on Bárrio del Carmen, a lively web of streets that unfolds north of Plaza del Mercado. Popular bars and pubs dot Calle Caballeros, starting at Plaza de la Virgen; the Plaza del Tossal also has some popular cafés, as does Calle Alta, off Plaza San Jaime.

Some of the funkier, newer places are in and around Plaza del Carmen. Across the river, look for appealing hangouts along Avenida Blasco Ibáñez and on Plaza de Cánovas del Castillo. Out by the sea, Paseo Neptuno and Calle de Eugenia Viñes are lined with clubs and bars, lively in summer. The monthly English-language nightlife and culture magazine *24/7 Valencia* (⊕ www.247valencia.com) is free at tourist offices and various bars and clubs; leisure guides in Spanish include *Hello Valencia* (⊕ www.hellovalencia.es) and *La Guía Go* (⊕ www.laguiago.com).

BARS AND CAFÉS

Café de las Horas

BARS/PUBS | This surreal bordello-style bar is an institution for Valencia's signature cocktail, Agua de Valencia (a syrupy blend of cava or Champagne, orange juice, vodka, and gin). The bar's warm atmosphere and convivial vibe are perfect for whiling away the hours at the start (or end) of the night. ⊠ *Calle del Conde de Almodóvar 1 ☎ 963/917336 ⊕ www.cafedelashoras.com.*

Café del Duende

CAFES—NIGHTLIFE | For a taste of *el ambiente andaluz* (Andalusian atmosphere), stop by this flamenco club in the heart of the Barrio del Carmen. It's open Thursday–Saturday from 10 pm (performances start at 10:30 pm on Thursday and at 11 pm on Friday and Saturday). On Sunday performances start at 8 pm. Get there early to secure a seat. ⊠ *Carrer Túria 62, El Carmen* ☎ *630/455289* ⊕ *www.cafedelduende.com.*

Tyris On Tap

BARS/PUBS | Valencia's first craft-beer brewery, Cerveza Tyris, has an animated bar opposite the Mercado Central. Visitors can sample a smorgasbord of locally brewed beers on tap and fill up on tapas, chili dogs, and burgers to a background of well-selected music. ⊠ *Carrer de la Taula de Canvis 6, El Carmen* ☎ *961/132873* ⊕ *www.cervezatyris.com.*

DANCE CLUBS

Calcatta

DANCE CLUBS | Need tangible proof that Valencia never sleeps? Find it at this Barrio del Carmen disco (Friday and Saturday only, from midnight), where a younger crowd parties to pop, R&B, and house music in a restored 17th-century palacio. Even if you drop by at 6 am, Calcutta will still be open. ⊠ *Calle Reloj Viejo 6, La Seu* ☎ *637/488505.*

MUSIC CLUBS

Jimmy Glass Jazz Bar

MUSIC CLUBS | Aficionados of modern jazz gather at this bar (check website for details as opening hours vary according to performances booked), which books an impressive range of local and international combos and soloists. ⊠ *Carrer Baja 28, El Carmen* ⊕ *www.jimmyglassjazz.net.*

Radio City

MUSIC CLUBS | The airy, perennially popular, bar–club–performance space at Radio City offers eclectic nightly shows featuring music from flamenco to Afro-jazz fusion. ⊠ *Carrer Santa Teresa 19, El Carmen* ☎ *963/914151* ⊕ *www.radiocity-valencia.com.*

🎭 Performing Arts

CINEMA

Filmoteca

FILM | The Filmoteca has changing monthly programs of films in their original language (look for *v.o.* for *versión original*) and an artsy haunt of a café. ⊠ *Pl. del Ayuntamiento 17* ☎ *963/539300* ⊕ *www.ivac.gva.es/la-filmoteca.*

MUSIC

Palau de la Música

CONCERTS | On one of the nicest stretches of the Turia riverbed is this huge glass vault, Valencia's main concert venue. Home of the Orquesta de Valencia, the main hall also hosts touring performers from around the world, including chamber and youth orchestras, opera, and an excellent concert series featuring early, baroque, and classical music. It's worth popping in to see the building even without concert tickets, and there is also an **art gallery,** which hosts free changing exhibitions by renowned modern artists. ⊠ *Passeig de l'Albereda 30* ☎ *963/375020* ⊕ *www.palauvalencia.com.*

Palau de les Arts Reina Sofía

CONCERTS | This visually arresting performing arts venue and concert hall, designed by Santiago Calatrava, hosts a rich calendar of opera and classical music throughout the year. ⊠ *Av. del Professor López Piñero (Historiador de la Medicina) 1* ☎ *902/202383 information and tickets* ⊕ *www.lesarts.com.*

🛍 Shopping

Nela

CRAFTS | Browse here, in the heart of the old city, for *abanicos* (traditional silk folding fans), hand-embroidered *mantillas* (shawls), and parasols. ⊠ *Calle San Vicente Mártir 2, Ciutat Vella* ☎ *963/923023.*

Plaza Redonda

GIFTS/SOUVENIRS | A few steps from the cathedral, off the upper end of Calle San Vicente Mártir, the restored Plaza Redonda ("Round Square") is lined with stalls selling all sorts of souvenirs and traditional crafts. ⊠ *Pl. Redonda, El Carmen.*

Albufera Nature Park

11 km (7 miles) south of Valencia.

South of Valencia, Albufera Nature Park is one of Spain's most spectacular wetland areas. Home to the largest freshwater lagoon on the peninsula, this protected area and bird-watcher's paradise is bursting with unusual flora and fauna, such as rare species of wading birds. Encircled by a tranquil backdrop of rice fields, it's no surprise that the villages that dot this picturesque place have some of the best options in the region for trying classic Valencian paella or *arròs a banda* (rice cooked in fish stock).

GETTING HERE AND AROUND

From Valencia, buses depart for the park from the corner of Sueca and Gran Vía de Germanías every hour, and every half hour in summer, 7 am–9 pm daily.

Sights

Albufera Nature Park

NATURE PRESERVE | This beautiful freshwater lagoon was named by Moorish poets—*albufera* means "the sun's mirror." The park is a nesting site for more than 250 bird species, including herons, terns, egrets, ducks, and gulls. Bird-watching companies offer boat rides all along the Albufera. For maps, guides, and tour arrangements, start your visit at the park's information center, the Centre d'Interpretació Raco de l'Olla in El Palmar. ⊠ *Ctra. de El Palmar s/n, El Palmar* ☎ *963/868050* ⊕ *www.albufera.com* ⓕ *Free.*

El Palmar

TOWN | This is the major village in the area, with streets lined with restaurants specializing in various types of paella. The most traditional kind is made with rabbit or game birds, though seafood is also popular in this region because it's so fresh. ⊠ *El Palmar.*

 Restaurants

Maribel Arroceria

$$ | SPANISH | So tasty is the paella here that even valencianos regularly travel out of the city to Maribel Arroceria, off the main drag in El Palmar. While you sit surrounded by the rice fields of Albufera Nature Park, during the week you can devour a fixed-price lunchtime *menu del dia* (€20) of four starters to share, a paella, and dessert, served in the contemporary, air-conditioned dining room or outside at pavement tables overlooking the canal. **Known for:** highly prized paellas; reasonable prix-fixe lunch menus, plus à la carte options; authentic setting in area considered the birthplace of paella. Ⓢ *Average main: €17* ⊠ *Carrer de Francisco Monleón 5, El Palmar* ☎ *961/620060* ⊕ *www.arroceriamaribel.com* ⓧ *Closed Wed. No dinner.*

Dénia

The stretch of coastline known as the Costa Blanca (White Coast) begins at Dénia, south of Valencia. Dénia is the port of departure on the Costa Blanca for the ferries to Ibiza, Formentera, and Mallorca—but if you're on your way to or from the islands, stay a night in the lovely little town in the shadow of a dramatic cliff-top fortress. Or, spend a few hours wandering in the Baix la Mar, the old fishermen's quarter with its brightly painted houses, and exploring the historic town center. The town has become something of a culinary hot spot and is home to award-winning restaurants, which for its compact size is something of an achievement.

GETTING HERE AND AROUND

Dénia is linked to other Costa Blanca destinations via Line 1of the Alicante–Benidorm narrow-gauge TRAM train. There's also regular bus service from major towns and cities, including Madrid (7¼–9 hours) and Valencia (1¾–2½ hours). Local buses can get you around all of the Costa Blanca communities.

The Playa del Arenal, a tiny bay cut into the larger one, is worth a visit in summer. You can reach it via the coastal road (CV736) between Dénia and Jávea.

VISITOR INFORMATION

CONTACTS Visitor Information Dénia. ✉ *Pl. Oculista Buigues 9* ☎ *966/422367* 🌐 *www.denia.net.*

Sights

Castillo de Dénia

ARCHAEOLOGICAL SITE | The most interesting architectural attraction here is the castle overlooking the town, and the **Palau del Governador** (Governor's Palace) inside. On the site of an 11th-century Moorish fortress, the Renaissance-era palace was built in the 17th century and was later demolished. A major restoration project is under way. The fortress has an interesting archaeological **museum** as well as the remains of a Renaissance bastion and a Moorish portal with a lovely horseshoe arch. ✉ *Av. del Cid–Calle San Francisco s/n* ☎ *966/422367* 🎫 *€3 (includes entrance to archaeological museum).*

Cueva de las Calaveras (*Cave of the Skulls*)

CAVE | **FAMILY** | About 15 km (9 miles) inland from Dénia, this 400-yard-long cave was named for the 12 Moorish skulls found here when it was discovered in 1768. The cave of stalactites and stalagmites has a dome rising to more than 60 feet and leads to an underground lake. ✉ *Ctra. Benidoleig–Pedreguera, Km 1.5, Benidoleig* ☎ *966/404235* 🌐 *www.cuevadelascalaveras.com* 🎫 *€4.*

Restaurants

El Raset

$$$ | **SEAFOOD** | Across the harbor, this Valencian favorite has been serving traditional cuisine with a modern twist for more than 30 years. From a terrace with views of the water you can choose from an array of excellent seafood dishes, including house specialties such as *arroz en caldero* (rice with monkfish, lobster, or prawns) and *gambas rojas* (local red prawns). À la carte dining can be expensive, while set menus are easier on your wallet. **Known for:** excellent seafood dishes; reasonably priced set menus; tasty paella. [$] *Average main: €20* ✉ *Calle Bellavista 7* ☎ *965/785040* 🌐 *www.grupoelraset.com.*

★ **La Seu**

$$$ | **SPANISH** | Under co-owners Fede and Diana Cervera and chef Xicu Ramón, this distinguished restaurant in the center of town continues to reinvent and deconstruct traditional Valencian cuisine. The setting is an architectural tour de force: a 16th-century town house transformed into a sunlit modern space with an open kitchen and a three-story-high wall sculpted to resemble a billowing white curtain. **Known for:** creative tapas; unbeatable midweek menu prices; inventive take on Valencian cuisine. [$] *Average main: €20* ✉ *Calle Loreto 59* ☎ *966/424478* 🌐 *www.laseu.es* 🕒 *Closed early Jan.–early Feb. Closed Mon.*

Hotels

★ **Art Boutique Hotel Chamarel**

$$ | **B&B/INN** | Ask the staff and they'll tell you that *chamarel* means a "mixture of colors," and this hotel brimming with charm, built as a grand family home in 1840, is certainly an eccentric blend of styles, cultures, periods, and personalities. **Pros:** friendly, helpful staff; individual attention; pet-friendly. **Cons:** no pool; not on the beach; rooms over the street are noisy. [$] *Rooms from: €110* ✉ *Calle Cavallers 3* ☎ *966/435007* 🌐 *www.hotelchamarel.com* 🛏 *15 rooms* 🍴 *Free Breakfast.*

★ **Hostal Loreto**

$ | HOTEL | Travelers on tight budgets will appreciate this basic yet impeccable lodging, on a central pedestrian street in the historic quarter just steps from the Town Hall. **Pros:** great central location in former nunnery; good value; broad, comfy roof terrace. **Cons:** no elevator; no amenities; rooms can be dark. [$] *Rooms from: €82* ✉ *Calle Loreto 12* ☎ *966/435419* 🌐 *www.hostalloreto.com* 🛏 *43 rooms* 🍴 *Free Breakfast.*

★ **Hotel El Raset**

$$$ | B&B/INN | Just across the esplanade from the port, where the Balearia ferries depart for Mallorca and Ibiza, this upscale boutique hotel has amenities that few lodgings in Dénia offer. **Pros:** staff is friendly, attentive, and multilingual; good location; good restaurant from same owners down the street. **Cons:** no pool; dim overhead lighting in rooms; pricey private parking. [$] *Rooms from: €160* ✉ *Calle Bellavista 1, Port* ☎ *965/786564* 🌐 *www.hotelelraset.com* 🛏 *20 rooms* 🍴 *Free Breakfast.*

★ **La Posada del Mar**

$$$$ | HOTEL | A few steps across from the harbor, this hotel in the 13th-century customs house has inviting rooms with seafront views; there's a subtle nautical theme, most evident in the sailor's-knot ironwork along the staircase. **Pros:** serene environment; close to center of town; lovely sea views. **Cons:** pricey parking; no pool; rooms overlooking the main road can be noisy. [$] *Rooms from: €198* ✉ *Puerto de Denia, Pl. de les Drassanes 2, Port* ☎ *966/432966* 🌐 *www.laposadadelmar.com* 🛏 *31 rooms* 🍴 *Free Breakfast.*

Calpe (Calp)

35 km (22 miles) south of Dénia.

Calpe has an ancient history, as it was chosen by the Phoenicians, Greeks, Romans, and Moors as a strategic point from which to plant their Iberian settlements. The real-estate developers were the latest to descend upon it: much of Calpe today is overbuilt with high-rise resorts and *urbanizaciónes*. But the old town is a delightful maze of narrow streets and small squares, archways and cul-de-sacs, with houses painted in Mediterranean blue, red, ocher, and sandstone; wherever there's a broad expanse of building wall, you'll likely discover a mural. Calpe is a delightful place to wander.

GETTING HERE AND AROUND

The narrow-gauge TRAM railway from Dénia to Alicante also serves Calpe, as do local buses.

VISITOR INFORMATION

CONTACTS Visitor Information Calpe. ✉ *Av. Ejércitos Españoles 44, Calp* ☎ *965/836920* 🌐 *www.calpe.es.*

Sights

Fish Market

MARKET | The fishing industry is still very important in Calpe, and every evening the fishing boats return to port with their catch. The subsequent auction at the fish market can be watched from the walkway of La Lonja de Calpe. ✉ *Port, Calp* 🕑 *Closed weekends.*

Mundo Marino

TOUR—SIGHT | Choose from a wide range of sailing trips, including cruises up and down the coast. Glass-bottom boats make it easy to observe the abundant marine life. ✉ *Puerto Pesquero, Calp* ☎ *966/423066* 🌐 *www.mundomarino.es* 🎟 *From €15.*

Dénia's massive fort overlooks the harbor and provides a dramatic element to the skyline, with the Montgü mountains in the background.

Peñón d'Ifach Natural Park

NATURE SITE | The landscape of Calpe is dominated by this huge calcareous rock more than 1,100 yards long, 1,090 feet high, and joined to the mainland by a narrow isthmus. The area is rich in flora and fauna, with more than 300 species of plants and 80 species of land and marine birds. A visit to the top is not for the fainthearted; wear shoes with traction for the hike, which includes a trip through a tunnel to the summit. The views are spectacular, reaching to the island of Ibiza on a clear day. Check with the local visitor information center about guided tours for groups. ✉ *Calp.*

 Restaurants

Patio de la Fuente

$$$ | **MEDITERRANEAN** | In an intimate little space with wicker chairs and pale mauve walls, this restaurant in the old town serves a bargain Mediterranean three-course prix-fixe dinner, wine included; you can also order à la carte. In summer, dine on the comfortable patio out back.

Known for: outdoor dining; good-value three-course dinner; divine Scotch egg. $ *Average main: €18* ✉ *Carrer Dos de Mayo 16, Calp* ☎ *965/831695* ⊕ *www. patiodelafuente.com* ⊗ *Closed Sun. and Mon. No lunch.*

Hotels

Pensión el Hidalgo

$ | **B&B/INN** | This family-run pension near the beach has small but cozy rooms with a friendly, easygoing feel, and several have private balconies overlooking the Mediterranean. **Pros:** beachfront location; reasonable prices; breakfast terrace with sea views. **Cons:** basic design; you must book far ahead in summer; weak Wi-Fi connection in some rooms. $ *Rooms from: €70* ✉ *Av. Rosa de los Vientos 19, Calp* ☎ *965/839862* ⊕ *www.pensionelhidalgo.com* ⇗ *9 rooms* ⊠ *No meals.*

Altea

11 km (7 miles) southwest of Calpe.

Perched on a hill overlooking a bustling beachfront, Altea (unlike some of its neighboring towns) has retained much of its original charm, with an atmospheric old quarter laced with narrow cobblestone streets and stairways, and gleaming white houses. At the center is the striking church of Nuestra Señora del Consuelo, with its blue ceramic-tile dome, and the Plaza de la Iglesia in front.

GETTING HERE AND AROUND
Also on the Dénia–Alicante narrow-gauge TRAM train route, Altea is served by local buses, with connections to major towns and cities. The old quarter is mainly pedestrianized.

VISITOR INFORMATION
CONTACTS Visitor Information Altea.
⊠ *Calle Sant Pere 14* ☎ *965/844114* ⊕ *www.visitaltea.es.*

 Restaurants

La Costera
$$$ | FRENCH | This popular restaurant focuses on fine French fare, with such specialties as house-made foie gras (simply called foie), roasted lubina (sea bass), and beef entrecôte. There's also a variety of game in season, including venison and partridge. **Known for:** bucolic outdoor terrace; in-season game; French specialties. $ *Average main: €20* ⊠ *Costera Mestre de Música 8* ☎ *965/840230* ⊕ *www.lacosteradealtea.es* ۞ *Closed Mon. No lunch Tues.–Thurs. No dinner Sun.*

Oustau de Altea
$$ | EUROPEAN | In one of the prettiest corners of Altea's old town, this eatery was formerly a cloister and a school. Today the dining room and terrace combine contemporary design gracefully juxtaposed with a rustic setting, and the restaurant is known for serving polished international cuisine with French flair. **Known for:** cuisine with French style; dishes named after classic films; contemporary artwork. $ *Average main: €15* ⊠ *Calle Mayor 5, Casco Antiguo* ☎ *965/842078* ⊕ *www.oustau.com* ۞ *Closed Mon. and Feb. No lunch.*

Hotels

Hostal Fornet
$ | HOTEL | The pièce de résistance at this simple, pleasant hotel, at the highest point of Altea's historic center, is the roof terrace with its stunning view; from here, you look out over the church's distinctive blue-tiled cupola and the surrounding tangle of streets, with a Mediterranean backdrop. **Pros:** lovely views; top value; multilingual owners. **Cons:** no pool or beach; small rooms; door is locked when reception is not staffed, and you have to call to be let in. $ *Rooms from: €49* ⊠ *Calle Beniardá 1, Casco Antiguo* ☎ *965/843005* ⊕ *www.hostalfornetaltea.com* ➥ *23 rooms* ⃝ *No meals.*

Alicante (Alacant)

82 km (51 miles) northeast of Murcia, 183 km (114 miles) south of Valencia, 52 km (32 miles) south of Altea.

The Greeks called it Akra Leuka (White Summit) and the Romans named it Lucentum (City of Light). A crossroads for inland and coastal routes since ancient times, Alicante has always been known for its luminous skies. The city is dominated by the 16th-century grande dame castle, **Castillo de Santa Bárbara,** a top attraction. The best approach is via the elevator cut deep into the mountainside. Also memorable is Alicante's grand **Esplanada,** lined with date palms. Directly under the castle is the city beach, the Playa del Postiguet, but the city's pride is the long, curved Playa de San Juan, which runs north from the Cap de l'Horta to El Campello.

GETTING HERE AND AROUND

Alicante has two train stations: the main Estación de Madrid and the local Estación de la Marina, from which the local FGV line runs along the Costa Blanca from Alicante to Dénia. The Estación de la Marina is at the far end of Playa Postiguet and can be reached by Buses C1 and C2 from downtown.

The slower narrow-gauge TRAM train goes from the city center on the beach to El Campello. From the same open-air station in Alicante, the Line 1 train departs to Benidorm, with connections on to Altea, Calpe, and Dénia.

VISITOR INFORMATION

CONTACTS Tourist Information Alicante. ⊠ *Rambla Méndez Núñez 41, Alicante* 🕾 *965/200000* ⊕ *www.alicanteturismo. com.* **TRAM.** ⊠ *Alicante-Luceros, Alicante* 🕾 *900/720472* ⊕ *www.tramalicante.es.*

 Sights

Ayuntamiento

BUILDING | Constructed between 1696 and 1780, the town hall is a beautiful example of baroque civic architecture. Inside, a gold sculpture by Salvador Dalí of San Juan Bautista holding the famous cross and shell rises to the second floor in the stairwell. Ask gate officials for permission to explore the ornate halls and rococo chapel on the first floor. Look for the plaque on the first step of the staircase that indicates the exact sea level, used to define the rest of Spain's altitudes "above sea level." ⊠ *Pl. de Ayuntamiento, Alicante* 🕾 *965/149100* ⊗ *Closed weekends.*

Basílica de Santa María

BUILDING | Constructed in a Gothic style over the city's main mosque between the 14th and 16th century, this is Alicante's oldest house of worship. The main door is flanked by beautiful baroque stone-work by Juan Bautista Borja, and the interior highlights are the golden rococo high altar, a Gothic image in stone of St.

Mary, and a sculpture of Sts. Juanes by Rodrigo de Osona. ⊠ *Pl. de Santa María s/n, Alicante* 🕾 *965/200000 tourist office (for information)* ⊗ *Closing times can vary due to religious services.*

★ **Castillo de Santa Bárbara** (*St. Barbara's Castle*)

ARCHAEOLOGICAL SITE | One of the largest existing medieval fortresses in Europe, Castillo de Santa Bárbara sits atop 545-foot-tall Monte Benacantil. From this strategic position you can gaze out over the city, the sea, and the whole Alicante plain for many miles. Remains from civilizations dating from the Bronze Age onward have been found here; the oldest parts of the castle, at the highest level, are from the 9th through 13th century. The castle is most easily reached by taking the elevator from Avenida Juan Bautista Lafora. The castle also houses the Museo de la Ciudad de Alicante (MUSA), which uses audiovisual presentations and archaeological finds to tell the story of Alicante, its people, and the city's enduring relationship with the sea. ⊠ *Monte Benacantil s/n, Alicante* 🕾 *965/152969* ⊕ *www.castillodesant-abarbara.com* ⊠ *Castle and museum free, elevator €3.*

Concatedral of San Nicolás de Bari

BUILDING | Built between 1616 and 1662 on the site of a former mosque, this church (called a *con*catedral because it shares the seat of the bishopric with the Concatedral de Orihuela) has an austere facade designed by Agustín Bernardino, a disciple of the great Spanish architect Juan de Herrera. Inside, it's dominated by a dome nearly 150 feet high, a pretty cloister, and a lavish baroque side chapel, the Santísima Sacramento, with an elaborate sculptured stone dome of its own. Its name comes from the day that Alicante was reconquered (December 6, 1248) from the Moors, the feast day of St. Nicolás. ⊠ *Pl. Abad Penalva 2, Alicante* 🕾 *965/212662* ⊠ *Free* ⊗ *Closed Sun. except services.*

Alicante's Esplanada de España, lined with date palms, is the perfect place for a stroll. The municipal brass band offers concerts on the bandstand of the Esplanada on Sunday evenings in July and August.

Museo Arqueológico Provincial

MUSEUM | Inside the old hospital of San Juan de Dios, the MARQ has a collection of artifacts from the Alicante region dating from the Paleolithic era to modern times, with a particular emphasis on Iberian art. ✉ *Pl. Dr. Gómez Ulla s/n, Alicante* ☎ *965/149000* 🌐 *www.marqalicante.com* 🎫 *€3* 🕒 *Closed Mon.*

Museu de Fogueres

MUSEUM | Bonfire festivities are popular in this part of Spain, and the ninots, or effigies, can be elaborate and funny, including satirized political figures and celebrities. Every year the best effigies are saved from the flames and placed in this museum, which also has an audiovisual presentation of the festivities, scale models, photos, and costumes. ✉ *Rambla de Méndez Nuñez 29, Alicante* ☎ *965/146828* 🎫 *Free* 🕒 *Closed Mon. Closed Sun. and Mon. in Aug.*

🍴 Restaurants

El Buen Comer

$$ | **SPANISH** | On the edge of the old town, this relaxed two-tier restaurant serves enticing dishes in plentiful portions. Downstairs, indulge in tapas and simpler dishes, or head to the fancier dining space upstairs for specialties like roast suckling pig, lamb chops, and sea bass baked in a carapace of salt. **Known for:** delicious rice dishes; great value for price; specialty meat and seafood dishes. [$] *Average main: €12* ✉ *Calle Mayor 8, Alicante* ☎ *965/213103* 🌐 *www.elbuencomer.es.*

El Portal

$$$ | **SPANISH** | Blending tradition with novelty is not always an easy task, but it is what draws people back to El Portal in droves. Chef Sergio Sierra runs a slick operation, from the restaurant's extravagant decor (think modern interpretation of Roaring '20s) to a menu that is committed to offering the best flavors of the region—from the freshest seafood to premium cuts of meat to

seasonal produce. **Known for:** montadito de solomillo de vacuno con trufa (steak sandwich with truffle oil); unique decor and DJ soundtrack; cocktails, wine, and dinner all in one place. [$] *Average main: €22* ✉ *C. Bilbao 2, Alicante* ☎ *965/144 444* 🌐 *www.elportaltaberna.es.*

★ La Taberna del Gourmet

$$$ | **TAPAS** | This wine bar and restaurant in the heart of the *casco antiguo* (old town) earns high marks from locals and international visitors alike. A bar with stools and counters offers a selection of fresh seafood tapas—oysters, mussels, razor clams—to complement a well-chosen list of wines from La Rioja, Ribera del Duero, and Priorat, and the two dining rooms are furnished with thick butcher-block tables and dark brown leather chairs. **Known for:** excellent wine list; fresh seafood tapas; reservations essential. [$] *Average main: €20* ✉ *Calle San Fernando 10, Alicante* ☎ *965/204233* 🌐 *www.latabernadelgourmet.com.*

Nou Manolín

$$$ | **SPANISH** | An Alicante institution, this inviting exposed-brick and wood-lined restaurant is generally packed with locals, here for the excellent-value tapas and daily menu. It's a superb place to tuck into fish freshly caught that afternoon, a tribute to the city's enduring relationship with the sea. **Known for:** market-fresh produce; authentic local vibe; a favorite of culinary superstar Ferran Adrià. [$] *Average main: €22* ✉ *Calle Villegas 3, Alicante* ☎ *965/616425* 🌐 *www.grupogastronou.com.*

🛏 Hotels

Hostal Les Monges Palace

$ | **HOTEL** | In a restored 1912 building, this family-run hostal in Alicante's central casco antiguo features lovingly preserved exposed stone walls, ceramic tile floors, and rooms furnished with eccentric artwork and quirky charm. **Pros:** personalized service; ideal location with rooftop terrace; lots of character. **Cons:** the newer, modern part is not as atmospheric; must book well in advance; bathrooms in standard rooms are small. [$] *Rooms from: €75* ✉ *Calle San Agustín 4, Alicante* ☎ *965/215046* 🌐 *www.lesmonges.es* 🛏 *24 rooms* 🍴 *Free Breakfast.*

🍸 Nightlife

El Barrio, the old quarter west of Rambla de Méndez Núñez, is the prime nightlife area of Alicante, with music bars and discos every couple of steps. In summer, or after 3 am, the liveliest places are along the water, on Ruta del Puerto and Ruta de la Madera.

El Coscorrón

BARS/PUBS | It's an Alicante tradition to start an evening out here, with El Coscorrón's generous mojitos. ✉ *Calle Tarifa 5, Alicante* ☎ *965/212727.*

👜 Shopping

Mercado Central

FOOD/CANDY | Bulging with fish, vegetables, and other local items, this is the place to stop by and discover Alicante's fresh produce, traded from this Moderniste-inspired building since 1921. ✉ *Av. Alfonso el Sabio 10, Alicante.*

Photo Credits

Front Cover: Lost Horizon Images/agefotostock [Description: Sagrada familia cathedral at sunset, Barcelona, Catalonia, Spain, Europe]. Back cover, from left to right: Boule/Shutterstock, ismel leal pichs/Shutterstock, Catarina Belova/Shutterstock. Spine: Jacekkadaj/Dreamstime. Interior, from left to right: Luciano Mortula (1). CEZARY WOJTKOWSKI (2). Solodovnikova Elena/Shutterstock (5). **Chapter 1: Experience Barcelona:** Krasnevsky/istockphoto (6-7). Mihai-Bogdan Lazar/shutterstock (8-9). Kert/shutterstock (9). Shootdiem/istockphoto (9). Danny Fernandez (10). Rafael Vargas/MACBA (10). Pere Sanz/dreamstime (10). Turisme de Barcelona (10). Pep Daude/Junta Constructora del Temple de la Sagrada Família. (11). Pere Pratdesaba/Fundació Joan Miró, Barcelona (11). La Vinya del Senyor (12). La Manual Alpargatera (12). Steve (12). nelgphotography/FC Barcelona (12). Christian Bertrand/shutterstock (13). Roger Colom/Ajuntament de Girona (14). Ingrid Prats/shutterstock (14). Turisme de Barcelona (14). Pe3k/shutterstock (14). Museu Nacional d'Art de Cataluyna (15). Catalunya La Pedrera Foundation (15). VitalyEdush/istockphoto (16). nito/shutterstock (16). Museu Picasso, Barcelona (16). Credit: Hemis/Alamy Stock Photo (17). Catedral de Barcelona, Guillem F. Gel (17). Isolda Delgado Mora (22). Cinco Jotas (23). Sergio G. Canizares/Espardenyes Torres (24). Art Escudellers (25). José Hevia. (26). Courtesy_POBLE ESPANYOL DE BARCELONA (26). Pere de Prada i Arana (26). Marco Rubino/dreamstime (27). CastecoDesign/shutterstock (27). KavalenkavaVolha/istockphoto (28). KavalenkavaVolha (29). Boule/shutterstock (30). peresanz/shutterstock (30). Pit Stock/Shutterstock (30). Iakov Filimonov/shutterstock (31). Georgios Tsichlis/shutterstock (31). Oso Media/Alamy (36). Pavel Kirichenko/iStockphoto (37). Luis M. Seco/Shutterstock (38). Public Domain (38). Zina Seletskaya/Shutterstock (38). Amy Nichole Harris/Shutterstock (38). Alfonso de Tomás/Shutterstock (38). Public Domain (39). Public Domain (39). zvonkomaja/Shutterstock (39). Iwona Grodzka/Shutterstock (39). Smackfu/Wikipedia (39). Solodovnikova Elena/Shutterstock (40). rubiphoto/Shutterstock (40). Synes/Flickr, [CC BY 2.0] (40). Jan van der Hoeven/Shutterstock (41). Quim Roser/age fotostock (41). Kalman89/Dreamstime (42). **Chapter 3: La Rambla:** LALS STOCK/shutgterstock (63). Luciano Mortula/LGM/Shutterstock.com (69). Matz Sjöberg/age fotostock (71). Steve Allen/dreamstimes (73). **Chapter 4: The Barri Gòtic:** ToniFlap/istockphoto (79). Xavier Caballé/wikipedia.org (86). Rafael Campillo/age fotostock (91). **Chapter 5: El Raval:** dymon/shutterstock (103). BORGESE Maurizio/age fotostock (107). Rafael Campillo/age fotostock (111). **Chapter 6: Sant Pere and La Ribera:** Marco Rubino/dreamstime (117) Ken Welsh/age fotostock (125). Ken Welsh/age fotostock (129). **Chapter 7: La Ciutadella, Barceloneta,Port Olímpic, and Poblenou:** eye35.pix/Alamy Stock Photo (137). S-F/shutterstock (142). **Chapter 8: The Eixample:** PumpizoldA/istockphoto (155). Marco Cristofori/age fotostock (162). Astroid/dreamstime (168). Robert Harding Product/age fotostock (169). Javier Larrea/age fotostock (170). Sylvain Grandadam/age fotostock (170). Jose Fuste Raga/age fotostock (170). Siobhan O'Hare (170). ccchan/Flickr, [CC BY 2.0] (171). Pepe Navarro/Temple de la Sagrada Família (171). Jsome1/Flickr, [CC BY 2.0] (172). Pep Daudé/Temple de la Sagrada Família (172). Achimh/Dreamstime (173). Hans Blosseyimagebro/age fotostock (173). Jose Antonio Sanchez/Shutterstock (174). MM Images/age fotostock (174). Rafael Campillo/age fotostock (174). Temple de la Sagrada Família (174). Achim Prill/iStockphoto (175). Temple de la Sagrada Família (175). ARCO/P Svarc/age fotostock (175). Harmonia Amanda (175). Wikipedia.Org (176). **Chapter 9: Gràcia:** Olga Visavi/dreamstime (203). dimbar76/shutterstock (212). **Chapter 10: Upper Barcelona:** silviacrisman/istockphoto (215). Solodovnikova Elena/Shutterstock (222). Ioseba Egibar/age fotostock (225). Javier Larrea/age fotostock (226). Daniel P. Acevedo/age fotostock (228). Sam Bloomberg-Rissman/age fotostock (228). Javier Larrea/age fotostock (228). J.D. Dallet/age fotostock (229). Jakub Pavlinec/Shutterstock (230). PHB.cz (Richard Semik)/Shutterstock (230). Fresnel/Shutterstock (230). Marta Menéndez/Shutterstock (230). Javier Larrea/age fotostock (230). J.D. Dallet/age fotostock (230). Fresnel/Shutterstock (230). Cephas Picture Library/Alamy (231). Mauro Winery (231). Alvaro Palacios Winery (231). Mas Martinet Winery (231). Mike Randolph/age fotostock (231). **Chapter 11: Montjuïc and Poble Sec:** Jordi Puig/age fotostock (235). Toniflap/Dreamstime.com (239). Catarina Belova/shutterstock (243). **Chapter 12: Catalonia, Valencia, and the Costa Blanca:** Robwilson39/Dreamstime.com (247). Patty Orly/Shutterstock (250). Mauricio Pellegrinetti/Flickr, [CC BY 2.0] (251). Mauricio Pellegrinetti/Flickr, [CC BY 2.0] (251). Oscar Garcia Bayerri/age fotostock (260). Carlos S. Pereyra/age fotostock (262). B&Y Photography Inc./agefotostock (265). Oscar Garcia Bayerri/agefotostock (268). Artur Bogacki/istockphoto (270). Helio San Miguel (277). Gitanna/Dreamstime (280). Alberto Paredes/agefotostock (284). Nils-Johan Norenlind/agefotostock (292). Igor Gonzalo Sanz/agefotostock (294). Charles Bowman/agefotostock (299). Hidalgo&Lopesino/agefotostock (301). Alan Copson/agefotostock (303). **About Our Writers:** All photos are courtesy of the writers.

Every effort has been made to trace the copyright holders, and we apologize in advance for any accidental errors. We would be happy to apply the corrections in the next printing of this publication.

Notes

Notes

Notes

Notes

Notes

Notes

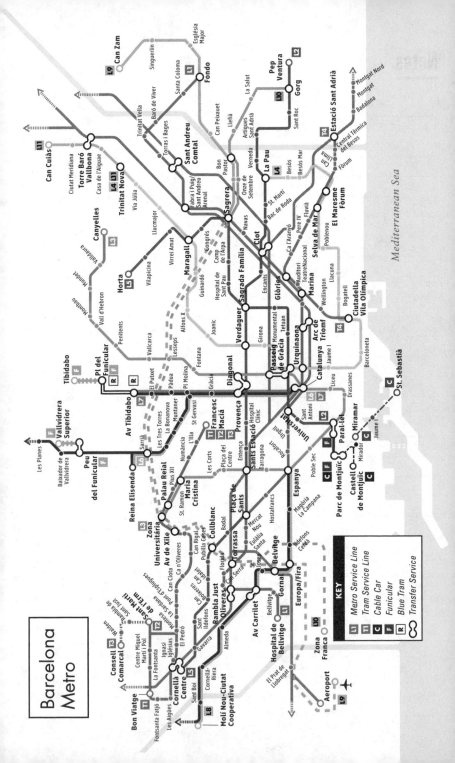

Barcelona Metro

Fodor's BARCELONA

Publisher: Stephen Horowitz, *General Manager*

Editorial: Douglas Stallings, *Editorial Director*; Margaret Kelly, Jacinta O'Halloran, Amanda Sadlowski, *Senior Editors*; Kayla Becker, Alexis Kelly, Teddy Minford, Rachael Roth, *Editors*

Design: Tina Malaney, *Design and Production Director*; Jessica Gonzalez, *Graphic Designer*; Mariana Tabares, *Design & Production Intern*

Production: Jennifer DePrima, *Editorial Production Manager*; Carrie Parker, *Senior Production Editor*; Elyse Rozelle, *Production Editor*; Jackson Pranica, *Editorial Production Assistant*

Maps: Rebecca Baer, *Senior Map Editor*; Mark Stroud (Moon Street Cartography), *Cartographer*

Photography: Jill Krueger, *Director of Photo*; Namrata Aggarwal, Ashok Kumar, Carl Yu, *Photo Editors*; Rebecca Rimmer, *Photo Intern*

Business & Operations: Chuck Hoover, *Chief Marketing Officer*; Robert Ames, *Group General Manager*; Tara McCrillis, *Director of Publishing Operations*; Victor Bernal, *Business Analyst*

Public Relations and Marketing: Joe Ewaskiw, *Senior Director Communications & Public Relations*; Esther Su, Senior *Marketing Manager*; Ryan Garcia, Thomas Talarico, Miranda Villalobos, *Marketing Specialists*

Fodors.com Jeremy Tarr, *Editorial Director*; Rachael Levitt, *Managing Editor*

Technology: Jon Atkinson, *Director of Technology*; Rudresh Teotia, *Lead Developer*; Jacob Ashpis, *Content Operations Manager*

Writers: Jacob Dean, Elizabeth Prosser, Steve Tallantyre

Editors: Jacinta O'Halloran, Debbie Harmsen

Production Editor: Jennifer DePrima

7th Edition

ISBN 978-1-64097-173-8

ISSN 1554–5865

Library of Congress Control Number 2019938462

All details in this book are based on information supplied to us at press time. Always confirm information when it matters, especially if you're making a detour to visit a specific place. Fodor's expressly disclaims any liability, loss, or risk, personal or otherwise, that is incurred as a consequence of the use of any of the contents of this book.

SPECIAL SALES
This book is available at special discounts for bulk purchases for sales promotions or premiums. For more information, e-mail SpecialMarkets@fodors.com.

PRINTED IN CANADA

10 9 8 7 6 5 4 3 2 1

About Our Writers

 Originally from the cloudy north of England, **Elizabeth Prosser** has embraced sunnier climes since she emigrated to Barcelona, Spain, in 2007. When she is not indulging in her passion for food and travel, she works as a freelance writer and editor covering a range of topics including travel, lifestyle, property and technology for a range of print and online publications. Elizabeth updated the Catalonia, Valencia and the Costa Blanca chapter, as well as Activities, Shopping, Sights, and Hotels content.

 Steve Tallantyre is a British journalist and copywriter. He moved from Italy to Barcelona in the late 1990s. Married to a Catalan native, with two "Catalangles" children, Steve writes about the region's restaurants, and food culture for leading international publications. He also owns a popular blog about Barcelona cuisine (⊕ *www.foodbarcelona.com*) and is the founder of a copywriting agency (⊕ *www.BCNcontent.com*). Steve updated our Where to Eat and Nightlife chapters.